Ignacio MÁRQUEZ ROWE

The Royal Deeds of Ugarit

A Study of Ancient Near Eastern Diplomatics

Alter Orient und Altes Testament
Veröffentlichungen zur Kultur und Geschichte des Alten Orients
und des Alten Testaments

Band 335

Herausgeber

Manfried Dietrich • Oswald Loretz

2006
Ugarit-Verlag
Münster

The Royal Deeds of Ugarit

A Study of Ancient Near Eastern Diplomatics

Ignacio MÁRQUEZ ROWE

2006
Ugarit-Verlag
Münster

Márquez Rowe, Ignacio:
The Royal Deeds of Ugarit.
A Study of Ancient Near Eastern Diplomatics
Alter Orient und Altes Testament Bd. 335

Herstellung: Druckhaus Folberth, Pfungstadt
Printed in Germany
ISBN 3-934628-86-9

Printed on acid-free paper

PREFACE

This book is the fruit of several years' labour after considerable migration. Although it originates from my Spanish dissertation (*El* ilku *en Ugarit*, PhD diss., University of Barcelona, 1995), scope and content have been extensively revised and totally rewritten in English.

The topic of the study as defined by the subtitle of the book touches upon two different disciplines, upon Assyriology and upon law. By training and profession I am a specialist on ancient Near Eastern languages and cultures, not a jurist, so that scholars dealing with diplomatics who would primarily qualify as jurists may find my discussion of legal matters unsophisticated. On the other hand, Assyriologists may find parts of my discussion rather superfluous. This is due to the fact that my goal has been to write a book also for the specialist in law or legal history as well as the generally interested scholar who has no familiarity with cuneiform documentation.

As will be apparent to the Assyriological reader, my treatment of the royal deeds of Ugarit has been deeply affected by the writings and teaching of Professor Wilfred van Soldt from the University of Leiden. As a matter of fact it was there, under his supervision during the years 1993 to 1996 that I laid out the foundations for this study. To him I owe a special debt of gratitude. Not only did he spend hours discussing with me various aspects of this study but also he most generously made available to me his files and collection of unpublished Ras Shamra material granting me permission to publish any interesting relevant data. Needless to say, his invaluable critics and help should not be held in any way accountable for the text's deficiencies, which remain entirely my own responsibility.

I am deeply grateful too to Manuel Molina for his support and personal concern during these last years in Madrid. His expert assistance has been crucial in preparing the camera-ready edition of this volume.

I wish to thank the authorities of the National Museum of Damascus who generously granted me permission to collate the royal deeds of Ugarit as well as to re-copy a few of them during my visits from 1993 to 1995.

My final thanks go to Professors Manfried Dietrich and Oswald Loretz for accepting my manuscript in the renowned series Alter Orient und Altes Testament and to Kai Metzler for his always kind and patient editorial work.

TABLE OF CONTENTS

INTRODUCTION

1. Discoveries: Ugarit, province of cuneiform law

Paradoxical as it may seem, it is a well-known fact that without conflagrations and catastrophic destruction the number of cuneiform records preserved to us would be drastically reduced. Indeed, if ancient Near Eastern cities had not been turned into desert hills we would have had no chance of finding the many thousands of clay documents from which cuneiform history is written. The site of Ras Shamra, the "Fennel Hill," on the Syrian coast, had remained more or less undisturbed for more than three millennia. The enemies who destroyed the flourishing city of Ugarit in the early 12th century BC abandoned the ruins allowing them to be covered by dust and vegetation and to eventually vanish into oblivion.

As is often the case, it was Lady Luck who opened the door to the modern archaeological discovery of the remains of the ancient buried city. In March 1928, near the beach of Minet el-Beida's bay, some eight miles north of Latakia, a farmer's plow hit and lifted by chance a stone slab that unexpectedly revealed a Late Bronze Age funerary vault. The following year, the Mission Archéologique Française, directed by Claude F.-A. Schaeffer, began the exploration and excavation of the harbor settlement as well as the neighbouring and archaeologically auspicious mound of Ras Shamra. As early as his first report in 1929, Schaeffer would conclude that "Minet el-Beida et Ras Shamra se sont révélés un centre de civilisation de haute importance."[1] The following seasons of work at Ras Shamra, which have continued right up to the present, have proven that his first assessment was far from wrong.[2] Clay tablets would be soon unearthed, written both in Akkadian and in a hitherto unknown language that used a cuneiform alphabetic script. The newly discovered (alphabetic) language, Ugaritic, its historical and geographical setting, and its literary expression immediately revealed close affinities with the world of the Old Testament, shedding important new light on questions of biblical literature and religion. To be sure, the great interest aroused in the scholarly world by the discovery of the Ras Shamra textual material,

---

[1] "Les fouilles de Minet-el-Beida et de Ras Shamra (Campagne du printemps 1929). Rapport sommaire," Syria 10 (1929):296.

[2] For a recent introduction to the ruins and history of ancient Ugarit, see Marguerite Yon, *La cité d'Ougarit sur le tell de Ras Shamra* (Paris, 1997).

dated to the last phase of the Late Bronze Age, was not because of the legal documents that came to light.

Shortly after the discovery of the first cuneiform tablet in 1929, Mariano San Nicolò postulated in his *Beiträge zur Rechtsgeschichte im Bereiche der keilschriftlichen Rechtsquellen* that Ras Shamra would sooner or later contribute to expand our knowledge on ancient Near Eastern law.[3] Paul Koschaker, in turn, recommended a certain reservation in expanding the universe of cuneiform law as far as the Mediterranean coast taking into especial consideration the culturally eclectic and distinct character of the Syrian area through the ages.[4] However, two years after the publication of his classic *Keilschriftrecht*, namely during the 8th campaign of excavations, Ugarit yielded the first five tablets of legal content written in Akkadian, three of them being published the same year by François Thureau-Dangin.[5]

This event marked the incorporation of Ugarit, or at least the larger area to which it belonged, to the world of cuneiform law.[6] But it was not until the excavation of the palace archives, after the long break following World War II, that Ugarit admittedly became a new and specific province of cuneiform law.[7] Indeed, over 250 private legal transactions as well as treaties and agreements between Ugarit and the neighbouring states and overlord had been recovered from the ruins of the royal palace.[8] And, most important, the majority of these documents, over two hundred, were actually composed by scribes from Ugarit. Today, after 62 campaigns of successful excavations at the site of Ras Shamra, the corpus of legal documents has increased in number and diversity, especially with the discovery of so-called private archives. The overall picture, however, remains necessarily incomplete. Only one sixth of the tell has been exposed on the surface, and the ever-increasing number of excavated tablets and fragments will inevitably correct and improve the picture we now have.

---

[3] In *Beiträge* (Oslo, 1931), n. 3 pp. 47-48.

[4] "Keilschriftrecht," ZDMG 89 (1935): 23.

[5] "Trois contrats de Ras-Shamra," Syria 18 (1937):245-255.

[6] Albrecht Alt, "Eine neue Provinz des Keilschriftrechts," WdO 1 (1947):78-92.

[7] See Georges Boyer, "La place des textes d'Ugarit dans l'histoire de l'ancien droit oriental, in *Le palais royal d'Ugarit*, vol. 3 (Paris, 1955), pp. 283-308; J. Klíma, "Die jüngste Provinz des Keilschriftrechtes," ArOr 24 (1956):123-130; and the definite inclusion in Victor Korošec's *Keilschriftrecht* (Handbuch der Orientalistik I/3, Leiden/Köln, 1964), in particular pp. 175-177.

[8] Published by Jean Nougayrol in *Le palais royal d'Ugarit* vol. 3.

2. Publication and previous studies of the legal material

The indebtedness of every scholar dealing with the Ugarit written material, like myself, to Jean Nougayrol is beyond any doubt. In charge of the decipherment of the Akkadian texts of Ras Shamra since 1951 until his death in 1975, his edition of texts, from literary and lexical texts to letters and records, can only be described as exemplary. With regard to the domestic legal documents, already on April 4th, 1952, before l'Académie des Inscriptions et Belles-Lettres in Paris, he would offer a magisterial analysis of the first important group of records, a total of thirty-eight texts, unearthed during the 15th campaign of excavations.[9] As he himself would later admit,[10] despite the abundant number of newly discovered deeds in the royal palace, the main outlines of his analysis would remain basically unchanged. The definite study he would eventually include in the edition of the more than 175 legal texts excavated during the 15th and 16th campaigns, namely in volume 3 of the series *Le palais royal d'Ugarit* (henceforth *PRU*), which has been so far the main reference guide to the domestic legal corpus. Deeds found in later campaigns were published in *Ugaritica* 5 and *PRU* 6. As stated above, Thureau-Dangin published the first three tablets of legal content unearthed at the site, and some years later Charles Virolleaud would edit two more texts.[11] After Nougayrol's death, Sylvie Lackenbacher and Florence Malbran-Labat, both currently epigraphers of the mission of Ras Shamra, have carried out the publication of a few legal documents. A number of texts still remain unpublished.

In his authoritative study, Nougayrol proposed to classify the domestic legal texts of Ugarit into three different categories. The first category of texts (or "*type 1,*" as he called it) would correspond to the transactions performed before a body of witnesses. The second type ("*type 2*") to the transactions presided over by the king of Ugarit, and the third ("*type 3*") to the king's own transactions, in which incidentally no mention of the witnessing party is made. This classification suggests, in turn, another valid and twofold division of the corpus: on the one hand, the royal deeds (or "*actes royaux*," in Nougayrol's words), including the transactions performed before and by the king (i.e. categories 2 and 3), and on

[9] "Textes de Ras-Shamra en cunéiformes syllabiques (campagne de 1951)," CRAIBL 1952:182-185.

[10] See "Les nouvelles tablettes accadiennes de Ras-Shamra (16e campagne: septembre-novembre 1952)," CRAIBL 1953:41.

[11] Virolleaud in "Cinq tablettes accadiennes de Ras-Shamra," RA 38 (1941):4-5, and "Six textes de Ras-Shamra provenant de la XIVe campagne (1959)," Syria 28 (1951):173-175, and Thureau-Dangin in "Trois contrats de Ras-Shamra" (see note 5 above).

the other the non-royal or "private" deeds (see our discussion in chapter 1).

The uneven distribution of these two groups of texts was manifest in the edition of *PRU* 3. Of the 179 documents published in this volume, only around ten did not belong to the category of royal documents. This circumstance and the fact that only a small number of royal deeds were found in subsequent campaigns explain that Nougayrol's treatment in *PRU* 3 has remained the main philological study of this corpus of documents. In the same volume, Georges Boyer provided a preliminary study on the law of Ugarit based on the published material. The obvious reason for the provisional or tentative character of his examination was the partial nature of the evidence. "Notre documentation" —he rightly remarked— "est presque exclusivement constituée par des pièces tirées des archives du palais royal et concernant des opérations où le roi intervient personnellement comme partie ou témoin qualifié." And he further predicted that "le jour où les fouilles exhumeront des textes appartenant à des archives privées, notre documentation sera certainement plus variée."

We can now say that Boyer's prediction was premonitory. Excavations at Ras Shamra have ever since brought to light the remains of a number of houses containing clusters of clay tablets, some of them of legal content, outside the walls of the royal palace. With the discovery and publication of these new "private" legal documents, our material has indeed become more varied. As regards the volume of new data, however, its less significant character is remarkable, especially as compared to the number of royal deeds dug up in the palace. The largest concentrations of private deeds have been found in the so-called archives of Rapʾānu and Rašapʾabu, the latter containing ten documents. One to five is the number of texts discovered in other, few houses, and it seems rather likely that these figures will not be substantially changed when other private archives come to light in forthcoming campaigns. What this means is that fifty years after Boyer's evaluation of the data, the picture offered by the royal deeds of Ugarit has not experienced a significant transformation. I am, of course, not saying that we have learned little or next to nothing of the legal life of Ugarit from the newly discovered and published texts.[12] What I mean is that the more varied material we now have has not overthrown, let alone endangered, the conclusions reached

---

[12] I cannot agree, for example, with Florence Malbran-Labat when she states (in "Langues et écritures à Ougarit," Semitica 49 [1999]:79) that "tel qu'il nous apparaît dans l'état actuel de notre documentation, le droit ougaritique est caractérisé, du point de vue de son contenu, par sa spécialisation: les actes concernent presque toujours la transmission de terres et l'enregistrement d'actes de propriété par l'autorité royale." This statement holds true for the state of the art in 1955, not at the time she wrote the article (see the discussion that follows).

by Boyer. As an example, we may quote the following text written in *PRU* 3, p. 287:

> La place tenue dans notre documentation par les actes royaux pourrait faire croire que la chancellerie du palais royal monopolisait presque complètement la rédaction des actes juridiques à Ugarit. Mais il ne faut pas oublier que nos textes proviennent en presque totalité des archives du palais royal. Les quelques documents d'origine différente sont au contraire des actes purement privés. Leur nombre s'accroîtra sans doute lorsque les fouilles s'étendront aux quartiers occupés par des habitations particulières. Il n'en reste pas moins que les actes royaux ont occupé une place importante dans la vie juridique d'Ugarit. Il convient donc de rechercher dans quelle mesure cette constatation peut correspondre à une originalité du droit protophénicien à l'égard des autres droits de l'Antiquité orientale.

The idea that lies behind the last sentence has been most influential in the field of ancient Near Eastern studies. In his introduction to Assyriological studies, for example, Wolfram von Soden wrote in 1985 about the legal life of Ugarit that "offenbar nahm hier der König besonders oft unmittelbar Einfluß auch auf privatrechtliche Vereinbarungen," a feature without any parallels in the large body of cuneiform documentary material.[13]

The first study that aimed at interpreting all the legal evidence of the kingdom of Ugarit was the doctoral dissertation *Studies in the Juridical Texts from Ugarit*, submitted by Gerald I. Miller in 1980 at The Johns Hopkins University. The author made clear from the outset that "primary focus has been made on the degree of royal involvement in the legal life of Ugarit."[14] "The conclusions reached —he continued— are derived from a systematic classification of the juridical texts which now include recently published tablets from private archives." As a matter of fact, the bulk of his work, which has remained unpublished, consists of an English annotated translation of all the domestic legal documents as well as a small number of administrative texts from Ugarit known up to 1980. The involvement of the king in the transactions is revealed by the relevant formulas and seal impressions present in the texts. Nevertheless, contrary to Miller's programmatic statement, the degree of the involvement is nowhere measured. The study is basically descriptive, and no analysis or

[13] *Einführung in die Altorientalistik* (Darmstadt, 1985), p. 133.

[14] P. ii.

synthesis of the pertinent data is made. The conclusion, which was expressly meant to focus "on the degree of royal involvement in the legal life of Ugarit,"[15] consists of a mere recapitulation of the evidence.[16]

On the other hand, the "systematic classification" of the legal texts proposed by Miller (royal grants, conveyances of private property, adoption contracts, and documents of claims and settlements) often proves, like so many modern classifications of ancient evidence, to be inadequate and even misleading. Indeed, as we shall see below, one single text can include two or more different transactions, and should accordingly be placed under more than one category. Such is the case of deeds recording a royal grant together with a conveyance of private property (Miller's first and second categories respectively).[17] In another document,[18] for example, we find both a conveyance of private property and an adoption (his second and third types) in which moreover the king appears explicitly involved. Royal grants, which constitute the first category, are certainly not easy to classify. Not only because they may appear together with other different transactions in the same document, as we have seen. But also because a number of transactions normally included as grants show particular features; some of them, for example, specify that the grantee has paid a certain amount of silver or gold to the donor-king.

These royal grants are the subject of another doctoral dissertation that has also remained unpublished. Clayton G. Libolt's *Royal Land Grants from Ugarit* was submitted in 1985 at the University of Michigan. The eighty-two documents selected in this work are distributed according to the different reigns and are presented in transliteration and translation, including a detailed commentary. This philological study is in turn introduced by an analysis of the formulary of the texts. The aim of Libolt's research, however, is not the philological examination of the documents but rather the sociological analysis implied by the texts, and more particularly how accurate this analysis can represent Ugaritic society. In his own words, the study "is directly concerned with the boundary between the palace and the village. It is in that boundary that the grant texts are located."[19]

[15] P. 10.

[16] Pp. 349-51.

[17] Such as RS 15.85.

[18] Such as RS 16.295.

[19] P. 19.

His attempt, therefore, clearly consists of applying the long-undisputed two-sector model, especially as designed by Mario Liverani, to the evidence of land grants. Indeed, it is his contention that these texts are not only important for the structure of Ugaritian society but also "for the social processes which were taking place near the end of the Late Bronze Age."[20] It is not my intention to thoroughly review his arguments and conclusions, for which I would now refer to David Schloen's discussion "Land Grants and the Question of Heritability" in his *The House of the Father as Fact and Symbol.*[21] I would simply like to express my reluctance to accept unilinear developments and the long-lasting tendency in humanities to integrate and interpret scanty, partial data into an overall evolutionary scheme. In historical research, especially when dealing with past civilizations, it has served the purpose of filling the inevitable gaps in our knowledge, or in other words, bridging the gaps often left very wide by the evidence. Concerning Libolt's evidence, it should be first noted that his eighty-two legal documents are neither uniform in content, as remarked above, nor all preserved in a perfect state, some of them being in a fragmentary condition. Secondly, one should bear in mind that they are distributed along one and a half century (as we shall see in detail in chapter 1); in statistical, admittedly figurative terms, the historical and social analysis would have to be based on less than two texts per year. And finally, attention should be drawn to the fact that the texts are, because of their very nature, usually short and always stereotyped in language, following a rigorous pattern and using frozen formulas and expressions (the subject of the present book). How then, we should ask, can these texts and the personal names they mention, mostly void of their real content, allow us more than a glimpse of the underlying social and historical context? I cannot agree with Libolt's methodological assumption that "the structure of the text reflects, even if only distantly, the structure of the society."[22] At least as excessive and unsubstantial is his conclusion that "the sudden shift in all sorts of small matters of style in the writing of the documents indicates a change in regime,"[23] or that allegedly according to the formulas of heritability Ugarit around 1250 BC "had cut itself off from its agrarian past," becoming "less and less of a

[20] P. 20. Note that on p. 441 he concludes that the scenario he has painted in his dissertation "agrees in broad outline with the scenario that Liverani has suggested for the social history of Late Bronze Syria."

[21] *The House of the Father as Fact and Symbol. Patrimonialism in Ugarit and the Ancient Near East* (Winona Lake, IN, 2001), pp. 241-46.

[22] P. 22.

[23] P. 437.

kingdom and more and more a commercial city."[24] Although the political circumstances around the second half of the 13th century may have favored a more flourishing trade, Ugarit remained to be a kingdom of the ancient world, as vitally dependent on agriculture as it was two centuries earlier.

Apart from the two doctoral dissertations just briefly reviewed, only a number of articles and short surveys on individual legal documents or small groups of documents as well as on particular legal aspects have appeared since Nougayrol's publication of texts in *PRU* 3. So, for example, the preliminary surveys on the law of succession and the status of women by Josef Klíma published in 1956 and 1957;[25] or the studies on the sale documents carried out by Richard Haase[26] and Burkhart Kienast.[27] The latter also published a contribution on the legal texts found at Ras Shamra written in the Ugaritic language, taking into especial account the analogies with their Akkadian counterparts;[28] a closer look at these bilingual equivalents in legal texts was later made by Lucio Milano.[29] Other scholars, such as Reuven Yaron,[30] Aaron Skaist,[31] Raymond Westbrook,[32] Jacob Hoftijzer and Wilfred van Soldt,[33] or Sylvie Lackenbacher[34] have also discussed individual texts, groups of texts or

---

[24] P. 439.

[25] "Untersuchungen zum ugaritischen Erbrecht (Auf Grund der akkadischen Urkunden aus Ras Šamra)," ArOr 24 (1956):356-374; "Sulla diseredazione secondo le fonti accadiche di Ugarit," RSO 32 (1957):655-660; "Die Stellung der ugaritischen Frau (Auf Grund der akkadischen Urkunden aus Ras Šamra)," ArOr 25 (1957):313-333 (= "Le statut de la femme à Ugarit d'après les textes accadiens de Ras-Schamra," Recueils de la Société Jean Bodin 11 [Bruxelles 1959], pp. 95-105).

[26] "Anmerkungen zum ugaritischen Immobilienkauf," ZA 58 (1967):196-210. Reference should also be made here to his "Zum Recht von Ugarit," RIDA 11 (1964):3-17.

[27] "Kauf. In Alalaḫ und Ugarit," RlA 5 (1976-80):532-537.

[28] "Rechtsurkunden in ugaritischer Sprache," UF 11 (1979):431-452.

[29] "Osservazioni sul bilinguismo ugaritico-accadico," VO 3 (1980):179-97, especially pp. 182-186.

[30] "A Document of Redemption from Ugarit," VT 10 (1960):83-90.

[31] "A Unique Closing Formula in the Contracts from Ugarit," in *Society and Economy in the Eastern Mediterranean (c. 1500-1000 BC)*, ed. M. Heltzer and E. Lipiński (Leuven, 1988), pp. 151-159.

[32] "The Price Factor in the Redemption of Land," RIDA 32 (1985):124-126.

[33] "Texts from Ugarit Concerning Security and Related Akkadian and West Semitic Material," UF 23 (1991):189-216.

[34] "Les textes judiciaires d'Ugarit," in *Rendre la justice en Mésopotamie. Archives*

particular clauses and formulas in single articles. Lackenbacher herself has recently translated into French an important number of Akkadian legal documents, basically following the version and interpretation of Nougayrol.[35] Finally, mention should be made here too of my two recent syntheses on the legal texts of Ugarit and the law of Ugarit.[36]

To date, however, no book has comprehensively dealt with a larger body of legal documents from Ugarit. And no study has been particularly focused on the broad and homogeneous corpus of royal deeds. Of course, aspects derived from their interpretation, such as the system of land grants and the more general and debated problem of land tenure and ownership, have been tackled in more or less depth by these and other scholars, such as more recently Schloen.[37] The same is true of the interpretation of single words and phrases belonging to the specific linguistic area of law.

3. Scope and plan of the present study

"The corpus" —wrote A. Leo Oppenheim with regard to the Mesopotamian literary texts— "has to be understood, appreciated, and utilized solely in terms of what it was meant to represent for those who created, maintained, and used it."[38] I would argue that this definition holds true for the study of any corpus of texts, thus including the mass of texts used to record the day-to-day activities of social and economic life. Indeed, the first question to be asked in order to understand and interpret (and also classify) a single document, whether ancient or modern, is the reason for its being written, implicitly including, of course, the question for whom it was written. Although the answers can admittedly differ from one document to another, one general consideration can, and must, be made about the addressee of ancient written sources. To put it again in the thoughtful words of Oppenheim, ancient Near Eastern texts, which are written in a language long dead, were not meant to speak to us, who

---

judiciaires du Proche-Orient ancient (IIIe-Ier millénaires avant J.-C.), ed. F. Joannès (Saint-Denis, 2000), pp. 317-320.

35 *Textes akkadiens d'Ugarit* (Paris, 2002), especially pp. 207-333.

36 "The Legal Texts from Ugarit," in *Handbook of Ugaritic Studies* (Handbuch der Orientalistik I/39), ed. W.G.E. Watson and N. Wyatt (Leiden/Boston/Köln, 1999), pp. 390-422; "Ugarit" in *A History of Ancient Near Eastern Law* (Handbuch der Orientalistik I/72-1), ed. R. Westbrook (Leiden/Boston, 2003), pp. 719-735.

37 Here I would also refer to my forthcoming "Land Tenure and Royal Administration in Late Bronze Age Ugarit" (to appear in Bibliotheca Orientalis).

38 *Ancient Mesopotamia. Portrait of a Dead Civilization* (2nd revised edition, Chicago/London, 1977), p. 20.

belong to a late and alien civilization.[39] This simple statement is crucial and must be kept in mind before attempting to interpret a cuneiform document or group of documents. For a wrong perspective from the outset is likely to mislead the whole study.

On the other hand, when selecting a number of texts for study we must ask ourselves about the legitimacy of our choice, that is, of both the inclusion and exclusion of documents. We have pointed out above the problems that can arise as a result of unconsciously applying our criteria and classifications, often inadequate, to the available ancient data. The question I would like to pose, therefore, in a sense echoing the *Eigenbegrifflichkeit* theorem, is whether the royal deeds of Ugarit represented an effective corpus for those who created, maintained, and used it. As I shall try to show in the following chapters, I believe the question must be answered in the positive. Not only are royal deeds characterized by the essential part played by the king in the transactions. The formal aspect is so distinctive that an illiterate Ugaritian from the 14th to the early 12th centuries BC, and also a modern scholar with little or no knowledge of cuneiform, would be able to easily recognize a royal deed. Moreover, an ancient Ugaritian would even be able to guess the place where it presumably belonged to since royal deeds were as a rule kept in one main royal archive. As for the *Eigenbegrifflichkeit* theorem, it should also be noted from the outset that the Ugaritic language had its own term to designate a royal deed proper.

To be sure, the corpus presents a number of important, practical advantages for its study. One that is obvious and essential, because it avoids the usual severe strain on Assyriological research placed by new finds, is that the royal deeds of Ugarit constitute a closed corpus. Indeed, even if original individual texts or copies of them can be discovered in private archives in future campaigns of excavations at Ras Shamra, the number of texts is not expected to significantly increase with these potential discoveries. And more importantly, the quality of the corpus will presumably remain basically unchanged. The royal palace where the group of tablets was found and obviously kept during the last phase of the Late Bronze Age has been mostly excavated. And this brings us to an additional, twofold profit for the study of the present corpus: the carefully recorded excavation of the tablets by Schaeffer and the masterful edition of most of the texts by Nougayrol.

These practical conveniences undoubtedly offer an excellent opportunity to look at and analyze the corpus of royal deeds. It goes without saying that since Nougayrol's publication and Boyer's legal examination new angles of vision have inevitably appeared. The early-predicted dis-

---

39 Ibid., pp. 12-13.

covery of private legal documents, for example, has shed indirect but important new light on our corpus. And the same is true of the recent discovery and publication of documentary material from other ancient Near Eastern sites. From a methodological point of view, the present study is therefore less concerned to dispute the opinions and interpretations of my predecessors than to build on them. It was usual of Nougayrol's analysis to pose relevant and interesting questions, sometimes modestly consigned to prolific footnotes, on the material he published. Our aim is to formulate them again, together with new ones, and attempt to answer them in the light of the new, broader perspective we now have. We have mentioned above that the corpus itself has not been the object of any particular and thorough study so far. It is this lacuna that this book wishes and intends to fill. Such investigation is no doubt required for the more general understanding of the nature of the administration of the palace of Ugarit, as well as for defining the scribal tradition of this Late Bronze Age province of cuneiform law.

The subtitle of this book precisely refers to the goal of this study. A legal document is by definition an instrument reduced to writing as a means of evidence, and as the means of giving formal expression to some act or contract. Therefore, as neatly and elaborately explained by John Nicholas Postgate, "it is not sufficient to consider only the words written on each tablet: its physical appearance (shape, sealing, arrangement of the inscription, etc.) also conveyed a message of its own, but more than that each legal or administrative document was but one cog in the administrative machine, and the message of its written words was understood by both writer and reader in relation to its function within the system as a whole." "For us to receive that message fully," he then wisely advised, "we must at least try to reconstruct that system, so that we too can interpret the tablet's information with the same awareness of its wider context."[40] Postgate's programmatic statement is but a complementary version of Oppenheim's words on how to understand a corpus of texts with which we opened this section. We need to deal with the questions of the creation, maintenance, and use of the royal deeds and what they meant to those who carried out these tasks if we wish to understand and appreciate the corpus.

This study of ancient Near Eastern diplomatics, namely of a significant part of the instruments of bureaucracy in Late Bronze Age Ugarit, therefore opens (in chapter 1) with a definition of the corpus announcing like an opera overture the main themes of the composition. The archaeological context of the tablets and fragments will lead to an archival examination of the corpus (chapter 2), i.e. the place in which this par-

[40] "Middle Assyrian Tablets: The Instruments of Bureaucracy," AoF 13 (1986):10.

ticular body of records was preserved and available for consultation. Chapter 3 deals with the professionals who created, maintained and used the archive and the documents kept in it. An analysis of the status of Akkadian, the language of the texts, and its training at Ugarit is the subject of chapter 4. Our discussion in the three following chapters focuses on the specific and technical legal language of the deeds proper. In chapter 5 we propose a new scheme of the deeds and discuss each of its parts, thus including a revaluation of the dynastic seal impressed on the tablets. The stereotyped formulary of the texts and a discussion of the legal notions underlying each phrase and term is the subject of chapter 6. And finally chapter 7 aims at determining, when possible, the different scribal hands, in an attempt to distinguish what is of legal significance and what is not, and also at tracing the origin and tradition of some items of the legal terminology used by notaries in Late Bronze Age Ugarit.

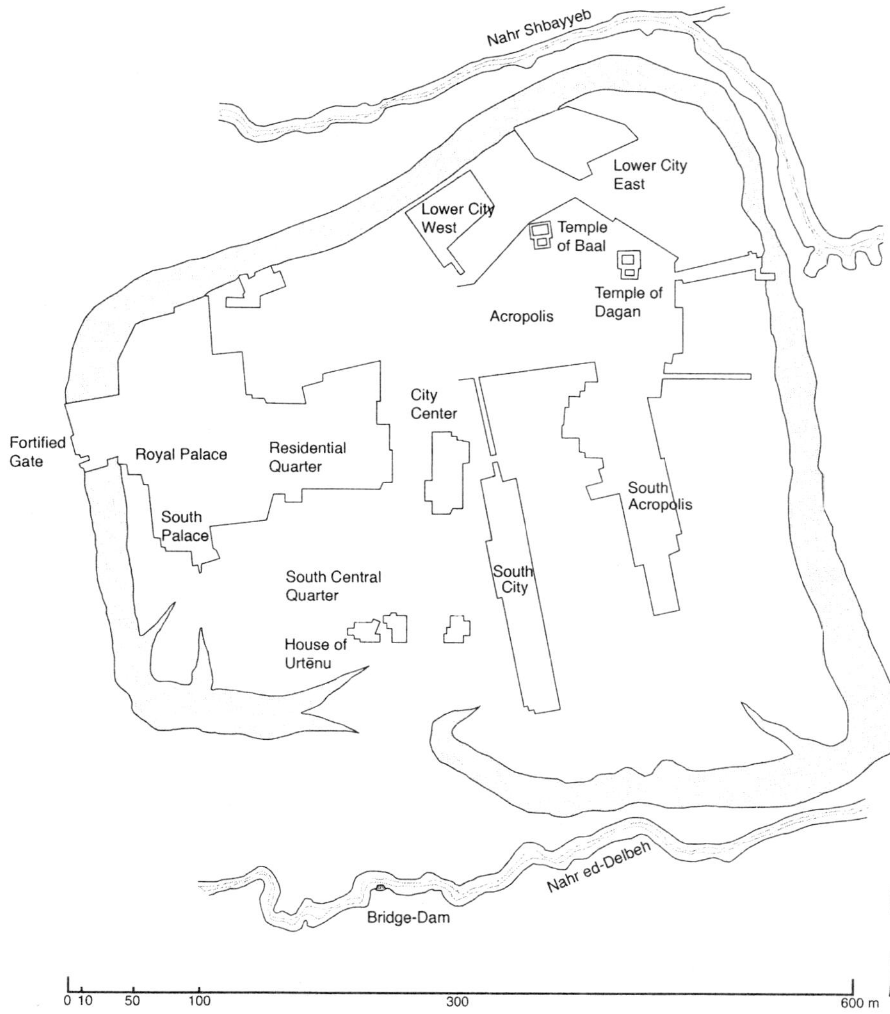

Fig. 1. Plan of the City of Ugarit. After *Études Ougaritiques I. Travaux 1985-1995*, ed. M. Yon and D. Arnaud (Paris, 2001), p. 4.

CHAPTER 1

THE CORPUS

The purpose of this chapter is to define and describe the broad lines of the body of royal deeds of Ugarit. The questions, what is a royal deed, and how is a royal deed to be distinguished from other legal documents, will, of course, be the starting-point of the discussion. On the other hand, several general characteristics of the texts must, and will, also be dealt with such as their find-place, chronological frame, language, and content. Needless to say, all these components represent the basis for our study. The complete list of royal deeds will therefore be followed by an introductory discussion of the different catalogue data as well as of all individual controversial cases, explaining and justifying the resulting inclusion or exclusion of texts from our corpus. If this analysis helps to fix the limits of the corpus, the conclusion that closes the chapter aims in turn at fixing the limits of the textual interpretation of the corpus.

1. Defining a royal deed

"Deeds shall be drawn up, sealed, and witnessed." This is part of the Lord's well-known promise to Jeremiah (Jer 32:10) that normal life would one day be resumed in the land that had been "delivered into the hands of the Chaldeans." Normal life naturally included traditional, correct legal procedure, in this particular case concerning the purchase or redemption of land in Judah. What interests us here, however, is not the law of property or succession in the days of Jeremiah, or the specific transaction with which the prophet was personally concerned, but the concept that lies behind the plain quoted words of God. For we have here a very sharp definition of a legal document in a source that belongs to a world devoid, as it is constantly repeated, of abstract statements. To be sure, a modern, Western definition could hardly improve it. What is a legal document but a written instrument signed or sealed, and validated or authenticated by the presence of witnesses?

This simple but accurate definition should allow us to identify and classify the legal texts in Ugarit into different, proper categories, as well as determine the scope of each of them. The nature of the recorded transaction, the owner of the seal impressed on the clay tablet, and the person or persons who appear witnessing or presiding over the transaction undoubtedly constitute the basis to carry out this necessary task.

The first distinction to be made is between the Ras Shamra documents that were written outside Ugarit and those composed at Ugarit. These two groups of texts would roughly correspond to the categories of diplomatic documents and domestic legal documents respectively. To the former belong all the treaties, agreements, decrees, as well as inter-state adjudications and arbitrations emanating from foreign chancelleries, especially those of the Hittite emperor and his viceroy for Syrian affairs, the king of Carchemish. Such documents, bearing the impression of the emperor's or viceroy's seal, were dispatched to the vassal king of Ugarit, or to one of his ministers, and would be subsequently kept in the palace archives, where they have been partly discovered.

The domestic legal documents, in turn, were written at Ugarit for internal use. They record private transactions concluded by the king or citizens of Ugarit in the areas of contract law, property law, family and inheritance law, and procedural law. As we have mentioned in the introductory chapter, it is possible, and also important, to further distinguish two categories among the domestic legal documents. On the one hand, the royal deeds (Nougayrol's "*actes royaux*"), that include all transactions performed before and by the king, and on the other the non-royal or "private" deeds recording transactions performed before a body of witnesses. As can be readily seen, this distinction is based on the essential elements defining a legal document.

In the case of royal deeds, the authenticity of the transaction (and the document) is provided by the presence of the king presiding over the transaction, whereas in the non-royal documents the transaction is validated by a number of witnesses listed at the end of the text. This aspect is formally emphasized in the text itself which mentions in the introduction whether the transaction took place "before king so-and-so" or "before witnesses," the basis for Nougayrol's classification of his types 2 and 1 respectively. As for his type 3, it goes without saying that the transactions performed *by* the king are also to be considered as performed *before* the king. The fact that the king was a party to the transaction, also formally appearing in the first lines of the text (most often granting real property), must have rendered unnecessary or otiose the inclusion of the pertinent clause stating that he was present presiding over it. Incidentally it should be mentioned that the formula "before king so-and-so" in the documents of type 2 or "before witnesses" in those of type 1 is occasionally omitted. On the other hand, some royal deeds list at the end of the document the names of a reduced number of witnesses, often including the scribe himself. These exceptional cases will be properly discussed in chapter 5 below. What I want to stress here is that the identification of a royal deed, and its distinction from other domestic legal documents, are not restricted to the presence of the witnessing formula. There is another essential, intimately related formal aspect that is determining for the correct, and also immediate, classification of a Ras Shamra tablet of legal content.

It was early realized that what automatically characterizes a royal deed is the seal impression. Tablets inscribed with a transaction performed before or/and by the king are consistently "signed" with the so-called "dynastic seal" of the rulers of Ugarit. This essential feature, which would allow even an illiterate person to quickly identify a royal deed, is directly related to the king's role of consenting and therefore ensuring the validity of the transaction and the document. Indeed, the presence of his seal impression on the tablet should *a priori* be an indication that he was himself present when the recorded transaction took place, or when the transaction was reduced to writing. Nougayrol, however, was not fully convinced about it: "Y assistait-il réellement ou symboliquement?" he would ask in one of his seminal footnotes. And he further expressed his reluctance to use as conclusive evidence the controversial document RS 16.145.[1] I would agree with him on the necessary cautious use of this, and, for that matter, any single document to draw ultimate general conclusions or answers. But I would certainly and strongly advocate for the inclusion and use of any potential, relevant source to attempt to answer any fundamental question. More so when the source presents some extraordinary and remarkable data, as is the case with this royal deed.

RS 16.145 bears the dynastic seal impression and describes two transactions, a land grant by the king and its subsequent sale by the grantee to a third person. The text shows several interesting exceptional features. To begin with, the donor king's name Yaqaru, without patronymic, is the name of the original owner of the dynastic seal, namely one of the ancestor kings who ruled Ugarit in the 15th century as we shall discuss below in chapter 5. Secondly, the text ends with a list of six witnesses to the transaction, a number typically found in non-royal legal documents, but unusual for a royal deed. As already mentioned the king's name and seal as a rule suffice to authenticate the transaction. Finally, the name of the last witness, ᶜUpsānu, is identified as a state official (*sākinu*) "who obtained the royal seal" (*ša uštēṣi kunuk šarri*). I would suggest that the three extraordinary features are interrelated. Here we exceptionally find a royal minister signing the royal deed with the dynastic seal, thus officially substituting the king ("By Order" we could say) and bestowing the necessary royal authenticity on the transaction. We do not know the reason why the ruler was absent at this transaction accordingly witnessed by six people; perhaps he was (a minor?) incapable of exercising the royal

---

[1] *PRU* 3, p. 29 n. 2. Boyer, in his legal study ("Étude juridique", p. 113), also expressed his doubts about the literal meaning of the formula "before king so-and-so." "Il est également possible —he wrote— que la présence du roi mentionnée dans ces textes fût purement fictive."

power and duties.[2] This would explain why the scribe wrote down the royal name Yaqaru (viz. the owner of the dynastic seal) as the donor king in the transaction.[3] This exception explicitly and no doubt requisitely recorded would prove the rule that no one else but the king would normally sign with the seal of the kings of Ugarit.[4]

This procedure may remind us of the famous passages in the book of Esther, which incidentally might have prompted Nougayrol's remark mentioned above. There it is described how the Persian king gave his

---

[2] That the *sākinu* of Ugarit could substitute the king in such special circumstances is suggested by a passage in a letter addressed to the former by the Hittite emperor in the following terms: "The king, your lord, is young and does not know anything" (RS 34.129:5-7); Itamar Singer ("A political History of Ugarit," in *Handbook of Ugaritic Studies*, p. 722) and van Soldt ("Studies on the sākinu-Official (2)", UF 34 [2002]:812) have suggested that the minor, incapable king referred to in the message was young ᶜAmmurapiᵓ, the last ruler of Ugarit (see the list of kings below).

[3] See Nougayrol, *PRU* 3, p. XXXVIII, or van Soldt who stated that the name "was obviously copied from the seal" (*Studies in the Akkadian of Ugarit. Dating and Grammar* [Neukirchen Vluyn, 1991], p. 14 n. 130); see also Kienast, "Rechtsurkunden in ugaritischer Sprache," p. 435, and Singer, "A Political History of Ugarit," pp. 612-13. It is also noteworthy that the king's patronymic is omitted (although mentioned in the seal inscription), contrary to the customary practice and formulary of the deeds (see chapter 7) —perhaps the omission was meant to make Yaqaru more explicitly "impersonal."

[4] Daniel Arnaud, however, has suggested that the donor was actually king Yaqaru ("Études sur Alalah et Ougarit à l'Âge du Bronze Récent," SMEA 37 [1996]:48 n. 6). And he accordingly dated the recorded transaction back to the early 15th century. As we shall see below, the archives of Ugarit belong to the last phase of the Late Bronze Age, beginning with the Hittite conquest around 1340 BC. The hypothetical interpretation proposed by Arnaud would then make of RS 16.145 a completely isolated royal deed, separated from the rest of the corpus by more than one hundred years (an idea that is neither suggested by the orthography of the text, cf. our chapter 7 below). On the other hand, I can neither agree with Arnaud that what was brought forth (or obtained) was not the royal seal but a sealed document (also Nougayrol's opinion in his preliminary *compte-rendu* in CRAIBL 1953:49). That the former alternative is impossible because "les scribes ne précisent jamais que le sceau royal aurait 'été' sorti et que tel ou tel l'aurait sorti, même quand le sceau est le sceau dynastique" is far from convincing. The fact that there is no parallel attestation does not, and cannot, regard as impossible such interpretation. Moreover, the word spelled ^{na4}kišib and its qualification ^{na4}kišib lugal are consistently used in the Ugarit corpus to designate the word "seal" (rather than "sealed document") and "royal seal," i.e. dynastic seal, respectively (as also pointed out by van Soldt in "Studies on the *sākinu*-Official (2)," p. 807 n. 12; see our discussion in chapter 5). As we shall see below, the document itself is called in the texts *ṭuppu* in Akkadian, and *spr* or *spr mlk* in Ugaritic.

seal first to Haman (3:10) and then to Mordecai (8:8ff.), saying to the latter: "Now you shall issue a writ concerning the Jews in my name, in whatever terms you think fit, and seal it with the royal signet." Of course the language of the royal deeds of Ugarit does not allow us to draw many conclusions on the life procedure that took place at Ugarit, neither to decide about the actual or fictitious meaning of the words "before king so-and-so." However, in the light of RS 16.145, it seems that the king's ministers only very rarely stood for the king and sealed his deeds, pointing to the probable fact that the king was normally present at the transactions signed with his seal.

It is a truism to say that the impression of the dynastic seal, and the king's presence (and consent), is directly related to the nature of a royal deed. But it may be of interest to point to the following evidence. Again one individual text provides the details. RS 15.125 is one of the few, exceptional royal deeds written in the native language of Ugarit in alphabetic cuneiform. Following the fragmentary operative part, the text (inscribed in lines 6-9) reads as follows: "Seal of Niqmaddu, king of Ugarit. Niqmaddu, king of Ugarit, has signed this document" (*mišmn . nqmd / mlk ugrt / nqmd . mlk . ugrt / ktb . spr hnd*). Closing the text on the lower edge of the tablet, the scribe literally designated the document as a "royal deed" (*spr mlk*). A short lexical discussion is here in order since the verb I have translated as "to sign" has been rendered differently, namely as "to write" since Virolleaud published this Ugaritic text.[5]

The reason for this commonly and unanimously accepted translation obviously lies in the general meaning the verb root (KTB) has in Hebrew. However, the Ugaritic language had and used another verb to denote the act of writing, namely SPR, where the noun *spr* (*/sipru/*) "writing, written document" derives from. Since there is no evidence that kings would be literate in Late Bronze Age Syria and it would indeed be difficult to imagine the ruler of Ugarit with a stylus in his hand inscribing a cuneiform text (that, as we know and shall discuss in following chapters, was the task of professional scribes), a translation "Niqmaddu, king of Ugarit wrote this document" can only make real sense if we understand it as "the king had it written," rather than literally.[6] Our proposed,

---

[5] *PRU* 2 no. 5. Virolleaud classified the text as a letter, and was followed by Manfried Dietrich, Oswald Loretz and Joaquín Sanmartín who gave the text a letter number, namely KTU 2.19 (so also in the second revised edition *The Cuneiform Alphabetic Texts from Ugarit, Ras Ibn Hani and Other Places* [Münster, 1995]). That the text was of legal content was already put forward by Kienast in "Rechtsurkunden in ugaritischer Sprache," pp. 445-446. Note, on the other hand, that Virolleaud misunderstood Nougayrol's designation "actes royaux" and also included under such category all Ugaritic royal letters (see *PRU* 2, pp. 17-35).

[6] The literal translation can be found, for example, in the dictionary of Ugaritic by

new rendering of the verb, however, is based on the technical legal meaning the same root has in Biblical Hebrew, for which only one attestation is available (like the Ugarit example). The context in which it appears is significantly Jeremiah's purchase of land mentioned above and its correct legal procedure. Following the word God had addressed to him, the prophet bought the field of Anathot from his cousin Hanamel, weighed the money to him, put the deed in writing, sealed it, and had men witness it. Then, we are told, he took the deed of purchase together with the copies and gave it to Baruch ben Neriah ben Mahseiah in the presence of his cousin and of the witnesses "who had signed (*ktwbym*) the deed of purchase."

To identify and classify a clay tablet or fragment as a royal deed should therefore pose few problems. Tablets inscribed with a text recording a transaction performed by or "before king so-and-so," and/or bearing the impression of the dynastic seal should undoubtedly form our corpus.[7] Here "and/or" unambiguously means "inclusive or," that is, we are referring to texts with one or both features. As a rule, and as we have already mentioned, royal deeds present both features. Exceptions, however, do exist. As we shall see below, the two most recently found texts of our corpus (written in Ugaritic) describe a royal transaction but bear no seal impression. And four royal deeds bear a royal seal impression other than the dynastic. The latter examples can be safely taken as exceptions to the rule; the two Ugaritic tablets, in turn, seem to be copies of original deeds.

The few problems of identification of royal deeds obviously appear when the document has come down to us in a fragmentary state, namely, when neither the seal impression nor the mention of the king as party to, or president over, the transaction is preserved. In such cases, the written text, and more particularly, the stereotyped formulas used in royal deeds can supply the lost information. The same holds true for the find-place of some damaged fragments. The fact that royal deeds were mainly

---

Gregorio del Olmo and Joaquín Sanmartín (*A Dictionary of the Ugaritic Language in the Alphabetic Tradition* [Handbuch der Orientalistik, I/67, Leiden/Boston 2003], p. 468); Kienast, in turn, preferred a contextual meaning "ausstellen" for KTB ("Rechtsurkunden in ugaritischer Sprache," p. 446).

[7] These were also the criteria proposed by Huehnergard to identify a legal text written at Ugarit (*The Akkadian of Ugarit* [Atlanta, 1989], p. 11). His three sufficient indications are: the mention of a judicial role or action of a particular king of Ugarit, the mention that some legal process took place in the presence of a particular king of Ugarit, and the presence of the royal seal of Ugarit. It should be stressed, however, that any of the indications would be sufficient to identify a royal deed but not any domestic legal text from Ugarit.

found in one palace archive can possibly serve as an argument to include fragmentary texts in our corpus.

2. The catalogue of royal deeds

The following list presents all the deeds that agree with the definition or characterization proposed above. The catalogue includes what we have considered to be the basic and relevant information of the tablets: find-place, date, language (and script) of the inscribed text, name of the scribe (if available), content of the deed, and the bibliographical reference to its *editio princeps*. Some of the aspects, such as the archaeological context, the language, and the content will have a separate, detailed treatment of their own in specific chapters of the book. Here only a brief and general introduction will be given, sufficient but also necessary, in order to properly frame the corpus of study. We shall accordingly restrict our discussion to the individual, controversial cases present in our material.

The task of completing the data of our catalogue has not been excessively painstaking thanks to the relatively recent publication of two comprehensive and complementary catalogues of the Ras Shamra texts. One is the mission's catalogue *La trouvaille épigraphique de l'Ougarit, vol. 1* (henceforth *TEO*) published by Pierre Bordreuil and Dennis Pardee, that includes all inscriptions discovered at Ras Shamra (and other related sites) up to 1988. The other is part of the monumental *Studies in the Akkadian of Ugarit. Dating and Grammar* (henceforth *SAU*) written by Wilfred van Soldt. Following these essential milestone works, texts are cited throughout this book according to their RS (Ras Shamra) inventory number. So that the reader can easily find the transliteration and copy of each cuneiform text, the first information given after the tablet number in the catalogue refers to the corresponding place of publication. The method of citation of the published texts is the one proposed by John Huehnergard in his *The Akkadian of Ugarit.*[8]

After the reference to the *editio princeps*, the find-place of the tablet is indicated. This information is also provided in both *TEO* and *SAU*. With the exception of a very few cases, tablets from Ras Shamra have been found in regular excavations, in other words, in their archaeological context. Because of the extraordinary great number of separate accumulations of tablets unearthed in the ruins of the city, the mission of Ras Shamra named these so-called "archives" after the buildings in which they were discovered. Within the walls of the royal palace, several concentrations of tablets came to light from various wings of the building. These were accordingly named after their respective spatial distribution,

---

[8] On p. 5.

e.g. "*Archives Centrales*," "*Archives Sud*," "*Archives Est*," and so on. Following van Soldt, we shall use the same designations in English translation, and also keep the abbreviation "PC" that stands for the original name given to the royal palace ("*Palais Central*"). The notation for tablets discovered in one of the palace archives accordingly follows the pattern: "PC/name of the archive."

It should be noted that not every locus where a tablet or a fragment has been found could be plausibly ascribed to an archive. In such cases, after "PC/" the number of the palace room is given. It should also be mentioned that after the preliminary revaluation of the palace architecture and spatial distribution recently carried out by Olivier Callot and Jean-Claude Margueron not only the function and nature of certain loci have been adjusted but also their nomenclature has been changed. For example, the identification of certain loci as open courts as understood by the excavator Claude Schaeffer has now been contested. Palace courts such as IV, V and VI have accordingly been renamed as rooms 152, 153 and 132, respectively.[9] The hyphen between two loci means that the tablet in question was found in the actual space between them.

On the other hand, private archives have been named after the alleged owner of the house in which they were found (incidentally suggested by internal textual data); so, for example, the houses, and corresponding archives, of Rašapᵓabu and Urtēnu.

A number of tablets and fragments have been recovered from the dump (*débris*) of excavations, becoming difficult and sometimes therefore speculative to establish the area or archive where they originally belonged. In other cases, only the more general find-place, but not the precise archaeological context, can be determined; so, for example, a tablet coming from the large residential area uncovered to the east of the palace, called by the mission "Residential Quarter."

Concerning the date of the texts, the only chronological fixed point is the name of the king under whose rule the text was composed or the name of other people mentioned in the text, especially the scribe who wrote it down. The deeds themselves, which could describe different kinds of transactions, were written either in Akkadian in word-syllabic cuneiform, or in Ugaritic, the native language, in alphabetic cuneiform.

---

[9] See for example and provisionally Jean-Claude Margueron, "Le palais royal d'Ougarit. Premiers résultats d'une analyse systématique," in *Le pays d'Ougarit autour de 1200 av. J.-C.*, ed. M. Yon et al. (Paris, 1995), pp. 188-190.

RS 8.98?
Publication: PRU 3 129b, pl. I
Find-place: Acropolis "Chantier I"
Language: Akkadian
Date: ^{c}Ammiṯtamru II? (fragm.)
Content: uncertain – small fragment with few signs preserved

RS 15.55?
Publication: unpublished
Find-place: PC/Eastern (53)
Language: Akkadian
Date: unknown (fragm.)
Content: uncertain – small fragment with few signs preserved

RS 15.70
Publication: PRU 3 130a, pl. XVII
Find-place: PC/Central (30)
Language: Akkadian
Date: ^{c}Ammiṯtamru II
Content: exchange of real property

RS 15.85
Publication: PRU 3 52f., pl. XIX
Find-place: PC/Central (30)
Language: Akkadian
Date: Niqmaddu II
Content: royal grant of real property & private gift of real property with royal confirmation

RS 15.86
Publication: PRU 3 51f., pl. XIX
Find-place: PC/Central (132)
Language: Akkadian
Date: ^{c}Ammiṯtamru II
Content: exchange of real property (between queen and another)

RS 15.88
Publication: PRU 3 88b, pl. XX
Find-place: PC/Central (21)
Language: Akkadian
Date: Niqmepa^{c}
Content: royal grant (confirmation) of real property
Scribe: Šapšumalku

RS 15.89
Publication: PRU 3 53b, pl. XX
Find-place: PC/Central (132)
Language: Akkadian
Date: Niqmaddu II
Content: royal grant of real property (transfer from uncle to niece)

RS 15.90
Publication: PRU 3 54a, pl. XX
Find-place: PC/Central (21)
Language: Akkadian
Date: Niqmaddu II
Content: division of family shares of real property

RS 15.91
Publication: PRU 3 75b, pl. XX
Find-place: PC/Central (132)
Language: Akkadian
Date: Arḫalbu
Content: royal grant of real property

RS 15.92
Publication: PRU 3 54ff., pl. XXI
Find-place: PC/Central (132)
Language: Akkadian
Date: Niqmaddu II
Content: adoption as son

RS 15.100
Publication: PRU 3 130b, pl. XXI
Find-place: PC/Central (31)
Language: Akkadian
Date: ^{c}Ammiṯtamru II
Content: uncertain (broken away)

RS 15.109+16.296
Publication: PRU 3 102ff., pl. XXII, XXIII
Find-place: PC/Central (30)
Language: Akkadian
Date: ^{c}Ammiṯtamru II (*Sammelurkunde* of deeds dated to Niqmepa^{c})
Content: royal grants of real property with payments (sales?)

RS 15.111
Publication: PRU 2 no. 9 (KTU 3.2)
Find-place: PC/Central (132)
Language: Ugaritic
Date: ^{c}Ammiṯtamru II
Content: royal grant of real property

RS 15.113
Publication: PRU 3 168c, pl. XXIV
Find-place: PC/Eastern (54)
Language: Akkadian
Date: Niqmaddu III
Content: uncertain (broken away)

RS 15.114
Publication: PRU 3 112f., pl. XXIV
Find-place: PC/Eastern (54) or PC/Central?
Language: Akkadian
Date: ^{c}Ammiṯtamru II
Content: royal grant of real property and a town

RS 15.117?
Publication: PRU 2 no. 7 (KTU 7.63)
Find-place: PC/Eastern (53)
Language: Ugaritic
Date: Niqmepa^c
Content: uncertain (fragm.)

RS 15.118
Publication: PRU 3 131a, pl. XXIV
Find-place: PC/Central (132)
Language: Akkadian
Date: ^{c}Ammiṯtamru II
Content: royal grant of real property with payment (sale?)
Scribe: Ya^{c}ḏirānu

RS 15.119
Publication: PRU 3 86ff., pl. XXV
Find-place: PC/Central (132)
Language: Akkadian
Date: Niqmepa^c
Content: purchases of real property with royal confirmation
Scribe: Karrānu

RS 15.120
Publication: PRU 3 56f., pl. XXV
Find-place: PC/Central (132)
Language: Akkadian
Date: Niqmaddu II
Content: will

RS 15.122
Publication: PRU 3 131f., pl. XXVI
Find-place: PC/Central (132)
Language: Akkadian
Date: ^{c}Ammiṯtamru II
Content: royal grants of real property with countergift

RS 15.123+16.152
Publication: PRU 3 89a, pl. XXVII
Find-place: PC/Central (132)
Language: Akkadian
Date: Niqmepa^c
Content: exchange (redemption?) of real property (with compensatory amount)

RS 15.125
Publication: PRU 2 no. 5 (KTU 2.19)
Find-place: PC/Central (31)
Language: Ugaritic
Date: Niqmaddu II or III
Content: royal exemption from service

RS 15.126
Publication: PRU 3 112a, pl. XXVII
Find-place: PC/Central (30)
Language: Akkadian
Date: ^{c}Ammiṯtamru II
Content: royal grant of real property with payment (sale?)

RS 15.127 (+)? RS 15.131
Publication: PRU 3 132b & 133a, pl. XXVIII
Find-place: PC/Central (30) & PC/Eastern (55) or Central?
Language: Akkadian
Date: Ammiṯtamru II
Content: royal grant of real property

RS 15.132
Publication: PRU 3 133f., pl. XXVIII
Find-place: PC/Central (30)
Language: Akkadian
Date: ^{c}Ammiṯtamru II
Content: royal grants of real property

RS 15.136
Publication: PRU 3 121f., pl. XXIX
Find-place: PC/Central (132)
Language: Akkadian
Date: ^{c}Ammiṯtamru II
Content: sale of real property
Scribe: Ya^{c}didu

RS 15.137
Publication: PRU 3 134f., pl. XXX
Find-place: PC/Central (21)
Language: Akkadian
Date: ^{c}Ammiṯtamru II
Content: royal grant of real property & promotion

RS 15.138+16.393B
Publication: PRU 3 101f., pl. XXX
Find-place: PC/Central (132-152)
Language: Akkadian
Date: Niqmepa^{c}
Content: royal grant of real property (transfer from father to son)
Scribe: Ḫuṣānu

RS 15.139
Publication: PRU 3 166f., pl. XXXI
Find-place: PC/Central (21)
Language: Akkadian
Date: Ibirānu
Content: purchase of real property with royal confirmation & ? (broken away)

RS 15.140
Publication: PRU 3 135f., pl. XXXI
Find-place: PC/Central (30-31)
Language: Akkadian
Date: ^{c}Ammiṯtamru II
Content: royal grant of real property
Scribe: Iltaḫmu

RS 15.141
Publication: PRU 3 136b, pl. XXXII
Find-place: PC/Central (30)
Language: Akkadian
Date: ^{c}Ammiṯtamru II
Content: royal grant of real property
RS 15.143+15.164
Publication: PRU 3 117, pl. XXXII
Find-place: PC/Central (152)
Language: Akkadian
Date: ^{c}Ammiṯtamru II
Content: royal grant of real property
Scribe: Nu^{c}merašpu

RS 15.145
Publication: PRU 3 122f., pl. XXXII
Find-place: PC/Central (132)
Language: Akkadian
Date: ^{c}Ammiṯtamru II
Content: royal grant of real property
Scribe: Munaḫḫimu

RS 15.146
Publication: PRU 3 58a, pl. XXXII (published as RS 15.146 + RS 15.161, but cf. *TEO*, p. 92)
Find-place: PC/Central (132)
Language: Akkadian
Date: Niqmaddu II or III
Content: conveyance of real property (fragm.)

RS 15.147
Publication: PRU 3 125, pl. XXXIII
Find-place: PC/Central (31)
Language: Akkadian
Date: ^{c}Ammiṯtamru II
Content: royal grants of real property
Scribe: Munaḫḫimu

RS 15.150
Publication: PRU 3 171a, pl. XXXIII
Find-place: PC/Central (31)
Language: Akkadian
Date: unknown (fragm.)
Content: conveyance of real property (with royal confirmation) (fragm.)

RS 15.155
Publication: PRU 3 118, pl. XXXIV
Find-place: PC/Central (30)
Language: Akkadian
Date: ^{c}Ammiṯtamru II
Content: royal grant of real property

RS 15.163+15.167
Publication: PRU 3 124, pl. XXXIV
Find-place: PC/Central (132)
Language: Akkadian
Date: ^{c}Ammiṯtamru II
Content: purchases of real property

RS 15.168
Publication: PRU 3 136f., pl. XXXV
Find-place: PC/Central (30)
Language: Akkadian
Date: ^{c}Ammiṯtamru II
Content: royal grant of real property
Scribe: Nu^{c}merašpu

RS 15.190
Publication: PRU 3 137b, pl. XXXVII
Find-place: PC/Central (132)
Language: Akkadian
Date: ᶜAmmiṯtamru II
Content: purchase of real property

RS 15.Y ([Varia 7] according to *TEO*)
Publication: PRU 3 78, pl. XXXVIII
Find-place: dump (PC/Central?)
Language: Akkadian
Date: Niqmepaᶜ
Content: royal grant of real property & promotion
Scribe: Šapšumalku

RS 15.Z ([Varia 8] according to *TEO*)
Publication: PRU 3 58f., pl. XXXVIII
Find-place: dump (PC/Central?)
Language: Akkadian
Date: Niqmaddu II
Content: royal grant of real property with payment (sale?)

RS 16.86+16.172
Publication: PRU 3 137f.+147b, pl. XXXIX, LVIII
Find-place: PC/Central (132)
Language: Akkadian
Date: ᶜAmmiṯtamru II
Content: royal grant of real property
Scribe: Munaḫḫimu

RS 16.131
Publication: PRU 3 138f., pl. XLII
Find-place: PC/Central (152)
Language: Akkadian
Date: ᶜAmmiṯtamru II
Content: sale of real property & exchange (redemption?) of real property

RS 16.132
Publication: PRU 3 140f., pl. XLIII
Find-place: PC/Central (132)
Language: Akkadian
Date: ᶜAmmiṯtamru II
Content: royal promotion & grants of real property & exemption from services

RS 16.133
Publication: PRU 3 59f., pl. XLIV
Find-place: PC/Central (132)
Language: Akkadian
Date: Niqmaddu II
Content: purchase of real property
Scribe: Šapšumalku

RS 16.134
Publication: PRU 3 141f., pl. XLIV
Find-place: PC/Central (132)
Language: Akkadian
Date: ᶜAmmiṯtamru II
Content: royal grant of real property

RS 16.135
Publication: PRU 3 89f., pl. XLV
Find-place: PC/Central (132)
Language: Akkadian
Date: Niqmepaᶜ
Content: sale of real property by the king

RS 16.136
Publication: PRU 3 142b, pl. XLV
Find-place: PC/Central (152)
Language: Akkadian
Date: ᶜAmmiṯtamru II
Content: royal grant of real property

RS 16.137
Publication: PRU 3 143a, pl. XLV
Find-place: PC/Central (152)
Language: Akkadian
Date: ᶜAmmiṯtamru II
Content: sales of real property

RS 16.138
Publication: PRU 3 143ff., pl. XLVI
Find-place: PC/Central (152)
Language: Akkadian
Date: ᶜAmmiṯtamru II
Deed: before the king
Content: royal grant of real property
Scribe: Yaᶜdidu

RS 16.139
Publication: PRU 3 145, pl. XLVII
Find-place: PC/Central (152)
Language: Akkadian
Date: ᶜAmmiṯtamru II
Content: purchase of real property

RS 16.140
Publication: PRU 3 45f., pl. XLVII
Find-place: PC/Central (152)
Language: Akkadian
Date: Niqmaddu II
Content: exchange of real property

RS 16.141
Publication: PRU 3 60b, pl. XLVIII
Find-place: PC/Central (152)
Language: Akkadian
Date: Niqmaddu II
Content: royal grant of real property and bride

RS 16.142
Publication: PRU 3 77b, pl. XLVIII
Find-place: PC/Central (152)
Language: Akkadian
Date: Arḫalbu
Content: royal grant of real property
Scribe: Šapšumalku

RS 16.143
Publication: PRU 3 81ff., pl. XLIX
Find-place: PC/Central (152)
Language: Akkadian
Date: Niqmepa^{c}
Content: royal grant of real property & transfer (from father to son) & private dispositions
Scribe: Šapšumalku

RS 16.144
Publication: PRU 3 76a, pl. L
Find-place: PC/Central (152)
Language: Akkadian
Date: Arḫalbu
Content: will ("last wishes") of king Arḫalbu

RS 16.145
Publication: PRU 3 169a, pl. L
Find-place: PC/Central (152)
Language: Akkadian
Date: unknown
Content: royal grant of real property & its subsequent sale

RS 16.147
Publication: PRU 3 90b, pl. LII
Find-place: PC/Central (152)
Language: Akkadian
Date: cf. scribe
Content: purchase of real property
Scribe: Šapšumalku

RS 16.148+16.254B
Publication: PRU 3 115f., pl. LII
Find-place: PC/Central (152)
Language: Akkadian
Date: ^{c}Ammiṯtamru II
Content: royal grant of real property

RS 16.149
Publication: PRU 3 176a (published as Pt. 383G)
Find-place: PC/Central (152)
Language: Akkadian
Date: cf. scribe
Content: conveyance of real property (fragm.)
Scribe: Šapšumalku

RS 16.150
Publication: PRU 3 47a, pl. LIII
Find-place: PC/Central (132-152)
Language: Akkadian
Date: Niqmaddu II
Content: royal grant of real property

RS 16.153
Publication: PRU 3 146f., pl. LIII
Find-place: PC/Central (132-152)
Language: Akkadian
Date: ^{c}Ammiṯtamru II
Content: royal grant of a town and taxes

RS 16.154
Publication: PRU 3 127f., pl. LIV
Find-place: PC/Central (132-152)
Language: Akkadian
Date: ^{c}Ammiṯtamru II
Content: sales of real property

RS 16.156
Publication: PRU 3 61f., pl. LV
Find-place: PC/Central (132-152)
Language: Akkadian
Date: Niqmaddu II
Content: sale of real property
Scribe: Yarimmu (cf. also Šapšumalku)

RS 16.157
Publication: PRU 3 83f., pl. LV
Find-place: PC/Central (132-152)
Language: Akkadian
Date: Niqmepa^{c}
Content: royal grant of real property & transfer (from father to son)
Scribe: Šapšumalku

RS 16.158
Publication: PRU 3 62b, pl. LVI
Find-place: PC/Central (132-152)
Language: Akkadian
Date: Niqmaddu II
Content: exchange of real property and dowry

RS 16.160
Publication: PRU 3 76b, pl. LVI
Find-place: PC/Central (132-152)
Language: Akkadian
Date: Arḫalbu
Content: royal grant of real property

RS 16.162
Publication: PRU 3 126, pl. LVI
Find-place: PC/Central (132-152)
Language: Akkadian
Date: ^{c}Ammiṯtamru II
Content: royal grant of real property

RS 16.163
Publication: PRU 3 169f,, pl. LVII
Find-place: PC/Central (132-152)
Language: Akkadian
Date: unknown (fragm.)
Content: conveyance of real property (fragm.)

RS 16.166
Publication: PRU 3 47f., pl. LVII
Find-place: PC/Central (132-152)
Language: Akkadian
Date: Niqmaddu II
Content: royal grant of real property

RS 16.167
Publication: PRU 3 62f., pl. LVII
Find-place: PC/Central (132)
Language: Akkadian
Date: Niqmaddu II
Content: royal grant of real property with payment (sale?)

RS 16.170
Publication: PRU 3 91a, pl. LVIII
Find-place: PC/Central (132)
Language: Akkadian
Date: Niqmepa^{c}
Content: royal confirmation of rights of ownership of real property located at the border area between Ugarit and Siyannu.

RS 16.171
Publication: PRU 3 147b, pl. LVIII
Find-place: PC/Central (132)
Language: Akkadian
Date: ^{c}Ammiṯtamru II
Content: royal grant of real property

RS 16.173
Publication: PRU 3 171b, pl. LVIII
Find-place: PC/Central (132)
Language: Akkadian
Date: unknown (broken away)
Content: royal promotion & conveyance of real property? (fragm.)

RS 16.174
Publication: PRU 3 63b, pl. LIX
Find-place: PC/Central (132-152)
Language: Akkadian
Date: Niqmaddu II
Content: purchase of real property with royal confirmation / royal grant of real property with payment (sale?)

RS 16.178
Publication: PRU 3 148a, pl. LIX
Find-place: PC/Central (132-152)
Language: Akkadian
Date: ^{c}Ammiṯtamru II
Content: royal grant of real property
Scribe: ^{c}Abdiltu

RS 16.182+16.199
Publication: PRU 3 148f., pl. LXI
Find-place: PC/Central (152)
Language: Akkadian
Date: ^{c}Ammiṯtamru II
Content: royal grants of real property

RS 16.184
Publication: PRU 3 149f., pl. LXI
Find-place: PC/Central (152)
Language: Akkadian
Date: ^{c}Ammiṯtamru II
Content: royal grants of real property, one with payment (sale?)

RS 16.186
Publication: PRU 3 168a, pl. LXII
Find-place: PC/62: Central?
Language: Akkadian
Date: Ibirānu
Content: royal grant of real property

RS 16.187B
Publication: PRU 3 91b, pl. LXII (published as 16.187A; see also the remarks in *TEO* p. 106)
Find-place: PC/Central (64)
Language: Akkadian
Date: Arḫalbu, Niqmepa^{c} or ^{c}Ammurapi$^{\supset}$
Content: uncertain (broken away)

RS 16.188
Publication: PRU 3 150b, pl. LXII
Find-place: PC/Central (132-152)
Language: Akkadian
Date: ^{c}Ammiṯtamru II
Content: royal grant of real property

RS 16.189
Publication: PRU 3 91f., pl. LXIII
Find-place: PC/Central (132-152)
Language: Akkadian
Date: Niqmepa^{c}
Content: royal grants of real property with payment (sales)

RS 16.190
Publication: PRU 3 64a, pl. LXIII
Find-place: PC/Central (132-152)
Language: Akkadian
Date: Niqmaddu II
Content: royal grant of real property

RS 16.191+16.272
Publication: PRU 2 no. 6 (KTU 3.4)
Find-place: PC/Central (152)
Language: Ugaritic
Date: from Niqmaddu II on
Content: redemption of enslaved people from abroad with provision concerning service

RS 16.191A
Publication: PRU 3 172b, pl. LXIII
Find-place: PC/Central (152)
Language: Akkadian
Date: cf. scribe
Content: uncertain (fragm.)
Scribe: Šapšumalku

RS 16.192A+16.205
Publication: PRU 3 153f., pl. LXVII
Find-place: PC/Central (62 & 132-152)
Language: Akkadian
Date: ^{c}Ammiṯtamru II
Content: release of people from claims after process
Scribe: Ya^{c}ḏirānu

RS 16.197
Publication: PRU 3 150f., pl. LXIV
Find-place: PC/Central (132-152)
Language: Akkadian
Date: ^{c}Ammiṯtamru II
Content: exchange of real property

RS 16.198B
Publication: PRU 3 168b, pl. LXIV
Find-place: PC/Central (132-152)
Language: Akkadian
Date: Niqmaddu III
Content: royal grant of real property? (broken away)

RS 16.200
Publication: PRU 3 64f., pl. LXV
Find-place: PC/Central (132-152)
Language: Akkadian
Date: Niqmaddu II
Content: adoption as son with royal confirmation

RS 16.201
Publication: PRU 3 151f., pl. LXV
Find-place: PC/Central (132-152)
Language: Akkadian
Date: ^{c}Ammiṯtamru II
Content: royal grant of real property
Scribe: Munaḫḫimu

RS 16.202
Publication: PRU 3 152f., pl. LXVI
Find-place: PC/Central (132-152)
Language: Akkadian
Date: ^{c}Ammiṯtamru II
Content: royal grant of a town

RS 16.204
Publication: PRU 3 119f., pl. LXVI, LXVII
Find-place: PC/Central (132-152)
Language: Akkadian
Date: ^{c}Ammiṯtamru II
Content: royal grant of real property
Scribe: Ya^{c}didu

RS 16.206
Publication: PRU 3 106a, pl. LXVIII
Find-place: PC/Central (132-152)
Language: Akkadian
Date: Niqmepa^{c}
Content: royal grant of real property with payment to PN (sale?)

RS 16.207
Publication: PRU 3 109b, pl. LXVIII
Find-place: PC/Central (132-152)
Language: Akkadian
Date: Niqmepa^{c}
Content: sale of real property
Scribe: Karrānu

RS 16.208
Publication: PRU 3 93a, pl. LXVIII
Find-place: PC/Central (132-152)
Language: Akkadian
Date: cf. scribe
Content: royal grant of real property
Scribe: Šapšumalku

RS 16.238+16.254
Publication: PRU 3 107f., pl. LXIX
Find-place: PC/Central (132-152)
Language: Akkadian
Date: ^{c}Ammiṯtamru II
Content: royal exemption from services

RS 16.239
Publication: PRU 3 79ff., pl. LXIX
Find-place: PC/Central (132-152)
Language: Akkadian
Date: Arḫalbu
Content: royal grant of real property & emancipation of a son

RS 16.240
Publication: PRU 3 173a, pl. LXX
Find-place: PC/Central (132-152)
Language: Akkadian
Date: unknown (fragm.)
Content: conveyance of real property? (fragm.)

RS 16.241+16.261+16.339
Publication: PRU 3 159f., pl. LXXXV
Find-place: PC/Central (132-152)
Language: Akkadian
Date: ^{c}Ammiṯtamru II
Content: purchase of real property
Scribe: Ya^{c}didu

RS 16.242
Publication: PRU 3 154f., pl. LXX
Find-place: PC/Central (132-152)
Language: Akkadian
Date: ^{c}Ammiṯtamru II
Content: royal grant of real property

RS 16.243
Publication: PRU 3 155f., pl. LXXI
Find-place: PC/Central (132-152)
Language: Akkadian
Date: ^{c}Ammiṯtamru II
Content: royal grant of real property
Scribe: Munaḫḫimu

RS 16.244
Publication: PRU 3 93b, pl. LXXI
Find-place: PC/Central (132-152)
Language: Akkadian
Date: Niqmepa^{c}
Content: royal grant of a town's taxes (to the town's governor)

RS 16.245
Publication: PRU 3 94f., pl. LXXII
Find-place: PC/Central (132-152)
Language: Akkadian
Date: Niqmepa^{c}
Content: royal verdict and transfer of real property
Scribe: Šapšumalku

RS 16.246
Publication: PRU 3 95f., pl. LXXII
Find-place: PC/Central (132-152)
Language: Akkadian
Date: Niqmepa^{c}
Content: exchange (redemption?) of real property (with compensatory amount)

RS 16.247
Publication: PRU 3 65b, pl. LXXIII
Find-place: PC/Central (132-152)
Language: Akkadian
Date: Niqmaddu II
Content: royal grant of real property

RS 16.248
Publication: PRU 3 48f., pl. LXXIII
Find-place: PC/Central (132-152)
Language: Akkadian
Date: Niqmaddu II
Content: royal grant of real property

RS 16.249
Publication: PRU 3 96ff., pl. LXXIV
Find-place: PC/Central (132-152)
Language: Akkadian
Date: Niqmepa^{c}
Content: royal grant/confirmation of real property (from father to son) & restitution of property after royal sentence

RS 16.250
Publication: PRU 3 85f., pl. LXXIV
Find-place: PC/Central (132-152)
Language: Akkadian
Date: Niqmepa^{c}
Content: royal grant of real property & transfer of real property (from father to son) & private dispositions
Scribe: Šapšumalku

RS 16.251
Publication: PRU 3 108f., pl. LXXV
Find-place: PC/Central (132-152)
Language: Akkadian
Date: Niqmepa^{c}
Content: royal grant of real property with countergift
Scribe: Šapšumalku

RS 16.252
Publication: PRU 3 66a, pl. LXXV
Find-place: PC/Central (132-152)
Language: Akkadian
Date: Niqmaddu II or III
Content: manumission of a slave woman and children (for marriage?)

RS 16.253
Publication: PRU 3 156f., pl. LXXVI
Find-place: PC/Central (132-152)
Language: Akkadian
Date: ^{c}Ammiṯtamru II
Content: gift of real and movable property (from husband to wife)

RS 16.254A
Publication: PRU 3 66b, pl. LXXVII
Find-place: PC/Central (132-152)
Language: Akkadian
Date: Niqmaddu II
Content: royal grant of real property (fragm.)

RS 16.254C
Publication: PRU 3 157b, pl. LXXVII
Find-place: PC/Central (132-152)
Language: Akkadian
Date: ^{c}Ammiṯtamru II
Content: royal verdict and transfer of real property

RS 16.254D
Publication: PRU 3 79a, pl. LXXVII
Find-place: PC/Central (132-152)
Language: Akkadian
Date: cf. scribe
Content: royal grant of real property
Scribe: Šapšumalku

RS 16.254E
Publication: PRU 3 173b, pl. LXXVII
Find-place: PC/Central (132-152)
Language: Akkadian
Date: unknown (fragm.)
Content: royal grant of real property? (fragm.)

RS 16.254F
Publication: PRU 3 158a, pl. LXXVIII
Find-place: PC/Central (132-152)
Language: Akkadian
Date: ᶜAmmiṯtamru II
Content: royal grant of real property (fragm.)

RS 16.255A+16.255E
Publication: PRU 3 67a, pl. LXXVIII
Find-place: PC/Central (132-152)
Language: Akkadian
Date: Niqmaddu II
Content: royal grant of real property (fragm.)

RS 16.255B
Publication: PRU 3 173c, pl. LXXVIII
Find-place: PC/Central (132-152)
Language: Akkadian
Date: unknown (fragm.)
Content: conveyance of real property (fragm.)

RS 16.255C
Publication: PRU 3 174b (published as RS 16.255H)
Find-place: PC/Central (132-152)
Language: Akkadian
Date: ᶜAmmiṯtamru II
Content: uncertain (broken away)

RS 16.255D
Publication: PRU 3 158b, pl. LXXVIII
Find-place: PC/Central (132-152)
Language: Akkadian
Date: ᶜAmmiṯtamru II
Content: royal grant of real property (fragm.)

RS 16.256
Publication: PRU 3 159a, pl. LXXIX
Find-place: PC/Central (132)
Language: Akkadian
Date: ᶜAmmiṯtamru II
Content: royal grant of real property with countergift

RS 16.260
Publication: PRU 3 98f., pl. LXXXIV
Find-place: PC/Central (152)
Language: Akkadian
Date: Niqmepaᶜ
Content: royal grant of real property with countergift

RS 16.262
Publication: PRU 3 67b, pl. LXXXVI
Find-place: PC/Central (132)
Language: Akkadian
Date: Niqmaddu II
Content: royal grant of real property

RS 16.263
Publication: PRU 3 49b, pl. LXXXVI
Find-place: PC/Central (132)
Language: Akkadian
Date: Niqmaddu II
Content: royal grant of real property & private gift of real property (from husband to wife) and subsequent sale (by wife)
Scribe: Šapšumalku

RS 16.267
Publication: PRU 3 110a, pl. LXXXVII
Find-place: PC/Central (132)
Language: Akkadian
Date: ᶜAmmiṯtamru II
Content: manumission of a slave woman (by the king, for marriage?) & provision *mortis causa* concerning real property

RS 16.269
Publication: PRU 3 68f., pl. LXXXVII
Find-place: PC/Central (132)
Language: Akkadian
Date: Niqmaddu II or III
Content: royal grant of real property & exemption from services as reward for having put to death a criminal

RS 16.270
Publication: PRU 3 41ff., pl. LXXXVIII
Find-place: PC/Central (132-152)
Language: Akkadian
Date: ᶜAmmiṯtamru II
Content: dynastic divorce

RS 16.275
Publication: PRU 3 50a, pl. LXXXIX
Find-place: PC/Central (132)
Language: Akkadian

Date: Niqmaddu II
Content: royal grant of real property

RS 16.276
Publication: PRU 3 69f., pl. XC
Find-place: PC/Central (132)
Language: Akkadian
Date: Niqmaddu II
Content: royal grant of a town with its taxes (as dowry?) & release of a man (son-in-law?) from obligations

RS 16.277
Publication: PRU 3 50f., pl. XC
Find-place: PC/Central (132)
Language: Akkadian
Date: Niqmaddu II
Content: exchange of real property (between queen and another)

RS 16.278
Publication: PRU 3 77a, pl. XCI
Find-place: PC/Central (132)
Language: Akkadian
Date: Arḫalbu
Content: uncertain (broken away)

RS 16.279
Publication: PRU 3 70b, pl. XCI
Find-place: PC/Central (152)
Language: Akkadian
Date: Niqmaddu II
Content: royal grant of real property? (broken away)

RS 16.281
Publication: PRU 3 161b, pl. XCI
Find-place: PC/Central (132)
Language: Akkadian
Date: ^{c}Ammiṯtamru II
Content: purchase of real property

RS 16.282
Publication: PRU 3 160f., pl. XCII
Find-place: PC/Central (132)
Language: Akkadian
Date: Ammiṯtamru II
Content: royal grant of real property with payment (sale?)
Scribe: Ya^{c}ḏirānu

RS 16.283
Publication: PRU 3 74b, pl. XCII
Find-place: PC/Central (132)
Language: Akkadian
Date: cf. scribe
Content: royal grant of real property with payment (sale?)
Scribe: Šapšumalku

RS 16.284
Publication: PRU 3 99b, pl. XCIII
Find-place: PC/Central (132)
Language: Akkadian
Date: Niqmepa^{c}
Content: purchase of real property
Scribe: Karrānu

RS 16.285
Publication: PRU 3 106f., pl. XCIII
Find-place: PC/Central (132)
Language: Akkadian
Date: Niqmepa^{c}
Content: sale of real property by the king
Scribe: Ḫuṣānu

RS 16.286
Publication: PRU 3 161f., pl. XCIII
Find-place: PC/Central (132-152)
Language: Akkadian
Date: ^{c}Ammiṯtamru II
Content: royal grant of real property with payment (sale?)

RS 16.295
Publication: PRU 3 70f., pl. XCV
Find-place: PC/Central (152)
Language: Akkadian
Date: Niqmaddu II
Content: gift of real and movable property (from grandfather to grandson) & subsequent adoption of grandson as son

RS 16.343
Publication: PRU 3 129a, pl. XCVI
Find-place: PC/Central (132-152)
Language: Akkadian
Date: ^{c}Ammiṯtamru II
Content: exchange (redemption?) of real property

RS 16.344
Publication: PRU 3 75a, pl. XCVI
Find-place: PC/Central (132-152)
Language: Akkadian
Date: Arḫalbu
Content: adoption as brother

RS 16.348
Publication: PRU 3 162f., pl. XCVII
Find-place: PC/Central (132)
Language: Akkadian
Date: ᶜAmmiṯtamru II
Content: royal promotion
Scribe: ᶜAbdiḫamanu

RS 16.353
Publication: PRU 3 113ff., pl. XCVIII
Find-place: PC/Central (132)
Language: Akkadian
Date: Ammiṯtamru II
Content: sale of real property

RS 16.356
Publication: PRU 3 71f., pl. XCIX
Find-place: PC/Central (132)
Language: Akkadian
Date: Niqmaddu II
Content: royal verdict and transfer of real property

RS 16.363
Publication: PRU 3 163f., pl. CI
Find-place: PC/Central (132-152)
Language: Akkadian
Date: ᶜAmmiṯtamru II
Content: royal grant of real property (fragm.)

RS 16.368
Publication: PRU 3 100a, pl. CII
Find-place: PC/Central (132-152)
Language: Akkadian
Date: Arḫalbu, Niqmepaᶜ or ᶜAmmurapiᵓ
Content: royal grant of real property (fragm.)

RS 16.371
Publication: PRU 3 72f., pl. CIII
Find-place: PC/Central (132)
Language: Akkadian
Date: Niqmaddu II
Content: exchange of real property & ? (fragm.)

RS 16.382
Publication: PRU 2 no. 8 (KTU 3.5)
Find-place: dump (PC/Central)
Language: Ugaritic
Date: ᶜAmmiṯtamru II
Content: royal grant of real property

RS 16.383
Publication: PRU 3 164b, pl. CIII
Find-place: PC/N of 52 or PC/Central?
Language: Akkadian
Date: ᶜAmmiṯtamru II
Content: exchange of real property (between king and another)

RS 16.384
Publication: PRU 3 165a, pl. CIII
Find-place: PC/Central (132-152)
Language: Akkadian
Date: ᶜAmmiṯtamru II
Content: royal grant of real property? (fragm.)
Scribe: Yarimmu

RS 16.385
Publication: PRU 3 73f., pl. CIV
Find-place: PC/Central (132-152)
Language: Akkadian
Date: Niqmaddu II
Content: royal grant of real property

RS 16.386
Publication: PRU 3 165f., pl. CIV
Find-place: PC/Central (132)
Language: Akkadian
Date: ᶜAmmiṯtamru II
Content: royal grant? (fragm.)
Scribe: Munaḫḫimu

RS 16.387
Publication: PRU 3 175b, pl. CV
Find-place: PC/Central (132-152)
Language: Akkadian
Date: unknown (fragm.)
Content: uncertain (broken away)

RS 16.413
Publication: PRU 3 166b, pl. CV
Find-place: dump (PC/Central?)

Language: Akkadian
Date: ᶜAmmiṯtamru II
Content: royal grant of real property? (fragm.)

RS 16.415
Publication: PRU 3 100b, pl. CV
Find-place: dump (PC/Central?)
Language: Akkadian
Date: Niqmepaᶜ
Content: uncertain (broken away)

RS 17.01
Publication: PRU 6 no. 27
Find-place: PC/Central (152)
Language: Akkadian
Date: ᶜAmmiṯtamru II
Content: royal grants of real property with countergift

RS 17.53 (= RS 17.113)
Publication: PRU 6 no. 25
Find-place: PC/Central (67)
Language: Akkadian
Date: Arḫalbu, Niqmepaᶜ or ᶜAmmurapiᵓ
Content: conveyance of real property? (fragm.)

RS 17.65
Publication: Ug 5 N no. 1
Find-place: Rašapᵓabu
Language: Akkadian
Date: Niqmaddu II
Content: uncertain (fragm.)

RS 17.113 see RS 17.53

RS 17.121
Publication: PRU 6 no. 56
Find-place: PC/Central (70)
Language: Akkadian
Date: unknown (fragm.)
Content: royal grant of real property? (fragm.)

RS 17.127
Publication: PRU 6 no. 26
Find-place: PC/Central (67)
Language: Akkadian
Date: cf. scribe
Content: uncertain (broken away)
Scribe: Šapšumalku

RS 17.147
Publication: PRU 6 no. 29
Find-place: PC/Central (66)
Language: Akkadian
Date: ᶜAmmiṯtamru II
Content: royal grant of real property

RS 17.322
Publication: PRU 6 no. 47
Find-place: PC/Central (132)
Language: Akkadian
Date: ᶜAmmurapiᵓ
Content: royal grant of real property? (fragm.)

RS 17.331
Publication: PRU 6 no. 21
Find-place: PC/Southern (153)
Language: Akkadian
Date: Niqmepaᶜ
Content: royal confirmation of conveyance of real property? (fragm.)

RS 17.350B
Publication: PRU 6 no. 46
Find-place: Residential Quarter
Language: Akkadian
Date: Niqmaddu III
Content: royal grant/confirmation of real property (fragm.)
RS 17.351B?
Publication: PRU 6 no. 61
Find-place: PC/Southern (68)
Language: Akkadian
Date: unknown (fragm.)
Content: conveyance of real property? (fragm.)

RS 17.363
Publication: PRU 6 no. 22
Find-place: PC/Southern (69)
Language: Akkadian
Date: Niqmepaᶜ
Content: conveyance of real property? (broken away)

RS 17.379A
Publication: PRU 6 no. 28 (published as RS 17.39)
Find-place: PC/Southern (69)

Language: Akkadian
Date: ^{c}Ammiṯtamru II
Content: royal grant of real property

RS 17.408
Publication: PRU 6 no. 33
Find-place: PC/Southern (68)
Language: Akkadian
Date: ^{c}Ammiṯtamru II
Content: royal grant of real property? (fragm.)

RS 17.410A(+)17.410B
Publication: PRU 6 nos. 34A + 34B
Find-place: PC/Southern (68)
Language: Akkadian
Date: Niqmaddu II, ^{c}Ammiṯtamru II or Ibirānu
Content: royal grant/confirmation of real property? (fragm.)

RS 18.21
Publication: PRU 6 no. 45
Find-place: PC/Southern (69)
Language: Akkadian
Date: Niqmaddu III
Content: private redemption of real property & royal grant of real property & slave
Scribe: Eḫliteššub

RS 18.22?
Publication: PRU 6 no. 55
Find-place: PC/Southern (153)
Language: Akkadian
Date: unknown (fragm.)
Content: conveyance (royal grants?) of real property (fragm.)

RS 18.53
Publication: PRU 6 no. 24
Find-place: PC/Central (132)
Language: Akkadian
Date: Niqmepa^{c}
Content: exchange of real property

RS 18.265A
Publication: PRU 6 no. 41
Find-place: PC/Southern (153)
Language: Akkadian
Date: Ibirānu? (fragm.)
Content: uncertain (broken away)
Scribe: AN-[

RS 18.280
Publication: PRU 6 no. 42
Find-place: PC/Southern (153)
Language: Akkadian
Date: Ibirānu
Content: uncertain (fragm.)
Scribe: Nu^{c}merašpu

RS 18.285
Publication: PRU 6 no. 30 (published as RS 18.500)
Find-place: PC/Eastern?
Language: Akkadian
Date: ^{c}Ammiṯtamru II
Content: royal grant of real property
Scribe: Iliramu

RS 19.98
Publication: PRU 6 no. 31
Find-place: PC/Southwestern (81)
Language: Akkadian
Date: ^{c}Ammiṯtamru II
Content: royal grant of real property
Scribe: Ya^{c}didu

RS 19.128
Publication: PRU 6 no. 32
Find-place: PC/75
Language: Akkadian
Date: ^{c}Ammiṯtamru II
Content: uncertain (fragm.)
Scribe: Iltaḫmu

RS 29.98
Publication: unpublished
Find-place: Residential Quarter
Language: Akkadian
Date: Niqmepa^{c}
Content: redemption of a slave woman (from the king by her husband?) and subsequent manumission together with her daughter

RS 94.2168
Publication: Bordreuil and Pardee, Manuel d'ougaritique, no. 38
Find-place: Urtenu
Language: Ugaritic

Date: ^{c}Ammiṯtamru II
Content: copy of an original Akkadian deed containing provisions of succession?

RS 94.2965
Publication: Bordreuil and Pardee, Manuel d'ougaritique, no. 39
Find-place: Urtenu
Language: Ugaritic
Date: cf. Ybnn/Yabninu (party to the transaction)
Content: excerpt of an original Akkadian deed describing a royal grant of real property?

3. The number of texts

Following the criteria established above, we have counted 176 royal deeds, to which five fragmentary texts could be added. Out of the five texts that defy a definite classification due to their state of preservation, three (RS 8.98, RS 15.55 and RS 17.351B) are very small, damaged fragments. The few signs preserved allow us to determine rather confidently the legal nature of the original documents. Their potential inclusion in the corpus of royal deeds is based, however, on very meager evidence. RS 8.98 preserves the last two signs of a king's name. And RS 15.55 and RS 17.351B seem to contain a clause concerning service owed to the palace only attested, as we shall see, in this category of legal documents. On the other hand, RS 18.22 describes what seems to be a multiple conveyance of lands in the manner of a royal deed. However, because no evidence of royal involvement is preserved (both the beginning and end of the text are missing), we have preferred to leave open, i.e. with a question mark, its inclusion in our corpus.[10]

The possible inclusion of RS 15.117 in our corpus is based on a new, alternative interpretation of the text, so that a more detailed commentary is required. The tablet (collated) is not fully preserved; the upper part of the obverse and the whole reverse is broken away. The text is in Ugaritic (KTU 7.63). The first three lines preserved are separated from the rest of the text by a ruling. They read as follows: [x x x *n*]*qmp*^{c} / [*bn nq*]*md* / [*mlk*] *ugrt*. Lines 4 to 9 read: ⸢*b*⸣ ^{c}*lṣdq* / *skn . bt* / *mlk . ṯǵr* / ⸢*m*⸣*lk bny* / ⸢*k*⸣$^{?}$. *lb . mlk* / [x x] ⸢*ṣmḫ*⸣$^{?}$.

This Ugaritic text has been generally taken to describe the royal titles of Niqmepa^{c}, tentatively restoring l. 1 as: [*šmt n*]*qmp*^{c} "'names' of Niqmepa^{c}"[11]. Edward Lipiński, in turn, interpreted it as a commemora-

[10] Nougayrol was neither certain about its attribution to his "type 3" (see *PRU* 6, p. 55).

[11] So Virolleaud, *PRU* 2, no. 7; John Gray, *Ugaritica* 6, pp. 289-290; del Olmo Lete, *La religión cananea según la liturgia de Ugarit* (Sabadell, 1992), p. 121; id., *Canaanite Religion according to the Liturgical Texts of Ugarit* (Bethesda, 1999), pp. 176-177; Dietrich, Loretz and Sanmartín, *Cuneiform Alphabetic Texts*, p. 528.

tive building inscription, taking *b*^{c}*lṣdq* in l. 4 as a personal name rather than a royal title.[12] Like him, I would understand *b*^{c}*lṣdq* as a personal name followed by his own titles "minister of the palace" and "royal gate-keeper." The following word *bny* poses, of course, more problems. One can tentatively take it, also in agreement with Lipiński, as a verbal form of BNY "to (re)build." In any case, the resulting partial translation does not really allow a full understanding of the record. I would doubt, however, that we are dealing with a building commemorative inscription. This kind of text is not commonly written on such tablets, nor would one expect to find such an inscription in the archives of the royal palace.

Concerning the first line of the text, one could possibly and tentatively restore [*l pn n*]*qmp*^{c} "before Niqmepa^{c}": it would fit in the broken space; it would describe the common introductory formula of legal documents (attested both in Akkadian and Ugaritic) in which the king appears presiding over the transaction (see chapter 6); and it would also explain the following ruling line after the complete formula (perhaps the royal dynastic seal was impressed on the lost upper part of the tablet —see chapters 5 and 6). It should be mentioned that van Soldt suggested in his catalogue of Ras Shamra texts the possible identification of RS 15.117 as a letter or a legal document, presumably then a royal deed.[13]

Also necessary for determining the total amount of texts is the identification of potential joins of legal fragments. Only two of the joins listed above were not published by Nougayrol, and are not accordingly included in *TEO*. Van Soldt suggested to join the fragments RS 15.127 and RS 15.131 (see *SAU*, p. 67), as well as RS 16.86 and RS 16.172 (see *SAU*, pp. 84, 568 and 570). The proposed joins seem very likely to me. RS 16.86 and 16.172 would join physically (they were found also together in the same find-spot). For the problem raised by the former join, namely the different provenance of the fragments RS 15.127 and RS 15.131, see the next section.

4. The find-place of the texts

As shown by the catalogue, most of the royal deeds come from the royal palace archives of Ugarit. Whereas this should not surprise us when dealing with royal documents, what is undoubtedly significant is the distribution of the texts within the palace itself. The majority of them

[12] "Recherches ugaritiques," *Syria* 50 (1973):40-42. The interpretation of *b*^{c}*lṣdq* as a PN was already suggested by Liverani, *Storia di Ugarit nell'età degli archivi politici* (Roma, 1962), p. 68.

[13] See *SAU*, p. 564, and my remarks in "The Legal Texts from Ugarit," pp. 413-414.

were found in one and the same accumulation of tablets, the one roughly located in the center of the building. Already in his "Exposé préliminaire" in *PRU* 3 Schaeffer defined the so-called palace central archive as "les archives juridiques par excellence du palais,"[14] and in the same volume Nougayrol further qualified it as "archives *royales*" (his own italics).[15] According to the catalogue of the mission, 152 texts out of 176 are reported to come from the central archive. To these one should probably add some texts found in the dump of excavations, some misplaced or wrong attributions in the inventory, as well as some stray finds.

Indeed, in his thorough study of the find-place of clay tablets and fragments discovered at Ras Shamra, van Soldt observed that the reported provenance of some of them contained more often than expected strong discrepancies. This, of course, may initially discourage any research on the archaeological context of the tablets. More so when one of the aims is to define and describe the different archives. "The dispersion of tablet fragments remains difficult to explain," he wrote with regard to the tablets of the first examined cluster of tablets, the so-called palace western archive.[16] "Especially the joins between fragments from the archive rooms and from the 'Place' in front of the Western Entrance is puzzling." "Similar problems," he then announced, "will be encountered with all the other archives," with particular reference to the central archive.[17] Intrusions among different archives are indeed attested.[18] And as

---

[14] P. XXIII.

[15] P. 23.

[16] *SAU*, p. 50.

[17] Ibid., p. 50 n. 29.

[18] Van Soldt pointed out stray finds and intrusions between a) the central and eastern archives (see *SAU*, p. 81); b) the southern and central archives (see *SAU*, pp. 81, 107; in note 98 p. 107 he significantly remarks the extraordinary dispersion of some fragments of treaties, "for example, 17.353+ found in IV-3, V-1, 83 and 69"); c) the southwestern and southern archives (see *SAU*, p. 121); d) rooms which do not belong properly to any archive with formal archives (see *SAU*, pp. 128, 131, 133); e) PC/PS, i.e. the open space between the royal palace and the so-called "South Palace," and palace archives such as the southern or southwestern ones (see *SAU*, p. 147); f) PS and the palace southern archive (see *SAU* pp. 153f.); g) the 'residential quarter' and the palace central archive (see *SAU*, pp. 161f.); or even h) between private archives such as the so-called library of the '*Lettré*' and Rašapʾabu's archive (see *SAU*, p. 164). Concerning the latter example, one should now refer to the recent conclusion drawn by Pierre Lombard according to which "les 24 tablettes attribuées au 'Lettré' ont toutes chances d'appartenir en fait au même lot que celles dites 'de Rashapabou'" ("Contexte archéologique et données épigraphiques. Quelques réflexions sur l'interprétation du gisement de 1973-1992," in *Le pays d'Ougarit autour de 1200 av. J.-C.*, p. 229). This archaeological revaluation would, of course, ex-

a result joins between far distant pieces remain unexplained.

In what follows we provide a list of the controversial cases that possibly, or even probably, belong to the central archive.

- RS 15.114: As pointed out by van Soldt (*SAU*, p. 66), Schaeffer admitted in *PRU* 3, p. XXII, that this tablet may have been wrongly attributed to the royal palace eastern archive and may plausibly come, instead, from the central archive.

- RS 15.127 and RS 15.131: As stated above, van Soldt suggested to join these two fragments (*SAU*, p. 67). This raises, consequently, the problem of the original find-place of the tablet since both fragments have been assigned rather distant find-spots: RS 15.127 from room 30 (central archive) and RS 15.131 from room 55 (eastern archive). If the join proves correct, as it seems, we could assume that RS 15.131 belonged to the central archive.

- RS 15.Y and RS 15.Z: These two tablets were found in the dump, out of their archaeological context. In *TEO*, p. 378, we can read that the provenance is unknown. However, the list of published texts in *PRU* 3, p. 275, states that they come from the dump of the palace central archive (so included, for example, by van Soldt in *SAU* in the list of legal texts on p. 235).

- RS 16.186, RS 16.192A + RS 16.205 and Room 62: Van Soldt included the palace room 62 among the "miscellaneous archives within the palace." Nevertheless, as he himself observed (*SAU*, p. 131), "it is uncertain if the mixed lot discovered in this room should be called an archive." More particularly, he believes that the legal texts RS 16.192A+ and RS 16.287 found there "most probably belong to the central archive." This is especially true of RS 16.192A which is part of the same tablet as RS 16.205 found in the space 132-152 that belongs to the central archive; "and —he added— the same may apply to 16.186" (ibid.).

- RS 16.382: As pointed out by Bordreuil and Pardee (*TEO*, p. 120), Virolleaud assigned in *PRU* 2, p. 20, the provenance of this tablet to the dump of the royal palace central archive.

- RS 16.383: According to *TEO* (p. 120), this tablet was found to the northeast of room 49. Also within the vicinity of the palace eastern archive, *SAU* (p. 71) catalogues the tablet as found, in turn, to the north of room 52. However, as pointed out by van Soldt himself, the find-spot of this tablet as well as the resulting inclusion in the eastern archive is doubtful; furthermore, as he himself noted, according to the list in *PRU* 3, p. 279, it comes from the central archive.

- RS 16.413 and RS 16.415: These two small fragments were all

plain the above-mentioned "intrusion."

found in the dump, without any further specific indication. Nevertheless, according to their publication number, their original find-place seems to have been the royal palace.

- RS 19.98: This tablet was found in the palace southwestern archive. As stated by van Soldt (*SAU*, p. 122), it "was kept here for unknown reasons." As he also pointed out, Schaeffer (*Ugaritica* 4, pp. 89ff.) was the first one to be puzzled about the find-place of the tablet, wondering whether it had been brought from the central archive, where it probably belonged to, in order to be baked in what he identified as the oven for tablets in the southwestern archive (the recent archaeological reappraisal by the Ras Shamra team has proved, however, that such oven did not exist).[19]

- RS 19.128 and Room 75: Isolated tablets in isolated rooms have also been found. This is the case of RS 19.128 from the palace room 75. One can only postulate, again with van Soldt, whether this royal document "may have come from the central archive" (*SAU*, p. 133).

To sum up, doubts will always exist as to the actual provenance of a number of tablets and fragments. This survey has shown that some find-spots are admittedly questionable, especially as far as joined fragments from different and distant loci are concerned. What needs to be stressed here is that the resulting number of texts that come from the palace central archive amounts to 160 (or 162, if we accept this archive as the original place of RS 19.98 and RS 19.128). In other words, more than 90 per cent of the total number of royal deeds stem from the palace central archive. Interestingly, the converse argument seems to be also true. That is, almost all legal texts and fragments discovered in the palace central archive are royal deeds. Accordingly, it is reasonable to suggest that the legal fragments excluded from our corpus due to the lack of indicative evidence could actually preserve part of royal deeds (see also below, chapter 2).[20]

As for the other palace archives, the southern concentration includes the largest number, namely eight documents and two fragmentary texts possibly preserving part of a royal deed.[21] One or two other documents

[19] See already Yves Calvet, "Les bassins du palais royal," Syria 67 (1990):39-40, and more recently Yon, *La cité d'Ougarit*, pp. 54-55.

[20] So, for example, RS 16.175, RS 16.203 ("Fragment avec traces de signes et empreinte de sceau," according to *TEO*, p. 108), RS 16.255F, RS 16.255G, RS 16.280D, RS 16.311, RS 16.414 (found together with RS 16.413 and RS 16.415 commented upon above), or the unpublished fragment RS 18.534 (catalogued in *TEO*, p. 188, as a "petit fragment de contrat").

[21] On the basis of the formulary, typical, although not exclusive, of royal deeds, it is posible that RS 18.274 also found in this palace archive is a fragment of a royal

(the find-place of RS 18.285 is not beyond doubt)[22] and two uncertain fragments come from the palace eastern archive (not included here are RS 15.114 and the possible joined fragment RS 15.131 discussed above). And concerning RS 19.98, the only royal deed reported to come from the southwestern archive, see the remarks above pointing to its possible origin in the central archive.

According to the catalogue of the mission, five royal documents (RS 17.65, RS 17.350B, RS 29.98, RS 94.2168, and RS 94.2965) and one small, damaged fragment with traces of what might be a royal deed (RS 8.98) have been found outside the walls of the royal palace. One of them, however, might belong to the palace southern archive.[23] The other four documents belong to private archives. The small fragment RS 17.65, perhaps the private copy of an original deed[24] was found in the house of Rašapᵓabu. This house was located in the residential area east of the palace where RS 29.98 was also discovered. As for RS 94.2168 and RS 94.2965, they are both written in Ugaritic and bear no (royal) seal impression. One can speculate and consider them Ugaritic copies of original royal deeds.

In closing this section, an obvious but important remark should be made. No royal deed, and more generally no legal document originating from Ugarit, has been found elsewhere than Ras Shamra. It would of course be surprising to find a text written by Ugarit scribes for Ugarit internal record outside the borders of the kingdom. One should incidentally mention that not even the archives of Ras Ibn Hani, a site hardly 5 km away from the capital (presumably the ancient town of Raᵓšu),[25] have yielded any legal documents. It can therefore be stated what one could have assumed *a priori*, namely that the archaeological provenance of the texts of our corpus corresponds to their scribal or linguistic provenance.

---

deed (see chapter 6).

[22] *TEO* (p. 169) assigns this tablet to the eastern archive (note that no locus is given). Van Soldt, however, does not list it among the tablets discovered in this archive (*SAU*, pp. 62ff.), or any other particular find-place within the palace. Note furthermore his observation that tablets from this archive "are only known from the 15th ... and 17th ... campaigns" (ibid., p. 61 n. 42).

[23] The inventory number RS 17.350B shows that it was discovered together with the finds of the palace southern archive, where an important group of royal deeds was kept. One should further note that van Soldt included it under this palace archive in his list in *SAU*, p. 236.

[24] As suggested by Nougayrol in *Ugaritica* 5, p. 2.

[25] As proposed by Michael Astour and van Soldt. See most recently Nadav Na'aman, "Raᵓshu, Reᵓsi-ṣuri, and the Ancient Names of Ras Ibn Hani," BASOR 334 (2004):33-39, with a survey of all proposed interpretations.

5. The language of the texts

The picture provided by the table above is fairly eloquent as far as the language of the texts is concerned. Of 176 royal documents, 170 are written in Akkadian in syllabic cuneiform, and only six texts are written in the native language of Ugarit in alphabetic cuneiform. As for the five uncertain fragments, four are written in Akkadian and one is in Ugaritic. To explain why scribes in Ugarit would not use Ugaritic but the language of Mesopotamia when they had to write a legal text (royal or private) it has been argued that Akkadian was at that time the lingua franca in the Near East, and particularly its western periphery.[26] Apart from the possible objections to the last statement (which will be discussed below in chapter 4), the argument itself does not seem to be convincing. A lingua franca is not directly related to, let alone determining, the use of the legal language, at least when domestic affairs are concerned. As is well known, administrative texts that usually deal with local matters are as a rule recorded in Ugaritic. Why then was Akkadian used to write royal deeds, which properly record domestic transactions? The answer seems to be intimately related to the genre of the texts.[27] But one essential question needs to be raised before we deal with the concept of legal language, and that concerns the time when the Ugaritic script was invented. For if, as it seems, the alphabetic cuneiform was not invented before the reign of Niqmepa^{c}, one should rather pose the question with a chronological reference, namely: why was Akkadian, and not Ugaritic, used to write the royal deeds of, say, ^{c}Ammiṯtamru II or Ibirānu? Although the date of the texts and the list of the kings of Ugarit who presided over the recorded and preserved transactions will be discussed in the next section, a word on the chronology of the Ugaritic script is here in order.

Until recently it was generally assumed that the Ugaritic alphabetic script was invented in the course of the 14th century. After a revaluation of the evidence, Bordreuil and Pardee have put forward that "il existe de bonnes raisons pour penser que la date de l'apparition de l'alphabet cunéiforme soit à situer dans la première moitié du XIIIe siècle." A few lines further, they go on to state in their *Manuel d'Ougaritique* that "l'absence de tout nom royal en cunéiformes alphabétiques antérieurement à Ammistamrou fils de Niqmepa, dont le règne s'est prolongé sur trois décennies à partir du milieu du XIIIe siècle, conforte cette hypothèse."[28] To the latter statement one should refer, however, to RS

[26] So, for example, Miller, *Studies in the Juridical Texts*, p. 317.

[27] As concluded by van Soldt in *SAU*, pp. 228-229 and 519. See already the remarks of Ephraim A. Speiser in his review article of *PRU* 3, namely "Akkadian Documents from Ras Shamra," JAOS 75 (1955):155-156.

[28] *Manuel d'Ougaritique*, vol. I (Paris, 2004), p. 32. See also the statement by

15.117 (KTU 7.63), discussed above. The Ugaritic text certainly mentions Niqmepa^{c}, king of Ugarit, and, if our interpretation proves correct, the fragment would be part of one of his royal deeds. Whether or not RS 15.117 becomes then the oldest datable extant text written in Ugaritic and accordingly the alleged date of the invention of the script is to be pushed back a few years, what remains probable is that the script itself did not exist in the time of, say, Niqmaddu II. It should accordingly not surprise us that the latter's deeds were all written in Akkadian. Why then in Akkadian? The answer is, I believe, self-evident.

As we shall discuss in detail in the following chapters, the Mesopotamian system of writing as well as the Mesopotamian language viz. Akkadian as well as the whole system of bureaucracy were adopted by the civilizations that surrounded Mesopotamia, naturally including the world of Ugarit. Indeed, the learning and use of Akkadian outside Mesopotamia came hand in hand with the script; this is another way of saying that writing in Akkadian meant nothing else than being literate. And it is, I believe, in this precise sense that we must understand Koschaker when he coined the word and the chronologically and geographically broad concept of "cuneiform law." By this, indeed, he did not understand a common or homogeneous legal system that would cover most of the Near East over the course of three millennia. The use of this relevant and original term he would justify with the following words:

> Nicht, daß Babylonien den Völkern, die es anzog oder auf die es einwirkte, sein Recht gegeben hätte. Vielmehr haben wir uns die Entwicklung dieser Rechte im wesentlichen als autonome vorzustellen. Was Babylon ihnen gab, war nicht der Inhalt, sondern die Form des Rechts: die Schrift, die Sprache und die Urkunde.[29]

As the term itself indicates, the concept strictly focuses on the formal expression of law. Ugarit was not yet a province of cuneiform law when Koschaker wrote his influential study. But as texts began to appear under the surface of the tell of Ras Shamra, his newly created forum of Oriental law would reach its western end at the shore of the Mediterranean. What is more significant of this province is that the exceptional Ugaritic royal deeds would still be written in cuneiform script and would present the form of the Akkadian documents. The shape and size of the tablets, the

---

Pardee, "il n'existe à présent aucune preuve que l'écriture cunéiforme alphabétique ait été inventée avant l'époque de ^{c}Ammiṯtamrou II" (in "Le traité d'alliance RS 11.722+," Semitica 51 [2001]:24); and the study by Anne-Sophie Dalix, "Šuppiluliuma (II?) dans un texte alphabétique d'Ugarit et la date d'apparition de l'alphabet cunéiforme," Semitica 48 (1998):5-15.

[29] "Keilschriftrecht," p. 27.

scheme and formulary of the texts would clearly reflect the Akkadian counterparts (see the discussion of the equivalent expressions in chapter 6).[30]

As to the *raison d'être* of these Ugaritic exceptions, it has been often suggested that these texts could be translations of Akkadian originals. If this may be true of the two tablets without seal impression recently found in Urtēnu's archive (namely RS 94.2168 and RS 94.2965), it seems unlikely for those showing the same formal aspect as the Akkadian documents that were kept in the archive of royal deeds *par excellence*. Indeed, what would have been the purpose of translating the Akkadian documents into Ugaritic? Why would the alleged copies be sealed with the dynastic seal and later kept in the central archive with the rest of "original" deeds? And finally, what happened then to the translated, original Akkadian deeds, or what were they meant for?

The general remark to be made is that the four royal deeds written in Ugaritic found in the palace central archive (RS 15.111 [KTU 3.2], RS 15.125 [KTU 2.19], RS 16.191 + RS 16.272 [KTU 3.4], and RS 16.382 [KTU 3.5]) were undoubtedly legally effective. All of them were sealed with the seal of the king of Ugarit.[31] As a matter of fact, it seems reasonable to ask why scribes who were admittedly biliterate (or biscriptal)[32] would not have written, if only exceptionally, legal documents in Ugaritic. We happen to know for example that Burqānu the scribe drew up at least three (private) deeds in Akkadian and one (also private) in his native language.[33]

---

[30] Especially in the cases of RS 15.111 (KTU 3.2) and RS 16.382 (KTU 3.5). See already the remarks by their editor Virolleaud, and the later examination of the Akkadian-Ugaritic equivalent expressions by Kienast ("Rechtsurkunden in ugaritischer Sprache," pp.434-444) and Milano ("Bilinguismo," pp. 183-186).

[31] See Kienast ("Rechtsurkunden in ugaritischer Sprache," p. 444), who excluded, however, RS 15.125 (KTU 2.19), taking it as an Ugaritic translation (like e.g. Huehnergard, *The Akkadian of Ugarit*, p. 187 n. 358). Nevertheless, that the royal seal must have been originally impressed on the tablet, viz. on the missing upper part of the obverse (the usual space for sealing in Ugarit tablets), is clearly suggested by lines 6-7 mentioned above: "Seal of Niqmaddu, king of Ugarit."

[32] That is, able to write one's native language and another with approximately equal facility. The term "biscriptal" was first used by van Soldt ("Babylonian lexical, religious and literary texts and scribal education at Ugarit and its implications for the alphabetic literary texts," in *Ugarit: ein ostmediterranes Kulturzentrum im Alten Orient. I. Ugarit und seine altorientalische Umwelt*, ed. M. Dietrich and O. Loretz [Münster, 1995], p. 186).

[33] The Akkadian texts are RS 8.145, RS 17.251 and RS 25.137; and RS 19.66 (KTU 3.8) is the one in Ugaritic. Van Soldt would still question whether the latter would not be a copy of an Akkadian original (see *SAU*, p. 27 n. 213). One should

Back to Koschaker's notion of cuneiform law, I certainly agree with the idea that the Babylonian "Form des Rechts" influenced the adoption of Mesopotamian bureaucratic practices by Ugarit scribes from the 14th to the early 12th centuries. But that is not a sufficient explanation. Why, and more importantly, under what circumstances and when would the Ugarit scribes adopt it? How did this "appealing" influence work? These questions will be properly dealt with in the chapter on the Akkadian language. Here I would simply state that legal life in Ugarit did certainly not start in the 14th century BC, in spite of the image projected by the extant sources. One should also keep in mind that legal language is characterized in all cultures by its traditional nature. The adoption, therefore, of Mesopotamian scribal practices in drawing up legal documents presumably had in Ugarit a longer history than what our sources could make us believe too soon. And it is precisely this long tradition, so closely linked to legal language and practice (as we shall also see in the corresponding chapter), that accounts for the continuing viz. conservative use of Akkadian to draw up legal texts despite the invention of a simpler script to write the vernacular (Ugaritic), used for example for administrative notes and records.

6. The date of the texts

"Due to the nature of the recording practices," wrote van Soldt in his introduction to the presently most comprehensive study on the chronology of the Ugarit archives, "no date in the strict sense of the word can be ascertained for any one text." "No eponyms," he explained, "year names or number systems were used."[34] Strangely enough, this is also true of legal texts. Scribes at Ugarit seem to have deviated from most legal traditions, including the Mesopotamian, where dating deeds was almost a requisite.

"The only fixed point," continued van Soldt, "may be the name of the ruling monarch, which is frequently mentioned in legal texts and letters." This is, of course, especially true of royal deeds. Together with the diplomatic documents, they are the more accurately dated texts of Ugarit and constitute the main evidence on which the chronological framework of this Late Bronze Age site has been built. In saying "more accurately," however, I do not mean that we are able to determine a

---

further note that if the tantalizing restoration proposed by Lipiński ("Aḫat-Milki, reine d'Ugarit, et la guerre de Mukiš," OLP 12 [1981]:113) is correct, RS 15.111 (KTU 3.2) would have been written by the well-known scribe of Akkadian royal deeds Nu^{c}merašpu (see chapter 5 section 3 below).

[34] *SAU*, p. 1.

fixed date, namely day, month and year, for any particular transaction. All that can be determined for any royal deed of Ugarit is a period of time as long as the duration of the rule of the king who presided over the recorded transaction. "This means," again in van Soldt's words, "that two texts with two different but successive kings can in fact be closer in time than two others dated to the same king." And the same holds true for the reference to individuals mentioned as relatives, vassals or officials of the king, especially the scribes of the documents. Šapšumalku, for example, was an active scribe during the successive reigns of Niqmaddu II, Arḫalbu and Niqmepaᶜ.

As shown by the catalogue, our corpus covers the reigns of seven successive kings, from Niqmaddu II down to ᶜAmmurapiᵓ, in all likelihood the last ruler of Ugarit.[35] In the absolute terms proposed by van Soldt (followed throughout this book), the royal deeds of Ugarit span a period of about one century and a half, namely from ca. 1330 BC down to the destruction of the city occurred between 1195 and 1175. This long period of time corresponds to the period of Hittite rule. Ugarit became a vassal kingdom of Hatti in the days of Niqmaddu II, and disappeared with the fall of the Hittite Empire. For the indispensable political background of our corpus, I refer to the excellent overview recently provided by Itamar Singer.[36]

The line of succession of the hereditary kings of Ugarit covered by our corpus is the following:

---

[35] A note on the numbering of the homonymous kings (in Latin characters) is here in order. For despite the recent discovery of several copies of the so-called "king list of Ugarit" and the corresponding line of succession of the rulers (see Arnaud, "Prolégomènes à la rédaction d'une histoire d'Ougarit II: les bordereaux de rois divinisés," SMEA 41 [1998]:153-173, and our discussion in chapter 5 below), we have kept the "traditional" names, as established by Nougayrol. Thus, our Niqmaddu II should now be renamed Niqmaddu III according to the king list, and our Niqmaddu III accordingly Niqmaddu IV; our Niqmepaᶜ would be the fifth ruler of Ugarit bearing this name, and our first Ibirānu would be the sixth with his name; our ᶜAmmiṯtamru II should be renamed "the third," and ᶜAmmurapiᵓ would be "the second." Our decision to use the "traditional" nomenclature is not only taken for the sake of convenience, viz. to make cross-references with the important works of our predecessors easier; one should also take into consideration the undoubtedly biased composition of the "king list of Ugarit." Its official character is already manifest with the exclusion of Arḫalbu from the list. How many other deliberate exclusions or inclusions there are we could only tell when new sources either from Ras Shamra or other sites come to light and illuminate the currently dark early phases of the history of Ugarit.

[36] "A Political History of Ugarit," pp. 603-733.

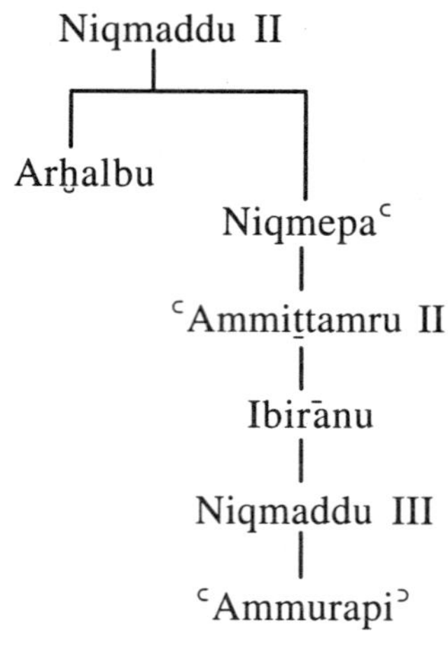

No break in the evidence is attested in this dynastic line of succession from Niqmaddu II until the destruction of Ugarit. Yet, a clear stop exists before Niqmaddu II in spite of the known dynastic succession. No legal documents are available from the time of Niqmaddu's father and predecessor ᶜAmmiṯtamru I, nor from earlier rulers.[37] The same is actually true of the major corpus of Ras Shamra tablets. What may be the reason for such textual discontinuity? It has been pointed out, more or less intentionally, that this interruption coincides with Ugarit's incorporation into the new Hittite Empire. Indeed, the preserved material runs parallel to the time of Hittite rule over this Mediterranean province. "With a few exceptions," concluded van Soldt, "no tablets are attested for the period preceding the Hittite conquest." In other, more deliberate words, he observed that "tablets dating from before the Hittite conquest had generally been thrown away."[38] Now, "whether the Hittite conquest should be held responsible for this phenomenon," he cautiously added, "remains unknown."

An alternative explanation, early put forward by Liverani,[39] is based on the report on Canaan that Abimilku, king of Tyre, sent to the Pharaoh, his overlord, by the time shortly before the Hittite conquest. "Fire destroyed the royal palace of Ugarit, (namely) half of it, the other half not," he wrote (EA 151:55-57).[40] Following this suggestion, the area

---

[37] For the interpretation of RS 16.145, see the discussion above.

[38] *SAU*, p. 141.

[39] See his "Ras Shamra. Histoire," Supplément au Dictionnaire de la Bible 9 (1979):1298, and, in more detail, his earlier treatment in *Storia di Ugarit*, pp. 27ff.

[40] William L. Moran translates the passage as follows: "Fire destroyed the palace at Ugarit; (rather), it destroyed half of it and so half of it has disappeared." (*The Amarna Letters* [Baltimore/London, 1992], p. 238). I prefer, nevertheless, his alter-

destroyed by the fire could have housed the archives where domestic legal texts and diplomatic documents were kept around the middle of the 14th century. It is generally assumed that the Hittite troops were not responsible for the fire. This is what Abimilku might have meant himself with the sentence that immediately follows in the message and that we would like to translate as: "It was not the Hittite troops, (though)." Singer suggested as potential authors of the conflagration the anti-Hittite confederacy of Mukiš, Nuḫašše and Niya, although this interpretation must necessarily remain tentative too.[41]

Whatever the cause of the fire, it is possible that the calamity brought about the destruction of the palace archives. The restoration of the palace and the leveling of the remains and debris of the destroyed half of the building would explain that no document earlier than Niqmaddu II was discovered in the palace archives. What seems also clear is that the imminent development of events in this northern Syrian area eventually leading to the Hittite conquest and lordship over the kingdom of Ugarit may have also prompted the definite death of former, allegedly destroyed diplomatic documents. Both the Emperor Šuppiluliuma I and his vassal king Niqmaddu II must have considered unnecessary to reproduce any old destroyed document proving Ugarit's former alliances.[42] It is more than unlikely that Niqmaddu II would some day write to his overlord in the terms once used by king Ribhadda of Byblos: "May the king inspect the documents of his father's house whether the ruler in Byblos has not been a loyal servant!"[43] The Hittite era had started, and was to last one century and a half.

native rendering suggested in his commentary in n. 5 p. 239. I would like to incidentally draw the attention to the West Semiticism made by the scribe in writing logographically the word for "palace." Instead of using the normative, well-known sign combination é.gal, he wrote é lugal, probably reflecting West Semitic */bêt malki/*.

[41] In "A Political History of Ugarit," p. 630. In this and the following page, Singer also discusses the archaeological evidence and interpretations, which he also finds inconclusive.

[42] The practice of reproducing diplomatic documents deteriorated by time is attested in the proper chancery of Ugarit. RS 17.334 is the reproduction of an older, broken tablet that contained a military agreement between Niqmaddu II and Šarri-kušuḫ of Carchemish. As stated in lines 20-23 at the end of the text: "This document was sealed by the king's (Ini-teššub's) grandfather, but it was broken. Now, the king Ini-teššub has sealed its duplicate."

[43] EA 74:10-12. I have borrowed the alternative translation proposed by W.L. Moran in *Amarna Letters*, p. 144 n. 3.

As for the royal domestic documents, however, the question of past loyalties and political alliances does not seem *a priori* to be relevant. The new international panorama did probably not invalidate or render obsolete the recorded past transactions allegedly destroyed by the fire. It is reasonable to assume, on the other hand, that the parties involved, naturally including their heirs, kept a copy of the documents. The fact, however, is that so far no private archive from Ras Shamra has yielded any legal text dated to before the reign of Niqmaddu II. The answer must thus remain open, aware of how misleading arguments *ex silentio* can be. Perhaps new findings will throw light to this presently obscure matter.

Back to the royal deeds, it should be mentioned that the long period of ca. 150 years is not evenly covered by the corpus. Less than ten deeds, for example, or in other words five percent of the whole corpus are attested for the last fifty years of Ugarit's history, namely for the reigns of Ibirānu, Niqmaddu III and ᶜAmmurapiᵓ. In contrast, at least 76 documents, i.e. over forty percent of the corpus, are dated to the time of one king, ᶜAmmiṯtamru II. 32 deeds are preserved from the reign of Niqmaddu II, and 26 from Niqmepaᶜ's. Speculative though it may be, it is significant to note that the highest number of transactions corresponds to the period of Ugarit's highest prosperity or the so-called "Pax Hethitica" subsequent to the peace treaty concluded between Egypt and Hatti after the battle of Qadesh.

Note that beside three of the dubious fragments that possibly belong to our corpus, 10 texts cannot be attributed to any particular reign due to their fragmentary condition. 16 other deeds can only be partially dated. An explanation of these ambiguous cases is here in order.

As stated in the catalogue, four deeds belong to either Niqmaddu II or Niqmaddu III. The reason is that in two texts (RS 15.125 [KTU 2.19] and RS 16.269) the king's name is mentioned without the usual patronymic. In the two other cases (RS 15.146+ and RS 16.252) the father's name is actually not preserved on the tablet. Concerning RS 15.125 (KTU 2.19), if we assume that the Ugaritic script was not invented before Niqmepaᶜ (see our discussion above), this fragmentary deed should accordingly be dated to Niqmaddu III.

On the other hand, three royal deeds (RS 16.187B, RS 16.368 and RS 17.53) do not preserve the king's name but only his father's name, namely Niqmaddu. They can therefore date to three different reigns, the one of Arḫalbu, the one of Niqmepaᶜ or that of ᶜAmmurapiᵓ.

A similar case is the fragmentary document RS 17.410A+B. The last two signs in line 2 can be read: *t*]*am*ˀ-*ri*. The restored king's name in the genitive case allows for three possibilities. ᶜAmmiṯtamru can either stand for the father's name, in which case the deed should be dated to either Niqmaddu II or Ibirānu, or the king who explicitly presided over the transaction (restoring the preposition "before" at the beginning of the line).[44] In view of the length of the line in question I would favor the former as the more likely interpretation.

RS 16.191+ is a complete tablet inscribed with an Ugaritic text (KTU 3.4). No mention of the king who presided over the transaction is made. His presence is evidenced by the impression of a royal seal. The seal impressed, however, was not the usual dynastic seal but one of Niqmaddu II. As shown by RS 17.147, a royal deed of ^{c}Ammiṯtamru II bearing the same seal impression, we can only use this evidence as a *terminus post quem.*[45] Nevertheless, if we again assume that the Ugaritic script was not invented before Niqmepa^{c}, the latter should be our *terminus post quem*. For a potential date to ^{c}Ammiṯtamru II on the basis of the grammar of the formulary, see our remarks in chapter 7.

Finally eight deeds can only be dated by means of the preserved name of a well-known person in the text. One of them is the royal official Yabnīnu, party to the Ugaritic transaction recorded in RS 94.2965, who probably lived in the so-called "South Palace," neighboring to the east of the royal palace, during the half-century preceding Ugarit's destruction.[46] Seven other documents preserve the name of the scribe Šapšumalku who, as stated above, wrote deeds of three successive kings: Niqmaddu II, Arḫalbu and Niqmepa^{c}.

Two other documents deserve a short commentary. RS 15.109+ is an extraordinarily large tablet presumably drawn up during the reign of ^{c}Ammiṯtamru II, since he appears in line 1 as the king presiding over the recorded act. The tablet, however, exceptionally bears a heading title that identifies it as a "deed of Niqmepa^{c} son of Niqmaddu" ([*ṭu*]*p-pu* ^{P}*níq-me-pa* dumu *níq-ma-*^{d}iškur). The content indeed describes a collection of transactions, namely conveyances that had one same person as transferee presided over by Niqmepa^{c}. Line 50 then recapitulates the multiple transactions as grants made by this very king. We have accordingly dated this *Sammelurkunde* to ^{c}Ammiṯtamru II noting that the transactions took place during his father's reign.[47]

---

[44] See Nougayrol, *PRU* 6, p. 35 n. 1.

[45] See *SAU*, p. 79.

[46] See *SAU*, pp. 155ff.

[47] Nougayrol (*PRU* 3, p. 102) did not, however, understand the text as a copy made during the reign of ^{c}Ammiṯtamru. He regarded the mention of ^{c}Ammiṯtamru in line 1 as showing that "le 'dauphin' a dû servir d'intermédiaire dans cette première opération" and that the title of "king" could only be applied to Niqmepa^{c}, i.e. exceptionally to the patronymic (ibid., n. 2; see nevertheless his remarks in the next footnote [no. 3]: "peut-être faut-il admettre que 15.109 a été établi sous le règne de Ammistamru"). Against this interpretation, Libolt proposed an alternative explanation. He understood the first sentence where ^{c}Ammiṯtamru is mentioned as a fictional clause. "On Niqmepa^{c}'s death," he wrote, "the grants made to Sinnaranu,

RS 17.322, on the other hand, is the only legal text that can be dated to the reign of ^{c}Ammurapi$^{\supset}$. This is based on a probable restoration of line 2 where the king's name is mentioned. The preserved (collated) traces read: [x x x (x) *a*]*p-i* dumu *níq-ma-*^{d}iškur.[48]

In closing this section one should emphasize once more the long period of time covered by the corpus. At the time of the destruction of Ugarit, an archive located in the central area of the royal palace stored documents that stretched back one century and a half. This brings us to the question of tablet preservation and record keeping, a subject we shall discuss in the following chapter. What is obvious is that not all kinds of texts were intended for permanent record thus being subject to storage on file. Only those that proved to be of lasting importance were kept for future reference.

7. The content of the texts

"Si nous nous penchons maintenant sur le *fond* des actes juridiques d'Ugarit," remarked Nougayrol in his introduction to the legal texts in *PRU* 3,[49] "nous ne manquons pas d'être frappés par leur caractéristique dominante: ils ne portent presque que sur des immeubles: maisons ou terres." A quick glance at our corpus indeed shows that except for a few cases royal deeds deal with the assignation of ownership of real property. Conveyances of land and houses, namely grants, sales and barters, constitute the bulk of the transactions recorded in royal deeds, viz. more than 90 percent of the corpus. It is significant that even the few extant cases of litigation are recorded as conveyance transactions. Boyer already observed that these acts do not formulate, as one would expect, oral processes or a summary of the procedure. Rather, he explained, they appear to be "un simple titre de propriété remis au gagnant du procès pour lui permettre de défendre son droit contre toute réclamation ulté-

---

grants of his father's property and others, were reviewed and regranted by Ammistamru at the very high price under the fiction that these properties had been sold to Ammistamru by his father" (*Royal Land Grants*, pp. 231-232). For the interpretation as a copy, see our remarks below.

[48] Thus confirming van Soldt's reading in *SAU*, p. 3 n. 29. There he noted that this king's name is usually spelled differently, namely ^{p}*a/am-mu-ra-pí*. It is known, however, that scribes at Ugarit do not follow one and the same spelling as far as personal names are concerned (including royal names, cf. our chapter 7 below). On the other hand, the writing *=ra-ap-i* or *=rap-i* to write the onomastic element *=rāpi*$^{\supset}$ is well attested (e.g., in legal texts, ^{f}dumu.mí-*ra-ap-i* in RS 16.156:4, 14, or $^{\ulcorner m\urcorner}$ìr-*rap-i* in RS 16.139:8).

[49] P. 25 (his own italics).

rieure, qu'elle vienne de son ancien adversaire ou de toute autre personne."[50] In other words, the purpose of these texts (such as RS 16.254D) clearly was to record the end-result or state of affairs subsequent to the litigation, thus serving, as Boyer put it, as a title to property.

There is in fact good reason to assume that the great majority of royal deeds can be characterized as title deeds. By these, however, we must not only understand conveyances, such as grants and sales, or deeds of adjudication of ownership of an estate, all of them explicitly recording the title to the granted, sold or disputed property. Deeds of adoption (e.g. RS 15.92 or RS 16.200) or wills (RS. 15.120 and even RS 16.144, Arḫalbu's so-called "last wishes") are also title deeds since they are intimately associated to rules of succession and property rights (see also RS 94.2168).[51] That family history is closely tied to the history of ownership can be seen from a royal deed such as RS 16.295. This document records a transfer of ownership of property from one grandfather to his grandson and is followed by another transaction, namely the grandfather's adoption of the grandson as his son. Another illustrative document is RS 16.239 that describes a royal grant of real property followed by the record of emancipation of one of the grantee's son.

The number of title deeds would accordingly constitute over 95 per cent of the corpus. There definitely was an interest to record the historical background of the ownership of the real property to be transferred. It is probably in this regard that the identification of the transferred house or field with the name of the former owner has to be understood (see chapter 6). Some deeds even include a sequence of transactions concerning the ownership of the property. RS 16.145, for example, describes a royal grant of an estate and the subsequent sale of the property by the grantee to a third party. RS 16.157, on the other hand, records first a royal grant of a property and next its transfer from the grantee to his son.

As shown by these examples, a number of deeds record more than one transaction. Nougayrol accordingly differentiated between "single" and "multiple" deeds; and he further distinguished among the latter between "*actes multiples homogènes*" and "*actes multiples hétérogènes*." Multiple deeds usually describe at least two more or less related transactions involving the same individual, as a rule the beneficiary party. Other examples are RS 16.142 recording a royal grant of real estate together with the grantee's promotion to a higher status by the king; or RS 16.154 recording two different sales of real property agreed by the same parties.

---

[50] *PRU* 3, p. 284.

[51] As will be discussed in chapter 6, RS 16.200 describing an adoption contains the warranty clause against eviction typical of deeds of conveyance of real property.

Their "heterogeneous" character, as opposed to the "homogeneous" one, is determined by the fact that the different transactions belong to Nougayrol's different types of deeds. RS 16.142 and RS 16.154 would accordingly belong to the homogeneous deeds. But RS 15.85 that describes an act by the king (his "*type 3*") in lines 1-10, and another transaction performed before witnesses (i.e. his "*type 1*") in lines 11-21 would be a heterogeneous deed. Here obviously lies one of the main sources of misleading modern classifications. For, as stated above, neither RS 15.85 nor RS 16.145, or RS 16.157 can be categorically classified as royal grants. A more detailed analysis of these multiple deeds and their possible interpretation as *Sammelurkunden* will be carried out below in chapter 3.

Among the few royal deeds that do not directly concern the ownership of property, one should mention the documents that deal with the fulfillment of, or exemption from, royal services (e.g. RS 15.125, RS 16.191+ or RS 16.238), as well as some deeds of manumission (such as RS 16.252 and RS 29.98).

In closing this section a brief discussion of two other deeds is here in order, since they have usually been classified under the group of diplomatic documents. Their inclusion in the present corpus is based on the fact that both tablets bear the impression of the dynastic seal of the kings of Ugarit. In addition, it should be mentioned that both documents were found in the same palace central archive where most royal deeds dealing with domestic affairs were kept. RS 16.170 records a royal decision on a longstanding dispute over bordering landed property between the kings of Ugarit and Siyannu (see the related documents RS 17.123 and RS 18.01 issued by the king of Siyannu, and the agreement issued by the emperor Muršili II RS 17.380+, all kept at the royal palace of Ugarit). Clearly the ownership of real property within the kingdom of Ugarit is here also at issue, which could explain why this "diplomatic" document sealed by Niqmepa^{c}, assuming therefore the obligation of the agreement, was kept together with the other royal deeds.[52]

RS 16.270 belongs to the large dossier concerning the dynastic divorce between ^{c}Ammiṯtamru II and the daughter of the king of Amurru. The king of Ugarit exceptionally signed the document with two seals: the dynastic seal and his personal signet ring thus assuming his obligation in the transaction. I have discussed elsewhere the origin of the text and its importance for the full dossier and case.[53] What I would like to point out

[52] Note that Nougayrol called it "une sorte d'édit royal" in *PRU* 3, p. 25 n. 2, and hesitated to define it as an "acte juridique international" in his re-edition of the text in *PRU* 4, p. 78.

[53] See my "The King of Ugarit, His Wife, Her Brother, and Her Lovers. The Mystery of a Tragedy in Two Acts Revisited," UF 32 (2000):365-372.

here is the fact that this is the only text of the dossier sealed by the divorced king, and to stress again that family history is closely tied to the history of ownership of property (cf. also Arḫalbu's "last wishes" in RS 16.144). With this regard, and although misplacement in this archive cannot be ruled out, it may be significant that RS 16.146+ recording the inventory of the dowry of the Amurrite princess was also found in the same palace archive beside RS 16.270.

8. Royal deeds: the prototype and an example

The aim of this section is to briefly recapitulate the evidence and remarks discussed so far about the corpus of study. In order to illustrate the general features of the documents we have considered it convenient to form an ideal type of a royal deed. The fictitious model is built on statistical grounds. That is to say it answers the question, what is a royal deed most likely to look like and contain? Aware that prototypes are not to be found in reality, we shall next provide one real, well-preserved example of a royal deed chosen from among the corpus.

The prototype of a royal deed, in Ugaritic *sipru malki* (the probable vocalization of the attested spelling *spr mlk*) and in Akkadian so far simply attested as *ṭuppu*, would be a carefully baked[54] clay tablet measuring 68 x 55 x 25 mm.[55] The top of the obverse would present the impression of the cylinder seal of the hereditary kings of Ugarit, the so-called dynastic seal. The finely inscribed cuneiform text would be written in Akkadian and record a conveyance of real property presided over by king ᶜAmmiṯtamru II who would also appear as the conveyor party to the transaction. The deed would of course have been stored and kept in the royal palace archive located at the center of the building.

The size of the tablets obviously varies from one deed to another. As is usually the case with clay tablets, a considerable number of texts have come down to us in an imperfect state of preservation, either fragmentary or with damaged parts, so that restorations of signs, words and lines are sometimes or even often required, only when possible of course. The example we have chosen to reproduce in hand-copy is RS 16.250, partly because of its excellent state of preservation (see the good photograph of both the obverse and reverse available in *PRU* 3, plate XIII). The tablet, found in the palace central archive, measures: 61 x 52 x 23. The inscribed Akkadian text records in 25 lines a grant of real property made

---

[54] See Schaeffer, *PRU* 3, p. XXIV, and Nougayrol, *PRU* 3, p. XXXV: "à peu d'exceptions près, tous ces documents sont d'argile *cuite*" (his own italics).

[55] My former estimation in "The Legal Texts from Ugarit," p. 395 should accordingly be corrected. The measurements of the tablets are taken from *TEO*.

by king Niqmepa^{c} to one ^{c}Abdu followed by ^{c}Abdu's transfer of the granted property to one of his sons. The text contains in addition a provision concerning the status of one of his wives, the mother of the beneficiary son, and her rights to the property. The text ends with the name of Šapšumalku the scribe of the royal deed written on the upper edge of the tablet and covering part of the top of the obverse.

The hand-copy of RS 16.250 at the end of the chapter (approximately reproducing its life size) made some years ago at the Museum of Damascus can be easily checked against the photograph mentioned above and the original beautiful copy made by Nougayrol.[56]

9. Conclusion

No doubt, the fact that a prototype of a royal deed can be built to a reasonable degree of probability suffices to realize the importance and homogeneity of the corpus under consideration. The few exceptions, such as the deeds written in Ugaritic or those found elsewhere than the palace central archive, can be obviously taken to illustrate the rule. The result of a closer examination at the number and quality of these texts has provided additional definiteness and precision to the preliminary view outlined in the introduction. 176 royal legal documents to which at least five other fragments of tablets can be added are attested without interruption from the reign of Niqmaddu II until the destruction of Ugarit, thus covering one and a half century of the history of this Eastern Mediterranean kingdom. The discussion has shown that not only the long period of time covered by the documents but also the language and the find-place of the deeds are closely linked to their genre and content. Akkadian is the

[56] Since the book is also addressed to non-cuneiformists, a word for lay readers to understand the cuneiform hand-copy is in order. The first remark to be made about a copy of a clay tablet concerns the perception and translation of a three-dimensional object (the cuneiform tablet) onto a two-dimensional surface (the page of paper). This process is held responsible for the signs and lines that run out of the drawn limits of the written surface (e.g. lines 3, 6, or 14). Actually, the signs that appear beyond the limits are inscribed along the edge and the opposite side of the tablet. The second remark to be made related to the previous one concerns the direction in which cuneiform tablets turn. Unlike the pages of a book, cuneiform tablets turned bottom to top. This is the reason why the right edge is used both in the text of the obverse and the reverse as the prolonged writing surface of too long lines. Finally, the dynastic seal was like most ancient Near Eastern seals a small cylinder made of stone. The signature thus consisted in rolling the seal upon the corresponding sealing space or surface of the clay tablet (in Ugarit, the top of the obverse), leaving a continuous impression of the carved scene in reverse. The continuous impression on RS 16.250 shows the "discontinuous" scene of the seal of the kings of Ugarit.

legal language of this province of cuneiform law during the Late Bronze Age. And the palace central archive was definitely meant to keep the royal title deeds, at least in the early 12th century BC. The description and nature of both the archive and the Akkadian language as characteristic elements of royal deeds will be discussed in length in two respective chapters.

The importance and homogeneity of the corpus, however, should not be exaggerated. It must not lead us, for example, to imagine, let alone believe, that its analysis will provide a vivid picture of the social or economic life in Ugarit during the Late Bronze Age. Cuneiform historians are too often expressing their happiness because of the wealth of preserved written material available to them. This is especially true in the field of economic and legal praxis for which the source record material is admittedly richer than what is found in the rest of the ancient world, such as Egypt, Greece and Rome. Our corpus, in particular, indeed can find no parallel in the ancient world. We have therefore every right to feel fortunate, but we must also bear in mind the limitations of our documentary material.

To begin with, the number of documents is important if we compare it to other ancient archives and also if we look at the rest of the legal material unearthed at Ras Shamra. A total of 60 legal texts and fragments have been so far discovered outside the walls of the royal palace belonging to a number of archives that come from some of the private houses at Ugarit (hence the usual designation as "private archives"). The number of texts per archive, however, is rather small. Two archives, for example, have only yielded two documents each, and the largest concentrations of tablets, such as the ones found in the houses of Rapᵓānu, Rašapᵓabu and Urtēnu, contain around ten deeds each. As compared to them, the palace central archive is undoubtedly outstanding. Nevertheless, we cannot fail to realize that the number of royal deeds is relatively meager, especially when we look at the chronological structure of the corpus. As stated above, not more than nine documents some of them in a fragmentary state of preservation are attested for the last fifty years of Ugarit's history. And the remaining deeds, that is, less than 170 texts and fragments, are distributed along one century.

The uneven distribution of legal texts found in the palace and the private houses brings us in turn to one of the distorting focuses with which we often look at cuneiform material. Palace or temple bureaucracies "necessarily leave more written evidence than family or clan organizations and private persons," observed Oppenheim. As a result of this documentary illusion, "the picture we obtain can hardly ever be trusted to correspond to facts," he concluded.[57] By definition, we are dealing

[57] *Ancient Mesopotamia*, p. 84.

with documents recorded probably by, in, and certainly for, the royal palace. With regard to the institutional use of writing, one should mention that the owners of the houses that have yielded clusters of tablets had clear and close connections with the palace. As remarked by van Soldt, they "were important persons who sometimes held important positions in the state bureaucracy."[58] As significant is the fact that many of these houses served as schools, as shown by the large number of school texts found in the archives. To judge from the available evidence, the sphere of writing at Ugarit seemed thus to be centered round the palace. The information they can yield will therefore necessarily be biased. The lens through which our illumination must pass, as metaphorically put by Postgate, are indeed the actual tablets. And our tablets are but the product of the administrative machine of the royal palace of Ugarit. Our inquiry in the next chapters will therefore focus on this machine, and will accordingly deal with the creation, maintenance and use of the royal deeds.

[58] "Private archives at Ugarit," in *Interdependency of Institutions and Private Entrepreneurs*, ed. A.C.V.M. Bongenaar (Leiden, 2000), p. 243.

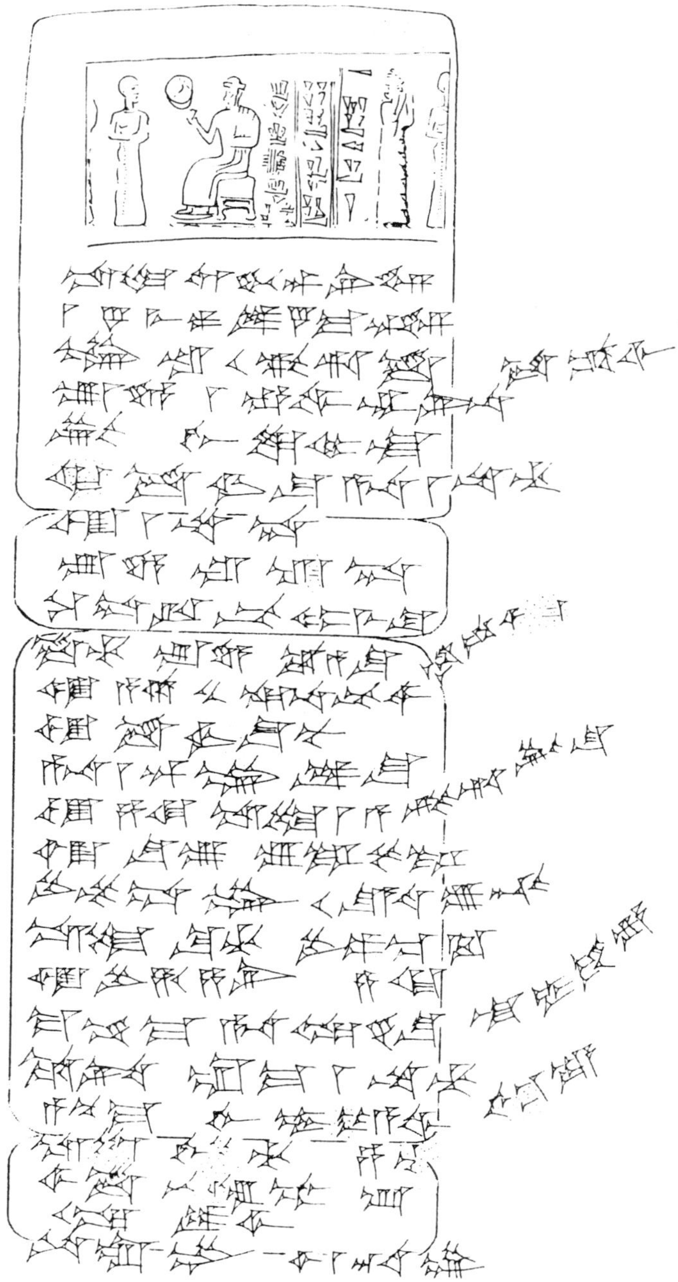

Fig. 2. RS 16.250

CHAPTER 2

THE ARCHIVE OF ROYAL DEEDS

1. Introduction

Only in recent years has there been any interest or systematic attempt to identify, reconstruct and understand cuneiform archives.[1] The blame, according to Ernst Posner, should not only be placed at the doorsteps of Assyriologists for not recognizing until recently the archival nature of their source material (he was writing at the beginning of the 1970s), but also of Archivists who, in his opinion, had long ignored the significance of the first great chapter in the history of their discipline.[2] But it is about the success in the interpretation of cuneiform archives and libraries, rather than the responsibility for failing to identify them, that we are here concerned. As is to be expected, this success could only be achieved as a result of the co-operation between the Assyriologist and the interested scholar in archival research.[3] It does not therefore come as a surprise that an Assyriologist turned, *malgré lui*, into a local archivist laid down the leading archival systematic approach to clay tablet accumulations. Indeed with Godefroy Goossens,[4] pointed out the architect of "archival science" Johannes Papritz, "zum erstenmal spüren wir sicheren Boden; Provenienzen und echte, große Archivkörper werden deutlich sichtbar heraus-

[1] See especially *Cuneiform Archives and Libraries*, ed. Klaas R. Veenhof (Leiden, 1986); the papers from the workshop "Les phénomènes de fin d'archives en Mésopotamie" held in Paris in 1995 collected in volume 89 (1995) of *Revue d'Assyriologie*; Olof Pedersén, *Archives and Libraries in the Ancient Near East 1500-500 BC* (Bethesda, 1998); and more recently *Ancient Archives and Archival Traditions. Concepts of Record-keeping in the Ancient World*, ed. M. Brosius (Oxford, 2003).

[2] *Archives in the Ancient World* (Cambridge, MA, 1972), p. 6.

[3] This sort of interdisciplinary collaboration was as a matter of fact the direction proposed by Oppenheim to bring the field of Assyriology out of what he diagnosed to be "the stagnation from which we suffer" (see his *Ancient Mesopotamia*, pp. 29-30).

[4] See his "Introduction à l'archivéconomie de l'Asie Antérieure," RA 46 (1952):98-107.

gestellt."[5] The words and essential principles of provenance and *respect des fonds* made finally their way into the broad and wealthy field of ancient Near Eastern studies.

In dealing thus with a proper archival study, we seem to be compelled to abandon the use of "cuneiform archive" in the manner that has so often been employed in Assyriology, and understand by these words something narrower than a simple cluster of clay tablets unearthed inside a building. It is rather in the modern sense of the word, namely in the meaning of a "fonds d'archives" that we ought to, and shall, use it here. Jean Favier provided a clear definition of this technical meaning. In his authoritative words, which opened his classic little handbook, "les archives sont l'ensemble des documents reçus ou constitués par une personne physique ou morale, ou par un organisme public ou privé, résultant de leur activité, organisé en conséquence de celle-ci et conservé en vue d'une utilisation éventuelle."[6] Creation, maintenance or preservation, and use are therefore essential, defining aspects of any group of records with archival value. Now, we should ask, how can these elements be recovered and identified from the ruins of ancient Near Eastern towns?

To be sure, two fundamental conditions need to be satisfied before one can safely identify any ancient archive. First, the archaeological record; without a more or less detailed description of the discovery of the texts made *in situ*, in the rooms proper, correlated with their general, ground plans, no possible analysis and eventual identification of a deliberately organized body of documents can be carried out. And secondly, text edition; for if the texts found more or less side by side inside a room or building remain unpublished, the scholar wishing to inquire into the potential archival nature of the group of documents would find himself at a dead-end. Cuneiform archival research, our particular concern, is not seldom seriously hampered because one of the two necessary conditions, or both, are missing. The term "silent archives" has actually been coined in Assyriology to designate groups of tablets with a common consistent origin whose archaeological context is irretrievable.[7] Silent cuneiform archives exist, for example, as a result of the earlier excavations when modern methods of archaeology had not yet been developed, and also as a result of the looting of archaeological sites such as the one consistently and massively carried out after the US-led recent invasion of Iraq.

---

[5] "Archive in Altmesopotamien. Theorie und Tatsachen," Archivalische Zeitschrift 55 (1959):16.

[6] *Les archives* (Paris, 1959), p. 5.

[7] See Corinne Castel, "Contexte archéologique et statut des documents: les textes retrouvés dans les maisons mésopotamiennes du I millénaire av. J.-C.," RA 89 (1995):131.

Compared thus to other colleagues, the scholar studying archival practices at Ugarit is in a favorable position. The reasons are several. To begin with, as already mentioned, texts were found at Ras Shamra *in situ*, with an undisturbed occupational level, that is, as they were left after the destruction of the city by the beginning of the 12th century BC. On the other hand, the two indispensable conditions, namely the record of the archaeological context of the tablets and their state of publication, are satisfactorily fulfilled. To the former has prominently contributed Claude Schaeffer's methodological approach and to the latter the magisterial work of the late epigrapher of the Mission de Ras Shamra, Jean Nougayrol. But the hardly disputable opinion that "Ugarit provides an almost ideal study ground for archivists," as recently stated by Wilfred van Soldt who carried out the most thorough research on these archives,[8] is due to an additional factor.

Already before the excavation of the palace would be completed, Schaeffer and Nougayrol deduced a remarkable deliberate distribution and organization of the royal archives. In Schaeffer's words, "nous avons à Ras Shamra l'avantage d'avoir pu établir le classement opéré par les auteurs mêmes des textes en cunéiforme trouvés dans le palais, celui qui fut adapté par l'administration royale d'Ugarit."[9] Indeed, at least two important accumulations of tablets then recently unearthed seemed to follow a clear pattern of distribution and arrangement according to their genre. Diplomatic texts such as inter-state treaties and agreements, were all discovered, i.e. must have been stored separately in a room, in the southern wing of the palace. And legal documents describing private legal transactions presided over by the king of Ugarit were concentrated, and thus must have been kept on file in another room, in the central area of the palace.

These so-called "Archives Sud" ("southern archive") and "Archives Centrales" ("central archive") respectively, must have clearly served a very precise purpose, indeed functioning as a royal "fonds d'archives." The eloquence and excellent publication of these examples undoubtedly account for the protagonist role that Ugarit played (beside Mari) in the studies of Goossens and Favier referred to above. In the latter's classic handbook, Ugarit and its royal archives cover almost one of the four pages devoted to archives in antiquity. Of course, one might easily suspect that chauvinism could lie behind the inclusion and favored treatment of Ras Shamra in his first chapter (where Tell Hariri is also mentioned). But the true reason lies elsewhere. As stated by Posner, "a study of the archives of Greece and Rome must rely almost exclusively on

[8] *SAU*, p. 48.

[9] See *PRU* 3, p. XI.

information derived from inscriptions and literary sources." "In the case of the archives of the ancient Orient," he continued, "literary sources are lacking; but, on the other hand, thanks to the excavations we can study the archives, or what is left of them, *in situ*."[10] That is no doubt the major advantage of Oriental case studies: the archaeological record. As for the prominent, particular role of Ugarit, I believe no other ancient Near Eastern site would have allowed Favier to state in 1959: "la répartition des documents dans les salles du dépôt d'archives du palais (...) permet d'affirmer que les fonds étaient scrupuleusement respectés et conservés selon un classement rigoureux."[11]

2. Description

"Le bâtiment couvre ainsi une superficie de près de dix mille mètres carrés. Tout Notre-Dame, sa clôture vers les quais comprise, y tiendrait donc à l'aise."[12] By the time Schaeffer wrote this illustrative description of the royal palace of Ugarit, the complete extent of the building had not yet been archaeologically realized. As a matter of fact, after the full excavation of the area, the actual limits of the most impressive, indeed imposing edifice in the city of Ugarit are still being re-examined and discussed.[13] What remains beyond doubt, in any case, is Schaeffer's first appreciation about the spectacular size of the palace. It was his belief that the building he unearthed at Ras Shamrra was to be counted among the most luxurious royal residences ever discovered in the Eastern Mediterranean world and, for that matter, in whole Western Asia. Unlike other ancient Near Eastern palaces, the walls of the residence of the kings of Ugarit were not made of mud brick but of quarried and finely dressed stone blocks. Timber, also naturally available in this Levantine area, played an essential role in the building of the monumental construction: elevation, to take the obvious example, basically rested on this material (viz. pillars, posts, columns and beam structure). In fact, the architectural importance of timber, and also its wide use, clearly account for the ravaging fire and the final collapse of the palace, together with the whole city, that took place by the beginning of the 12th century.

The important cluster of tablets found in the remains of the central

---

[10] *Archives in the Ancient World*, p. 26.

[11] *Les archives*, p. 10.

[12] Schaeffer, *Ugaritica* 4, p. 7.

[13] As already mentioned above, Callot and Margueron have announced their forthcoming architectural revaluation of the royal palace. For the time being, mention must, and will, be made of the provisional study written by the latter "Le palais royal d'Ougarit. Premiers résultats d'une analyse systématique."

area of the royal palace, which was accordingly named the "Archives Centrales," was brought to light in 1951 during the 15th campaign, and its excavation was completed two years later in the course of the 17th campaign. According to Schaeffer's first report, the tablets were found scattered in several rooms on two different levels.[14] Such a relevant and significant observation, however, was nowhere analyzed or further studied. Curiously enough, Schaeffer would not tackle this problem in later publications. Only the recorded find-spots of the tablets, the so-called "points topographiques," were left behind in the reports of the mission, almost constituting all the data that could be used to reconstruct the scene.[15] To be sure, reconstituting original record groups and archival installations is the basic commitment of any archival study. That is the reason why Goossens rightly recommended Assyriologists to respect the original state of the discovery by publishing the texts by rooms or groups of rooms. Once this step was fulfilled, he explained, can the documents be arranged and an analytical inventory of them prepared. Van Soldt seemed to follow Goossens' programmatic approach when he undertook thoroughly and successfully the wanted task of reconstituting this and other original record groups of Ugarit.[16]

The "points topographiques" of Ras Shamra fix the place of discovery of an object both horizontally and vertically. On the basis of the horizontal data, van Soldt distinguished in the "central archive" three separate accumulations of tablets surrounding room 152 (former court IV). This division of the "central archive" would prove, in his terms, "basically correct" once the genre of the tablets would be considered.[17] Indeed, the legal documents, namely royal deeds, were concentrated in one of the sections, what he termed "the northern wing" that also contained the largest number of tablets. The core of this northern wing can be situated in the passage connecting rooms 132 and 152 (i.e. former courts VI and IV respectively). As shown by the catalogue and the more elaborate list below, in this small space were actually found more than a third of the total amount of royal deeds.

---

[14] "Nouvelles fouilles et découvertes de la mission archéologique de Ras Shamra dans le palais d'Ugarit (campagne 1951)", Annales Archeólogiques de Syrie 2 (1952):13, and id., "Fouilles à Ras-Shamra-Ugarit (Campagne 1951)," CRAIBL 1952:237.

[15] For the complete, official list of tablets and inscribed objects together with their find-spots, see now *TEO*.

[16] The archival study constitutes chapter two of his first part of *SAU*, covering almost two hundred pages.

[17] *SAU*, p. 90.

This simple observation immediately suggests that those royal deeds were not originally lying on the floor, neither were they stored there on a shelf or a niche. A doorway leading from one room to another is obviously not the right place to keep such, or for that matter, any records. There is therefore every reason to assume that if, as one expects, tablets fall vertically after the collapse of the building, the original place of storage must consequently have been on the upper floor. This would be supported by the fact that royal deeds were discovered scattered within the northern wing of the "Archives Centrales," namely as defined by van Soldt, in rooms 21, 30, 31, the northern parts of rooms 152 and 132, and the above mentioned passage between the latter (see fig. 3).[18]

Fig. 3. The Royal Palace. After J.-Cl. Margueron, "Le palais royal d'Ougarit. Premiers résultats d'une analyse systématique", p. 194.

---

[18] *SAU*, p. 88.

Van Soldt provided again the most accurate analysis of the evidence to confirm this hypothesis. This he did by carefully examining this time the vertical reading of the "points topographiques."[19] He reconstructed the general floor level and calculated the distance from the surface level. "If we average the elevations for the various areas," he wrote with regard to the northern wing, "we arrive at a surface level of approximately +20.10m, which provides a depth of 2.20m for the 'ground-floor' (destruction level) previously set at +17.90m."[20] Tablets, on the other hand, as he pointed out, were seldom found in the level of the destruction layer, the bulk being concentrated at the higher elevations, "most notably in the N. Wing." It may be noted, for example, that the bulk of tablets from the space 132-152 "were found between –0.70m and –1.50m."[21] Given the remarkable distance between the two levels and the find place of the tablets, "it seems inescapable to conclude —he wrote— that many of the texts had been stored on an upper story (the first 'étage')."[22] It should be noted that Schaeffer himself had come to the same conclusion for the so-called "Archives Sud," where diplomatic texts were kept, "Archives Est" and "Archives Sud-Ouest," apparently on the basis of the discovery of the remains of staircases in adjacent rooms.[23] The fact, however, as stated above, is that he would not re-evaluate the archaeological record of the central archive in the light of the later discoveries and hypotheses.[24]

The first remark we should make is that the picture we now have of the palace central archive is not so ideal for archivists as it has been often depicted. It is simply not possible to reconstruct the archival room where royal deeds were presumably kept on file. Hardly anything is left of the original installations. All the evidence we have of the existence of an upper floor, apart from the recorded and calculated different destruction layers, seems to be the remains of staircases in the vicinity of the relevant area. As usual in these cases, all we can do is guess; for example, how big

---

[19] His methodology is summarized in "The Palace Archives at Ugarit," in *Cuneiform Archives and Libraries*, ed. K.R. Veenhof, pp. 198-199. For a parallel, preliminary study of the alleged upper story of the palace, see Liverani, "Il primo piano degli archivi di Ugarit," SEL 5 (1988):121-142.

[20] *SAU*, p. 91,

[21] Ibid., p. 83.

[22] Ibid., p. 92.

[23] "Nouvelles découvertes à Ras Shamra-Ugarit et à Enkomi-Alasia (Chypre) en 1953," CRAIBL 1954:102; id., *Ugaritica* 4, pp. XV, 47; id., "Les fouilles de Ras Shamra-Ugarit, quinzième, seizième et dix-septième campagnes (1951, 1952, et 1953), rapport sommaire," Syria 31 (1954):23.

[24] See Liverani, "Il primo piano", pp. 125-126.

was the room, what storage systems were used, or how were the documents organized and consulted. We cannot even establish how the other two alleged wings (east and south) of the "central archive" were related to one another and to the northern counterpart. As deduced by van Soldt, the eastern and southern wings of the central archive also showed two distinct levels and a roughly similar pattern of tablet distribution.[25] The genre and content of the texts, however, is somewhat different.[26] Were there then different archival rooms on the upper floor? Or was there rather a single large room with different sections where documents were arranged (perhaps on shelves) according to content? And if, as indicated by the vertical reading of the "points topographiques," texts were also kept on the ground floor, what was the purpose of it? Van Soldt suggested that "tablets still in use may have been stored temporarily on the lower level;" "although," as he later admitted, "this cannot be proven."[27] Interesting in this regard is a three-record group found on the destruction level from the so-called southern wing (perhaps kept there because they would still be in use, following van Soldt's suggestion). The three documents record the sale of land to Ṯaryelli, queen of Ugarit, and are witnessed by the same official Ṯipiṭbaᶜlu.

Our second remark concerns the so-called "northern wing" of the central archive. 130 royal deeds come from this area (see the list below). In other words, almost three-quarters of our corpus have been found in an area of approximately one hundred square meters, centered in the passage connecting rooms 132 and 152. Taking into account the collapse of the building, and specifically the upper floor where the deeds were kept, it is reasonable to suggest that the archive of royal deeds was located just above the "center of gravity" 132-152. It is also likely that the royal deeds found close or around this northern wing were originally placed in, and were part of, the same archival room, the distant find-spot thus reflecting the "expansive wave" of the collapse. In support of this assumption, but also keeping in mind the phenomenon of stray finds discussed in the previous chapter, one may refer to several joins between fragments of tablets from different sections and wings (see the list below). Van Soldt himself tentatively included the western section of room 132 in the northern wing,[28] where eleven royal deeds were found, precisely on account of the similar type of tablets and the attested various joins with tablets from 132-152, room 30 and the northern section of

---

[25] *SAU*, p. 92.

[26] Ibid., p. 90.

[27] Ibid., p. 93.

[28] Ibid., p. 88.

152.[29] To judge from the find-spots of the tablets and the direction taken by what we have termed "the expansive way," it is possible following a suggestion made to van Soldt by Maurits van Loon that the walls of the archival room carrying the shelves collapsed to the south.

I believe we are indeed justified in speaking of a specific archive of royal deeds. Not only on the basis that these were mainly found concentrated in the northern wing of this central accumulation of tablets; but also because the converse statement is also true. The northern wing "corpus" almost exclusively contained royal deeds[30] (see especially the content of the significant find place 132-152). Of course it is not possible to determine in this state of affairs whether and in what way the few and often broken administrative texts and letters mostly written in Ugaritic found beside royal deeds were kept in the same archival room. The same is true of the interesting group of Egyptian alabaster vases. Indeed, a number of fragments of vases bearing inscriptions of pharaohs Amenophis III, Amenophis IV and his wife Nefertiti, Horemheb, and Ramesses II were exceptionally discovered beside royal deeds in the northern wing accumulation.[31] One of these alabaster fragments seems to evince the marriage between king Niqmaddu II and an Egyptian court lady.[32] This evidence may obviously raise the question whether the items proper were considered archival records. One should note with this regard that the archive of royal deeds included the tablet RS 16.146+ that records the dowry of the Amurrite princess, wife of another king of Ugarit, ᶜAmmiṯtamru II. And that close to it was also found the diplomatic document RS 16.270 dealing with the divorce between the Amurrite princess and ᶜAmmiṯtamru II.

To sum up, on the basis of the archaeological record and the content of the tablets, we can safely assume that a royal archival depository existed on the upper floor, just above the ground-floor passage that linked rooms 132 and 152. There the royal secretaries maintained and preserved around 1200 BC a well-defined and homogeneous group of records created by their predecessors: title deeds that concerned the king(s) of Ugarit. These documents stretched back to the time of Niqmaddu II; that is to say that by the time of the final conflagration that destroyed the palace and the city of Ugarit, the archive contained records one hundred and fifty years old. The number of documents preserved included the

---

[29] Ibid., p. 86.

[30] Ibid., p. 90.

[31] See Schaeffer, "Fouilles à Ras-Shamra-Ugarit (Campagne 1951)," p. 237; id., *PRU* 3, p. XXIII; id., *Ugaritica* 3, p. 164-168; and van Soldt, *SAU*, p. 75.

[32] See also Alan R. Schulman, "Diplomatic Marriage in the Egyptian New Kingdom," JNES 38 (1979):185, with n. 39.

160 texts and fragments recovered from the ruins of the accumulation of tablets from the central area of the palace. The deeds were properly organized, perhaps on shelves, and, following van Soldt's suggestion, possibly according to "dossiers" (see below) or kings.[33]

To conclude this section, a word must be said about the current understanding of the spaces and circulation of guests, ministers and secretaries, and of course the king and his family within this central area of the palace (see fig. 3). Margueron has identified the large room 132 (formerly interpreted as a court) as an assembly hall.[34] There, he suggests, would take place banquets or solemn official receptions. It is in this context that Margueron has deduced from a revaluation of the remains of the locus 78 south of the hall the presence of a dais, where, as he believes, the king would sit during, and preside over, the ceremonies. The guests or assembled people would reach the large hall through court 128 (formerly I), the porch 72 and room 20. The hall 77 and the stairway (76-85) that led to the upper floor where, according to the French archaeologist, the royal apartments were located connected the platform and what he identified to be the throne room (71). The king thus had direct access to perform his official functions from the upper floor where his private rooms were situated. The archive of royal deeds would then have been, according to this reconstruction, part of the king's private quarters of the palace.

3. The list of deeds from the archive

We have mentioned that the room (or perhaps rooms) of the archive of royal deeds is forever lost to us. All we have are the recorded remains of the collapsed installation originally situated on the upper floor. The difficulty presented to the scholar interested in archival research is therefore to identify all the pieces that had once belonged to the archive. This may be schematically attempted by drawing an imaginary line on the plan of the ground floor of the palace central area that would include the alleged remains, especially textual, of the archival room(s). Van Soldt's proposal of a "northern-wing area" has proved as we have seen rather convincing. The wing would thus enclose rooms 21, 30, 31, the northern parts of rooms 132 and 152, the passage between 132 and 152, and possibly also the western section of 132. The list of archival deeds that follows is accordingly based on the thorough study carried out by van Soldt, and has also profited from the systematic catalogue of the mission (*TEO*).

---

[33] *SAU*, p. 92.

[34] See "Le palais royal d'Ougarit," pp. 188-190. See also Yon, *La cité d'Ougarit*, pp. 46-50.

Room 21

RS 15.88
RS 15.90
RS 15.137
RS 15.139

Remarks:
No other texts or inscriptions were found in this locus.

Room 30

RS 15.70
RS 15.85
RS 15.109+
RS 15.126
RS 15.127(+)?
RS 15.132
RS 15.141
RS 15.155
RS 15.167+
RS 15.168

Remarks:
Apart from the major group of royal deeds, this room has yielded a very fragmentary Ugaritic administrative text (RS 15.156), a fragment of a Sumero-Akkadian incantation (RS 15.152), and two pieces of alabaster vases with Egyptian hieroglyphic inscriptions of Amenophis IV (RS 15.203) and Ramesses II (RS 15.201). Note that the awkward RS 15.152 was found isolated from the rest of documents ("point topographique" 161, -0.40m), perhaps pointing to the fact that it was stored or kept separately (at least from royal deeds). The find-spot (cf. also its fragmentary state) actually suggests that it was found out of the original place (had it been reused as floor material, as proposed by van Soldt for other peculiar pieces?).[35]

As for the joined fragments of royal deeds, RS 15.109 belongs to the same tablet as RS 16.296A and RS 16.296C from locus 132-152 as well as RS 16.296B from the northern part of 132; RS 15.167 joins RS 15.163 from room 132 W section. Another fragment (RS 15.127) seems to join a fragment (RS 15.131) reported to come from a far-away room in the palace (55) belonging to the accumulation named "Archives Est" (see the discussion in chapter 1 above). Note with this regard that an

[35] See, for example, the other fragment of an incantation found in the palace room 62 (*SAU*, p. 131).

administrative fragment (RS 15.42) found in this eastern archive (namely in room 53) basically of an administrative content, joins a fragment from room 30 (RS 15.110), perhaps to be considered then a stray find.

Room 31

RS 15.100
RS 15.125
RS 15.147
RS 15.150

Remarks:
Like the previous locus, this room basically yielded royal deeds. The exceptions are a very fragmentary text (RS 15.124) tentatively identified as a letter (see Nougayrol, *PRU* 3, p. 21; van Soldt, *SAU*, pp. 75 and 564) and two fragments of alabaster vases with Egyptian hieroglyphic inscriptions of Amenophis IV (RS 15.202) and Niqmaddu (presumably II), king of Ugarit (RS 15.239).

Locus 30-31

RS 15.140

Remarks:
In this passage only this tablet was found.

Locus 132-152

RS 15.138+
RS 16.150
RS 16.152+
RS 16.153
RS 16.154
RS 16.156
RS 16.157
RS 16.158
RS 16.160
RS 16.162
RS 16.163
RS 16.166
RS 16.174
RS 16.178
RS 16.188
RS 16.189
RS 16.190
RS 16.197

RS 16.198B
RS 16.199+
RS 16.200
RS 16.201
RS 16.202
RS 16.203
RS 16.204
RS 16.205+
RS 16.206
RS 16.207
RS 16.208
RS 16.238 + RS 16.254
RS 16.239
RS 16.240
RS 16.241+
RS 16.242
RS 16.243
RS 16.244
RS 16.245
RS 16.246
RS 16.247
RS 16.248
RS 16.249
RS 16.250
RS 16.251
RS 16.252
RS 16.253
RS 16.254 (see RS 16.238+)
RS 16.254A
RS 16.254B+
RS 16.254C
RS 16.254D
RS 16.254E
RS 16.254F
RS 16.255A+E
RS 16.255B
RS 16.255C
RS 16.255D
RS 16.255E (see RS 16.255A+)
RS 16.255F
RS 16.255G
RS 16.270
RS 16.286
RS 16.296A + RS 16.296C+

RS 16.296C (see RS 16.296A+)
RS 16.343
RS 16.344
RS 16.363
RS 16.368
RS 16.384
RS 16.385
RS 16.387
RS 16.393A

Remarks:

This locus has yielded the largest number of royal deeds, and hardly any other texts but royal deeds have been found therein. The only clear exceptions are one Ugaritic administrative text (RS 16.198[A]) and three small Ugaritic fragments (RS 16.378A, B, and C, perhaps of letters). On this account it is reasonable to argue that fragments of (Akkadian) tablets of legal content such as RS 16.203 and RS 16.255G, and perhaps also RS 16.255F, are pieces of royal deeds (see already chapter 1 above). Also significant is the discovery in this small passage of the non-inscribed tablet RS 16.393A, which exclusively presents the impressions of the dynastic seal and its replica (for a detailed description, see chapter 5 below).

Note that six fragments from 132-152 join pieces found in other adjoining loci of this northern wing: RS 15.138 joins RS 16.393B from room 132 N section; RS 16.199 joins RS 16.182 from room 152 N section; RS 16.241 joins RS 16.261 and RS 16.339, both from room 132 N section; RS 16.254B joins RS 16.148 from room 152 N section; RS 16.296A and RS 16.296C join RS 16.296B from room 132 N section, and RS 15.109 from room 30; RS 16.152 joins RS 15.123 from room 132 W section; and finally RS 16.205 joins RS 16.192A from room 62 (for this room, see chapter 1 above).

Room 132 N section

RS 15.91
RS 15.92
RS 15.136
RS 15.145
RS 15.146 + RS 15.161
RS 15.161 (see RS 15.146+)
RS 16.86 + RS 16.172
RS 16.132
RS 16.133
RS 16.134
RS 16.135

RS 16.161+
RS 16.167
RS 16.170
RS 16.171
RS 16.172 (see RS 16.86+)
RS 16.173
RS 16.175
RS 16.185
RS 16.256
RS 16.261 + RS 16.339+
RS 16.262
RS 16.263
RS 16.267
RS 16.269
RS 16.273
RS 16.275
RS 16.276
RS 16.277
RS 16.278
RS 16.281
RS 16.282
RS 16.283
RS 16.284
RS 16.285
RS 16.296B+
RS 16.311
RS 16.339 (see RS 16.261+)
RS 16.348
RS 16.353
RS 16.356
RS 16.371
RS 16.386
RS 16.393B+

Remarks:

Since most of the texts found in the northern section of room 132 are royal deeds, it can again be reasonably argued that some fragments of allegedly legal content such as RS 16.175, RS 16.311, and RS 16.185 could be part of royal deeds. Note that the latter piece was tentatively taken by Nougayrol as a school text, namely a vocabulary (*PRU* 3, p. 213); we rather consider, following van Soldt's suggestion, that it is of a legal nature (*SAU*, pp. 83 and 570). In this locus was also found RS 16.161 joining RS 16.146 from room 152 N section, the tablet describing the dowry of the Amurrite princess, wife of king ᶜAmmiṯtamru II.

As for the joined fragments, RS 16.261 and RS 16.339 join RS 16.241 from 132-152; RS 16.296B joins RS 15.109 from room 30 and RS 16.296A + RS 16.296C from 132-152; and RS 16.393 joins RS 15.138 from 132-152, all of them belonging to the common northern-wing area.

RS 16.273 is a fragment of a non-domestic legal document; the transaction is lost but we know it took place before Takḫulinu, a royal official of Carchemish. Of interest is the fact that it was found isolated ("point topographique" 541) at the lowest level (-2.75m), thus apparently kept at the time of the conflagration in a room at the ground-floor, apart then from the corpus (and archive) of royal deeds.

Beside this legal material, the northern section of room 132 has yielded five fragmentary Ugaritic administrative texts, at least two of them (RS 16.193 and RS 16.194) dealing with field allotment (the remaining damaged texts are RS 16.195, RS 16.280, and RS 16.372); a small fragment of a Ugaritic letter (RS 16.196); and some other fragmentary, almost unintelligible pieces also written in Ugaritic (RS 16.280A, B, C, and E).

Room 152 N section

RS 15.143+
RS 16.131
RS 16.136
RS 16.137
RS 16.138
RS 16.139
RS 16.140
RS 16.141
RS 16.142
RS 16.143
RS 16.144
RS 16.145
RS 16.146+
RS 16.147
RS 16.148+
RS 16.149
RS 16.181
RS 16.182+
RS 16.184
RS 16.260
RS 16.279
RS 16.295

Remarks:

The epigraphic content of the northern section of room 152 mainly consists of royal deeds too. It is thus possible that the fragment RS 16.181 describes a legal transaction rather than an administrative operation (as tentatively interpreted by Nougayrol, *PRU* 3, p. 197; for its possible legal nature, see *SAU*, pp. 79 and 570). Note that RS 16.146, joining RS 16.161 from room 132 N section, is part of the tablet with the inventory of the Amurrite princess' dowry.

All joined fragments come from the northern-wing area: RS 15.143 joins RS 15.164 from room 132 W section, RS 16.148 joins RS 16.254B from 132-152, and RS 16.182 joins RS 16.199 from 132-152.

Beside these texts were found a Ugaritic letter addressed to the queen (RS 16.137bis), a Ugaritic administrative record on landed property (RS 16.376), a fragment of a text that may be somehow related to the treaty corpus between Hatti and Ugarit (RS 16.259), and a fragment of an alabaster vase with an Egyptian hieroglyphic inscription of Amenophis III (RS 16.340). Concerning RS 16.259, one should mention that in the southern section of this very room was found strangely enough RS 17.04, a piece belonging to a treaty text from the "southern archive." Both fragments could therefore be intrusive.

Room 132 W section

RS 15.86
RS 15.89
RS 15.111
RS 15.118
RS 15.119
RS 15.120
RS 15.122
RS 15.123+
RS 15.163+
RS 15.164+
RS 15.190
RS 18.53

Remarks:

We have mentioned that van Soldt tentatively included this area to the so-called northern wing of the "Archives Centrales" on the basis of the attested joins with tablets from the loci dealt with above as well as the presence of a similar type of tablets. Indeed, the major group of tablets corresponds to royal deeds (five administrative texts and a tag all written in Ugaritic were also found there). And all joined fragments come from the northern-wing area: RS 15.123 joins RS 16.152 from 132-152, RS 15.163 joins RS 15.167 from room 30, and RS 15.164 joins RS 15.143 from room 152 N section.

The rest of deeds found in the greater central archive

From the area surrounding the northern wing were recovered a number of royal deeds. According to what has been stated above, it can be argued that these documents reached their find-place somewhat removed from the core passage 132-152 as a result of the "expansive wave" of the collapse of the upper floor, their original place being the archival room proper. Furthermore one should note that in one case (RS 16.192A), the fragment actually joins another fragment found in the locus 132-152.

The surrounding area naturally includes the southern section of room 132 (RS 17.322), the southern and eastern sections of room 152 (S: RS 17.01, E: RS 16.191 + RS 16.272 and RS 16.191A), rooms 62 (RS 16.186 and RS 16.192A+), 64 (RS 16.187B), 66 (RS 17.147), 67 (RS 17.53 and RS 17.127), and 70 (RS 17.121). Note that a fragment of legal content found in room 152 E section (namely RS 16.191B) might also be part of a royal deed.

We also mentioned (in chapter 1) that five royal deeds had been recovered from the dump of archaeological work carried out during the excavation of the palace central archive. It is therefore possible, or even probable, that their original place was the archive of royal deeds located upstairs. The tablets are: RS 15.Y, RS 15.Z, RS 16.382, RS 16.413, and RS 16.415.

Finally, we should recall the potential misplaced tablets or stray finds previously discussed in chapter 1, whose place of origin might well have been the archive of royal deeds. Four of them are reported to come from the accumulation of tablets east of the palace (so-called "Archives Est"): RS 15.131+ from room 55 (already mentioned above), RS 15.114 (from room 54), RS 16.383 found to the north of room 52, and RS 18.285. The other two royal deeds with awkward find-spots are RS 19.98 from the palace southwestern archive and RS 19.128 from the palace room 75.

4. A royal registry

The starting-point of this section and discussion will be once more a brief appreciation of the excavator of the palace. The reason lies in the fact that Schaeffer's incidental definition of the "Archives Centrales" he had recently dug up was going to have an important echo (probably more important than he would have imagined), finding a significant place in the later discussion of ancient archives. On p. XXIV of his "Exposé préliminaire" in *PRU* 3, he opened a section dealing with the dynastic seal of the kings of Ugarit with the following words: "Ce vaste notariat royal que constituaient les Archives Centrales (...)." Whereas an Assyriologist would probably go on reading Schaeffer's text to learn about the extraordinary dynastic seal of Ugarit (for which see chapter 5 below), every Archivist would certainly stop there and underline the words "notariat royal." This can be seen, for example, in the long essay written by Papritz on cuneiform archives, and in Posner's landmark study on ancient archives.

In his characteristic fastidious style, the German scholar aimed to demonstrate, against the opinions expressed by early Assyriologists such as Morris Jastrow, that the ancient Near East did not know any sort of central record office comparable to the Athenian Metroon or Rome's Tabularium. "Nichts dergleichen ist in Altmesopotamien zu verspüren!" he would drastically conclude;[36] or further: "nach den bisherigen Ausführungen müßten wir also auch bezüglich des Typs der Gesta municipalia feststellen, daß ihn keine überzeugenden Funde in Altmesopotamien bezeugen."[37] In view of his negative tone and approach, it is significant that after the last sentence he would positively consider that "in diesem Licht erhalten die im 'Zentralarchiv' von Ugarit gemachten Entdeckungen ihr besonderes Gewicht."[38] And after a short, though not completely accurate,[39] description of these archival records, he would close the survey on potential Oriental examples of his "Gesta-municipalia-Typus" referring to Schaeffer's designation of the Ugarit archive "als 'vaste notariat'." Perhaps prompted by Papritz' exceptionally indulgent treatment of this Oriental example, Posner would allow himself to go one step further. "Did the beginning of a 'royal notariat' in Syrian Ugarit —he would ask in the introduction to his *Archives in the Ancient World*— influence developments in the Greek cities of Asia Minor and on the Greek mainland, where the notarial function became an integral part of the duties of the city archives?"[40] And among the six "basic types of records that may be called constants in record creation," he would list, presumably having in mind the tablets from the Ugarit palace central archive, what he termed "'notarial' records of state agencies or state-authorized persons that safeguard private business transactions between individuals."[41]

This interpretation on the part of such expert Archivists undoubtedly

---

[36] "Archive in Altmesopotamien," p. 40.

[37] Ibid., p. 42.

[38] Ibid., p. 43.

[39] For example when he mentions that "die Verwendung unterschiedlicher Siegel Rückschlüsse auf verschiedene Verfahren zuläßt;" as we already mentioned, only one seal, the dynastic, was used as a rule to provide the king's "Zeugenschaft" (see the discussion in chapter 5 below).

[40] *Archives in the Ancient World*, pp. 9-10.

[41] Ibid., p. 4.

rests on more solid ground than the simple, though eloquent, couple of words written down by the excavator of Ras Shamra. We are not being naïve, nor were Papritz and Posner. The seminal volume *PRU* 3 published in 1955 not only included the archaeological report and edition of the royal deeds that convincingly established the idea of the existence of a record office within the royal palace of Ugarit. Boyer also contributed to the book an appendix that was to become the main reference to the legal interpretation of the deeds. There he expressed the influential notion (followed among other scholars by Schaeffer, Papritz and Posner) that the royal deeds of Ugarit manifestly evidence the state involvement in private transactions between individuals. "L'intervention de l'autorité publique dans les actes de droit privé" would be the title of the first and main section of his study.[42] It is this general assumption (we shall discuss in detail further below), clearly reflected in Posner's definition of "notarial records," that lies behind the common interpretation of the archive as a state registry.

It goes without saying that the dichotomy between the private and the public domain is one of eternal dispute and discussion, not only among Archivists and Assyriologists. The distinction is, for example, essential and effective in law both in practice and in theory more or less since Roman times. Jurists, however, are well aware of the ambiguous criteria that define it and have expressed different, sometimes opposite, ideas about them. But let us return to archival science. Favier, as for one, significantly recommended in his introduction to his handbook to define as quickly as possible what we understand under public archives.[43] Given the importance of the issue, it seems worthwhile quoting the passage in full.

> On a, depuis longtemps, considéré comme publics les documents constituant les titres politiques ou domaniaux de l'État, ou constitutés par l'État pour son utilité propre, comme les traités, les originaux de lois, les registres des actes du pouvoir. La notion de propriété de l'État se fondait alors sur l'origine gouvernementale ou administrative des documents. Mais, à partir du XVIIe siècle, une nouvelle doctrine s'est fait jour à la faveur du renforcement du pouvoir monarchique : c'est l'intérêt général, et en particulier celui du prince, qui établit la nature publique de documents d'archives ; des pièces n'ayant jamais été conservées comme partie du domaine public en raison, non de leur origine, mais de leur na-

---

[42] See *PRU* 3, pp. 283-293.

[43] *Les archives*, p. 6.

ture : papiers d'un ministre, d'un diplomate, en tant qu'ils concernent les affaires de l'État.

According to Favier, what shaped the new concept of public records after the 17th century, becoming validated by the end of the 19th century, namely the notion of "general interest," was paradoxically enough the particular interest of the ruler. Perhaps one should refer in this context to the famous exclamation "l'État, c'est moi!" supposedly made by the young Sun King in April 13, 1655, when the president of the Parliament pointed to the interest of the state to persuade him about a controversial fiscal decision he had taken. This modern understanding of what is to be considered a public archive, continued the French Archivist, would then enable the state to bestow the rights of claims on a larger number and kind of records, as well as to preserve them, use them, and even remove them if need be. Some archives could even be destroyed by order of the ruler, as was the case for example of some archives of American presidents. As for the consequent unsettled debate on the nature of state archives, one needs simply to recall the unique and eloquent archival case of the Watergate affair. As is well known, a lengthy and complex legal discussion took place during the trials about the ownership of the tapes of conversations held in the Oval Office. How often in history, clearly including the most recent, would a state president or a ruler consider all the records in the office resulting from his official activities his personal property?

Regarding now, for instance, the Middle Ages in Europe or Antiquity in the Near East, our particular concern, the problem admittedly is not less entangled. In both these worlds the close connection between ownership rights and positions in the ruling hierarchy makes the distinction between the private and the public sector at least as blurred. There is then one question that inevitably forces out of the discussion and that is whether, and to what extent, such a modern concept is applicable in any meaningful way to our ancient Oriental world.

I believe it can be argued that the modern definition of public records hinting at their nature rather than their origin has been directly influenced by the classical definition of the two branches of law referred to above. "Publicum ius est, quod ad statum rei Romanae spectat; privatum, quod ad singulorum utilitatem pertinet." The emphasis of the legal distinction instituted by Justinian and still in use today is indeed laid on the intended addressee of the enacted norm, rather than on the origin of the norm. If the interest is addressed to the global community, or to put it in twenty-first century terms, if the interest is of a "general" character, the norm is said to belong to the area of public law. But if the interested party is a single individual, then the area concerned is that of private law. We have already mentioned that Jurists feel seldom satisfied with these criteria, and keep on discussing the legal meaning and correct use of so crucial a word as "interest." This, as we have seen, seems to be also true in archival science.

To be sure, the ambiguity of the definition does not concern documents such as laws, treaties, and decrees. Their official nature is as doubtless as their official origin. Therefore, in the case of an accumulation of diplomatic documents, such as the palace southern archive of Ugarit, it seems we are safely justified to speak of a state archive. But can we speak of a state record office in the case of the neighboring archive of royal deeds? If we stick to the modern concept of public archives and records, the answer can only be reached by answering the essential question, in whose interest were royal deeds enacted?

We have already seen that royal deeds are characterized by the recorded regular presence of the king at the transactions. In other words, all legal business recorded in these documents came before the ruling monarch. Whereas this should not surprise us in the well-attested case of royal grants, what is undoubtedly significant, as well as interesting, is that the corpus includes an important number of transactions between private individuals, such as sales or barters. Why were these private legal business made before the king? That is indeed another way of asking our central question, who was the interested party in these enacted transactions?

We have already mentioned that Boyer's legal interpretation of royal deeds did, and still does, enjoy a wide acceptance among scholars. Following his opinion, it is commonly assumed that with the impression of the dynastic seal on the document (directly linked to the absence of [other] witnesses in the text) the king of Ugarit bestowed not only his but the whole dynasty's protection over the transaction and title deed.[44] The involvement of the king would have accordingly been meant, as implied in Posner's definition of "notarial records," to "safeguard private business transactions between individuals." This interpretation can of course be taken to answer our crucial question. For, according to this view, the king would have participated in these transactions not so much in his own interest but in the individual parties'. In modern archival terms, we would then be entitled to speak of public records, and identify the archive located on the upper floor in the central area of the palace as a public title office. On the other hand, since most deeds deal, as we have quickly seen and will see in detail later, with the ownership of estate or landed property, the office or "notariat" would correspond to some kind of land registry.

---

[44] *PRU* 3, pp. 285-287. This interpretation will be discussed in the following pages and in chapters 5 to 7, paying special attention to the relevant, challenging legal view of Skaist ("A Unique Closing Formula," pp. 151-159).

"In neither case is there any reason to suppose that the state takes an interest in the transaction on its own behalf: it is there to act as an impartial arbiter, and to lend its authority to render the sale valid in the eyes of the law." The British Assyriologist John Nicholas Postgate was not commenting upon the deeds of Ugarit. He was referring to the two-stage intervention of the authorities of Assur known to have taken place at private sale transactions between individuals during the second half of the second millennium BC, thus roughly corresponding to the time of the Ugarit archives.[45] Two groups of sources (accordingly termed Middle Assyrian) provide the relevant information, namely the land-sale documents and the so-called tablet B of the Laws, in particular its sixth paragraph.

The first stage of the state intervention referred to by Postgate consisted in supervising the public announcement of the (private) sale. The buyer, as stipulated in the Laws, would have the herald make a proclamation of his business intentions three times during the course of one month both within the city of Assur and within the town where the property to be sold is situated. This first stage, aimed at giving official confirmation that the sale may proceed once the property was declared free of claims, is also provided for in the Middle Assyrian sale records. There it is typically concisely expressed by means of the clause "he (i.e. the buyer) shall 'clear' the land (from claims)" (e.g. *eqla uzakka*). This is in fact the first of a three-clause set of provisions regularly present in land-sale documents. The two other subsequent clauses would correspond in Postgate's scheme to the second stage of state intervention. This consisted in measuring the property with the "royal rope" and "drawing up the strong deed before the king" (e.g. *ina ašal šarri imaddad u ṭuppa dannata ana pāni šarri išaṭṭar*). The text of the law is unfortunately broken off when it comes to describe the writing of documents and no mention of the "strong tablet" is preserved. In view of the clause often attested in sale documents that states that "until the strong deed is written before the king, this (deed) is (the) strong (one)" (e.g. *adi ṭuppa dannata ana pāni šarri išaṭṭurūni annītuma dannat*), it seems reasonable to understand the *ṭuppu dannatu* as a sort of royal title deed.[46] No doubt the royal confirmation of the transaction was meant to provide evidence of title to the property sold, and accordingly safeguard the buyer against eviction.

---

[45] "Land Tenure in the Middle Assyrian Period: A Reconstruction," BSOAS 34 (1971):514-520; the quoted sentence is on p. 515.

[46] Note also the Old Assyrian text quoted by Postgate himself in note 78 p. 516: *kīma ṭuppi dannati laberti annītu ṭuppu dannat* (Gelb-Sollberger, JNES 16 [1957]:163ff., lines 35-37).

Given the characteristic features of this legal procedure, Postgate concluded that the so-called "strong tablet" or "valid tablet," as he would first call it (our "royal title deed"), would differ only in two respects from the "interim" sale documents we have. "First —he wrote—, it gave evidence of the confirmation of the transaction by the authorities, perhaps in the form of seal impressions of the officials concerned; and second, it contained the exact details of the land or property sold, giving in particular its location (...) and its dimensions, which had to be established with a standard official measure." "No example is known to me —he would then admit— of a Middle Assyrian tablet which answers to this description."[47] Today, more than thirty years later, we must still confess that no such tablet has come to light in any Assyrian site or modern collection of clay cuneiform tablets. The case, however, is that, as is already evident by the description we have proposed, the royal deeds of Ugarit show striking affinities to this very description.[48]

To begin with, as we have seen, the royal title deeds of Ugarit are characterized by the royal confirmation of the transaction in the form of the dynastic seal impression. One should further note that an essential feature of the Middle Assyrian "royal title deeds" is that they were written "before the king." And we have seen that exactly the same wording appears at the head of, indeed defining the royal legal documents from Ugarit. With this regard, I can only agree with Postgate's suggestion that the confirmation of the transaction by the authorities in Assur was made in the form of official seal impressions. In the light of the Ugarit parallel, however, perhaps the impression on the "strong tablet" was not made with the seals of a number of officials, but with that of the monarch himself.[49] On the other hand, if I may carry the parallel a little further, I would like to suggest that the description of the property sold in the Middle Assyrian "royal title deed" did not need to include its dimensions, as proposed by the British scholar. The fact that it had to be measured "with the royal rope" does not mean that the final record would necessarily specify the dimensions. The royal nature and

[47] "Land Tenure in the Middle Assyrian Period," p. 516. For the Middle Assyrian *ṭuppu dannatu*, see also his later contribution "Middle Assyrian Tablets: The Instruments of Bureaucracy," AoF 13 (1986):17-18; an earlier, important treatment can be seen in Koschaker, *Neue keilschriftliche Rechtsurkunden aus der El-Amarna Zeit* (Leipzig, 1928), pp. 32-36.

[48] The institutional parallels were already pointed out by Boyer, *PRU* 3, p. 290, followed by Miller, *Studies in the Juridical Texts*, pp. 31-32.

[49] If so, the only possible candidate for an actual "strong tablet" suggested by Postgate ("Land Tenure in the Middle Assyrian Period," p. 516 n. 77), namely the fragment BM 123367, should be discarded.

authentication of the document and transaction would undoubtedly suffice, for it would imply that the previous, official step was concluded. As we shall see in detail in chapter 6, the royal deeds of Ugarit concerning conveyances of land as a rule did not record the dimensions of the property (no doubt officially measured). This would be simply described in the common terms: "the field/house of PN_1, son of PN_2, (which is situated) in the area of TN (toponym)." One should note that this is exactly the same description we find both of the property to be sold as announced by the herald and of the estate sold in sale documents. The former text indeed describes it with the following words: "the field or house of so-and-so, son of so-and-so, (situated) within the area of the town in question" (*eqla u bēta ša annanna mār annanna ina ugār āle annie).*[50]

Whether or not the description of the property in the title deed would mention its dimensions, the coincidence between the depiction of the Middle Assyrian *ṭuppu dannatu* and the royal deeds of Ugarit is remarkable. As far as we know, the scribes of Ugarit did not designate their deeds (at least in written form) in the same Assyrian terms. They rather used the common Akkadian word *ṭuppu* without further qualification. This, however, is not a serious objection. It does not mean, for example, that in the hypothetical case that a scribe of Ugarit would have seen a "strong deed" from Assur he would not have recognized it as the Assyrian counterpart of his royal deeds. The latter, as we have seen, undoubtedly differed from other legal documents in the "*verstärktem* Rechtsschutz"[51] conferred by the presence of the king and the royal seal impression.

Perhaps some day the spade of a lucky archaeologist working in an Assyrian capital will bring to light at least a fragment of what we could safely identify as a *ṭuppu dannatu* and eventually confirm or disprove the proposed correspondence. If this alleged and certainly desired circumstance would really happen, it is to be expected that the excavator would not find just one single text or fragment. According to what has been stated above, it is likely that the find would consist of a larger number of examples. This probable guess is based on the assumption that, just like the Ugarit royal documents, Middle Assyrian "strong deeds" were presumably kept all together in some archive within the capital. As

[50] For the most recent edition of the Middle Assyrian law-book, in particular Tablet B §6, see Martha Roth, *Law Collections from Mesopotamia and Asia Minor* (2nd Printing, Atlanta, 1997), pp. 177-178.

[51] That is how Papritz described the royal deeds of Ugarit ("Archive in Altmesopotamien," p. 43). Note that Nougayrol also wrote that the state intervention conferred to the transaction "une vertu spéciale, une *force* nouvelle" (*PRU* 3, p. 25). The italics in both passages are mine.

has been recently put on the basis of the reading of the relevant passage in the law-book, "Assyria must have had a public registry of land-sale contracts."[52] It will be remembered that the archive unearthed in the central area of the royal palace of Ugarit has precisely been commonly characterized as a land registry. As we shall see in the next chapter, several scribal practices incidentally referred to in our corpus point to a notarial activity of the institution responsible for this Ugarit archive. But before closing the present chapter a word must be said about the alleged public nature of the archive of title deeds. The name "central archive" that was given by the excavator of Ras Shamra should not mislead our interpretation. As we have already mentioned, it simply referred to the topographic location of the accumulation of tablets within the palace.

To begin with it should be stated that the concept and institution of state archives conferring protection and legitimacy on private documents did not occur in the Classical world before Hellenistic times; and not even then was it generalized. The Metroon, the central archive in fourth-century Athens so often quoted in archival discussion, mainly housed decrees of the *boule* and assembly that would be read out to the jury and help decide cases at court. It seems, therefore, that Posner's question on the influence of "the beginning of a 'royal notariat' in Syrian Ugarit" in the Greek cities of Asia Minor and on the Greek mainland is not actually suitable to the evidence. Regarding the Ugarit "royal notariat," it is true that the people who appear buying land in sale transactions presided over by the king obtained thereby protection and legitimacy. The property they acquired became, as Boyer would put it, "dynastically" safeguarded against eviction. But there can be little doubt that the king of Ugarit, lord over his land and subjects, also derived his own benefit from his personal involvement in these "private" transactions. In other words, recalling the crucial and difficult question we asked at the beginning of the discussion, the king of Ugarit presumably took an interest in them on his own behalf, probably the same he took when he granted land. It should be remembered that not only land grants by the king and private transactions belong together in the corpus of royal deeds, but also that both kinds of transaction can, and do, appear side by side inscribed on the same tablet.

"Since all pertinent information is based on the meager written evidence and supplemented by inference, the nature of the text material is bound to influence our judgment." It is necessary to recall Oppenheim's essential forewarning[53] to keep in mind that our corpus was created by the palace bureaucracy and kept in a special archive within the royal

---

[52] Sophie Lafont, "Middle Assyrian Period," in *A History of Ancient Near Eastern Law*, ed. R. Westbrook, p. 547.

[53] *Ancient Mesopotamia*, p. 84.

palace, namely located in the king's private quarters, indeed to be used by the king or his secretaries when necessary. The king, therefore, or rather, the whole dynasty was a, probably the main, interested party in the enacted transactions. Now, where exactly lay his interest?

This is not the right place to discuss the relevant content of royal deeds or the much-debated subject of land tenure.[54] Suffice it to mention here that the particular involvement of the king in private land-sales beside, or should we say associated to, his activity as grantor of land to individuals already suggests that the land conveyed was held on condition that the holder would do some kind of service for the king. This, as we shall see, is confirmed by the fact that the provision of the liability to royal obligations (such as the typical Mesopotamian *ilku*-service) is only attested in royal deeds. At this point reference should be made to the fact, sometimes neglected, that private deeds have also been unearthed at Ugarit. The land-sale documents RS 17.22+ and RS 17.149, for example, were recovered from the so-called house of Rašapʾabu, east of the royal palace. Both transactions were made before a number of witnesses and record the sale of land to Rašapʾabu (in RS 17.149 together with his wife). It is probably no coincidence that in non-royal deeds dealing with conveyances of land such as these no mention of services is made. In other words, it can be reasonably argued that the lands conveyed in royal deeds, either by grant from the king or by sale between individuals, were subject to fiscal liability to the king, unless, as is also attested in these texts, the king chose to grant exemption to the tenant. If this interpretation is correct, the lands must necessarily be considered as part of the landed patrimony of the king or dynasty.[55] The "general interest" implicitly attributed by scholars to the state intervention in private transactions at Ugarit would therefore correspond here too to the particular interest of the ruler. The land registry situated in, thus operating from, the royal palace would have been meant to control the organization of the royal landed estate. Should we then be asked to tentatively describe the archive of royal deeds in modern terms, we would accordingly suggest calling it a crown land registry.[56]

---

[54] For which I refer to my forthcoming "Land Tenure and Royal Administration in Late Bronze Age Ugarit."

[55] See also Skaist, "A Unique Closing Formula," p. 158.

[56] Similar royal registration offices seem to have existed in other periods and areas of the ancient Near East. Apart from the contemporary potential case of Assur already mentioned, one should refer to Hammurapi's Babylonia (as suggested by the so-called Šamaš-ḫazir's correspondence) and perhaps Eshnunna in Early Old Babylonian times (see Klaas R. Veenhof, "Cuneiform Archives: An Introduction," in *Cuneiform Archives and Libraries*, pp. 25-27).

CHAPTER 3

THE ROYAL NOTARIES

No serious study on diplomatics or legal language can neglect an investigation, no matter how thorough, on the professionals who wrote the documents. This is what the present chapter is about. To use once more the words with which we defined the scope of the book, we would now accordingly turn to the group of persons who created, maintained, and used the well-defined body of royal deeds at the court of Ugarit from Niqmaddu II (second half of the fourteenth century) to ᶜAmmurapiʾ (first quarter of the twelfth century). After an introduction to the role of writing (and non-written communication) and bookkeeping in law, we shall consider the training of scribes at Ugarit. The following inquiry will attempt to answer the difficult, but necessary, question of how did these notaries or secretaries create, maintain, and use the deeds. In other words, we shall investigate on the administrative machine of the royal palace and the bureaucratic techniques that were practiced. To close the chapter, we shall draw our attention to the identity, social position and institutional background of the notaries.

1. Writing and Law

Ugarit in the two centuries that preceded its final destruction was not a literate society. This statement may obviously cause surprise, especially when we know that the Late Bronze Age level of Ras Shamra has yielded texts inscribed in five different scripts and that the one used to write the native Semitic language (Ugaritic) is one of the oldest alphabets in the world.[1] How often has it been echoed that the ease of alphabetic reading and writing must have favoured the development of literate societies and, for that matter, even of political democracies? I am of course not questioning the important impact of writing, whether word-syllabic or alphabetic, on human societies. The influence of this major mode of communication on social organization has been amply demonstrated since the leading studies of Jack Goody, who took a special interest in the ancient

[1] Beside alphabetic cuneiform Ugarit has yielded inscriptions in word-syllabic cuneiform, Egyptian hieroglyphs, Hittite hieroglyphs, and the Cyprian script (close to Linear B).

Near East no doubt for having been the birthplace of early "literate civilizations," possibly including the first one in southern Mesopotamia. What I want to say and stress, however, is that the impact or influence of writing should not be exaggerated. The world of Ugarit, like the broader (and abstract) world of the ancient Near East to which it belongs, was a world of talk, not of writing. Communication at all levels was generally and customarily carried out orally. It can naturally be argued that this holds also true for our modern world. But the difference is self-evident. Writing in Ugarit and the ancient Near East was, unlike today, severely, and socially, restricted. Only a limited group of the population had access to texts and was able to read and write. This minority, on the other hand, moved within the narrow circles of the elite, especially the so-called great organizations such as, in Ugarit, the royal palace. And also unlike our highly and daily written-intercommunicative world, not all fields of social interaction were affected by writing. We can therefore conclude that despite the image we may have of the thousands of clay tablets unearthed in the desert soil of Near Eastern sites and nowadays kept in museums all over the world, we are faced to oral cultures with a component of literacy. This conclusion must incidentally persuade us that the interpretation of any such civilization is of extreme difficulty and substantially limited since what has come down to us is but a fraction of what was written and next to nothing of what was spoken.

In law, to come to the field of social interaction we are concerned with, the spoken word plays, and no doubt has always played, a prominent part.[2] As a matter of fact, when legal language is attacked or even ridiculed (a practice already evidenced in the days of Cicero), its critics are usually referring to the legal spoken language, or in the terms of its detractors, to the specialized language that only lawyers can speak, emphasizing thereby the remoteness of the language of the law from ordinary speech. In the ancient Near East there were no lawyers, not even *iuris consulti* or orators who would legitimately defend their clients. To be sure, one cannot speak of jurists in this area in the strict sense, namely as professional interpreters of law and statutes, possibly not even during the Hellenistic period. But despite the absence of more or less professional pleaders, Ugarit and every ancient Near Eastern city had courts and juries who would hear disputes and trials, call upon persons to give verbal testimony, and eventually render verdicts, sometimes after long

[2] See also the remarks of Raymond Westbrook on "Written and Oral" in his "Introduction: The Character of Ancient Near Eastern Law," in *A History of Ancient Near Eastern Law*, pp. 12-13; and the contribution by Dominique Charpin, "Le geste, la parole et l'écrit dans la vie juridique en Babylonie ancienne," in *Écritures, systèmes idéographiques et pratiques expressives*, ed. A.-M. Christin (Paris, 1982), pp. 65-73.

interrogation and the taking of solemn oaths. All these spoken words have left but a faint trace in the cuneiform written record. "A case that might have consumed an hour," wrote Edward Chiera in his popular, posthumous, book *They Wrote on Clay*, "had to be condensed into a tablet that could be read in one-tenth that time. Consequently —he explained—, we have there no stenographic report but merely a summary."

The reason why the actual spoken words were not taken down is not to be sought in the inadequacy of the writing material or the writing system of Mesopotamian civilization but in the simple premise that a document tells us no more information than what its author wished to convey. And the authors of the documents, the subject of the present chapter, apparently wanted to record the state of affairs existing after litigation. The very few documents, including royal deeds, of Ugarit that happen to mention legal procedures indeed record the end-result of a case, for example which of the litigant parties had the title (or rights of ownership) to the disputed property (and of course which had not). In short, it seems we shall never know what utterances were spoken by the parties, witnesses and jury during the different moments of the procedure. With regard to the remarkable silence of the sources, it must be pointed out that we know only incidentally that oaths were taken and that witnesses were summoned by the court of Ugarit. Curiously enough the information does not come from the legal texts themselves but from messages sent by foreign or outside officials (accordingly mostly dealing with inter-state disputes) containing requests such as "May so-and-so together with his witnesses swear!" or "May they (viz. the witnesses) enter the temple!" implicitly meaning "and swear!"[3]

It is likewise significant that, for example, no lease contract or marriage agreement has been found so far at Ras Shamra. It is always possible to attribute this lack of evidence to the chances of discovery and preservation. But it is at least as possible, and indeed tantalizing, to suggest that such kind of legal transactions were not committed to writing at Ugarit between the fourteenth and twelfth centuries before our era. We happen to have a literary source, namely a (fragmentary) myth written in Ugaritic that describes a divine marriage presumably reflecting the practice operative at earthly Ugarit. Yarḫu the moon-god arrives on the scene requesting to Nikkal's father that the bride be given to him or, in other words, that the young goddess Nikkal enter his house. The following, necessary step apparently consisted in the groom's payment of the bride-price to the head of the bride's family, since the final scene shows Nikkal's family making ready the scales (to weigh the silver).[4] This sort of

[3] See the letters RS 20.21, RS 20.22, and RS 20.239.

[4] The Ugaritic myth is inscribed on RS 5.194 (KTU 1.24).

beautifully, though fragmentary and somewhat concise, exemplified ceremonies is more often than not lacking in the picture we have of legal life in ancient Ugarit. The wealth of documentary material in the cuneiform world contrasts with the relatively meager information we have from literary sources, indeed the reverse image Classical and Biblical scholars are used and bound to. Vivid examples of a land-sale transaction such as the one described in the Book of Jeremiah (32), for instance, are simply absent in our source material.

As a result, the so-called symbolic ceremonialism and the employment of various acts and formal ceremonies so typical a means to conclude an agreement (such as marriage) are usually lost to us together with the also essential words that were uttered during the transaction. All that is left of the gestures or rites that undoubtedly were publicly and ceremoniously performed on these occasions is a handful of attested legal formulas that may refer to symbolic acts. Likewise, the only utterances preserved in our records consist of a limited body of quotes from the parties to the transactions,[5] and a few frozen, conventional sentences or words that have been significantly defined as speech acts. The latter designation is meant to characterize the uttered words not only, or not so much, as something said but of an action done. So, for example, when the ancient Mesopotamian husband who wished to divorce his wife spoke out the words "You are not my wife;" here the utterance typically carried what has been termed a performative function (note that among Muslims the parallel speech act "I repudiate you" needs to be uttered three times).[6] Namely in the royal deeds of Ugarit we find the speech act "You are not our lord, another king is our lord."[7]

As for the non-oral, non-written accepted conventional procedures, one may refer from the Ugarit legal corpus to the symbolic formulas "to pour oil on one's head" as part of the ceremony of manumission of a slave, or "to place/leave one's garment on the door bolt or the stool" as the act symbolically performed by the repudiated son before departing his father's house.[8] One cannot decide, however, whether or not the

---

[5] Recourse to direct speech in legal texts is usually attested for wills and deeds generally dealing with the transfer of family property (see e.g. the provisions in the royal deed RS 16.143:23-29).

[6] John L. Austin who introduced the concept of speech act (in his classic *How To Do Things with Words* [Cambridge, MA, 1975]) referred on p. 5 to the modern, well-known example "I do (sc. take this woman to be my lawful wedding wife)."

[7] It is actually attested in a provision contained in a royal grant (RS 16.353). The grant is to be revoked, as stated in lines 17-20, "if PN (the grantee) or his children, his children's children, his progeny, his progeny's progeny speak to the king of Ugarit as follows: 'You are not our lord, another king is our lord'."

[8] See Meir Malul, *Studies in Mesopotamian Legal Symbolism* (Neukirchen-Vluyn,

words quoted were indeed taken down directly from the flowing speech of the parties and the symbolic legal formulas referred to actually performed rites. The problem, I believe, lies in the complex relationship between the written and the non-written, especially the oral, levels. For at issue are not, as might be too quickly deduced from Goody's writings, two qualitatively distinct modes of human communication but two different kinds of expression. Each played its specific part simultaneously and complementarily in what we have called oral societies with a component of literacy, such as the one of ancient Ugarit. But only the remains of one of them, the written, have come down to us. This circumstance must of course not influence our judgment and make us give preeminence of one over the other.

It is a commonplace among scholars to state that transactions and legal business can be committed to writing more than other social interactions. I say "can" because this may not be true of all kinds of legal transactions and procedures. It has been observed, for example, that Mesopotamian criminal proceedings were apparently not recorded on tablets.[9] And we have seen that this may also have been the case in Ugarit regarding marriage agreements and lease contracts. Of course we do not know whether these transactions were not actually put into writing during the 14th to the 12th centuries or examples have simply not survived from antiquity. One should always keep in mind how misleading arguments *ex silentio* can be; how often has a new discovery altered the picture! Still, one can also speculate for the time being and suggest that such transactions were not considered indispensable to record, and that a simple verbal agreement sufficed, perhaps because the property relations were recorded elsewhere and the personal relations did not go beyond the lifetime of the parties (and witnesses). The last statement is especially relevant and illuminating since it brings us directly to the intimate relation between writing and law. For was not writing precisely invented to overcome the urgent need to store information over time? And is not a reliable and long memory a necessary (and sufficient) condition to prove a claim or title to property, especially if required long after it was settled?

It is well known that titles to property, when not sold away, were (and are) kept and transferred from generation to generation usually through the successive heads of the family to provide evidence of (family) rights of ownership in case of litigation.[10] The recording and filing of land-sale

---

1988), pp. 44ff. and 93ff. respectively.

[9] Oppenheim, *Ancient Mesopotamia*, pp. 283-284.

[10] Note that in Babylonia from the days of Hammurapi on the titles transferred were termed *ṭuppāt* (or *kanīkāt*) *ummātim* (see Charpin, "Transmission des titres de propriété et constitution des archives privées en Babylonie ancienne," in *Cuneiform*

contracts, land grants, barters and gifts, adoptions and wills for future reference is, regardless of the size of the documentary material, at the origin of bookkeeping. Letters and administrative records were probably also susceptible to be stored for some period of time; but their use and therefore lifetime was definitely less long lasting than contracts and titles. Because they were precisely intended for permanent record clay tablets inscribed with a legal text, such as the royal deeds of Ugarit, could be baked, unlike administrative documents and letters. Indeed, the importance of a written agreement is self-evident. To own the tablet recording a land-sale transaction impressed with the seller's (or obliged party's) seal essentially meant to have rights of ownership over the land itself, as a rule rendering them irrevocable. The Akkadian clause *ṭuppu annû ileʾʾēšu* found at the end of a number of contracts and agreements[11] precisely means that the tablet in question cannot be contested.[12] Disputes could immediately and easily be decided on the spot on the basis of the evidence contained in the produced tablets (*ana pī ṭuppi*)[13]. Concerning royal deeds, we have seen that their very nature made the transactions recorded absolutely irrevocable. No one and nothing could contest the rights of ownership established by a royal deed. That obviously explains the implications and the actual circumstance of the case of forgery of the dynastic seal as reported to us in one of the documents.[14] The aim of the culprits was nothing but to create (forged) royal deeds or, in other words, (forged) irrevocable titles to property. This incident shows, on the other hand, that at least as important as the written word, in the sense of legally effective, was the seal impression on the tablet, a fact that brings us back to the phenomenon of literacy and illiteracy.

Archives and Libraries, ed. K.R. Veenhof, pp. 121-140). As shown by Charpin, the person who received a property automatically acquired all former tablets relating to the property itself. That is the way archives were constituted and enlarged in the course of time.

[11] E.g. RS 16.270:43. The legal clause is typically found in agreements drawn up in Carchemish (e.g. RS 17.145:19f., RS 17.158:25, RS 17.337:24f.) and in contracts from Emar.

[12] Compare also the Old Babylonian practice that had one of the litigant parties draft a "tablet of forbearance" (*ṭuppi lā ragāmim*) (see now Westbrook, "Old Babylonian Period," in *A History of Ancient Near Eastern Law*, pp. 371-372; and for an example in OB Alalakh, my corresponding chapter on p. 698).

[13] See RS 16.245:4'. Note that the Akkadian expression (literally meaning "by the mouth of the tablet") significantly evokes the interrelationship of the written and spoken levels of communication discussed above (see also Charpin, "Le geste, la parole et l'écrit," p. 70).

[14] RS 16.249.

Of course a seal impression (like a modern signature) alone, without a text, would not suffice to claim the rights to a property purchased recently or several decades ago. Seals cannot stand in such cases instead of writing, but one can say that their impression on legal documents could and presumably did stand in place of reading. We have mentioned earlier that a royal deed could be readily recognized by a modern scholar without any knowledge of cuneiform as well as by an illiterate Ugaritian living between the 14th and the early 12th centuries BC. In fact to own a title deed such as a land-sale or adoption document does not necessarily imply that the owner could read it. It obviously did not matter whether or not he or she could decipher the text. What really mattered is that the holder of the title deed knew the content of the text(s) he kept. Admittedly a citizen of Ugarit would have doubted the authenticity of a title deed written on papyrus and signed, say, by the pharaoh Ramesses II; but he would have been as amazed and suspicious before a cuneiform title deed from Hammurapi's Babylon. The reason of his or her astonishment can be understood by recalling our prototype of a royal deed. What I mean to stress is that the physical appearance of the deed, that is, the nature and position of the seal impression on the tablet, the shape of the tablet itself, and the arrangement of the inscription conveyed a message of their own; a message that even the larger body of illiterates of a society such as Late Bronze Age Ugarit could read. I cannot imagine, for example and specifically, that the kings of Ugarit were able to read the text of the title deeds they kept in an archive beside their bedroom (not only because the written language, Akkadian, was not their mother tongue). For such purpose they particularly supported and maintained specialized personnel, technically trained and prepared to read and write for them.

2. Scribal education

"Although they differ in essential respects," wrote Oppenheim concerning the various cultures surrounding Mesopotamia, "a number of attitudes are common to all these civilizations." The first and foremost is that "they accepted the Mesopotamian system of writing (cuneiform signs on clay), and, to varying degrees, Mesopotamian language and literary tradition."[15] Man's history has shown through multiple examples that a new technology spreads farther and more quickly than any other social or cultural experience. And also that its adoption by a foreign people need not (very often does not) go hand in hand with the phenomenon of immigration. Writing is a good example. It is now known, and it was cer-

[15] *Ancient Mesopotamia*, pp. 67-68.

tainly believed already by the ancients in the Near East, that writing emerged in Mesopotamia. This new technology was then adopted more or less rapidly, and progressively, by its neighbors to the east, north and west. Like any other craft in a traditional world such as the ancient Orient, writing was transmitted in a somewhat rigid fashion, through painstaking, established training from apprenticeship to working, professional status. This explains why so different civilizations who imported the cuneiform script (speaking so different mother-tongues) as the Hittites, Hurrians, Elamites or Levantines learned the Mesopotamian writing system in the languages proper of Mesopotamia, naturally foreign to them; and nothing else explains why we find almost identical school exercises spread all over the Near East through two long millennia.

Because the raw material of the scribal craft was clay many final, but also initial and midway, products of "writing industries" unearthed both in and outside Mesopotamia have survived. By initial and midway products I mean the important evidence of the different stages of scribal training. As a rule we find school exercises wherever the new technology was adopted. Indeed, virtually all sites where cuneiform tablets have been discovered, however small the number may be, have yielded at least one text typical of Mesopotamian educational practice. Even in the Egyptian capital of Amarna, nearly two hundred miles up the Nile, a number of cuneiform didactic tablets were found beside the major and renowned corpus of Akkadian letters.[16] At least as remarkable is the fact that the only cuneiform evidence extant from Ashkelon is a fragment of a syllabary;[17] and almost the same is true for other Levantine sites.[18] Despite the very scarce cuneiform material that has come to light from ancient towns such as Byblos, Kumidi, Megiddo, Tel Aphek or Hazor, there is significantly consistent evidence of school activity in all of them (note that the syllabary fragment found at Byblos dates to as early as the late third millennium).[19] Of course, the more productive the "writing

[16] See now Shlomo Izre'el, *The Amarna Scholarly Tablets* (Groningen, 1997).

[17] See Huehnergard and van Soldt, "A Cuneiform Lexical Text from Ashkelon with a Canaanite Column," IEJ 49 (1999):184-192.

[18] See Karel van der Toorn, "Cuneiform Documents from Syria-Palestine. Texts, Scribes, and Schools," ZDPV 116 (2000):97-113.

[19] For Byblos, see Georges Dossin, "Fragment de syllabaire de la III Dynastie d'Ur," Mélanges de l'Université Saint-Joseph 45 (1969):245-249; for Kumidi, see Dietz O. Edzard, "Ein neues Tontafelfragment (Nr. 7) aus Kāmid al Lōz," ZA 70 (1980):52-52; for Megiddo, see Albrecht Goetze and Selim Levy, "Fragment of the Gilgamesh Epic from Megiddo," ᶜAtiqot 2 (1959):121-128; for Tel Aphek, see Anson F. Rainey, "Two Cuneiform Fragments from Tel Aphek," Tel Aviv 2 (1975):125-128, and id., "A Tri-Lingual Cuneiform Fragment from Tel Aphek," Tel Aviv 3 (1976):137-138; and for Hazor, see Hayim Tadmor, "A Lexicographical

industry," the more voluminous the corpus of "initial and midway products" is likely to be. Ugarit provides a good testimony, as does Emar on the Euphrates. These latter examples, as well as Amarna in Egypt, attest to the time of broadest extent of the cuneiform world, namely between the early 14th and 12th centuries BC. By then Akkadian had become the language of diplomatic texts all over the Near East. As we shall discuss in detail in the next chapter, treaties and inter-state correspondence would be written as a rule in this Mesopotamian Semitic language.

The importance of the school texts discovered at sites such as Ras Shamra will be readily realized when we take into account first that it was in the course of the 12th century BC that the uniformity of teaching materials, that is, of what has been termed the "canonization" of the cuneiform lexical and literary books, took place in Mesopotamia; and secondly, that the educational handbooks from "peripheral" towns (such as Ugarit, Emar, Boghazköy or Amarna) are contemporary to the important Mesopotamian textual gap between the late Old Babylonian period (around 1600 BC) and the library of Ashurbanipal (7th century BC), only imperfectly filled by the texts from the so-called "library of Tiglath-pileser I" (end of 12th century BC). Before the didactic corpus would be fixed, various local recensions, that is, slightly different versions of the same teaching material existed in Mesopotamia. The question that immediately arises regarding the school texts discovered at Ras Shamra is then which of the existing recensions or didactic curriculum was followed at the Ugarit schools? What accepted body of textbooks did teachers use to introduce and educate Ugarit individuals in the craft of reading and writing?

The question is not easy to establish. To begin with, not all pre-canonical recensions are known to us. On the other hand, it must be kept in mind that the tradition followed at Ugarit during the 14th to 12th centuries was not necessarily directly imported from its original Mesopotamian school center. When Oppenheim wrote that civilizations outside Mesopotamia "accepted the Mesopotamian system of writing" he did not mean that they adopted it straight from the land between the Tigris and the Euphrates. They could have taken it from intermediate civilizations. Ugarit, like Emar and the towns from the Mediterranean fringe, might well have imported the cuneiform writing system from a school center situated in Anatolia or northern Syria, which in turn could have directly or indirectly imported it from Mesopotamia. It should be noted with this

---

Texts from Hazor," IEJ 27 (1977):98-102, and Wayne Horowitz, "A Combined Multiplication Table on a Prism Fragment from Hazor," IEJ 47 (1997):190-197. One should note that also at Ras Ibn Hani (probably the ancient Raʾšu belonging to the kingdom of Ugarit) there has been found one educational text (RIH 77/24+28/13).

regard that part of the school material of Ugarit, namely vocabularies, include readings in the Hurrian language or also that the literary tablet RS 25.44 containing the "Message of Ludingira to His Mother" was in all likelihood copied at Boghazköy.[20] A thorough and overall study of all the peripheral didactic material would probably throw important light on the subject.[21] For the time being, however, answers cannot be definite. It cannot be said, for example, which traditional school center was directly responsible for the training of scribes at Ugarit, neither which was the one ultimately responsible, although we can safely state which was not: in particular, the well-known Nippur tradition. We can also establish that the original school was in Babylonia proper. This is clear for instance from the names of water courses copied in the Ugarit geographical lists as well as the fish names in the lexical exercises, all of them native to South Mesopotamia but absolutely foreign to and indeed very distant from the Mediterranean world. The chronological frame can also be roughly established. The kings of the First Dynasty of Babylon listed in the texts, especially the last royal name Samsuditana, provide the *terminus post-quem* for the recension taught at Ugarit. We can therefore conclude that scribes at Ugarit were trained according to a late Old Babylonian (or early Middle Babylonian) tradition.

Now, what did the scribal training consist of? What was the content of the traditional educational material and the method practiced at the schools of Ugarit? To be sure, writing cannot be learned without a language behind it. The Mesopotamian cuneiform writing system, namely the first and main script in the ancient Near East was traditionally learned in the languages of Mesopotamia proper. Consequently, as we have already said (and more will be said in the next chapter), when a non-Mesopotamian student undertook to learn the Sumero-Akkadian writing system, or in other words, literacy with the help of teachers and textbooks he was at the same time learning a foreign, second language. In Ugarit, and other "peripheral" schools, this language was Akkadian. The training and knowledge of Sumerian, the other Mesopotamian native language, by then already long dead, was very much restricted: words had to be pronounced and understood, but outside Mesopotamia it hardly represented a written language.

Instruction at school began with manual work: how to make clay

[20] See for the latter Nougayrol, *Ugaritica* 5, p. 310.

[21] For the texts from Boghazköy (with reference to Ugarit and Emar and Hurrian mediation), see Gary Beckman, "Mesopotamians and Mesopotamian Learning at Ḫattuša," JCS 35 (1983):97-114; and for the Ugarit material, including important references on the texts from Emar, see the thorough study of van Soldt, "Babylonian Lexical, Religious and Literary Texts and Scribal Education at Ugarit and Its Implications for the Alphabetic Literary Texts," pp. 171-212.

tablets and handle the stylus traditionally made of reed was the preliminary step in the education of future scribes.[22] The first stage in the acquisition of literacy was based on the traditional lines of repeated reading, recitation and writing of signs, from the simplest to the more complex cuneiform arrangements. Here mention should be made again, however incidentally, to the essential oral tradition of memorizing signs and schooling in general, of which only very light traces are left (such as the written names of the signs). Without the verbal component, wrote both Miguel Civil and Antoine Cavigneaux in their respective thoughtful and thorough contributions on lexical lists, the texts we have are but lifeless bones.[23] The "bones" discovered at Ras Shamra tell us that in Ugarit[24] beginners learned first by rote the list of elementary syllabic signs, known as the *tu-ta-ti* exercise; then they practiced writing personal names and the derived list of logograms (namely Sumerograms) called by Benno Landsberger "Silbenalphabet A" which could in turn add a column with their Akkadian translation (the so-called "Silbenvokabular A"). This repertoire was followed by another list of simple logograms ("Syllabary Sa"). The bilingual version of this list in the Mesopotamian curriculum ("Vocabulary Sa") was enlarged at Ugarit with translations into Hurrian and Ugaritic.[25] Students were also trained at this stage in the archaic forms of the signs (this list is accordingly termed by Assyriologists "Paleographic Sa"). The quadrilingual vocabulary is followed in the same tablet by the so-called "Weidner God List," a sequence that is also attested in Mesopotamia proper. Which exercise was to come next in the strict and rigid training of a scribe at Ugarit, however, is not clear. No catch-line at the end of a text and no combination of properly identified series in one and the same tablet are attested at this point.

---

[22] Schaeffer reported the find of a few bronze styli during the excavation of room 3, what he called a "secrétariat," in the royal palace ("Reprise des recherches archéologiques à Ras Shamra-Ugarit. Sondages de 1948 et 1949 et campagne de 1950," Syria 28 [1951]:14). To the best of my knowledge the items have unfortunately remained unpublished.

[23] Civil, "Lexicography," in *Sumerological Studies in Honor of Thorkild Jacobsen on his Seventieth Birthday, June 7, 1974*, ed. S.J. Lieberman (Chicago, 1975), p. 130; Cavigneaux, "Lexikalische Listen," RlA 6, p. 612.

[24] Our description of the curriculum of Ugarit follows the leading authoritative study by van Soldt "Babylonian Lexical, Religious and Literary Texts and Scribal Education at Ugarit and Its Implications for the Alphabetic Literary Texts" mentioned above. The relevant sources can accordingly be found in his contribution.

[25] A new example of Vocabulary Sa with Hurrian translation came to light in the 1994 campaign of excavations (RS 94.2939); see Béatrice André-Salvini and Mirjo Salvini, "Un nouveau vocabulaire trilingue sumérien-akkadien-hourrite de Ras Shamra," SCCNH 9 (1998):3-40.

In Mesopotamia, the list of divine names sometimes precedes the large thematic series Ḫarra-ḫubullu with which the second phase of the elementary education started. This important list of words consisted at Ugarit of some fifteen tablets or chapters. The pupil had to learn by heart the Sumerian and Akkadian terminology of legal and administrative documents contained in the first two chapters of the series, and then proceed with the remaining tablets that formed a sort of cultural encyclopedia with several thousand entries (including, for example, names of trees and wooden objects, pottery, or domestic and wild animals). A list of human occupations and conditions, the so-called "Lu-series," followed; and the training continued with the memorization of another vocabulary, the "Izi-list," that was usually copied at Ugarit in its bilingual version (Sumerian and Akkadian), and a long, difficult list of compound logograms (the "Diri-list"), difficult because their reading cannot be deduced from the individual components. Copies of other advanced textbooks have been found at Ras Shamra such as the typical exercise of grammatical elements and lexical forms with their Akkadian translations (the so-called "Grammatical Texts"), the well-known "Ea sign list," and the vocabularies named "Nigga" and "Erimḫuš." Their exact place within the curriculum, however, cannot be established for the time being. And the same is true of the "Table of Measures" that was practiced at the schools of Ugarit. It is possible that the latter completed the elementary instruction of the pupil perhaps combined together with exercises in the writing of contracts as well as arithmetic calculations.

After being familiarized with the whole repertoire of cuneiform signs and words, students would be then introduced to a number of literary compositions from Mesopotamia. No evidence or even hint of the curricular order of the didactic literary corpus of Ugarit (such as a catalogue text) is available to date. Copies of some forty Sumero-Akkadian texts belonging to this second, higher level of education have been recovered from the ruins of a number of schools at Ras Shamra. Although they all ultimately clearly originate from Babylonia, it is significant that the corpus has strong parallels in "peripheral" schools such as Boghazköy and Emar. Also of interest is the fact that the texts are not lengthy, usually covering not more than one tablet, unlike the long epics or scholarly series of Mesopotamia. There are incantation texts (against Lamaštu, *šimmatu* or *samānu*), a few prayers and omen texts (such as copies of *Šumma izbu* or *Enūma Anu Enlil*), and examples of what modern scholarship regards as literature proper. Among the latter, we can mention copies of "wisdom texts" (e.g. a version of the Righteous Sufferer, the Admonitions of Šubê-awīlim to His Son, the so-called Poem of Early Rulers, or fables), as well as copies of more traditional Babylonian tales such as the flood story (presumably as part of Atraḫasis) and Gilgamesh[26]. The limited corpus of didactic literature contrasts with the scribal curriculum known to have been practiced at Mesopotamian centers and is probably an indication of the relatively low degree of proficiency in Akkadian and no doubt in Sumerian achieved by the scribes of Ugarit (an aspect we shall discuss in the next chapter). Significant with this regard is the considerable amount of aberrant mistakes present in the copies of these texts.

The reason for the inaccuracies and the relatively poor understanding of Akkadian (and Sumerian) of apprentice scribes is self-evident. It is a tautology to say that the Mesopotamian system of writing and the Mesopotamian language(s) and literary tradition were not learned in their natural setting. The students', and generally the teachers', mother tongue was Ugaritic and instruction was presumably conducted in the native language. Evidence for the linguistic setting of the classrooms at Ugarit is the Ugaritic column of the "Sa vocabulary" referred to above. If, as it is generally agreed, the more and better trained the pupil, the more concisely he would write his exercises, it seems reasonable to argue that the more he wrote, the more he reflected the oral instruction. When we deal with the Akkadian language at Ugarit in the next chapter, reference will be made to the interference of the Ugarit scribes' mother tongue in their Akkadian written texts. What we need to stress now is that the scribal craft at Ugarit was not completed without instruction in the script created at this very school center probably late in the 14th or the beginning of the 13th century BC to write the native language.[27]

It goes without saying that learning an alphabet is a much easier and quicker task than studying a complex word-syllabic writing system. The Ugaritic script which adopted the Mesopotamian technique of writing cuneiform signs on clay, consisted of thirty-one signs: twenty-seven consonantal signs, three syllabic signs (the *alif* combined with the three vowels /a, i, u/), and a word-divider (namely a small vertical single wedge). Repeated writing and recitation of the thirty phonetic signs clearly constituted the first stage of the Ugaritic curriculum. Several copies of lists of signs, so-called "abecedaries," have been found at Ras Shamra (and one was discovered as far south in the Levantine coast as Beth Shemesh)[28].

---

[26] The wealthy epigraphic harvest of the 1994 campaign of excavations at Ras Shamra includes a complete tablet of a Gilgamesh text, reportedly very fine and to-date unpublished. For a brief but recent survey of the wisdom literature found at Ugarit, I would refer to my "Scribes, Sages, and Seers in Ugarit," in *Scribes, Sages, and Seers. Wise Men and Women in the Eastern Mediterranean World. A Prospectus*, ed. Leo Perdue (Göttingen, in press).

[27] See already our remarks in chapter 1 section 5.

[28] See the proper identification of the text in Avraam G. Loundine, "L'abécédaire de Beth Shemesh," Le Muséon 100 (1987):243-250 (abecedary in the so-called short

Once familiarized with this relatively small repertoire of signs, the student would practice the script in context. Parallel to the word-syllabic curriculum, lists of personal names seem to have been a normal writing exercise at this stage. Exercise letters and religious and literary compositions (amounting to not more than forty), such as the famous epics of Kirta and Aqhatu or the so-called cycle of Ba^{c}al, would then complete the student's education. It is significant that whereas Sumero-Akkadian literary texts copied by apprentice scribes were as a rule limited in size, the Ugaritic myths and epics could cover several tablets.

It can therefore be stated that education at Ugarit was "biliterate" or "biscriptal," as van Soldt has put it[29] (of course as soon as the Ugaritic script was invented and in use). These two learning tasks were then pursued independently but probably in parallel, for a scribe, say around 1250 BC, would not be a competent professional until the two scripts had been mastered. Naturally the Sumero-Akkadian writing system would pose more problems and difficulty than a pseudo-alphabet of thirty signs with which the trainee would write his mother tongue. That this two-sided instruction was conducted in parallel or simultaneously can be deduced from a number of school tablets inscribed with exercises both in Ugaritic and Sumero-Akkadian cuneiform. RS 20.148+, for example, is a four column tablet which has the same excerpt of the Grammatical Texts repeated three times; following the Sumero-Akkadian text of the first column the scribe wrote a series of Ugaritic abecedaries, and still another one is written along the vertical lines that separate column three from column four. A further example is RS 22.225 that has an Ugaritic incantation against the evil eye on the obverse of the tablet and the syllabary exercise *tu-ta-ti* together with an acrographic list of what seem to be personal names on the reverse. And RS 20.136 is another mixed exercise tablet with an excerpt of the Weidner God List on the obverse and an Ugaritic one-line text on the reverse.[30] From these examples it cannot be established how the two curricula were combined by the teacher. RS 22.225 shows an elementary word-syllabic exercise beside an alleged example of Ugaritic high-level education. By contrast, RS 20.148+ pre-

cuneiform alphabet and *halaḥam*-order written from right to left). Note that the situation resembles the one described above for Levantine sites and the high proportion of Mesopotamian didactic text finds. Indeed this school exercise is the only cuneiform text found at Beth Shemesh.

[29] "Babylonian Lexical, Religious and Literary Texts and Scribal Education at Ugarit and Its Implications for the Alphabetic Literary Texts," p. 186.

[30] For this text in particular, as well as other examples, see my "Syllabic and Alphabetic Texts. A Further Note on Scribal Education at Ugarit," UF 28 (1996):457-462.

sents the basic Ugaritic abecedary exercise alternating with a repeated excerpt of a relatively complex word-syllabic textbook. At a more balanced level, we find an abecedary with syllabic equivalents (RS 19.159) and an exercise text with mixed alphabetic and word-syllabic signs and words (RS 20.147). The problem is that we unfortunately hardly know anything about the didactic methods that were practiced at the schools of Ugarit (and other places as well). What we know, however, is that once the student reached the master's stage and became a professional scribe, especially in the administration, he could and would use (when necessary or convenient) both scripts side by side or independently. A number of Ugaritic administrative texts, for example, bear a summary or caption written in Sumero-Akkadian cuneiform.[31] And, as already mentioned, a scribe like Burqānu was the author of at least four legal documents, three written in Akkadian in word-syllabic cuneiform, and one in Ugaritic in alphabetic cuneiform.[32]

As it can be deduced from these last examples, on completion of their training scribes could normally expect (one can say that they were generally meant) to enter the administration, perhaps after a period of assistantship in which they would become familiar with the bureaucratic tasks.[33] Most of the final products of the writing industry of Ugarit during the 14th to 12th centuries are records of the day-to-day activities that concerned the elite of Ugarit, namely letters, legal documents, and administrative texts written either in Ugaritic or in Akkadian, following the conventions established by the scribal craft. Of interest is the fact that the adoption of the Mesopotamian writing material (the clay tablet) and technique (impressing wedged-shape signs from left to right) to write

---

[31] See the list in Dietrich, Loretz and Sanmartín, *Die keilalphabetischen Texte aus Ugarit* (Neukirchen-Vluyn, 1976), p. 506 ("Akk. und sum. Angaben"), and also Huehnergard, *The Akkadian of Ugarit*, p. 322 (Appendix 4: "Ugaritic Economic Texts with Sumero-Akkadian Summaries"), as well as my "Summaries of Ugaritic Texts and Some New Reading Suggestions," UF 24 (1992):259-262; to this list one should add now the texts RS 92.2001+ (passim) and RS 92.2013 (line 1), published respectively as RSOu 14 nos. 35 and 41 (see my review to *Études ougaritiques, I. Travaux 1985-1995*, ed. M. Yon and D. Arnaud [Paris, 2001], in Or NS 74 [2005]:140).

[32] RS 8.145, RS 17.125 and RS 25.137 in Akkadian, and RS 19.66 (KTU 3.8) in Ugaritic. If the restoration of RS 15.111 (KTU 3.2):19 proposed by Lipiński is correct ("Aḫat-Milki, reine d'Ugarit, et la guerre de Mukiš," p. 113), the notary Nu^{c}merašpu, author of the Akkadian deeds RS 15.143+, RS 15.168, RS 18.280, and RS 15.127 (+)$^{?}$ RS 15.131, would also have drawn up the Ugaritic royal deed (see, however, our remarks in chapter 5, especially note 103).

[33] This last phase of specialization is known to have been at work in Mesopotamia proper.

Ugaritic texts went hand in hand with the adoption of tablet formats. Ugaritic letters, for example, were clearly patterned after the Akkadian or word-syllabic prototype.[34] And the same is true for the few Ugaritic royal deeds, as we shall see in chapters 4 and 5, or the literary texts such as the epic works and myths typically divided in columns following the classic Babylonian pattern.

In view of the expected future, namely administrative, tasks of apprentice scribes it may seem paradoxical that no model contract has been found at Ugarit such as the sample didactic documents known to have been taught at Mesopotamian schools. Because the curriculum at Ugarit must have more or less strictly followed a Late Old Babylonian scribal training, we have suggested above that at the end of the first, elementary level of education, that is, before the introduction to the Mesopotamian literary corpus, the pupil at Ugarit would have practiced the writing of legal documents. We know that this was indeed the case in the Babylonian curriculum, especially at Nippur. As stated by Stephen J. Lieberman, model contracts together with proverb texts were taught "as students were making the transition from writing single words to phrases." Both kinds of writing drills, he continued, "were put on the same side of tablets with metrological exercises."[35] This seems to be further confirmed by a Sumerian literary composition known to Assyriologists as the school dialogue "Edubba D" in which two students of an imaginary Babylonian school in the first quarter of the second millennium discuss and boast about the extent of their respective scribal knowledge. At a certain point one of them describes his abilities in writing metrological exercises as well as all kinds of contracts: deeds of sale and adoption, deeds of lease and pledge, and marriage contracts.[36]

---

[34] Apart from the size and shape of the tablet itself one should further note the occasional adoption or rather adaptation of the arrangement of the three alphabetic signs {*r-g-m*} for the introductory verb form /*rugum*/ "speak!" after the standard Akkadian equivalent tri-syllabic word {*qí-bi-ma*} for /*qibīma*/.

[35] "Nippur: City of Decisions," in *Nippur at the Centennial*, ed. M. de J. Ellis (Philadelphia, 1992), p. 131. See also more recently Niek Veldhuis, *Elementary Education at Nippur. The Lists of Trees and Wooden Objects* (Groningen, 1997), pp. 40, 60-61; and Eleanor Robson, "The Tablet House: A Scribal School in Old Babylonian Nippur," RA 95 (2001):39-66. A comprehensive treatment of the model contracts used in Old Babylonian schools was being prepared by Lieberman himself together with William W. Hallo and Fatima Yildiz (entitled "The Manual of Sumerian Legal Forms"); see also recently, Hallo, "A Model Court Case Concerning Inheritance," in *Riches Hidden in Secret Places. Ancient Near Eastern Studies in Memory of Thorkild Jacobsen*, ed. Tzvi Abusch (Winona Lake, IN, 2002), pp. 141-154.

[36] See Civil, "Sur les 'livres d'écolier' à l'époque paléo-babylonienne," in *Miscella-*

These paired Old Babylonian curricular exercises and the fact that the Sumero-Akkadian handbook of the "Table of Measures" was taught at Ugarit allowed us to speculate that the writing of contracts was also practiced at these "peripheral" Late Bronze Age schools. It is relevant and significant to note in this regard that the copying of contracts was part too of the scribal training in first-millennium Babylonia.[37] Are we then to blame again the accidents of discovery, or rather to pause and respect the always dangerous *argumentum ex silentio*? Should the absence of model contracts at Ugarit be explained on account of the fundamental oral instruction of scribes? But then, how do we explain the practice of writing letters, as evidenced by a few Ugaritic copies found at Ras Shamra? Is it possible, one finally needs to ask, that examples of sample legal documents have been unearthed but have not been recognized thus far? Perhaps the reason for the absence of such texts is not to be sought through only one of the questions we have posed. It is, for example, possible that of the two modes of instruction used to teach students how to write legal documents, namely the "paradigmatic approach" (i.e. with lexical texts) and the "pattern practice" (i.e. with model contracts),[38] only the former entered the (written) curriculum at Ugarit, and that the latter was substituted by oral instruction, the few exceptions to the rule having escaped so far the spade of the archaeologist or the eye of the Assyriologist. Indeed, regarding the latter question, how can one safely distinguish a true transaction (or message, for that matter) from a fictitious, didactically intended example?

There is undoubtedly very much (indeed too much) that we do not know, and shall probably never know. But there are also indications that we can expect to discover so as to be able to offer more or less speculative impressions. For example, duplicates or triplicates of a contract can be plausibly taken as repeated exercises of a model transaction; a tablet inscribed with two contracts or with a contract and a literary passage (such as a Sumerian proverb in Old Babylonian times) is most likely to

nea Babylonica, Mélanges offerts à Maurice Birot (Paris, 1985), pp. 67-78, notably lines 40-48. It may be of interest to incidentally mention that a similar text describing Old Babylonian school activities was practiced in the schools of Ugarit both in Sumerian and Akkadian (RS 17.10 and RS 17.80 respectively; see Nougayrol, *Ugaritica* 5, pp. 23-28, and Civil, "An Edubba text from Boghazköy," NABU 1987/47).

[37] Not only excerpts of contracts but also full records would be copied and practiced in the course of the first level education at Neo-Babylonian schools (see Michael Jursa, *Das Archiv des Bēl-Rēmanni*, [Leiden, 1999], pp. 13-31, and cf. Petra Gesche, *Schulunterricht in Babylonien im ersten Jahrtausend v. Chr.* [Münster, 2001], pp. 147-148).

[38] See Lieberman, "Nippur: City of Decisions," p. 129.

be identified as a school text. And even a tablet inscribed with a legal text relatively full of blatant mistakes in orthography and grammar or very coarsely written can be interpreted as a "midway product" of an inexperienced student or beginner; concerning the latter case, however, one should consider at least conceivable that professional scribes with a low proficiency of Akkadian (the language of the text) could have worked at "peripheral" bureaucracies (a subject we shall discuss in the next chapter). From this follows a further problem. For what if the pupil who wrote a model contract was a competent, careful student? How could we, modern scholars, distinguish such an admittedly "midway product" from a finished, original functional record?

It can be suggested that the absence of witnesses, for instance, could uncover the legal inefficacy of the text pointing to its didactic nature;[39] more decisive of course should be the absence of a seal impression or any personal mark on the tablet as well as the archaeological context of the tablet itself. It may thus be worthwhile considering (or reconsidering) under this light a few examples of legal documents without witnesses or any impression on the reserved sealing space of the tablet unearthed among the largest concentration of didactic material so far discovered at Ras Shamra. The so-called "house of Rapʾānu" has yielded some 235 didactic texts, that means, more than half of the total finds at Ras Shamra; conversely, the bulk of the textual content in this house (almost 70 per cent) is of a didactic nature.[40] Non-sealed legal texts are: RS 20.146, RS 20.176, RS 20.214B, RS 20.235 and RS 20.236 (the latter two texts also omit the normative list of witnesses). It is true that this school, and others in Ugarit, has yielded scribal training exercises beside actual records such as sealed legal documents, letters, and administrative texts. How should we then interpret these non-sealed documents of legal content? Were they kept as memoranda or private copies of original transactions? Or could at least one of them be part of the important didactic body of texts taught at the school at the time of the final collapse of the building (and city)?

Even if it is more judicious to leave these questions open for the time being, I would still like to briefly draw the attention to one of the texts, namely RS 20.235. The tablet shows a number of significant irregular features. To begin with, as already stated, it lacks the seal impression on

---

[39] Sumerian model contracts, for example, lack witnesses (and also the prescriptive date); in some cases the text would indicate their absence by replacing them with the notation "its witnesses, its month, its year" (see Lieberman, "Nippur: City of Decisions," p. 130 n. 18, and Hallo, "A Model Court Case Concerning Inheritance," p. 142).

[40] See van Soldt, *SAU*, pp. 165-180.

the properly reserved space on the upper part of the tablet. Secondly, it seems that the scribe's lack of application rather exceptionally led Nougayrol to misread the second line of the text; what the (apprentice?) scribe wrote (and apparently carelessly erased) was the usual introductory phrase of legal documents *ana pāni šībūti* "before witnesses."[41] The names of the witnesses, however, normally necessarily listed at the end of the tablet are missing. Furthermore, the transaction itself is completely shapeless: only one of the parties is mentioned (by name) and the verb defining the nature of the business is again missing. As for the inventory of movables listed in the text (metal ware, beds, chairs, etc.), one should also note the peculiar last items, namely "oxen together with the shepherd, servant of the goddess Aṯtartu (?)."[42] In view of the remarkable number and quality of odd features as well as the find-place of the tablet it seems reasonable to suggest that the author of the text was an apprentice scribe.

Whether or not the speculation about the nature of RS 20.235 proves correct,[43] what seems clear in view of the epigraphic finds is that if writing contracts was practiced at Ugarit schools it was only done exceptionally. One should incidentally note that mathematical exercises, to put a simple, clear example, have not been discovered thus far from among the Late Bronze Age ruins of Ras Shamra, despite the very probable guess that teaching arithmetic calculations, however elementary, belonged in the scribal curriculum. As a matter of fact, the so-called "paradigmatic approach" may have sufficed to train students in their future tasks of drawing up legal documents at this elementary level. This method consisted in teaching the (naturally smaller) units of a contract, namely the individual contractual clauses and words. The knowledge of these formulas and terminology would without much difficulty eventually allow the scribes to combine them into actual, complete contracts. We have seen that in Ugarit the scribal curriculum included learning by rote a series of words, phrases, and clauses typical of cuneiform legal compositions, indeed constituting the first two chapters of the elementary encyclopedic handbook Ḫarra-ḫubullu. At this point, and given the scope of the present study, it may be worthwhile pausing and summarizing the interesting development of these Mesopotamian paradigms of

---

[41] The French epigrapher transliterated the second line of the text as follows (in *Ugaritica* 5, p. 178): *a-na mišil 2* ?[ ]?. But it must probably be read: *a-na pa*$^{!}$-*ni*$^{!}$ ^{I}[$^{\text{ú?.meš?}}$*ši*$^{?}$-*bu*$^{?}$-*t*]*i*.

[42] Lines 17-18: gu$_4$.hi.[a] *qa-du* ^{lú}sipa / ^{lú}ìr ^{d}eš-dar.

[43] As mentioned above, RS 20.236 from the house of Rapʾānu also lacks the list of witnesses and the seal impression (note the scribal lapsus in line 7, namely the omission of the sign MA).

legal formularies, clauses and words.[44]

It is known that the Mesopotamian lexical series Ḫarra-ḫubullu originally began with the list of trees, that is, with Tablet III of the twenty-four-chapter canonical recension. Tablets I and II were accordingly deliberately affixed to the original elementary series in a somewhat artificial fashion, their style being admittedly alien to the remaining chapters. The two-tablet "independent" composition seems to have been first compiled in Old Babylonian times, as shown by extant texts (so-called forerunners [of the canonical series]) coming from cities such as Sippar. The oldest dated precursor copy is from the fifteenth year of the Babylonian king Samsuiluna. This composition derives from a list of legal terms and phrases belonging to the old collection of "model contracts" as well as from forerunners of the "Izi"-lexical-list. Another legal textbook very similar in style and content was developed in parallel and used in Old Babylonian Nippur schools. Its Sumerian title *ki-ulutin-bi-šè* may in fact be subtly referred to by one of the students in the school literary dialogue "Edubba D" mentioned above.[45] The canonical version of this series, called after its Akkadian translation *ana ittišu*, is comprised of seven tablets and must have included some 1,800 entries. The extant sources of this handbook are all library texts (mostly from the collection of Ashurbanipal) and no copy dates to earlier than the twelfth century.

The late Old Babylonian curriculum adopted in schools at Ugarit did not include the Nippur legal textbook *ana ittišu*, which must have followed different ways of transmission, but had instead incorporated, as we have seen, the other parallel, sometimes overlapping, two-chapter collection of legal phrases and words into the longer teaching series Ḫarra-ḫubullu. Copies and excerpts of the two first chapters were written down by apprentice-scribes at Ugarit in both monolingual (Sumerian) and bilingual versions (Sumerian-Akkadian; there is also one example of Sumerian-Hurrian).[46] As we have already said, by practicing and memorizing

[44] Unfortunately the comprehensive, updated study of Ḫarra-ḫubullu I-II and their Old Babylonian forerunners "and the like" planned by Lieberman (cf. "Nippur: City of Decisions," p. 130 n. 20) has remained unpublished. The following description is accordingly based on the critical editions of Hh I-II and the series *Ana ittišu* published by Landsberger in *MSL* volumes 5 and 1 respectively, as well the later outlines offered by Civil ("Lexicography," pp. 127-173), Roth (*Scholastic Tradition and Mesopotamian Law: A Study of FLP 1287, a Prism in the Collection of the Free Library of Philadelphia* [Ph.D. diss. University of Pennsylvania, 1979], pp. 13-14), Cavigneaux ("Lexikalische Listen," p. 631), and Veldhuis (*Scribal Education at Nippur*, pp. 69 and 79).

[45] See Civil, "Sur les 'livres d'écolier'," p. 77 (ad line 36).

[46] See the complete list in van Soldt's table in "Babylonian Lexical, Religious and Literary Texts and Scribal Education at Ugarit and Its Implications for the Alpha-

these lists the scribe was trained in the correct use of Sumerian and Akkadian contractual phraseology. We therefore agree with Daniel Arnaud when he wrote that Ḫarra-ḫubullu (namely, Tablets I and II)[47] was "un manuel destiné à apprendre leur métier aux notaires mésopotamiens;" but the accent needs modification when he went on to state that "son entrée dans le cursus académique syrien [specifically meaning Ugarit] ne se comprend que parce qu'il faisait partie d'un ensemble plus vaste pour la pédagogie du sumérien et de l'accadien." His drastic conclusion that "nous sommes donc là en Syrie dans le domaine des Belles-Lettres et absolument pas dans celui de la pratique juridique occidentale" seems to be partly deduced from the severe errors and the poor understanding of the Sumerian words copied by the pupil on the Ras Shamra tablet he published (RS 1979.22), namely a monolingual exercise of Ḫarra-ḫubullu I, as well as by the fact that the legal formulas of the text "n'appartiennent pas au droit ougaritique, qui les ignore."

It is beyond doubt, as we have tried to show, that the fifteen-chapter textbook was part of the broader curriculum of scribes, and also that many words and chapters were hardly used and useful for the future scribe (such as the names of water-courses in the Babylon region or the names of fish only found in south Mesopotamian marshes). Moreover, it is true that not all the legal formulas used by professional scribes of Ugarit to write legal documents were contained in the lexical series (in particular, the lines preserved in RS 1979.22). But what one needs to take into consideration is that this genre of texts was as a rule written at Ugarit in the Sumero-Akkadian writing and in the Akkadian language. Whatever the understanding of the Sumerian language by the scribe-to-be, the first two chapters of Ḫarra-ḫubullu contained an important part of the terminology needed to write a legal document at Ugarit. Akkadian, as we said, was the language of the deed and presumably the language recited while the student wrote with more or less proficiency the Sumerian legal words and phrases (possibly also followed by their Ugaritic translation). Legal terminology in use at Ugarit (to be discussed in detail in chapter 6) such as Akkadian *zittu* "share," usually written with the Sumerogram ḫa.la, or words such as igi for *šību* "witness," šu-du$_8$-a for *qātātu* "guarantor," šám til.la.bi.šè for Akkadian *ana* / *ina šīmišu gamri* "(for its) full

betic Literary Texts," p. 198. It seems likely that future finds at Ras Shamra will increase the number of examples.

47 "Les textes cuneiformes suméro-accadiens des campagnes 1979-1980 à Ras Shamra-Ougarit," Syria 59 (1982):199.

price;"[48] verb forms used to build up the formulas that specify the nature of the transaction such as *ilqe*, *ileqqe*, *ileqqū* from *leqû* "to take," *ublam*, *ubbal* and *ubbalū* from *abālu* "to bring, to carry," *ipṭur*, *ipaṭṭar*, *ipaṭṭarū* from *paṭāru* "to redeem," *iddin*, *inaddin*, *inaddinū* from *nadānu* "to give;" or phrases such as Akkadian *ana arkat ūmi amēlu ana amēli* "in the future one to / against the other," or *ana mārūtišu* "in sonship (i.e. legal status as son)," or *ana aḫḫūtišu* "in brothership (i.e. legal status as brother)," were all learned through repeated writing and recitation of Ḫarra-ḫubullu I and II. It is possible, or even probable, although not provable, that apprentice students became familiar with the characteristic formulas and pattern of a legal document of Ugarit during their alleged assistantship in the state bureaucracy, but there can be little doubt that the elementary textbook served as a first tool to teach the future notaries of Ugarit how to write royal deeds.

3. *The responsibilities of palace notaries*

Civil closed his contribution on education in Mesopotamia with a reference to a Sumerian literary passage. "The post of a scribe 'who regularly comes and goes in the palace' —he wrote— was considered a most enviable one, a divine blessing to be preferred to material riches."[49] To be sure, literacy, especially in traditional oral cultures, was highly valued and intimately linked to power; and an intimate, indeed prestigious, connection to the ruler can indeed be desired more devoutly than any material riches, although, one should add, both ambitions were (and are) admittedly not incompatible. The indispensable presence of an educated or literate official in an ancient Near Eastern palace was obviously associated to a high social status and to generous wages. This twofold nature of literacy is echoed in another wisdom text, namely a bilingual Sumero-Akkadian proverb: "The scribal art —it says— receiving a handsome fee is a bright-eyed guardian, the need of the palace."[50] The discussion on the social status of a palace notary of Ugarit and his relationship to power will be dealt with in the next section. It is to the related indispensable

---

[48] Note that the Mesopotamian cuneiform words that appear mixed with cuneiform alphabetic signs in the school exercise RS 20.147 (KTU 5.15) mentioned above are significantly: šám.ti.la (sic) *ša* géme and *ḫu-bu-la*[?].

[49] In *The Anchor Bible Dictionary*, vol. 2, p. 305. Civil kindly referred to me the passages in Enlil and Namzitarra (end of the composition) and Gilgamesh, Enkidu and the nether world (line 263).

[50] Quoted by Laurie E. Pearce in her "The Scribes and Scholars of Ancient Mesopotamia," in *Civilizations of the Ancient Near East*, vol. 4, ed. Jack M. Sasson (New York, 1995), p. 2265.

tasks and responsibilities he had that we now turn.

The royal palace based in the city was "the great organization" in Ugarit. It represented the major economic unit and upon it was centered the administration of the whole kingdom. However deliberately overemphasized the tone of the biblical denunciation of kingship by Samuel (1Sam 8:10-18), there can be little doubt that the ancient Oriental state, like most ancient states, was primarily, whatever its size, a system for extracting taxes and forming armies, and that the king or dynasty that ruled it was or became the most important landowner in his country.[51] Modern ethnological and anthropological studies have shown that the administration of such a system can exist without writing. And yet, when writing is available, the Mesopotamian proverb can hardly be questioned: the palace becomes then vitally dependant on the scribal art. The technical ability to write and read allows the ruler, certainly by way of his scribes, to communicate with his allies and overlords as well as his dependencies, and to record his political agreements, legal transactions and all (or most) state business and fiscal activities. It was actually to control the palace administration system and keep the accounts of the master's treasury that royal scribes established a bureaucratic organization.

We have seen in the previous chapter that the scribes of Ugarit had established before 1200 BC an office or registry on the upper floor of the royal palace that was meant to control the organization of the royal landed estate and accordingly an important section of the royal tax revenue. We have occasionally called these professional scribes "notaries," not however in the modern sense of a public officer authorized to authenticate contracts, acknowledge deeds, or take depositions, but rather in its obsolete, specifically historical meaning of an officer certified by the king whose duty was to write, witness, care for, and otherwise take care of documents. These fundamental tasks of notaries are well attested at Ugarit. We know that they designed the royal deeds; on the other hand, their names and profession often appear at the end of these records specifying their role as (usually only) witnesses to the transaction (see the discussion in chapter 5); and the reconstructed archives such as the one of royal deeds located in the palace together with a number of references to bureaucratic practices in the texts show that they carefully filed, used, and preserved the documents *ex officio*. As is readily clear, the study of the functions of the notary's office at Ugarit relies exclusively on information derived from the archaeological record and the excavated documentary material. No literary sources, ancient manual or description of

---

[51] The subject is developed in my forthcoming "Land Tenure and Royal Administration in Late Bronze Age Ugarit."

the professional tasks are available.

Notaries designed royal deeds at Ugarit through at least one and a half centuries. But they did not design them as lawyers do nowadays. Their proficiency was not with law or legal interpretation. As I have insisted throughout the discussion, notaries were essentially professionals of the craft of writing and reading. Drawing up legal documents, however, was not and is not like writing other kinds of day-to-day records such as letters or bills and receipts. One of the fundamental differences lies in the distance between the sender and the receiver of the message. For in the case of legal texts, unlike letters for example, the distance is not measured in miles but in years or even centuries. As we mentioned above, a legal document is characterized by its potential long life, namely the duration imposed by the legal relationship established by the recorded transaction. It is this temporary importance that explains the accordingly necessary strict formalism of legal texts. A notary from the time of the last king of Ugarit, i.e. around 1200 BC, had to be able to read and understand a royal deed sealed by ᶜAmmurapiᵓs grandfather's great-grandfather, say drawn up in 1340 BC. Not however through painstaking efforts of interpretation or decipherment but as though the text would have been written by one of his contemporary colleagues. A quick glance at the royal deeds immediately shows that this was true at Ugarit. The formal aspect and the wording of the texts remained basically unchanged through the generations.

Although we shall deal with the legal language in the forthcoming chapters, mention must be made here of the characteristic technical wording of this genre of documents. The presently much-criticized remoteness of the language of legal documents from ordinary speech was a reality too in Late Bronze Age Ugarit. Not only, as we shall see, because Akkadian was hardly spoken, if at all, in this Mediterranean area of the Near Eastern world, but also because the documents present particular, obscure features familiar to anyone who has read a modern contract, such as a rigorous pattern, long sentences, archaizing expressions, or the technical meaning of words. Some modern scholars dealing with this kind of documentary material have complained that every phrase is technical and legal to an extent that often defies translation. The reason for the "obscurity" of the legal language lies in the temporal importance of legal relations, as mentioned above. So that the message could be properly and accurately conveyed, indeed a requisite in legal matters, the code was to remain basically unchanged and transmitted from one generation to the next in a well-established, rigid fashion.

It is this pedagogical specialization that a notary had to accomplish. We have seen that his training was a hard and complex one; he began as a student the craft of reading and writing and would become through his indispensable days as apprentice of his teacher (*kabzuzu* in Akkadian and *lāmidu* in Ugaritic) an expert scribe (*ṭupšarru emqu*), as one of the well-known notaries of Ugarit living around 1300 BC once called himself.[52] The difficulty to master the rigid formal aspect of royal deeds was, however, relative. Scribes meant to become royal notaries had to learn what must have often been an obscure archaic and technical verbiage, but on the other hand the practiced repertoire and pattern of phrases and formulas was rather limited and definitely frozen. The choice of standard or stock phrases used and mastered by notaries will be dealt with in chapter 6. It is to the question how and when these notaries created their documents that I would like to turn now, even if the answers must remain once more speculative given the scarcity of evidence.

It is possible that deeds were designed in the presence of the king during the audience in which the transaction took place. This seemed to be the practice in contemporary Assur concerning the so-called "strong tablets." It will be recalled that once the seller had freed the property of claims and the sold property had been measured with the royal rope would the definite "strong tablet be written *before the king*" (my italics). This is what was established in the three-clause set of provisions regularly present in Middle Assyrian land-sale documents discussed in the previous chapter. With regard to the plausible presence of the king of Ugarit during the recording of royal deeds one should naturally refer again to the regular, indeed essential, impression of his seal on the tablets. The reconstructed, and necessarily hypothetical, picture we suggest would accordingly be the following.[53] The parties to the transaction would be allowed to enter the palace by the gatekeeper and would be then introduced into the assembly or audience hall (room 132). Once inside they would face the king sitting on his throne on a dais at the end of the room (locus 78). A reduced number of royal guards and officials would stand close to the ruler, and in front of him would sit the notary or secretary. After hearing the parties and considering the business presented to him or initiated by him (for example in the case of a grant of land), the king would ceremoniously, and irrevocably, decide before a number of witnesses. At this stage, it is possible that the ruler would pronounce similar words to those spoken by the Persian king to his secretary Mordecai as reported in the Book of Esther (8:8ff.): "Now you shall issue a writ (...) in my name, in whatever terms you think fit, and seal it with the royal signet." The royal

[52] Šapšumalku in RS 16.142:16.

[53] For the interpretation of the layout of the palace, see chapter 2 above, and fig. 3.

notary would then shape the tablet and roll the cylinder seal of the kings of Ugarit, previously solemnly handed over to him by the king, over the surface of soft, damp clay on the upper part of the tablet, parallel to its short side.[54] And with his stylus he would inscribe the text of the decision immediately below, parallel to the seal impression, in the concise, accurate and standard (as a rule Akkadian) terms of royal deeds, and in a remarkable fine script. Closing the document, he would often write his own name, sometimes specifying his role as witness to the transaction (this is especially true in the case of the "expert" notary Šapšumalku).[55] Only exceptionally would he write the names of other witnesses present in the audience hall.[56]

It seems also possible that the secretary made then a copy of the title, which was given to its new holder. Some texts, in particular the few legal decisions after litigation, indeed refer to the king's handing over of tablets to the rightful owner of the title.[57] On the other hand, three more or

---

[54] The interpretation of RS 15.125 (KTU 2.19), namely the meaning we have proposed above for the Ugaritic verb KTB could suggest that the king himself, perhaps only occasionally, signed (viz. rolled his cylinder seal on) the deeds.

[55] As noted by Nougayrol in *PRU* 6, p. 28 n. 1. Here is the list of royal deeds in which he appears as witness: RS 15.Y, RS 16.133, RS 16.143, RS 16.149, RS 16.156, RS 16.157, RS 16.191A, RS 16.245, RS 16.250, RS 16.251, RS 16.263, RS 16.283, RS 17.127, and perhaps also RS 16.147 and RS 16.254D.

[56] The exceptions are RS 15.138+, RS 16.156 and RS 16.285 (possibly also RS 16.192+). I cannot agree with Nougayrol when he wrote that "sans doute doit-on voir là des actes auxquels le roi n'assistait pas *en personne*" (*PRU* 3, p. 230, his own italics). There is in principle no decisive contradiction between the recorded presence of one or two more individuals, some of them royal officials, during the transaction and the presence of the king himself presiding over it. As stated in the previous chapter, RS 16.145 seems to be the only clear attestation of the absence of the king, officially substituted by one of his ministers and accordingly expressly recorded in the text. For further discussion, see chapter 5 below under section 4. In this chapter we shall see that legal documents in Ugarit are phrased in objective style, following the Mesopotamian classic pattern. With regard to the role of the scribe, I cannot agree with Johannes Renger's opinion according to which Mesopotamian legal texts "are styled as a protocol written from the viewpoint of the witnesses" ("Legal Aspects of Sealing in Ancient Mesopotamia," in *Seals and Sealing in the Ancient Near East*, ed. Mc Guire Gibson and Robert D. Biggs [Malibu, CA, 1977], p. 75); I rather believe Wilhelmus F. Leemans was right when he replied that "c'est le scribe qui fait figurer les contractants comme de tiers personnes, relatant ce qu'ils ont fait ou déclaré, et non les témoins" ("La fonction des sceaux des contrats vieux-babyloniens," in *Zikir Šumim, Assyriological Studies Presented to F.R. Kraus on the Occasion of his Seventieth Birthday*, ed. G. van Driel et al. [Leiden, 1982], p. 222).

[57] RS 16.245:6'f. and RS 16.356 :10ff. The tablet said to have been taken "before

less fragmentary royal deeds (RS 17.65, RS 17.350B and RS 29.98) are reported to come from outside the palace, namely from the so-called "residential quarter" of the city. One of them (RS 17.65) was discovered in the house of Rašapʾabu and the other two presumably belonged to other private archives. The same holds true for what seem to be two Ugaritic (non-sealed) copies of royal deeds found in the recently excavated house of Urtēnu.[58]

As mentioned above, the royal notaries made a remarkable careful and fine job. The shape of the inscribed wedges is extraordinarily neat and regular, undoubtedly intended for future generations of secretaries to have no problems whatsoever to read each and every sign inscribed on the tablet. As a matter of fact, the only reproach one can make, as pointed out by Nougayrol, is their "mise en page," that is, the exact arrangement of some lines of the text.[59] Notaries did not always measure properly the length of a line or sentence. We do find examples of lines stretching beyond the edge of the tablet and running well into the middle of the opposite side, the signs thus appearing upside down when the document was turned over for reading purposes.[60] The remarkable carefulness in the design of such documents, indeed free of mistakes, is to be explained on account of the nature of the message, as stated above. And the same holds true for the baking of the tablets. By baking them notaries prevented anyone from attempting to alter the message of royal deeds, namely by moistening the clay and rewriting a name or word. The alternative means to secure a legal document, i.e. placing it in envelopes of clay, well attested for example in Old Babylonian times (also in the Syrian area)[61], was not practiced at Ugarit. Once successfully baked somewhere within the palace,[62] the tablet would eventually be brought upstairs into the archive of royal deeds next to the king's apartments where it was permanently filed in its corresponding place.

---

the king" in RS 16.263:19f. was probably not a copy of the royal deed itself but the old title (sale document) to the estate newly acquired.

58 Note that neither RS 94.2168 nor RS 94.2965 present the normative reserved sealing space on the tablet.

59 *PRU* 3, p. XXXV.

60 See our hand-copied example RS 16.250 at the end of chapter 1.

61 For example in Alalakh.

62 Not, however, in the "four aux tablettes" in the vicinity of the so-called "palace southwestern archive" early identified by Schaeffer. As stated above, the recent archaeological reappraisal by Callot and Margueron has discarded Schaeffer's interpretation.

As we mentioned in the previous chapter, the collapse of the first floor of the royal palace during the conflagration that put an end to Ugarit has left us very little information on the possible way the archive of royal deeds was organized. Given the fact that notaries built up specific palace archives to keep different kinds of records, namely one for royal title-deeds and one for state diplomatic documents, it is reasonable to argue that elaborate (we might say modern) systematic bureaucratic practices were used at Ugarit during the two centuries that preceded the final destruction. We may therefore conjecture that royal deeds were filed (on shelves?) following a certain order, possibly according to the kings who sealed the documents, that is, in chronological order, and perhaps also according to "dossiers."[63] In his edition of the texts Nougayrol grouped a number of royal deeds into "dossiers" following the observation that some individuals would rather often appear as benefiting from several royal grants and privileges, as well as contracting parties in sale transactions;[64] so, for example, the seven-record "dossier" of Nuriyānu (RS 16.140, 16.150, RS 16.166, RS 16.248, RS 16.263, RS 16.275 and RS 16.277), or the one of ᶜAbdu (RS 16.143, RS 16.157, RS 16.239, RS 16.250 and RS 16.254D). Concerning their distribution in the archive, it may be worthwhile mentioning that except for one royal deed the documents that constitute ᶜAbdu's file were all found together in the same locus, the doorway between rooms 132 and 152, where also three of the documents of the "dossier" of Nuriyānu were reportedly discovered.[65] The hypothetical distribution of deeds according to date and "dossiers" would have clearly served the bureaucratic purpose of quickly finding the right evidence to produce it in case of trials or appeals, but also when fiscal matters had to be checked.

It is tempting to see in the so-called "multiple deeds" a similar bureaucratic practice. It will be recalled that these documents record at least two explicitly unrelated transactions involving the same individual, as a rule the beneficiary party. Did the different transactions, one should ask, take place at the same time before the king as described in the reconstruction suggested above? The answer is clearly negative in the case of a "heterogeneous multiple deed," that is, when one recorded transaction is said to have come before the king and another one before witnesses (such as RS 15.85). Of course one may still question whether the latter transaction (either in written form or by producing the eye witnesses) was not brought before the king in order to receive royal confirmation. As for the so-called "homogeneous multiple deeds," did the different

---

[63] As proposed by van Soldt in *SAU*, p. 92.

[64] *PRU* 3, pp. 29-30.

[65] See van Soldt, *SAU*, p. 83.

recorded sales of real property, say in RS 15.119, take place simultaneously at the palace audience hall? Did the same buyer acquire them from distinct sellers on the same day? Or was the palace ceremony meant to bestow validity to the different, independent past transactions, in a way comparable to the Middle Assyrian "strong tablets"? Or still could it be that a palace notary simply put together in his archival office two original single-transaction royal deeds in one new document for bureaucratic purposes? It is significant with this regard that thus far only royal deeds record more than one transaction. No multiple deeds before witnesses are extant.

Even if, as it seems once again, such questions will have to remain open unless new decisive evidence comes to light, one should refer here to the already discussed exceptional *Sammelurkunde* RS 15.109+. For not only the extraordinary size of the tablet and design of the text, but also the chronological references (viz. the kings' names) attest to the sophisticated work of the palace administrative machine. A notary of king ᶜAmmiṯtamru II seems to have collected one of the "dossiers" from the archive of royal deeds, the one of Sinarānu the merchant constituted by some thirteen royal deeds signed by Niqmepaᶜ, and copied the transactions each in a distinct paragraph on a new, naturally large tablet previously signed by the ruling monarch, son of Niqmepaᶜ.[66] Whether the royal notary drew up RS 15.109+ sitting before the king or in his bureau can not be decided, although the latter seems more likely given the particularly complex scribal work.[67] According to these remarks, it is possible that our picture of the writing of royal deeds reconstructed above would need some modification. Perhaps the notary designed his documents, not during the transaction in the audience hall, where he would actually note down (on wax-covered wooden boards?) the necessary data, viz. names of the parties, nature of the transaction, location and name of the conveyed real property, obligations, etc., but in his office. Van Soldt suggested that "the rooms on the ground-floor [in the central palace area] probably served as secretariate."[68] There he would accordingly carry along his notes and the dynastic seal, and the king would not directly see how he would carefully roll it on the definite tablet (neither whether he would attempt to make a forgery of it).

Archivists such as Papritz and Posner have pointed out one of the serious drawbacks (probably the most serious one) of administration on

---

[66] Cf. Nougayrol, *PRU* 3, p. 102 n. 3.

[67] That would explain the presence of some inaccuracies or equivocal passages, especially concerning the change of (elliptic) subject in contiguous sentences (e.g. lines 50-52, and presumably also the first lines of the text).

[68] See *SAU*, p. 521.

clay.[69] Updating clearly being one of the requisites of bookkeeping, how could cuneiform scribes add new entries or the necessary modifications of outdated records on dried, even baked clay tablets?[70] Obviously, we should answer, by writing them down in a new document and discarding or throwing away the old one(s). Indeed, when rights and obligations expired, the customary practice in the ancient Near East consisted in breaking the clay tablet that established them, sometimes, if not regularly, before witnesses. Contracts establishing the new legal situation could thus provide a penalty against the party who would produce another, presumably meaning an old and therefore invalid, deed.[71] Concerning our example from Ugarit, it seems rather reasonable to argue that the tablets constituting the old "dossier" of Sinarānu, just like other outdated documents, were destroyed once they had been registered anew onto the royal deed RS 15.109+. Two extant exceptions can be taken to prove the rule and be possibly understood as the result of notaries' unusual omission. RS 15.138+ is precisely one of the royal deeds from the dossier of Sinarānu included in RS 15.109+, namely the first recorded transaction in the first paragraph. And the same seems to hold true for RS 16.142. This tablet records a grant of real property made by king Arḫalbu stipulating in addition the service the grantee is bound to perform. Some years later RS 15.Y was to outdate RS 16.142. There the same real property is said to be granted (we should then rather say confirmed) by the succeeding king Niqmepa^{c} and the grantee is promoted from the status established in the earlier record to a presumably higher one, being accordingly bound to perform another, more prestigious service.[72]

It is likely that the drawback of registration on clay may be held responsible for the cases of royal re-grants or non-explicit confirmations of grants made by the predecessor king. (One should incidentally mention that when no information is available there is no way to ascertain whether a recorded and preserved grant was actually made by the grantor king or by one of his predecessors on the throne of Ugarit.) The needs of new business may have required the recording of such "fic-

---

[69] Papritz, "Archive in Altmesopotamien," p. 46; Posner, *Archives in the Ancient World*, p. 51.

[70] See nevertheless the devices invented by cuneiform scribes, such as the ones of Mari drawing a red stripe on the tablet to cancel it, in Charpin, "Une pratique administrative méconnue," MARI 3 (1984):158-159; and also id., "Corrections, ratures, annulations: la pratique des scribes mésopotamiens," in *Le texte et son inscription*, ed. R. Laufer (Paris, 1989), pp. 57-62.

[71] As in the "private" deed RS 17.36:10-12.

[72] See, nevertheless, our remarks in chapter 6 footnote 76.

tions." Apart from the illustration provided by RS 15.Y and RS 16.142, we can find further support in the "dossier" of ᶜAbdu mentioned above. We happen to know that three of the fields granted by Niqmepaᶜ to the noble ᶜAbdu in RS 16.157 are but "confirmations" of grants made to him by Arḫalbu, as recorded in RS 16.239.[73] The fact that ᶜAbdu decided, probably in his old age, to transfer part of his granted estate to his sons and have the transaction(s) accordingly registered in the archive of royal deeds must have prompted such formal "revision." This incidental change of ownership decided by the head of the family resulting in new "entries," namely new royal titles, provides a beautiful example of an interesting bureaucratic practice. As explicitly stated in one of the deeds of the "dossier" (RS 16.143), it was ᶜAbdu's initiative to bring his sons' shares or allotments into the palace,[74] that is, to have them registered according to his wish, in all likelihood after having been granted the essential king's audience and consent to the transactions. As a matter of fact, these new titles and allotments constitute the major part of the "dossier." The three new "entries" (RS 16.143, RS 16.157 and RS 16.250) were properly recorded and duly witnessed by one and the same royal notary, Šapšumalku, probably on the same day.[75] When put side by side, one can hardly fail to recognize exactly the same design, style, and "expert" hand in the three documents that were later carefully kept in the archive of royal deeds.[76]

4. The status of the royal notaries of Ugarit

> And as is the custom in the kingdom of Abgar the king, and in all kingdoms, that everything which the king commands, and everything that is said before him

---

[73] The field of ᶜAbdiʾanti son of Šuwandanu, the *ṣibbīru* field, and the orchard in "Spring-field" in RS 16.239 lines 5, 6 and 8 respectively correspond to the field of the son of Šuwā, the *ṣibbīru* field, and the orchard in "Spring-field" in RS 16.157 lines 6, 7 and 9; for the equivalence of the second field, see already Nougayrol, *PRU* 3, p. 83 n. 1. Note furthermore that the *kannapīyu* field in RS 16.239:7 appears too in RS 16.250:11, as noted by Nougayrol (*PRU* 3, p. 85 n. 1).

[74] Lines 16-17: *ᶜAbdu zittīšunu ana ekallim ušērib*. See now also the interpretation suggested by Sophie Lafont *apud* Lackenbacher, *Textes akkadiens d'Ugarit*, p. 305 n. 1102.

[75] RS 16.250 is the example of royal deed we chose to reproduce in hand-copy in chapter 1.

[76] In chapter 7 we shall attempt to prove that it is possible to attribute anonymously written deeds to specific known royal notaries precisely on the basis of the formal aspect of the tablet and the orthography of the text.

> is written down and placed among the records, so also Labubna, the son of Semnac, the son of Abshadar, the king's scribe, wrote these things of Addai the Apostle, from the beginning to the end. Hannan also, the Tabularius, the king's Sharrir, set the hand of witnesses, and placed it among the records of the writings of the kings, where are put the commands and laws, and the contracts of those who buy and sell are kept there with care, without any negligence.

This paragraph closing the famous Syriac text of *The Teaching of Addai, the Apostle*,[77] probably written around 400, describes important aspects of bureaucracy we have deduced and imagined in the previous pages for Late Bronze Age Ugarit. The considerable distance in time (not so much in terms of space) should not be too surprising for although Abgar, presumably V, ruled the kingdom of Edessa in the days of Jesus, the custom described in the colophon (which could even be tinged by the later world of the Syriac author) expressly applies to "all kingdoms." Every decision uttered by the ruler, especially within the walls of the palace audience chamber, was noted down in the most accurate and concise manner by his scribe and duly and carefully kept in the royal archives by his notary. The royal archives in Edessa on the other hand not only contained the kings' decrees and edicts, but also deeds of sale that concerned his subjects and kingdom, a picture that has actual parallels at Ugarit.

It is most probable, however, that in the palace of Ugarit the tasks of the royal scribe, the keeper of the archives and the notary (the latter two related if not equivalent offices possibly translating the Latin word Tabularium and Syriac Sharrir)[78] were fulfilled by one and the same professional, what we have called "notary" or also "secretary." The latter designation seems fairly appropriate in our context given the privileged position of trust and privacy these professionals enjoyed with the ruler.[79] As we have seen, notaries like Šapšumalku worked inside the royal palace, sat regularly in front of the king, rolled the cylinder seal of the kings of Ugarit on the tablets, wrote down title deeds that concerned property rights of the dynasty and the kingdom, and kept and cared for the documents in palace archives located upstairs within the king's private apartments. We know that they also issued and witnessed diplomatic

---

[77] In the classic English translation by George Phillips published back in 1876.

[78] As rendered by Javier Teixidor, *La filosofía traducida* (Sabadell, 1991), p. 79.

[79] See also the remarks of van der Toorn, "Cuneiform Documents from Syria-Palestine. Texts, Scribes, and Schools," p. 101.

documents,[80] and it is very likely that the same professionals would write their master's messages addressed to overlords, allies and officials, as well as read the mail to the king. No doubt royal notaries would see and hear very much of what was done and said in the palace, especially important matters concerning the state.[81] Were they actually not required to put down in clay tablets everything which the king commanded and everything that was said before him, as stated several centuries later in *The Teaching of Addai*?

Even if the secretary's role would have been mainly restricted to written matters and record custodial functions, his potential influence on the management of state affairs should surely not be underestimated. As a matter of fact, we happen to know that a number of royal notaries of Ugarit also bore the title of "vizier" (Akkadian *sukkallu*) of the king.[82] Because the title is so far only attested in Ugarit with scribes, the translations "royal secretary" or "secretary-of-state" have been proposed.[83] The importance of the office is underlined by the fact that its holder is mentioned in the treaties between Hatti and Ugarit as one of the privileged Hittite court people benefiting from the tribute.[84] Secretaries were presumably certified by the ruler and appointed for life, and could therefore hold the office through successive kings, such as Šapšumalku who was notary of Niqmaddu II and of his sons Arḫalbu and Niqmepaᶜ.[85]

---

[80] The royal notary Iltaḫmu, for example, is the author of RS 17.299 and a witness to the inter-state agreement RS 17.371+, a deed designed in turn by another royal notary, Nuᶜmerašpu, also author of RS 18.02.

[81] See e.g. the study of Oppenheim, "A Note on the Scribes in Mesopotamia," in *Studies in Honor of Benno Landsberger on His Seventy-Fifth Birthday* (Chicago, 1965), pp. 253-256; and van der Toorn, "Cuneiform Documents from Syria-Palestine. Texts, Scribes, and Schools," pp. 100-105

[82] Namely, the notary Karrānu (see RS 17.137:6'), his son Iltaḫmu (see RS 17.371+RS 18.20:11), Nuᶜmerašpu (see RS 17.77:13'), and Eḫliteššub (se RS 18.21:34). If, as suggested by van Soldt, the Ugaritic office title *ṯᶜy* corresponds to Akkadian *sukkallu*, the famous scribe Ilimalku, the author of most Ugaritic extant literary texts, would also have been "vizier" of king Niqmaddu III; see his "The Title *ṯᶜy*," UF 20 (1988):313-321, and his revised, updated conclusions in "Babylonian Lexical, Religious and Literary Texts and Scribal Education at Ugarit and Its Implications for the Alphabetic Literary Texts," p. 189. Pardee, however, rather believes that the Ugaritic title denotes a cultic function (see his commented translation of Ugaritic literature in *The Context of Scripture. Volume 1: Canonical Compositions from the Biblical World*, ed. W.W. Hallo [Leiden/New York/Köln, 1997], p. 343 n. 103).

[83] Van Soldt, "The Title *ṯᶜy*," p. 321.

[84] Ibid., p. 319.

[85] See below the appendix to the chapter.

I agree with Alan K. Bowman and Greg Woolf when they wrote that "literacy does not of itself promote economic growth, rationality or social success," probably expressing their disagreement with the exaggerated positions professed by a number of "graphocentric" scholars especially in the 1980s and early 1990s.[86] But I believe that literacy, especially in essentially oral societies such as the ones in the ancient world, did promote some people, namely royal secretaries, to their own economic prosperity and social and political success. This is certainly the meaning of the Mesopotamian literary passages quoted above. The scribal craft (or art) was not like the craft of a carpenter or a smith. Literacy was in the ancient Orient, and in Ugarit in particular as we have seen, intimately linked to power. Of course there must have been different levels of achievement in the career of a scribe. Not every apprentice was meant, or could expect, to become one of the privileged and prestigious officials "who would regularly come and go into the palace." To be sure, the rank of a royal (confidential) secretary was only entrusted to few, selected scribes. We only know thirteen different names of notaries for the whole period covered by the royal deeds, namely about one century and a half. It is possible, however, that the number of actual secretaries was not much higher. Every ruler, on the other hand, could have at his service more than one secretary: nine, for example, are attested by name for ^{c}Ammiṯtamru II.[87]

Scribal education at Ugarit may have actually been institutionalized, that is, conducted and controlled from the great organization. We had conjectured above that during the last stage of the rigorous scribal training some advanced students would become assistants of royal notaries learning then how to prepare royal legal and administrative documents and state letters. Notaries-to-be may thus have been early pre-selected from among the whole group of apprentice-scribes, perhaps according to ability, social background, or both. It is only "the good scribe" who "is indefatigable and enters the palace easily," as stated in the Sumerian poem of *Gilgamesh, Enkidu and the nether world*. And with regard to the Ugaritic script, whether its invention a little earlier or later than 1300 BC was imagined by an individual scribe or decreed by the ruler himself (Niqmepa^{c}?), there can be no doubt that the latter had to give his consent it and institutionalize it.

The concentrations and find-place of what we have called initial and midway products of the writing industry at Ugarit manifestly show that in the royal palace, that is, the main center of administration of the king-

[86] "Literacy and Power in the Ancient World," in *Literacy and Power in the Ancient World*, ed. A.K. Bowman and G. Woolf (Cambridge, 1996), p. 3.

[87] See the appendix to this chapter.

dom, there was paradoxically no center of learning. Schools in the city of Ugarit were run in what is usually called "private" houses.[88] It is now generally agreed, however, that the term "private" can here too be misleading. The accumulations of tablets discovered in these buildings contain, besides school material, documents of state, such as letters from foreign officials and rulers and records of home administration.[89] The owners of these houses, therefore, were in all likelihood people who held important positions in the state bureaucracy. Some of them probably were scribes who would regularly come and go in the palace to read letters to the king sent to him from abroad and to note down the ruler's replies. But they would also write messages for other court officials (such as the *sākinu*'s) and design contracts concluded between citizens of Ugarit.[90]

Royal secretaries must have owned large houses in the city where some of them probably had their office and school. For who could teach writing and reading but the restricted number of literate professionals who would be normally engaged in administrative functions issuing written documents and reading messages received at Ugarit? If the literal meaning of a cuneiform school is that of "a house that issues tablets" (the probable though not undisputed etymology of Sumerian *edubbaʾa*)[91] we might speculate whether it does not refer to the administrative building where scribal education actually took place. Whatever the exact meaning, the idea of government-operated or institutionalized education at Ugarit certainly gains ground. There can hardly be any doubt that the palace

---

[88] A situation that holds also true for Old Babylonian times. The schools of Ugarit have been thoroughly dealt with by van Soldt. Here we shall again follow his results summarized in "Babylonian Lexical, Religious and Literary Texts and Scribal Education at Ugarit and Its Implications for the Alphabetic Literary Texts," especially pp. 178-180. Four major school centres in the city were: the so-called house of Rapʾānu discussed above, the "Tablet House" or "Maison-aux-tablettes," the house of "Lamaštu", and the house of the "Lettré." Although only few, some school texts are reported to come from the royal palace (see *SAU*, p. 140). Especially noteworthy are several Ugaritic abecedaries. Were they the result of the students' stage as assistants of royal scribes?

[89] See more recently the study of van Soldt, "Private Archives at Ugarit," pp. 229-245.

[90] Royal notaries such as Iltaḫmu or Munaḫḫimu recorded transactions performed before witnesses; the former is author of RS 17.88, RS 17.356 and RS 17.358; and the latter designed RS 17.77, RS 18.267, RS 29.100 and perhaps also RS 22.223 (we assume that he is the same scribe of royal deeds on the basis of the orthography of the texts; see *SAU*, pp. 29-30 and below chapter 7).

[91] See most recently Konrad Volk, "Edubba'a und Edubba'a-Literatur: Rätsel und Lösungen," ZA 90 (2000):3.

administrative machine, by far the largest writing industry in the kingdom, required a constant flow of individuals technically trained (in "official" school-houses) and able to write and read to keep it working. But where were these pupils drawn from?

Crafts in the ancient Near East were normally transmitted from father to son, or at least within the family, and the scribal craft does not seem to have been an exception. The available evidence from Ugarit is too scanty to provide a clear answer but it seems eloquent enough.[92] Indeed, it is significant that at least three royal notaries took over their father's office: Yaᶜḏirānu son of Ḫuṣānu, Munaḫḫimu son of Yarimmu, and Karrānu's son, Iltaḫmu who also became like his father a royal "vizier."[93] Moreover, thanks to the preserved colophons of the school texts, we know that the family of the notary Nuᶜmerašpu was a family of scribes. Of the many conditions the ruler had to consider when he selected a secretary from among the potential candidates, the most important, such as ability, knowledge, and social background, were clearly fulfilled if his father had held the same office successfully. For not only the code of written messages had to be transmitted from one generation to the next, but also the behavioral code had to be properly assimilated. Good manners were certainly a requisite to become a companion of the king, and their acquisition must have been an important part of the boy's instruction (since indeed only boys could become professional scribes). But as already implied by the literal meaning of the office itself, the main condition of a secretary was his reliability. As we mentioned above, a notary certified by the king was by his profession entrusted with the secrets of state and it was his duty to protect them. Because all sorts of precautions must have been taken to prevent the potential publication of the ruler's secrets, it is possible, though not provable due to the lack of evidence, that the king of Ugarit imposed a loyalty oath to his most immediate officials, naturally including his secretaries. This we know to have been the usual practice for instance in the palace of Mari in the eighteenth century and one millennium later in the palace of the kings of Assyria.[94]

---

[92] See van Soldt, "Babylonian Lexical, Religious and Literary Texts and Scribal Education at Ugarit and Its Implications for the Alphabetic Literary Texts," pp. 181-182.

[93] See RS 17.371+18.20:11. If the Iliramu of RS 16.114:rev. 14' is the homonymous notary of ᶜAmmiṯtamru II then he also took over his father's (the expert Šapšumalku's) trade (see van Soldt, *SAU*, p. 29).

[94] For Mari, see Jean-Marie Durand, "Précurseurs syriens aux protocols néo-assyriens," in *Marchands, diplomates et empereurs. Etudes sur la civilisation mésopotamienne offertes à Paul Garelli*, ed. D. Charpin and F. Joannès (Paris, 1991), pp. 13-71.

Whether or not they took an oath before entering the service of the king, the truth is that secretaries and scribes were not always faithful to their master. The famous case of the forgery of the dynastic seal and royal deeds speaks eloquently enough. As reported in RS 16.249 lines 14-19, two people "committed a great crime by making a duplicate seal of the dynastic seal and designing forged deeds within the city of Ugarit."[95] That at least one of the offenders was a royal notary is beyond any doubt.[96] How else could he (or both of them) have had access to the dynastic seal, and then drawn up (forged) royal deeds? His or their privilege to come and go into the palace is explicitly referred to in the text some lines further. After the culprits had been seized, as the text reports (in lines 20-25), king Niqmepa^{c} did not punish them to death in what seems to have been an act of clemency but instead they and their sons were forbidden to ever enter the palace again (and the whole area of Ugarit).[97] The fact that the children are also mentioned in the king's decision may incidentally point to the hereditary character of the office discussed above.

Less fortunate was another scribe named Yatarmu who "became an enemy of the king, his lord."[98] We would like to know more about the circumstances of this interesting episode in the kingdom of Ugarit. What the text of the royal deed (RS 16.269) says is that a certain Gabānu put to death the rogue scribe and gave subsequently (back) one of the towns of the kingdom to king Niqmaddu. As a result, no doubt the main interest of the record, Gabānu was rewarded with a house and fields and exemption from royal service. Whatever approximation or guess we make given the lack of information about the incident, what seems clear is that a scribe could succeed (at least temporarily) in raising himself (unlawfully) to a position of authority over the king's jurisdiction. This of course was only possible if he had previously achieved high social status and a large measure of power.

---

[95] *^{c}Abdirašpu mār ^{c}Abdimir u [Mun]aḫḫimu ḫiṭṭa rabâ ītepš[ū] kunukka meḫer kunuk šarri rabî ītepšū u ṭuppāti sarrūti ina libbi Ugarit išaṭṭurū* (*sic*).

[96] The verbal forms are all in plural, but it seems likely that only one of them was responsible for making the duplicate seal, pointing perhaps to a different handcraft trade (a seal-cutter?).

[97] Unless the culprits were given another chance, Munaḫḫimu the forger should not be confused with the homonymous notary of ^{c}Ammiṯtamru II.

[98] RS 16.269:7-8: *inūma nakir Yatarmu ṭupšarru itti šarri bēlišu*. See also Rainey, "The Scribe at Ugarit. His Position and Influence," Proceedings of the Israel Academy of Sciences and Humanities, III/4 (1969):145-146.

As a matter of fact, "receiving a handsome fee" was essential to the scribal art, as predicated by the Mesopotamian proverb. To be sure, royal notaries or secretaries derived influence, power and prestige from their lifetime function as officials, but also income. Social progress and economic prosperity, as we mentioned above, go more often than not hand in hand. As is customary in the ancient Near East, it is very likely that notaries, like other "civil servants" in Ugarit were supported by the king through grants of real property.[99] In the light of the cases of crime reported in the preserved royal deeds of Ugarit, it is possible that the king considered that the more numerous the gifts the more loyal (or the less treacherous) the secretary would be. Unfortunately we are unable to trace even the general steps of one royal notary's progress. The economic activities of Yaᶜḏirānu, our best-known example, can only be gleaned through the stereotyped and laconic language of three preserved royal deeds. Thus we know that he owned a house that was conveyed away during the reign of Arḫalbu (in RS 16.239:4), that he purchased land from the wealthy merchant Sinarānu with the royal consent of Niqmepaᶜ (RS 16.206), and that he received from ᶜAmmiṯtamru II, that is in his old age,[100] a whole town with its tithe, grazing rights and other taxes (RS 16.153), perhaps as a reward for past outstanding, loyal service.

Appendix: Attested royal notaries[101]

ᶜAbdiḫamanu	RS 16.348
ᶜAbdiᵓiltu	RS 16.178
Eḫliteššub	RS 18.21
Ḫuṣānu	RS 15.138+, RS 16.285
Iliramu	RS 18.285
Iltaḥmu	RS 15.140, RS 19.128, RS 16.353
Karrānu	RS 15.119, RS 16.207, RS 16.284
Munaḫḫimu	RS 15.145, RS 15.147, RS 15.190, RS 16.86+, RS 16.201, RS 16.243, RS 16.255C, RS 16.255D, RS 16.386
Nuᶜmerašpu	RS 15.143+, RS 15.168, RS 18.280, RS 15.127 (+)? RS 15.131, RS 15.111 (KTU 3.2)(?)[102]

[99] It is possible that the grantee Yarimmu in RS 16.141 should be identified with the homonymous royal notary of Niqmaddu II.

[100] As remarked by van Soldt (*SAU*, p. 8), "he cannot have been much younger than 60 years by the time ᶜAmmiṯtamru II took power."

[101] Cf. Nougayrol, *PRU* 3, pp. XXXVIII-XXXIX.

[102] See footnote 32 above.

Šapšumalku	RS 15.88, RS 15.Y, RS 16.133, RS 16.142, RS 16.143, RS 16.147, RS 16.149, RS 16.157, RS 16.191A, RS 16.208, RS 16.245, RS 16.250, RS 16.251, RS 16.254D, RS 16.263, RS 16.283, RS 17.127 (cf. RS 16.156)
Ya^cdidu	RS 15.136, RS 16.138, RS 16.204, RS 16.241+, RS 19.98
Ya^cḏirānu	RS 15.118, RS 16.192A+, RS 16.282
Yarimmu	RS 16.156, RS 16.384[103]
AN-[ ]	RS 18.265A

Arranged according to the kings they served:

Niqmaddu II:	Yarimmu, Šapšumalku
Arḫalbu:	Šapšumalku
Niqmepa^{c}:	Šapšumalku, Ḫuṣānu, Karrānu
^{c}Ammiṯtamru II:	^{c}Abdiḫamanu, ^{c}Abdi$^{\supset}$iltu, Iliramu, Iltaḥmu, Munaḫḫimu, Nu^{c}merašpu, Ya^{c}didu, Ya^{c}ḏirānu, Yarimmu
Ibirānu:	Nu^{c}merašpu, AN-[ ]
Niqmaddu III:	Eḫliteššub

[103] Van Soldt assumed the identification of Yarimmu the scribe of RS 16.156 with Yarimmu the author of RS 16.384, despite the distance in time between both deeds. "As to Yarimmu's age, he wrote (*SAU*, p. 8): he was apparently a full-blown scribe already in the time of Niqmaddu [II] (16.156); this means that he cannot have been much younger than 20 years, even if he had been an advanced student. Consequently, his age must have been around 70 by the time of ^{c}Ammiṯtamru's accession." On the basis of the different orthographic habits, however, the identification is not beyond doubt (cf. our discussion in chapter 7). As for potential cases of casual homonymy, one may refer to the Munaḫḫimu forger of royal deeds and the notary of ^{c}Ammiṯtamru II.

CHAPTER 4

AKKADIAN IN UGARIT

The Akkadian language was not the speech current in Ugarit, neither for that matter in any other town in Late Bronze Age Syria. Because scholars at Ugarit created late in the fourteenth or in the first half of the thirteenth century a new (alphabetic) script to write their own tongue on clay tablets, we are fortunate to know (of course only imperfectly) the grammar and part of the lexicon of the native Semitic language spoken in this northern Levantine area during at least the last third of the second millennium. Beside tablets written in the vernacular, known today as Ugaritic, other epigraphic finds from the Late Bronze Age levels of Ras Shamra attest to the fact that many different languages concurred in Ugarit. That is hardly surprising. Throughout history Near Eastern Levantine cities have played a major role in commercial and social relations. At the crossroads of east-west and north-south traffic, from Istanbul to Alexandria, populations of different origin and mother tongue have met through the millennia in these Mediterranean harbors to conduct their affairs. The Levantine pattern was in the second millennium before our era —as at other, more recent times, as beautifully described by Amin Ma'alouf in *Les échelles du Levant*—, the mingling of distinct peoples side by side. In Ugarit, indeed one of the "échelles du Levant" during the Late Bronze Age period, Cretan, Cypriot, Hittite, Egyptian, Phoenician and other foreign voices must have got relatively often mixed with the noise and bustle of a city day. Now, were Akkadian voices also heard in the narrow and twisted streets of the city, at least as often as the written documents we have can make us assume? Was the language of Mesopotamians used, as can be understood by a casual reading of the most recent literature on the subject, to bridge the linguistic gap that obviously existed between, say, a Cypriot and an Ugaritic merchant? It is to these questions and the generally accepted idea that Akkadian became the lingua franca in the Late Bronze Age Near East and in Ugarit in particular that we shall turn first. In the second section, we shall focus our discussion on the status and nature of Akkadian as the fully established formal language to write legal documents at Ugarit.

1. Akkadian as lingua franca

> Il est des langues qui semblent porter dans leur destin la vocation à l'universalité. L'akkadien fut sans doute la première d'entre elles. Au deuxième millénaire avant notre ère, son usage et celui de l'écriture cunéiforme sont communément répandus dans tout ce qui, de l'Égypte à l'Élam, constitue autour de la Mésopotamie le monde civilisé du temps. Il l'est non pas à la façon d'un jargon bâtard que des soldats vainqueurs essaiment sur leur passage ou que les marchands propagent autour de leurs comptoirs, mais sous la forme la plus relevée qui soit, une langue de haute culture qu'adoptent volontairement les chancelleries, les cercles politiques, les juristes et les savants.

I begin with this quotation from René Labat[1] because it briefly but eloquently describes the common Assyriological assessment of what became known as Peripheral Akkadian at the close of the 1960s. By then a number of important sites outside Mesopotamia such as Ras Shamra in Syria or Amarna in Egypt had yielded enough remarkable evidence to prove that the language and writing indigenous to the land between the Tigris and the Euphrates became in the Late Bronze Age Near East the accepted language of international correspondence and diplomacy. Being a language used by non-native speakers, Peripheral Akkadian tends to offer, again in Labat's own words, "moins de résistance à la contamination des idiomes parlés dans les pays qui l'emploient comme langue internationale."[2] Studies in the Akkadian of the texts from Byblos and Amurru in the Amarna period, or from Boghazköy, Nuzi, Alalakh, and Ugarit have indeed shown that, and to what degree, the scribes who wrote them allowed their mother tongue to influence the ecumenical, diplomatic Mesopotamian language.[3] In view of the high linguistic

---

[1] "Le rayonnement de la langue et de l'écriture akkadiennes au deuxième millénaire avant notre ère," Syria 39 (1962):1.

[2] Ibid., p. 14.

[3] See the works of Moran on Canaanite Akkadian, including his doctoral dissertation *A Syntactical Study of the Dialect of Byblos as Reflected in the Amarna Tablets*, now collected and edited by Huehnergard and Izre'el in *Amarna Studies. Collected Writings* (Winona Lake, IN, 2003). For studies on other varieties of Peripheral Akkadian, see Labat, *L'akkadien de Boghaz-köi. Étude sue la langue des lettres, traités et vocabulaires akkadiens trouvés à Boghaz-köi* (Bordeaux, 1932); Huehnergard's *The Akkadian of Ugarit*, and van Soldt's *Studies in the Akkadian of Ugarit*; Izre'el, *Amurru Akkadian. A Linguistic Study* (Atlanta, 1991); Gernot Wilhelm, *Untersuchungen zum Hurro-Akkadischen von Nuzi* (Neukirchen-Vluyn,

"contamination" of the Akkadian of, for example, Canaanite Amarna letters, Nuzi, or Alalakh, scholars writing before the 1970s used to characterize unaffectedly the language as "barbarized Akkadian."[4]

As a result of the development of new trends and preoccupations in the scientific study of language in the last third of last century, a number of scholars began to approach the study of Peripheral Akkadian from a different viewpoint. Indeed in the past two decades there has been a noticeable explosion of interest in sociolinguistic theory among Assyriologists, especially as far as the phenomena of bilingualism and languages in contact are concerned, a subject surely suitable to the complex, multicultural situation of the ancient Near East. Thus, for example, the notion of "languages in contact" itself has been proposed to replace or render obsolete the traditional Assyriological concept of "barbarisiertes Akkadisch;"[5] the name of "lingua franca," on the other hand, is a now commonly accepted label for second-millennium Akkadian,[6] and terms such as "pidginized language" or "language mixing" can be found to describe the nature of Late Bronze Age Levantine Akkadian. As part of the volume of recent writing on the subject, it is also worthwhile referring to a study that has claimed the identification of the Akkadian used during the thirteenth century in the Phoenician city of Tyre as the first beach-la-mar in man's recorded history.[7]

Because of the danger of easily assigning wrong or inadequate labels in Assyriological linguistic exercises, Shlomo Izre'el, one of the leading

---

1970); my "Notes on the Hurro-Akkadian of Alalaḫ in the Mid-Second Millennium BCE," in *Past Links. Studies in the Languages and Cultures of the Ancient Near East* (IOS 18), ed. S. Izre'el, I. Singer and R. Zadok (Winona Lake, IN, 1998), pp. 63-78; or Arnaud, "Le dialecte d'Alalah: un examen préliminarire," AuOr 16 (1998):143-186.

[4] For example, Landsberger, "Assyrische Königsliste und 'dunkles Zeitalter'," JCS 8 (1954):48; Oppenheim, *Ancient Mesopotamia*, p. 278; see also Cord Kühne, *Die Chronologie der internationalen Korrespondenz von El-Amarna* (Neukirchen-Vluyn, 1973), p. 5. An outline of the present discussion was given in my lecture "Akkadian as a Contact Language" in the symposium "Lenguas en contacto. I coloquio internacional" held at Madrid and Toledo in October 2003 (published as "Reflexiones sobre el acadio como lengua de contacto en el antiguo Oriente," in *Lenguas en contacto: el testimonio escrito*, ed. P. Bádenas et al. [Madrid, 2004], pp. 17-34).

[5] See Wilhelm, "Introduction," in *Nuzi at Seventy-Five*, SCCNH 10 (1999):10-11.

[6] See recently, for example, John Huehnergard and Christopher Woods, "Akkadian and Eblaite," in *The Cambridge Encyclopedia of the World's Ancient Languages*, ed. Roger D. Woodard (Cambridge, 2004), p. 219.

[7] See Arnaud, "Une bêche-de-mer antique. La langue des marchands à Tyr à la fin du XIIIe siècle," AuOr 17-18 (1999-2000):143-166.

scholars in the study of the Akkadian lingua franca of the western periphery, counselled caution and rightly warned against the perilous confusion between "pidgin and creole *languages*" and "pidgin and creole *linguistics*" (his own italics).[8] One thing, he noted, is to use the analytic tools and notions that have been developed in the relatively recent study of languages in contact to understand a variety of Peripheral Akkadian, and another very different matter is to understand such a Peripheral Akkadian as a pidgin language. "Incontrovertibly," he concluded, "pidgin languages are not ones to which any of the Peripheral Akkadian dialects should be compared. It is the so-called pidginization and creolization processes of both types of languages (named after the extreme cases where such features are attested) to which the linguistic affinities found in any contact language should be compared."[9] And he further stressed that "none of the Peripheral Akkadian dialects known hitherto, not even the mixed language of the Canaanite Amarna letters, can be termed 'pidgin'." I believe this preliminary warning to be essential, and I would still add (and discuss later) that even the name and label of lingua franca for Peripheral Akkadian can be misleading if interpreted too literally. In view of this and Izre'el's arguments, one is inclined to consider that the subject of Akkadian around Mesopotamia has not seldom been wrongly or inaccurately addressed, and furthermore that the sociolinguistic approach to our sources might actually require modification or readjustment.

The difference between a linguist and an Assyriologist dealing with bilingualism or languages in contact is a sharp one and also self-evident. The former is basically concerned with the identification of the more universal social factors involved in people's choice of language, and in showing how their choice is manifested in terms of language, dialect, variety, style, variant, etc. His subject matter is verbal forms of behaviour, and his data are drawn from direct observation and interview techniques. In contrast, an Assyriologist, and for that matter any scholar dealing with bilingualism in antiquity, has no live informants and will never be able to hear one single speech-sound of his vernacular of study, unless of course new sophisticated technologies eventually develop a device that can neatly recover the dead voices of the past. For the time being, then, the scholar dealing with ancient bilingualism must content himself with the remains of written dead languages.[10]

---

[8] In his review to Huehnergard's *The Akkadian of Ugarit*, BiOr 49 (1992):171.

[9] Ibid., with special reference to Huehnergard's remarks on word order (*The Akkadian of Ugarit*, p. 224) and grammatical simplification and reduction (ibid., p. 272)

[10] See the recent relevant remarks made by James N. Adams and Simon Swain in

Uriel Weinreich wrote in his classic book *Languages in Contact* that "for an analysis that can do justice to the complexity of linguistic facts, the data must be obtained, first and foremost, from the flowing speech of bilinguals in the natural setting of language contact." "The usual sort of evidence —he continued— taken from relatively well established languages cannot be a substitute."[11] Nor, we should conclude, the written evidence. The speech of, say, ancient Ugaritian potential bilinguals stopped flowing not yesterday but before yesterday, namely more than three millennia ago, and the corresponding natural setting of language contact vanished along with it. As we defined above, the cultures of the ancient world, and in particular the ancient Near East, were essentially oral cultures (with a component of literacy). What we have in our thousands of clay cuneiform tablets, if I may insist once more, is only a fraction of what was written and next to nothing of what was spoken. The clues we have to discover the oral world are extremely vague and chiefly indirect. How then can we properly deal with the essential sociolinguistic question of "who *spoke* what language to whom and when"?[12] In sum, the complexities of cultural and linguistic contact as matters characteristic of verbal communication can almost only be guessed when dealing with a (long) dead written tradition.

We can for example make the reasonable guess that pidgins or sabirs did exist in the Eastern Mediterranean harbour towns in the second millennium before our era, in the same way as they existed in the Middle Ages (such as the historical lingua franca or beach-la-mar). Why not? It is indeed possible that merchants from, say, Ugarit and Egypt, longing to make good and stable business, bridged the linguistic gulf that separated them by inventing a mutually intelligible, simple language, no doubt assisted with grins and gestures. Guess work can of course be taken further: perhaps the sabir was based on a rudimentary grammar of a prestigious language, for instance Akkadian, and a restricted vocabulary from another language, such as Ugaritic. But these are of course only scholarly guessing games. My interest and intention here, however, is to point out that should this or other pidgins have existed they would have left no trace behind them, that is, in the written record. The beach-la-mar voices would have vanished together with the accompanying gestures ages, actually millennia, ago. Writing, it will be remembered, was like

the "Introduction" to *Bilingualism in Ancient Society. Language Contact and the Written Word*, ed. J.N. Adams, M. Janse, and S. Swain (Oxford, 2002), pp. 1-20.

[11] I quote from the second printing edition of *Languages in Contact. Findings and Problems* (The Hague, 1963), p. 44.

[12] The question (without italics) is the title of Joshua A. Fisman's seminal contribution in La linguistique 2 (1965):67-88.

any other craft in the hands of a professional, comparatively small group, and merchants would not belong to the technically literate minority who wrote cuneiform signs on clay tablets. On the other hand, as discussed in the previous chapter, scribes at Ugarit, and in all likelihood in the whole ancient Levant, were chiefly employed by the "great organization," so that the sources we have are essentially the products of palace administrations and chanceries. There can hardly be any doubt for example that palace scribes were the authors of the Canaanite Amarna letters. And the same holds true for those who wrote the less than fifteen extant Akkadian letters and fragments written at Tyre in the thirteenth century. One should note that when preserved the sender of these messages is the ruler himself or one of his officials.[13] The interpretation of the language of these texts as a beach-la-mar in the sense that it represents "the spoken language of Tyrian merchants" is therefore difficult to sustain.[14] Likewise, I cannot agree with the label of trade jargon for the Akkadian of the preserved cuneiform letters of the Phoenician city of Sidon.[15] It is impossible to prove, but also hard to believe, that the language of the texts corresponds to the language spoken by those ancient Sidonians engaged in trade business. As a matter of fact, it is even difficult to ascertain that it corresponds to any spoken language at all. The Akkadian of Tyre, Sidon or Ugarit, as we know it, was but a written language, namely the internationally accepted language of diplomatic texts and correspondence.

After what has been said in the lines above about our unavoidably limited knowledge of verbal communication in the ancient Near East, the last sentence must make us pause for a moment and consider whether the text material we have may not be influencing our judgment, as it too often does. Can we speak of Akkadian, as is sometimes found in Assyriological literature, as the accepted language of international diplomacy in the second millennium? What we know is that it was the accepted language of international *written* diplomacy: treaty texts and cor-

---

[13] See the list given by Arnaud, "Une bêche-de-mer antique," p. 166. All the letters found at Amarna are addressed by Abimilku, the king of Tyre. As for the letters unearthed at Ugarit, four are sent by the ruler of Tyre (RS 17.397B+, RS [Varia 25], RS 94.2174, RS 94.2595), and the other five tablets that preserve the head of the message (RS 34.167+, RS 94.2286, RS 94.2412, RS 94.2416+, RS 94.2485) are all addressed to the same individual named Ur-Teššub, that is, in all likelihood Urtēnu, the well-known palace official of Ugarit.

[14] Arnaud, "Une bêche-de-mer antique ," pp. 143 and 161-165.

[15] As recently suggested by Arnaud himself in "Le jargon épistolaire de Sidon à la fin de l'âge du Bronze récent," in *Études Ougaritiques. I. Travaux 1985-1995*, ed M. Yon and D. Arnaud (Paris, 2001), pp. 291-322; followed by Malbran-Labat, "Langues et écritures à Ougarit," p. 78.

respondence between different and distant courts, speaking different and often distant mother tongues (such as Hittite, Egyptian, Hurrian, Cypriot, or Ugaritic), were conventionally and as a rule written in the language native to Mesopotamia. But does this written Akkadian evidence necessarily mean that spoken communication between the plenipotentiaries or rulers of the different nations was carried out in that same language? Akkadian in Ugarit, as we have seen in the previous chapter, was a specialized, "scribal" language. It indeed came (ultimately) from Mesopotamia together with the script. And the same holds true for other cities outside Mesopotamia. This is exactly what Labat meant in the text with which we opened the section. Akkadian, he wrote, was introduced together, and, I would stress, indissolubly, with the cuneiform script in the periphery of Mesopotamia; that is another way of saying that the acquisition of Akkadian went hand in hand with the acquisition of literacy. From this follows the second essential reflection of Labat: Akkadian outside its home land was not used "à la façon d'un jargon bâtard que des soldats vainqueurs essaiment sur leur passage ou que les marchands propagent autour de leurs comptoirs, mais sous la forme la plus relevée qui soit, une langue de haute culture." What I am trying to suggest, in sum, (and more will be said later) is that the Akkadian of our texts corresponds to the ecumenical (imported) Mesopotamian language learned by scribes at school, and that there is no evidence to assume that Akkadian was used in Ugarit or any other Levantine city outside the academic circle.

I would like to insist on the fact that the task of learning this foreign language was pursued in parallel with the acquisition of the Mesopotamian script. One may therefore suggest in the light of the scribal curriculum we have described in the previous chapter that the acquisition of Akkadian as a second language was progressively divided up, as early as the second millennium before our era, into pronunciation, vocabulary, and grammar. The repeated recitation and copy of cuneiform syllabaries, vocabularies, and literary texts, in that didactic order, would respectively train the student in the phonetic, lexical, and syntactical components of the language. It is superfluous to say that the process of learning Akkadian outside Mesopotamia, such as in Ugarit, did not take place in a natural setting. Indeed the evidence we have shows that it was carried out, at Ugarit for example, but also at the capitals of Egypt (Amarna) and Hatti (Boghazköy), through formal and traditional classroom instruction. The question we should now raise is whether or not the teachers themselves were native speakers of Akkadian.

It has been convincingly shown that in the course of history scribes from Mesopotamia would sometimes migrate or be sent abroad to hold temporarily or for life a position in a "peripheral" local administration. The origin of the names of a number of scribes of Nuzi, for example, and a thorough examination of their writing habits led Pierre M. Purves to suggest that the early generation of professional literate people working in the administration of this Hurrian region of northern Mesopotamia were Akkadian speaking immigrants, presumably coming from Babylonia.[16] The presence of Mesopotamian scribes in the Hittite country during the Late Bronze Age period has also been adduced on the basis of their Akkadian names and the relatively common institutionalized exchange of technicians between both countries as referred to in their preserved correspondence. "It is probable," wrote Gary Beckman, the author of this study,[17] "that Anu-šar-ilāni was also an expert on loan from the Babylonian government, and that he similarly made himself at home in Ḫatti: he sired children, instructed them in his craft, and thereby founded a scribal family." The mobility of scribes who travelled from one country to another must have been a fairly normal practice in most periods of ancient Near Eastern history. Suffice it to mention here the famous call of Yasmakh-Addu to his father, the emperor Samsī-Addu, asking him to send to Mari a scribe who could read Sumerian.[18]

As for Ugarit in the Late Bronze Age period, only about fifty names of scribes who signed their Mesopotamian cuneiform texts are fully preserved. None, however, is of Mesopotamian origin.[19] Not surprisingly most names from the time of Niqmaddu II to the dramatic end of the city in the early twelfth century are Ugaritic, such as Šapšumalku, Nu^{c}merašpu, Munaḫḫimu, Ya^{c}didu or Ya^{c}ḏirānu, and, generally speaking, Ugaritic is the language that more often interfered in the Akkadian texts composed by the scribes themselves (i.e. legal documents, administrative records, and letters). After a careful and thorough study of the whole corpus, van Soldt "observed strong *Hurrian* influence in the documents written under the earlier kings of Ugarit, especially in the syllabary." "In the documents written under the *later* kings," he continued, "we observed a growing *Assyrian* influence, and even more clearly, a growing *Ugaritic* influence" (his own italics).[20] The "linguistic evolu-

---

[16] "The Early Scribes of Nuzi," AJSL 57 (1940):162-187.

[17] "Mesopotamians and Mesopotamian Learning at Ḫattuša," JCS 35 (1983):97-114; the quote is from p. 107.

[18] The text is M.7930+. See Charpin, "Les malheurs d'un scribe ou de l'inutilité du sumérien loin de Nippur," in *Nippur at the Centennial*, ed. M. deJong Ellis (Philadelphia, 1992), pp. 24-25; and also Durand, "Unité et diversités au Proche-Orient à l'époque amorrite," in *La circulation des biens, des personnes et des idées dans le Proche-Orient ancien*, ed. D. Charpin and F. Joannès (Paris, 1992), p. 124.

[19] See in particular van Soldt, *SAU*, pp. 19-32.

[20] *SAU*, p. 521. The sentence of Malbran-Labat, namely "dans ces actes (viz. Akkadian legal documents) la tradition paléo-babylonienne a subi des influences où se

tion" of the Babylonian-based Akkadian written in Ugarit, especially the peculiar sequence of Hurrian-Assyrian influence, he explained in the light of the political situation of the period roughly covered by the documentary material.[21] As is well known, in the course of the thirteenth century, Assyria succeeded the Hurrian speaking power of Mittanni (or Hanigalbat) in northern Mesopotamia and began to spread its influence, naturally including its own cultural contribution, to the west. It is possible therefore that the Late Old Babylonian scribal material used in school (discussed in the previous chapter) entered Ugarit through Mittannian mediation before the fourteenth century.[22] It seems, nonetheless, that the definite answer to this and other questions, such as the exact mechanics behind the growing Assyrian influence in the thirteenth century, will have to remain open for the time being.

It is nevertheless of interest for the present discussion to note a further observation van Soldt made about the content of three particular concentrations of tablets found at Ras Shamra. "The discussion of the morphological features has shown that the Akkadian of Ugarit was a blend of a variety of influences," he wrote.[23] As far as the archaeological distribution of the morphologically "influenced" Akkadian texts is concerned, he remarked that "three archives stand out." "Two of these —he specified— by their relatively high proportion of Assyrian forms, one by its Babylonian character."[24] Especially relevant for us are the texts discovered in the so-called "Tablet House" in the "South City" area, and those from the so-called "Lamaštu archive" unearthed within the "South Acropolis" quarter. Not only because of the detectable Mesopotamian native flavour of the Akkadian language of the texts, but also because the evidence is chiefly composed of school texts. The didactic material of the latter school house is exceptionally written "in almost pure Babylonian," as described by van Soldt,[25] and that from the "Tablet House" in

mêlent des éléments cassites, hourrites, hittites" ("Langues et écritures à Ougarit," p. 79), cannot accordingly be taken literally.

[21] *SAU*, p. 522.

[22] Nougayrol already remarked "l'importance du facteur hourrite (...) en tant qu'*intermédiaire* des traditions babyloniennes" in his contribution to the 1961 Rencontre Assyriologique Internationale ("L'influence babylonienne à Ugarit, d'après les textes en cunéiformes classiques," Syria 39 [1962]:35 [his italics]); cf. also Kühne, *Die Chronologie der internationalen Korrespondenz von El-Amarna*, pp. 6-7, and van Soldt, *SAU*, p. 375.

[23] *SAU*, p. 471.

[24] Ibid., p. 474.

[25] Ibid., p. 474. Note the main features: the 3p feminine genitive and accusative singular suffixes (*-ša/-ši* respectively) are not confused, the Babylonian ending of

classical Assyrian.[26] Unfortunately we do not know the precise date of these texts and cannot situate them in the historical line of political events, nor do we know whether the scribes who brought, and taught with, this allegedly genuine Mesopotamian material were of Babylonian or Assyrian descent respectively. It seems, however, that a better guess can be made regarding our third archive.

The so-called "South Palace," a large building that was probably the residence of a certain Yabnišapšu (or Yabnīnu), yielded an important group of tablets that chiefly consist of records written in Akkadian. The "Assyrianizing character" of this Akkadian was early recognized by van Soldt.[27] In a more recent study, the same author has meticulously analyzed every single feature of the texts.[28] The careful examination of the palaeography, for example, allowed him to conclude that there is "a strong Assyrian influence in the archive."[29] The spelling habits (such as the use of the sign ŠÁ, the spelling of /s/ with S-signs, or the regular use of the ᵓA-sign) also stand out pointing to "a strong Mesopotamian influence;" "the orthography —he then wrote— seems to favour an Assyrian origin of at least one of the scribes" of this office.[30] As for the language of the texts, a number of morphological features are also clearly Assyrian in origin (e.g. the genitive in *–e*, and the verbal forms *tadin* and *epāše*). In the light of this evidence, van Soldt reasonably argued that a scribe trained in Assyria worked in the "South Palace" of the city of Ugarit. On the basis of a fragmentary letter found within the archive addressed to a scribe named Naḫeši-šalmu, a clearly Mesopotamian name attested in contemporary Assyria, van Soldt has suggested to identify him with the author of the documents.

But that is all we have thus far about scribes at Ugarit as potential Akkadian native speakers: the Assyrian name (preserved in a broken letter)

---

the genitive singular and the oblique plural (*-i*/*-ī* respectively) occurs almost without exception, verbs *primae aleph* have *i-* as a prefix, verbs with a so-called weak radical "aleph 3-5 and 7" use only /*–e-*/, and almost no cases of anomalous use of prepositions are attested.

[26] For example, as opposed to Babylonian Akkadian, these texts use the *–e*/*-ē* ending of the genitive singular and the oblique plural, or the *e*-prefix in verbs *primae aleph*.

[27] *SAU*, p. 474.

[28] "Naḫiš-šalmu, an Assyrian Scribe Working in the 'Southern Palace' at Ugarit," in *Veenhof Anniversary Volume. Studies Presented to Klaas R. Veenhof on the Occasion of His Sixty-fifth Birthday*, ed. W. van Soldt et al. (Leiden, 2001), pp. 429-444.

[29] "Naḫiš-šalmu, an Assyrian Scribe," p. 437.

[30] Ibid., p. 440.

of a scribe associated with an "Assyrianizing" administrative office of Ugarit, and two concentrations of tablets of didactic content showing strong Mesopotamian influence, one Babylonian and one Assyrian. The evidence is indeed meagre. The problem, furthermore, is that we cannot ascertain that Naḫiš-šalmu, the properly spelled Assyrian name of the scribe, was indeed working for the administrative machine of Ugarit: no extant text is signed with his name; and the fact that no Mesopotamian school texts have been found associated to the archive does not even allow us to suggest that he was engaged in teaching his presumably native language to Ugarit students. Of course we can speculate and try in a more or less artificial fashion to bring together some of the preserved elements of the disconnected picture. Perhaps Naḫiš-šalmu indeed migrated from an Assyrian town to eventually reach Ugarit, establishing himself in a house in the "South City" area, namely the one called by archaeologists the "Tablet House." There he might have taught students the scribal art he had learned himself in his home country, using the didactic material that was partially recovered by the French Mission of Ras Shamra. Given his skill and origin, he would not have had to wait for long before finding a job, namely at the office of the state chief-administrator (*šatammu rabû*) Yabnīnu. But perhaps Yabnīnu had actually called for him, a native Assyrian scribe, profiting the international political overture of his time (second half of the 13th century BC?).[31] Once appointed, it is also possible that Naḫeši-šalmu, as he was inaccurately called by his colleagues at Ugarit, would have decided to spend the rest of his life at this Mediterranean harbour town: he then would have adopted some of the writing habits of his new colleagues,[32] and would have hardly spoken his mother tongue outside the academy. No doubt after some years working for Yabnīnu he would have achieved a fairly fluent control of the language he would then use daily to communicate, namely Ugaritic (naturally with Assyrian accent and from time to time resorting to idioms or syntactic features of his mother tongue).

The story we have imagined, possible as it may be, is again nothing but guess work. But it may at least help, I hope, to illustrate my point that Akkadian in Ugarit was very seldom heard outside the academy where it was dictated, constantly recited and copied, and only very exceptionally pronounced by either teacher or student without any Ugaritic accent. As I have stressed above, Akkadian was a language specifically learned by a minority in the long and painstaking process of becoming technically literate. In his description of Akkadian as lingua franca in the western periphery, Izre'el precisely wrote that this language was used "by just a

---

[31] For the possible date of the archive, see van Soldt, *SAU*, pp. 155ff.

[32] As pointed out by van Soldt in "Naḫiš-šalmu, an Assyrian Scribe," p. 443.

small group of speakers. These were scribes of specific schools or scholarly traditions." "In various cases," he then added between brackets, "it is also possible that Akkadian may also have been used by diplomats, administrators, and other kinds of officials as well."[33] The tentative inclusion of diplomats, administrators, and other officials in the alleged bilingual group is presumably derived from the applied general concept of lingua franca itself we shall discuss later. Agustinus Gianto, in turn, writing on Amarna Akkadian as a contact language, distinguished "different degrees of bilingualism in Syria-Palestine."[34] "In general we can say that the northern area exhibits stronger and more widespread bilingualism among the population than the southern regions." And he further stated that "it can be assumed that throughout the area the regional languages were being spoken although in a number of regions Akkadian was the official language for business, legal, political and, to some extent, literary and religious purposes." One can say that Gianto's judgment has been victim of the illusory influence of the source material we are commonly subject to. For it is not bilingualism the issue of his discussion but "biliteralism." Akkadian was not the spoken official language for business, legal, political, and let alone literary and religious purposes in "northern" Ugarit or in "southern" Jerusalem. Administrative records, legal and diplomatic documents, and literature were indeed written in Akkadian in Ugarit, as we have seen, and perhaps also in Jerusalem. But rituals, lawsuits, or governmental decisions were no doubt normally spoken in Ugaritic and Jerusalemite respectively. On the other hand, the fact that Ugaritic, apparently unlike the Late Bronze Age Jerusalem native Semitic dialect, was written (and is luckily preserved) on clay tablets does not mean that Ugarit exhibited a "stronger and more widespread bilingualism among the population." The availability of the sources should not constitute a linguistic criterion. Furthermore, as discussed above, Ugaritic-Akkadian or Jerusalemite-Akkadian bilingualism, if exhibited at all, would have been probably restricted to the literate minority of the population. As stated by Gianto himself some paragraphs later, Amarna Akkadian "was developed and used mainly among scribes of the local southern courts, so that it is never spread to larger population."[35]

As I have been trying to suggest, the same is true for the whole Levant during the Late Bronze Age period. The process of learning Akkadian as a second language in those countries outside Mesopotamia followed, I believe, the same steps: through the standard and traditionally

---

[33] *Amurru Akkadian*, p. 9.

[34] "Amarna Akkadian as a Contact Language," in *Languages and Cultures in Contact*, ed. K. van Lerberghe and G. Voet (Leuven, 1999), p. 125.

[35] Ibid., p. 127.

established acquisition of the Mesopotamian script. What differs is of course the level of proficiency achieved by the scribes, something that depended on a large variety of factors such as the ability and competence of the apprentice scribe but obviously also the proficiency of the teacher himself, the number and quality of clay textbooks, and the distance between the two linguistic systems, that is, mother tongue and target language. It should be stressed that this set of variables is important but is only a selection. On the other hand, the less proficiency attained by the apprentice scribe in the target, foreign language, or the greater is the learning difficulty and problem, the more important and conspicuous is the potential interference of the mother tongue. I believe the question of the nature and wide range of varieties of Peripheral Akkadian lies largely in this complex, but socially very restricted, sociolinguistic situation of second language acquisition, as we shall discuss in detail below.

The wealth of Akkadian documentation from Ugarit, especially as compared to other Levantine "southern" centres, provides good examples of the relevant variables involved in second language acquisition and proficiency outlined above. Let us briefly review a representative sample. Concerning the learning process of Mesopotamian writing and Akkadian language, we have exercises of apprentices belonging to different stages. The following illustrative description with examples is taken at length from van Soldt's study "The Akkadian of Ugarit: Lexicographical Aspects":[36]

"Quite a few words that were written in lexical texts can be identified only with difficulty and sometimes not at all, partly because the scribe apparently did not understand what the teacher told him, partly because the teacher did not remember the word in its correct form. Some examples from a few hundred cases will suffice [the transcribed words in brackets stand for the normative form of the Akkadian words]:

ú.KI.KAL.ḫi.li.a = *la-a-a-ri-tu* (*lardu*), Hh [= Ḫarra-ḫubullu] 16-17, MSL 10, 108:24.

ú.nab.na.du = *mu-ri-da-di-lu* (*murdudû*), ibid., line 35.

ú.ᵈDÌM.ME = *na-ma-li-te* (*lamaštu*), ibid., 111:112.

giš.sag.kul.lá.lá = *sú-ku-ru za-gi-ri* (*sikkūr šāqili*), Hh 5b-6, MSL 6, 28:273.

giš.suḫur = *ma-gi-qu* (*mekkû*), ibid., 96 :148.

[36] Published in SEL 12 (1995):205-215. The following full quote comes from pp. 206-207.

The number of examples can easily be multiplied. In literary texts, too, we find this kind of mistake:

dal-ḫat-e-re-tum = *dalḫā têrētu*, U 5, 162 [= Righteous Sufferer]:5'.
ul iq-bu-ú a-da-mur-ṣi-ia = *ūl iqbû adān murṣiya*, ibid., line 8'.

In many cases the mistakes of the apprentice scribe make it hard for us to understand what he meant and, due to lack of parallels, some texts still remain partly unintelligible."[37]

I believe that the written words and sentences are not only confusing and unintelligible to us. I can easily imagine that a native Mesopotamian would have been unable to understand them had he heard the student's or even teacher's recitation, or casually read (if literate of course) the school tablets on which they were written.

"Naturally —explained subsequently van Soldt—, the documents which the scribes composed after the completion of their study do not suffer from these mistakes to the same degree. The scribe was well aware of the meanings of the words which he wrote down. However, unexpected peculiarities may point to a lack of proficiency, and possibly of education, on the part of the scribe." Learning Akkadian in Ugarit was not performed "effectively" as it would be advertised nowadays. Proof of it is what may be considered the relatively frequent temptation faced by professional scribes to resort, consciously or unconsciously, to features of their mother tongue when composing Akkadian texts. To be sure, these substrate interferences affected in various degrees all aspects of language use, thus ranging from vocabulary to syntax, including morphology and phonology. The two relatively recent impressive works on the Akkadian of Ugarit have so thoroughly dealt with this subject that our task will limit itself to some main references.[38]

Let us briefly list some examples of deviations from native Akkadian (i.e. either Babylonian or Assyrian) morphology presumably due to Ugaritic influence:[39] the confusion of the third person feminine genitive and accusative singular suffixes, the presence of case-endings on singular and feminine plural nouns in construct state, the use of the verbal prefix */t-/*

---

[37] The interpretation of these and other examples as mistakes made by the student, namely "Hörfehler" was put forward by Wolfram von Soden in "Bemerkungen zu einigen literarischen Texten in akkadischer Sprache aus Ugarit," UF 1 (1969):189-195; see also e.g. GIM MU.PÀD.DA for *kīma upāṭi* in RS 17.155:39. Huehnergard, however, in his *The Akkadian of Ugarit*, pp. 108-109, prefers to list this and other examples under the heading "crasis and sandhi."

[38] We mean of course the ones written by Huehnergard and van Soldt.

[39] See the summary with the corresponding references of Huehnergard, *The Akkadian of Ugarit*, pp. 280-281, and 271-276; and van Soldt, *SAU*, p. 472.

for the third person feminine singular form, the non-use of the subjunctive marker, the anomalous use of a number of prepositions, and the wrong gender of words such as "town" (*ālu*) and "field" (*eqlu*). As for the syntax of the texts,[40] the fact that word order in clauses is much freer than in Mesopotamian Akkadian or that the verb is seldom placed at the end can be reasonably taken as a result of Ugaritic influence; probably of Ugaritic origin too are the construction of the predicate of nominal clauses without the enclitic *–ma*, the use of the conjunction *u* to introduce a main clause, and the construction of *yānu* with the accusative. Not less significant for the realization of language interference is the more than 180 Ugaritic words attested in the Akkadian administrative and legal documents, occasionally marked by scribes with a gloss-sign.[41] Although many of them are names or designations of local regions and estates, common Ugaritic words can also be found beside Akkadian-Ugaritic hybrid formations such as the verb forms spelled *i-ṣa-ʾa* (with the meaning "it went out") or *i-bi-la* ("he brought").[42]

That the more inexperienced the scribe the more he allowed his mother tongue to interfere his (non-normative) Akkadian is clearly shown by a number of exceptional examples. Two texts, of legal content, stand out: RS 17.388 and RS 22.223. The former contains a number of aberrant spellings especially for verbal forms:[43] *e-na-da-ni* for *inaddin* (line 7), *e-te-e-ru* for *itūrū* or *iturrū* (line 15), and *te-ṣa-bi-*tu_4 for expected *iṣabbatū* (line 16), the latter clearly attesting to Ugaritic morphological interference. As thoughtfully remarked in a footnote by Nougayrol who edited the text, "c'est la langue accadienne plutôt que l'écriture babylonienne (cf. les Np.) qu'il maltraite."[44] Concerning RS 22.223, an unpublished text quoted by van Soldt,[45] the scribe's lack of proficiency is shown by repeated cases of haplography (*<i>-túr-ru* in line 8, *ú-<ma>-lu-ú* in line 11, and *qa-<ti>* in line 12), and again aberrant verbal forms influenced by Ugaritic grammar: note the *–u* ending of the singular forms following the Ugaritic indicative norm, and the more eloquent

[40] See Huehnergard, *The Akkadian of Ugarit*, pp. 280-281, and van Soldt, *SAU*, p. 518.

[41] See in general the thorough study by Huehnergard, *Ugaritic Vocabulary in Syllabic Transcription* (Atlanta, 1987).

[42] See Huenhergard, *Ugaritic Vocabulary*, p. 133, and van Soldt, *SAU*, p. 437.

[43] See Nougayrol, *PRU* 6, p. 50 n. 1; Huehnergard, *The Akkadian of Ugarit*, p. 11 n. 13; and more recently van Soldt, "The Akkadian of Ugarit: Lexicographical Aspects," p. 207.

[44] See the previous footnote ("Np." obviously stands for "noms de personnes").

[45] *SAU*, p. 441. There he also mentions other examples of aberrant verbal forms influenced by Ugaritic.

yaqtulu-form *ia-tu-ru* (in line 13).[46]

Before going any further, it is essential to make a distinction between the three sets of examples listed above attesting to the errors and interferences made by Ugaritic scribes when writing Akkadian texts. The first category is clearly that of isolated mistakes made by students in their process of learning Mesopotamian cuneiform. The incorrect understanding of Akkadian words and sentences as they were dictated (perhaps inaccurately) by the teacher in the classroom cannot be taken as part of the process of attempted meaningful performance: it is likely that the students were not trying to express meaning when they (incorrectly) spelled the words, especially because they probably did not understand what they heard (e.g. *la-a-a-ri-tu* for *lardu*, or *dal-ḫat-e-re-tum* for *dalḫā têrētu*). As opposed to these examples, the other two sets of non-normative instances belong to the category of produced (written) language, namely by professional scribes. The first important remark to be made about the listed deviations from native Akkadian morphosyntax is that they show a regular, consistent pattern; they are recurrent features in the scribal production of Akkadian in Ugarit. In other words, the interference phenomena (such as the construct state with triptotical declension or the much freer word order in clauses) were established and "normalized" features that were accordingly taught at schools. That is another way of saying that the Akkadian language norm academically *defined* in Ugarit clearly differed from the native Akkadian norm. Finally, the examples RS 17.388 and RS 22.223 stand as exceptional scribal productions of Akkadian; as stated above the errors made by both scribes reflect the poor knowledge they had of the Mesopotamian language as defined and learned in Ugarit: they knew the meaning of the words they wrote, and they were able to write Mesopotamian cuneiform (as noted by Nougayrol); their level of proficiency in (Ugarit) Akkadian morphosyntax, however, was far from satisfactory, as eloquently shown by the "Ugariticized" written verbal forms.

We can say that what is exceptional of the Akkadian of Ugarit seems to be the rule in the Amarna texts, especially the letters from Byblos. There indeed the verbal system is almost completely permeated with elements of Byblian, the native Semitic dialect spoken in this Levantine area. As is well known, the usage of *qatala*, *yaqtulu*, *yaqtul*, and *yaqtula* forms appears consistently in the letters, and scribes occasionally had also recourse to hybrid formations consisting in an Akkadian prefix conjugation that served as base for a Byblian suffix conjugation (such as

[46] The fact that the document is sealed and records a list of witnesses, including the scribe himself, rules out a priori the possible interpretation of the text as a scribal exercise (see our discussion in the previous chapter).

tašapparta or *irtiḫat*).[47] This particular linguistic evidence has led some scholars to draw a line in the linguistic map of Peripheral Akkadian. Here belongs the distinction referred to above between a northern and a southern area as far as the alleged phenomenon of bilingualism in the Late Bronze Age period is concerned. Moran speaks of a transformation of the Babylonian language in the southern tradition. "Indeed," he wrote, "so radical is the transformation that one may ask whether the language of this tradition, even when qualified as 'extremely barbarized,' should be called Babylonian at all. It is a pidgin in which the Babylonian component is mainly lexical, whereas the grammar is profoundly West-Semiticized, most notably in the word order and, most important of all, in the verbal system." "The language —he concluded— can only be described as an entirely new code, only vaguely intelligible (if at all) to the West Semite because of the lexicon, and to the Babylonian because of the grammar."[48] Izre'el would of course rightly object to using the label "pidgin" for this special, newly developed dialect, but would agree on the particular different linguistic situation in the southern region of Canaan, as compared to the rest of varieties of Peripheral Akkadian. The newly developed dialect he would describe in similar terms: "its lexicon —he wrote— was almost entirely Akkadian, while the grammar was mostly Canaanite, the mother tongue of the scribes who wrote these letters;" but he would rather designate it as "a mixed language."[49] Gianto, in turn, has proposed to call this entirely new code an "institutionalized interlanguage," thus interestingly referring to the process of second language acquisition we have been dealing with above.[50] But let us allow

---

[47] Apart from Moran's leading thorough studies, see also Gianto, *Word Order Variation in the Akkadian of Byblos* (Rome, 1990); Rainey, *Canaanite in the Amarna Tablets: A Linguistic Analysis of the Mixed Dialect Used by the Scribes from Canaan* (Leiden, 1996); and Izre'el, *Canaano-Akkadian* (Munich, 1998).

[48] *The Amarna Letters*, pp. xxi-xxii.

[49] The quote is taken from his "The Amarna Glosses: Who Wrote What to Whom? Some Sociolinguistic Considerations," IOS 15 (1995):102. See also his *Canaano-Akkadian*, and "Some Methodological Requisites for the Study of the Amarna Jargon. Notes on the Essence of that Language," to appear in *Tell el-Amarna, 1887-1987*, ed. B.J. Beitzel and G.D. Young (Winona Lake, IN).

[50] The notion he introduced in his *Word Order Variation in the Akkadian of Byblos*, pp. 10-11; and he further dealt with it in "Amarna Akkadian as a Contact Language," pp. 126ff. Rainey showed less interest in these theoretical or methodological issues we are here concerned with as is obvious from his indistinct use of various labels; as noted by Huehnergard in his review to the four-volume work on Canaanite in the Amarna Tablets (BASOR 310 [1998]:61), "Rainey refers to the language as a 'code' (II 32); he also mentions 'the peripheral jargon' (II 121), 'pidgin developments' (II 133), and the important notion of an 'interlanguage' (e.g.

him to describe this sociolinguistic or psycholinguistic notion notably developed by Larry Selinker in 1972, as applied to the Byblos variety of Akkadian in the Amarna period.

"In learning a foreign language," wrote Gianto,[51] "the learner develops a temporary code to facilitate the understanding or the reproduction of the target language. This code is neither the native language nor the target language. Such a code is an adaptation of the learner's native language rather than the target language since one cannot simplify a code one has not fully mastered. Usually the effect of this code is not lasting because the learner keeps making progress in mastering the grammar of the target language. But where the corrective role of native speakers is not available, this interlanguage will remain and become fossilized."

This is according to him exactly what happened in Byblos. The situation in the southern region of Syria-Palestine he then describes as follows: "scribes must have received some training in cuneiform writing and in the Akkadian language. Yet their training seems to stop within their own circles. There was no corrective element from the native scribal tradition nor were there native speakers of Mesopotamian Akkadian." Furthermore, "it is obvious that the scribes were trained to produce just a few operations. Thus —he concluded— the interlanguage code became institutionalized. This seems to be the situation in the south." The new, interesting sociolinguistic label proposed by Gianto for this variety of Peripheral Akkadian can, however, be also misleading if understood too literally.

Selinker called interlanguage the "linguistic system based on the observable output which results from a learner's attempted production of a target language norm."[52] In this narrow sense, the Amarna letters from Byblos can hardly be compared to the subject matter of interlanguage research. It is not only that Selinker's (and other modern sociolinguists' or psycholinguists') observable linguistic data were and are obtained first and foremost from the flowing speech of second-language learners. Strictly speaking, none of the written letters can be designated as "a learner's attempted production" of normative Akkadian. The texts themselves are "finished products" made by professional scribes. The authors of the letters are not *learners*, the subjects of Selinker's study, but actually *learned* people. And the Akkadian inscribed in these clay tablets is not a language which the scribe is in the process of learning. It is neither

---

II 135, 346);" note furthermore that the subtitle refers to the notion of "mixed dialect."

[51] "Amarna Akkadian as a Contact Language," p. 127.

[52] "Interlanguage," International Review of Applied Linguistics in Language Teaching 10 (1972):214.

an interim grammatical system nor the result of a "*grammatica interrupta*," as implied in Gianto's text. The Akkadian of the Byblos letters, like the one of Ugarit, however different from the native Mesopotamian Akkadian, was locally and scholarly normalized and accordingly became the proper, and academically fulfilled, target language at schools, as shown by the many examples of the scribal production. Gianto, of course well aware of this linguistic situation, qualified then the alleged interlanguage as "fossilized and institutionalized." Although, as quickly pointed out, the newly proposed label "interlanguage" may be misleading, the introduction of the notion of second language acquisition is not only important but, I believe, necessary for the linguistic study of Peripheral Akkadian.

Two aspects we have already referred to throughout the chapter need to be stressed when dealing with the process of learning Akkadian as a foreign, second language in the Near East. The first one is essential because it establishes an original difference with our modern concept of second language acquisition. As we have repeatedly noted, Akkadian in, say, Ugarit or Byblos, unlike modern English in Spain for example, was not learned for its own sake. It was learned in the essential process of becoming literate. Akkadian was the language expressed in (cuneiform) writing. It may be exaggerate to qualify Akkadian acquisition as a secondary goal in school training outside Mesopotamia, but stress needs to be made that the essential goal of the training was to become literate. As Moran put it himself, "the Amarna letters are manifestations of the 'cuneiform culture' that was shared in the fourteenth century B.C. throughout the ancient Near East."[53] The important implication of understanding Peripheral Akkadian as a manifestation of "cuneiform culture" (or "cuneiform scribal *koinē*," as it has been also designated again using terms from the field of sociolinguistics)[54] is that any borderline in the linguistic map is not necessary, and that its study requires incorporating the different varieties of Akkadian (from Byblos, Ugarit, Tyre, Boghazköy or Alalakh) into a single discourse. Indeed the process of learning Akkadian as a second language beside the acquisition of literacy took place in all schools in the Near East. The degree of proficiency, not in literacy but in Akkadian, is the second important aspect in this process of second language acquisition. As stated above, one must distinguish between the degree attained by an individual learner whose target Akkadian will be the one established by the local school, and the degree of proficiency of a local scholarly tradition as compared to the native Mesopotamian lan-

---

[53] *The Amarna Letters*, p. xviii.

[54] See for example Jerrold S. Cooper, "Sumerian and Semitic Writing in Most Ancient Syro-Mesopotamia," in *Languages and Cultures in Contact*, p. 74.

guage. In either case, the resulting Akkadian cannot be literally called a pidgin or an interlanguage, even if structural features of the language, such as the overgeneralization of grammatical rules, are common to these linguistic systems.

Let us now recapitulate our main arguments. What the traditional and still valid name "Peripheral Akkadian" implies is the existence of common elements that justify taking all varieties together: the Akkadian of Ugarit, Byblos, Jerusalem, Tyre, Alalakh, Boghazköy, etc. The common framework is that these Akkadian varieties, whatever their sometimes important differences, are all manifestations of the same "cuneiform culture" originally spread from Mesopotamia (hence the designation peripheral). The Near Eastern centres that adopted cuneiform culture (including bureaucracy) also share the linguistic condition that Akkadian was not their mother tongue. "No people on earth, I suspect, when they get writing, write their own language," as a scholar has rightly put it.[55] Every cuneiform school centre outside Mesopotamia developed, and taught consecutive generations of scribes, a variety of written Akkadian (with cuneiform signs on clay tablets) that deviates from core Akkadian usage. Another common element of these written varieties is therefore their imperfect proficiency in normative native Akkadian. The different degree of divergence from it can be taken to establish the mutual differences of these linguistic systems (the nature of which still defies a precise linguistic categorization). This degree is proportional to, and indeed responsible for, the degree of interferences of the vernacular spoken at the different schools. The higher the degree the more "barbarized" can thus be characterized the Peripheral Akkadian.[56] One last important point needs, however, to be discussed, and that is whether or not Peripheral Akkadian was really spoken, and if so, what was its social context; in other words, who spoke this language to whom and when? Naturally this inquiry will bear upon the label "lingua franca" generally agreed for second-millennium Akkadian.

Some pages earlier we have referred to the presently accepted opinion among Assyriologists that scribes constitute the core of the Peripheral Akkadian speech community. A number of scholars have also suggested

---

[55] I take the quote by Alton Becker originally applied to Old Javanese literature from Piotr Michalowski who used it to close his seminal contribution "Language, Literature, and Writing at Ebla," in *Ebla 1975-1985*, ed. Luigi Cagni (Naples, 1987), p. 175.

[56] Note incidentally that the shape and aspect of some of the tablets (e.g. the letters from Lachish or Megiddo) can also be qualified as "barbarized," as compared to the standard, Babylonian pattern. This is not without interest given the intimate link that existed between Akkadian language and writing Mesopotamian cuneiform signs on clay tablets.

including other, few members of the society, such as diplomats, administrators, and other officials. We also noted above that the tentative inclusion of these additional people presumably derived from the assumption that Akkadian was used as a lingua franca throughout the Near East, just like Aramaic one millennium later. Indeed it seems that international negotiation in both the written and oral levels was regularly carried out in Aramaic during most of the first millennium before our era. Two eloquent sources are usually brought forth. One is the notorious passage in the Second Book of Kings (18:16); there it is reported that by the time of Hezekiah Aramaic was known by (three) Judean government officials and used by them to conduct negotiation with Sennacherib's official. The second well-known example is the letter found at Saqqara addressed to the Pharaoh by Adon, the king of Ekron, attesting this time to the written diplomatic use of Aramaic around 600 BC. As we have seen, eight hundred years earlier Akkadian was used between the same distant regions to conduct diplomatic relations in written form. But was Akkadian, like Aramaic, also the accepted spoken language of international diplomacy? We are not helped much by the sources to answer this crucial question. The Old Testament makes unfortunately no reference to the sociolinguistic situation of the Late Bronze Age Levant in particular or the second millennium Near East in general. And our cuneiform sources are undoubtedly of a different nature. As stated above, the clues we have to discover this sociolinguistic situation are extremely vague and chiefly indirect. I propose to look quickly at two vague and indirect references from the Ras Shamra corpus material that may help illuminate the dark picture.

The first one I have chosen because of its singular, ironic character. RS 17.109 is exceptional because it represents the only record written in the Hittite language found at Ugarit.[57] Shortly after its discovery within the remains of the royal palace diplomatic ("southern") archive, Hittitologists, too, agreed with the uniqueness of this cuneiform clay tablet because not only was it (and still is) the first Hittite legal document found outside the Anatolian homeland of the Hittite empire but also the only source that could shed light on the form of Hittite private legal practice. A further exceptional feature is that RS 17.109 represents the only deed of deposition thus far unearthed at Ugarit. Whatever the reasons lying behind the linguistic choice of the text proper, it is nonetheless ironic that the only text from ancient Ugarit that exclusively records an actual verbal testimony is written in the Hittite language. This incidental evidence should obviously warn us of the danger of drawing too fast conclusions

[57] For a last treatment with full bibliography, see my "The Legal Texts from Ugarit," pp. 420-422.

on past, no doubt complex sociolinguistic situations from our extant written sources. On the other hand, it should remind us that Akkadian was not the exclusive written language used for diplomatic relations among Near Eastern states. I hasten to recall, for example, that the pharaoh's correspondence with the Anatolian kingdom of Arzawa in the Amarna period (EA nos. 31 and 32) was made in Hittite, as expressly requested by the Arzawa scribe in his letter (EA 32:24f.): "The tablets that are brought here always write in Hittite!"[58] And that of the twelve preserved letters sent by the Mittannian emperor to the Egyptian court, one (EA 24) is written in Hurrian, the sender's mother tongue, instead of the usual Akkadian.[59]

My second indirect reference to the sociolinguistic situation in thirteenth century Ugarit comes from an Akkadian transaction between Hittite and Ugaritian dignitaries. According to the find-spot of the cuneiform tablet, RS 17.251 was like RS 17.109 originally filed in the diplomatic archive of the royal palace. The inscribed text describes the sale of a slave from the Hittite princes Taki-Šarruma and Tulpi-Šarruma apparently then posted in Carchemish to ᶜUzzēnu the *sākinu*-minister of Ugarit.[60] Of potential interest for the present discussion are two probably related pieces of information contained in the text. One is that the scribe of the text is Burqānu, the only scribe of Ugarit who is known to have written texts in both Akkadian and his native language (note that he properly declined the personal names in the text, following the Ugaritic scribal habit).[61] The other is that one of the six named witnesses to the international transaction is a certain Nuᶜmēnu, an interpreter (with a clear Ugaritic name).[62] Why, we should hasten to ask, was Nuᶜmēnu present at the transaction? Why was there a need for an interpreter if Akkadian, the language of the document written by Burqānu, was the lingua franca at that time? If, as it seems, Hittite and Ugaritic were the languages spoken

58 I follow Volkert Haas' translation in Moran, *The Amarna Letters*, p. 103.

59 We may incidentally mention that this letter has long represented (and in a sense still represents) the basic source for our knowledge of the Hurrian grammar.

60 For the identity of the two Hittite "brothers," see Singer, "A Political History of Ugarit," p. 654, and more recently, id. "The Great Scribe Taki-Šarruma," in *Hittite Studies in Honor of Harry A. Hoffner Jr. On the Occasion of his 65th Birthday*, ed. G. Beckman et al. (Winona Lake, IN, 2003), pp. 341-348.

61 See van Soldt, *SAU*, p. 27 n. 213. Burqānu and his written productions have already been discussed in previous chapters. As already mentioned too, Nuᶜmerašpu may also have been the author of a Ugaritic royal deed if we accept Lipiński's restoration of RS 15.111 (KTU 3.2); see note 32 of chapter 3, and our forthcoming remarks in chapter 5 note 103.

62 Line 23: igi ᵖ*nu-me-nu* ˡᵘ́*tar-gu-um-ia-nu*.

by highest officials of the countries of Hatti and Ugarit to negotiate and settle a slave-sale business that presumably took place at Ugarit (since the document is composed by an Ugaritic scribe and Nu^{c}mēnu is possibly of Ugaritic origin),[63] is it legitimate to posit, let alone assume, the existence of a lingua franca?

Indirect and isolated as the latter instance is (it is the only extant attestation of a dragoman in the Ras Shamra documentary material), it raises one fundamental question: was there normally an interpreter during inter-state negotiations conducted by plenipotentiaries speaking different mother tongues? Did usually states with political, military, or commercial interests resort to actual bilingual (or multilingual) speakers to bridge the language gap existing among them? Is the almost complete silence of sources about them, such as the tablets of Ugarit, a sign of the habit pattern, that is, of the regular presence of interpreters in official inter-state affairs? And is accordingly the exceptional reference to Nu^{c}mēnu in RS 17.251 due to his casual role as witness to one of the transactions he officially usually interpreted?

Cuneiform sources provide considerable documentation about the existence of interpreters of various languages spoken throughout the Near East between the third millennium down to the late first millennium. This is not the place for a survey, however brief, of this material or for a descriptive account of the status and role of the interpreter in the ancient Near East. For our purposes, that is, in order to realize the consistent presence of interpreters at Oriental courts, it may be sufficient to mention the often quoted report of king Assurbanipal when he received the unexpected visit of a messenger from the land of Lydia: "Of all the tongues from East to West that (my god) Ashur has granted me —he said— there was no one here who could speak his tongue which was completely foreign and unintelligible."[64] At least as illustrative, although probably more significant, is the fact that our term "dragoman" is but a loan word from Akkadian (*targumānu* / *targumannu*).[65] How many words (together with their notions) have travelled such a long and uninterrupted way from this far-away language? The originality of the word and notion, however, should not surprise us. For is it not precisely in the

---

[63] Apart from the linguistic habits (such as the triptotically declined personal names referred to above or the introductory legal formula), one should note that the seal, namely a Hittite ring-seal, is impressed in the Ugaritic style, i.e. on top of the obverse (see the detailed discussion in the next chapter).

[64] Piepkorn Asb. 16 v 1-13.

[65] See Ignace J. Gelb, "The Word for Dragoman in the Ancient Near East," Glossa 2 (1968):93-104; more recently Frank Starke has proposed a Hittite etymology of the Akkadian word in "Zur Herkunft von akkad. *ta/urgumannu(m)* "Dolmetscher"," WdO 24 (1993):20-38.

heart of Mesopotamia where the mythical landscape of the original confusion of languages is set? If not "invented," an adjective that may sound fairly inappropriate in this context, interpreters were certainly early and steadily institutionalized in the Near East.

From the considerable cuneiform documentation on dragomen, I have chosen one single example because of its relevance for the present discussion. It is one of the very few attestations of pre-Late-Bronze-Age Ugarit, namely a casual reference in an Akkadian administrative text from Mari. The tablet itself (ARM 23 556) belongs to the dossier of the notorious journey that the king Zimri-Lim of Mari made to the Mediterranean in 1765 BC;[66] in lines 29-31 mention is made of an interpreter, literally "the interpreter of the Cretan chief-merchant who was at Ugarit."[67] What we do not know is exactly what languages he mastered. In view of his employer or superior, one can easily imagine that the native language spoken in eighteenth-century Crete was one of them, possibly his mother tongue, and another one might have been the Middle Bonze Age dialect of Ugaritic; perhaps he had some notion of Amorite too to render intelligible the Cretan terms of the transaction uttered by the chief-merchant to Zimri-Lim's officials at Ugarit. Or was Akkadian, indeed the language of the Mari text, used to communicate? It is difficult, if I may insist again, to draw a sociolinguistic picture from a handful of casual references. We mentioned above the message sent by Yasmakh-Addu to his father the emperor asking him to send as quick as possible a scribe who could read Sumerian. The cuneiform text actually adds: "and who speaks Amorite," attesting to the vernacular of the addressor.[68] Another indirect clue comes from a message of a high official of Mari posted somewhere in the Upper Khabur area; there he reported to have met someone who "masters Akkadian, Amorite, and Hurrian."[69] The available evidence is too laconic and slim to provide a clear answer but I believe it is sufficiently significant. Kings and merchants in the ancient

---

[66] See Pierre Villard, "Un roi de Mari à Ugarit," UF 18 (1986):387-412; in view of the forthcoming, more complete study in Charpin's, "'Année où Zimri-Lim est allé en renfort du Yamhad' : une campagne des armées de Mari dans le royaume d'Alep," see provisionally Dominique Charpin and Nele Ziegler, *Mari et le Proche-Orient à l'époque amorrite. Essai d'histoire politique* (Paris, 2003), pp. 214-216 (cf. also Charpin's "Le voyage d'un roi de Mari," Le Monde de la Bible 146 [2002]:25-29).

[67] The text reads: ^{lú}*ta-ar-ga-ma-an-nim* / ugula [dam.gà]r *k*[*a*]*p-ta*$^{!}$*-ra-i* / *i-na ú-ga-ri-tim*^{ki}.

[68] See above footnote 18.

[69] The text is A.109, and the official is a *merᶜûm*; see Durand, "Unité et diversités au Proche-Orient à l'époque amorrite," p. 125.

Near East apparently were no bilinguals and were in constant search and need of interpreters. Only with their help and knowledge could they establish direct contacts and communications with foreign countries to conduct political negotiations and trade business.[70] The boasting of Shulgi who ruled the land of Sumer and Akkad, and beyond, during the first half of the 21st century claiming to have spoken and administered justice in five different languages can be taken as proof of the unusual bilingual competence of ancient Near Eastern monarchs.

That every king and probably also every chief-merchant (like the one of Crete) had at least one interpreter to help bridge the language gap between his mother tongue and the native language of his most direct, in the sense of politically dependent or economically indispensable, neighbour or partner should seriously question the assumption of the existence of a lingua franca in the narrow sense of the expression as well as the alleged attestation of written pidgins and trade jargons, in particular in the Late Bronze Age Levant. The presence of an interpreter in the transaction recorded at Ugarit in the 13th century BC between Hittite and Ugaritic highest officials is revealing in this regard. On the other hand, and this is what especially matters here, had there been a bilingual or even trilingual king or minister of Ugarit, I believe Akkadian would not have been among his mastered vernaculars; Hittite, Egyptian or Cypriot would have been much more probable, certainly more useful, candidates.

To be sure, Akkadian voices must have been occasionally heard at the Mediterranean fringe of the Near East presumably uttered by merchants coming from Babylonia and Assyria,[71] apart from those pronounced (with foreign accent) by teachers and students in scribal schools. Furthermore, Akkadian was during the Late Bronze Age period the internationally accepted language of written diplomacy (with cuneiform signs on clay tablets). It was learned in schools as part of the training to become technically literate, as we have stressed above. But the native Mesopotamian language does not seem to have been used by diplomats or plenipotentiaries speaking different mother tongues to conduct oral international negotiation during the second half of the second millennium. Peripheral Akkadian seems indeed to have been basically (perhaps exclusively) used as a contact written language. The implications are of utmost importance because we would accordingly have to

[70] See in general Samuel A. Meier, *The Messenger in the Ancient Semitic World* (Atlanta, 1988), that includes a survey of the Amarna material; for ambassadors and interpreters in Mari, see the remarks by Durand, *Documents épistolaires du palais de Mari*, vol. I (Paris, 1997), p. 592.

[71] As evidenced, for example, by Hattušili's letter to Kadašman-Enlil (KBo 1 10, rev. 14-25), referring to the murder of Babylonian merchants in the lands of Amurru and Ugarit.

linguistically analyze the different varieties not as dialects but as strictly written linguistic systems.[72] As a result too, I would propose to slightly modify the commonly accepted label for Peripheral Akkadian into *lingua scripta franca*. Although in Bloomfieldian terms, our research would be based on no more than a secondary, graphic representation of language, the linguistic "diamesic" variation of language, referring to the medium used to communicate, is not without linguistic interest. The new approach would require formulating the sociolinguistic question "who spoke Peripheral Akkadian to whom and when?" in other, accordingly more relevant terms, namely: Who wrote Peripheral Akkadian to whom and when?[73]

The question is clearly not a difficult one. Naturally the language-using individuals, i.e. what we could call the locus of the particular language contact, are the scribes. They were the only people who could write, and read, Akkadian in Mesopotamian cuneiform. Indeed, in the Akkadian communicative process the scribe stood at both ends, as issuer and receiver of the (written) message (that is incidentally what we pointed out in the previous chapter about the communicative process of legal messages). The implied sociolinguistic situation is of especial importance and may help understand the phenomenon of more or less "barbarized" Peripheral Akkadian discussed in the preceding pages.

We quoted above Moran's appreciation of the Byblos letters in the Amarna period as a language that "can only be described as an entirely new code, only vaguely intelligible (if at all) to the West Semite because of the lexicon, and to the Babylonian because of the grammar." This apparently paradoxical condition becomes congruous when we realize that the message was issued and received by scribes trained in the same school tradition. The Akkadian cuneiform "peripheral code" that was used to communicate in written form, no matter how "new" or deviated from the native Akkadian language, was transmitted from one generation to the next in a well-established, rigid fashion at the local schools.[74] The messages technically written by Canaanite scribes were not meant to be

---

[72] That was already proposed by van Soldt for the Akkadian of Ugarit; note his explicit remarks that "the Akkadian attested in the records found at Ugarit of the Late Bronze Age (LB III/3) has to be regarded as a written rather than a spoken language," or further that "we cannot speak of the Akkadian 'dialect' of Ugarit" in "The Akkadian of Ugarit: Lexicographical Aspects," pp. 205 and 206 respectively.

[73] Cf. already the title of Izre'el's paper on Amarna glosses published in IOS 15 mentioned in note 49 above.

[74] One should nevertheless keep in mind that the corpus of Amarna letters from Byblos covers hardly forty years and that next to nothing is known of the number or name of the scribes who wrote them.

read by their Babylonian colleagues, neither by Assyriologists, but by themselves.[75] It is true, as put by Gianto in his discussion of interlanguage, that the corrective role of native speakers was certainly not available; but the case in point is rather whether it was needed at all.[76] What we might call "barbarizing" scribes carried out their professional task: they drew up written texts that were intelligible to those who read them; they produced written communication. As for the code itself, the Amarna letters, for example, but also the royal deeds of Ugarit as we shall see in the next chapter, show that scribes were not required to use Akkadian, or their knowledge thereof, in a wide variety of literary contexts. The choice of phrases and expressions was rather limited. In Gianto's terms, "scribes were trained to produce just a few operations."[77]

In his thoughtful essay on translating Akkadian texts and more particularly Akkadian letters, Oppenheim wrote that "the intended message and the actual wording of the letter are separated by a gap that can be considerable. The immediacy of the dictated or otherwise suggested content is bound to be hampered by the linguistic and stylistic inadequacies or propensities of the scribe *who in this civilization stands typically between message and letter*" (my italics). "Our search for life communication —he would conclude a few lines further— is forestalled by the medium: letter and scribe."[78] This is the more true for the Late Bronze Age Levant since, as we have seen, letters written in (Peripheral) Akkadian were in all likelihood not read aloud in (Peripheral) Akkadian. How could they when Akkadian was almost exclusively the means of written expression, only intelligible to the scribe who read it (especially in the case of the Byblos letters, as we have seen)? Civil, writing on bilingualism in logographically written languages, made an interesting side trip to the adaptation of Chinese script to Japanese literature. The important lesson he drew from it, especially relevant for our discussion, is "that the language in which a text is written is not necessarily the language in

---

[75] A more thorough discussion of the communicative process, including the interpretation of glosses, lies beyond the scope of the present chapter. It will be taken in an individual, forthcoming study. For the interpretation of glosses, see especially, Izre'el, "The Amarna Glosses," pp. 101-122; and id., "Vocalized Canaanite: Cuneiform-Written Canaanite Words in the Amarna Letters. Some Methodological Remarks," Dutch Studies (NELL) 5 (2003):13-34; and van der Toorn, "Cuneiform Documents from Syria-Palestine," pp. 104-105.

[76] Note that if Naḫiš-šalmi was indeed the scribe of the texts found in Yabnīnu's administrative office, his native Akkadian would have even been "contaminated" by the writing rules and habits of his Ugaritic colleagues (see footnote 32 above).

[77] "Amarna Akkadian as a Contact Language," p. 127.

[78] *Letters from Mesopotamia* (Chicago/London, 1967), p. 65.

which the same text is read."[79] In the Late Bronze Age Levant, the written word and the spoken word clearly belonged to two different linguistic systems. The Akkadian written word was a graphic representation of a word originally spoken, or otherwise suggested, in the vernacular of the addressor of the message (for instance, southern Byblian or northern Ugaritic);[80] and the Akkadian written word subsequently became speech again (in Byblian or Ugaritic) in the mouth of the scribe who read it aloud.[81] Akkadian was, in sum, the internationally accepted language of the written medium of communication in the Near East during the second millennium BC. Palace scribes from fourteenth-century Byblos or Ugarit wrote in (their local variety of) Akkadian because that was almost the compulsory way, namely the conventional operation, to render the verbal expression into written form.[82]

---

[79] "Bilingualism in Logographically Written Languages: Sumerian in Ebla," in *Il bilinguismo a Ebla*, ed. L. Cagni (Napoli, 1984), p. 76.

[80] Note here the West Semiticism made by the scribe in writing logographically the word for "palace" in EA 151:55 (as suggested above in ch. 1, n. 40). Instead of using the cuneiform normative logogram é.gal, the Tyrian royal scribe wrote é lugal, probably reflecting the Tyrian expression for "palace" */bêt malki/* dictated by the king.

[81] Eva Von Dassow has recently dealt with the problem of Canaanite Akkadian (in her detailed review of Rainey's four-volume study: "What the Canaanite Cuneiformists Wrote: Review Article," IEJ 53 [2003]:196-217); there, especially on pp. 215-216, she has asked some of the questions we have raised and has occasionally and independently reached similar answers. Particularly interesting is her conclusion that "one might almost characterise the Canaanite scribes' use of cuneiform as Akkadographic, and the texts they wrote as tablet-length Akkadograms, punctuated by occasional Canaanite words and explanatory glosses" (p. 215). The understanding of Canaanite Akkadian as a case of alloglottography (as she titled her lecture at the London 2003 Rencontre Assyriologique Internationale I did not have the pleasure to attend) seems to agree in general terms with our interpretation outlined above. Our main point of disagreement, apart from her accepted use of the label "interlanguage," is, however, her conclusion "that the true *lingua franca* shared by Canaanite scribes and their correspondents in the Late Bronze Age was not Akkadian, as is usually assumed, but Canaanite" (p. 216). What I have tried to show (I hope convincingly) in this chapter is that there probably was no lingua franca in the Late Bronze Age Near East. Akkadian, let alone Canaanite, did not seem to serve to bridge the language gap that existed between, say, the Egyptian and the Hittite courts. The recourse to interpreters seems to have been the rule to solve the numerous situations of mutual "deafness" in the Near East during the second millennium. As a matter of fact, interpreters constituted the real bilingual (or multilingual) speech community.

[82] Note the similar observation made by Durand for the Akkadian written in the Amorite period ("Apologue sur des mauvaises herbes et un coquin," AuOr 17-18 [1999-2000]:192).

2. Akkadian as legal language

> A suit might most conveniently have been brought in this way: "The Sabine property is mine." "No, it is mine"—then the trial. The lawyers would not consent to so simple a statement. "A property," he says, "which is situate in the district which is designated as Sabine." Well, that is prolix enough, but see what follows: "This I affirm to be my property by Quiritary title." What next? "From this place, I formally summon you to that place yonder to join issue with me according to law."

The ironic tone of the passage may resemble one of Yale Law Professor Fred Rodell's sarcastic quips on the legal profession and language. But it is not. It is part of Cicero's speech held in Rome for the defense of Murena in a case of electoral corruption in 63 BC.[83] The often criticized convoluted, arcane and obscure language used by lawyers today indeed stands at the end of a long tradition. In this chapter, however, no pretense is made to stretch the tradition further back in time and claim another cuneiform "first" in man's recorded history. The main reason being that we are not concerned here with law talk as the talk of judges to lawyers, lawyers to lawyers, or even lawyers to clients as we understand it today or as it existed in the Republican Rome. As we have already had the occasion to point out, in the ancient Near East there were no *iuris consulti*, nor were there orators who would legitimately defend clients, striving with their elaborate rhetoric to impress judges and influence juries. In fact one cannot speak of jurists in this area in the strict sense, that is, as professional interpreters of law and statutes, possibly not even during the Hellenistic period. Given the absence of more or less professional pleaders, the spoken words in ancient Oriental cases of litigation rather seem to reflect what Cicero, and so many people today, would positively characterize as convenient, ordinary language. Suffice it to mention the words spoken by the two plaintiff-women before King Solomon's court in Jerusalem (1Kings 3:22): "No; the living child is mine; yours is the dead one." "No; the dead child is yours; mine is the living one"—then the celebrated, magnificent and wise trial.

What we are here concerned with is not then the language used in courts, mostly gone for ever with the winds that blew through the gates and streets of ancient Near Eastern towns, but with the language of legal writing. The evidence we have is documentary, namely cuneiform legal texts inscribed on clay tablets. The legal language preserved in these clay

---

[83] *Pro L. Murena* XII.26. The translation is by Louis E. Lord in The Loeb Classical Library volume.

documents is not, therefore, the specialized language that, as has been both posited and attacked, only lawyers can speak or design; rather, we are dealing with an alleged specialized language that only professional scribes could write. As we have seen in previous chapters, the correct design of cuneiform legal documents was taught in schools as part of the scribal education; legal education proper, as taught for instance by *iuris consulti* (also in private houses) in the Republican Rome, did not exist in Ugarit in particular or the ancient Near East in general. The difference between both careers is self-evident and did apparently also concern the duration of study. For if we may trust Cicero, anyone (particularly including himself) could become a *iuris consultus* in three days, whereas Daniel, for one, needed three years to complete his training as a Mesopotamian scribe at the court of Nebuchadnezzar, according to the biblical Book of Daniel.[84] We may reasonably presume that both sources are biased, no doubt for different reasons; in the case of Cicero's *Pro Murena*, the text is admittedly overflowing with irony and sarcasm. But however exaggerated or distorted the real duration of studies, the difference must have been considerable. An apprentice scribe at Ugarit, just like Daniel at Babylon, had to learn not only the complex Mesopotamian cuneiform system, but also Akkadian as a second, foreign language. For the fact is that although the language normally spoken at the court of Ugarit was Ugaritic (as Hebrew was certainly the tongue heard at Solomon's court in Jerusalem and Latin the language in which Cicero expressed his renowned rhetoric), legal documents in Late Bronze Age Ugarit were not (but for a very few exceptional cases) drawn up in the Semitic Levantine vernacular but in Akkadian.

After what has been said in the previous section of this chapter, the use of Akkadian to write legal documents in Ugarit from the 14th to the 12th century BC should not come much as a surprise. Akkadian was the ecumenical written language of the Near East during most of the second millennium. Its teaching at school was an essential part of, and was therefore closely linked to, the traditional scribal training. Indeed it was built on didactic material that remained basically unchanged for centuries. Copying, reciting and learning the classic schoolbooks and pieces of literature, such as excerpts from the Epic of Gilgamesh or the Righteous Sufferer, helped the non-Mesopotamian student fix the Akkadian language. Labat, it will be remembered, thus defined it as "une langue de haute culture qu'adoptent volontairement les chancelleries, les cercles politiques, les juristes et les savants." As we have seen, Akkadian was certainly a language of high culture adopted together with the Mesopotamian script by all the chanceries outside Mesopotamia giving rise to a

[84] See respectively, *Pro L. Murena* XIII.28, and Dan 1:5.

common bureaucratic *koinē* in the Near East during the second millennium. And it was the language in which political, legal, and scholarly documents were written. Royal scribes, notaries (rather than jurists), secretaries, and scholars were all drawn from the schools in which writing was learned. But it is especially in the field of law that Akkadian enjoyed an additional advantage. Indeed it was the remarkable traditional, centuries-old stability of Akkadian as a written language that presumably favoured its choice as the legal language par excellence. For what characterizes best a legal writing but continuity and tradition?[85]

Law, it is generally agreed, is very much about obeisance to the past and control of the future. As an instrument of temporal and spatial generality, law shows an overriding concern for precise, consistent and traditional linguistic usage. Indeed in no other variety of language are the meaning of words and the history of linguistic usage of so much importance. We mentioned above that the distance between the sender and the receiver of a legal message is not measured in miles but in centuries. At Ugarit, for example, a century and a half had intervened between the oldest and the most recent extant royal deed, and yet the text of both records hardly presents any linguistic difference. Legal language is traditional by definition: what is written today should be understood by scribes or notaries in the future, in the same way as today notaries understand what their predecessors wrote centuries ago. Here lies the conservative character of legal language, a language that does not aim at linguistic originality or creativity but on the contrary, at the prestige of tradition. It is on the other hand this obeisance to the past that makes the words of law authoritative for the present and for future generations. "There is a certain legal language, Quintus," explained Cicero in *De legibus* with his usual sarcastic tone, "not so antiquated as that of our ancient Twelve Tables and Sacred Laws, and yet, to give greater authority, a little more archaic than the language of the present day."[86] The use

---

[85] I prefer this explanation to the suggestion recently made by Lackenbacher according to which the choice of Akkadian as legal language may be due "au fait que le pouvoir hittite devait avoir la possibilité d'exercer un certain contrôle" (*Textes akkadiens d'Ugarit*, p. 214). I can hardly imagine the Hittite emperor or chancery regularly inspecting or checking his vassal's home landed transactions. I would rather agree with Boyer when he wrote that "le protectorat exercé par l'empire hittite ne semble pas avoir porté d'atteinte sérieuse à la souveraineté interne du roi d'Ugarit. Celui-ci exerce sur ses sujets et sur le territoire de son royaume une autorité sans partage qui s'étend à tous les domaines de l'administration" ("Royauté et droit public dans les textes d'Ugarit," in *Mélanges d'histoire du droit oriental,* vol. 2 [Paris. 1965], p. 163).

[86] II.18. The translation is by Clinton W. Keyes in the Loeb Classical Library volume.

of archaic expressions and constructions is still today a distinctive feature of legal language. Old and Middle English words no longer in general usage and Latin terms and phrases are rather commonly found in current English legal writing, bestowing on it, as Cicero would put it, authoritative status. It is a traditional belief that the older the words of the law (and the law itself), the higher their quality. Given then the normal dependence of the written legal language on traditional, prestigious models it seems reasonable to argue, back to our subject, that if Akkadian was the legal language in thirteenth-century Ugarit it is because it had been used centuries earlier there to write legal documents in a very similar fashion.

The words and phrases produced by the scribes of Late Bronze Age Ugarit must therefore very likely reflect a Levantine or Syrian usage that goes back at least to some point in the Middle Bronze Age period. What this implies, I hasten to add, is that although the language chosen and used to write legal documents was ultimately imported from Mesopotamia (together with the writing system and the characteristic bureaucratic techniques), the scribes of Ugarit did not follow the Mesopotamian pattern and style of deeds.[87] As stated by Oppenheim, the bureaucratic techniques were accepted in all those administrative centers outside Babylonia proper, but they were all together modified and adapted for the use of each and every palace.[88] The Akkadian language too, as we have seen, differed in terms of orthography and grammar from one school centre to another, and especially between the peripheral traditions and the core. Obeisance to the past, or in other words custom, is one of the salient features of both the law and the words of the law. Every area or sphere in the Near East had its own, particular past and thus remained faithful to its own legal tradition and custom through time. It is worth noting, for example, that Sumerian, rather than Akkadian, was the legal language adopted and used by Mesopotamian scribes proper early in the second millennium although Sumerian was no longer the vernacular, simply because in the land of Babylonia (or Sumer and Akkad) this language enjoyed then the advantage of centuries-old stability and usage. In the Levant and Syria, as we have said, the prestigious, traditional written language was Akkadian (for a discussion, see chapter 7 section 2 below).

[87] This is what Arnaud meant when he wrote about the Mesopotamian Ḫarra-ḫubullu Tablets I and II that "les formules juridiques ci-dessous n'appartiennent pas au droit ougaritique, qui les ignore" (in "Les textes cuneiformes suméro-accadiens des campagnes 1979-1980," p. 199; for a discussion see chapter 3).

[88] *Ancient Mesopotamia*, p. 277.

In defining and listing the texts of our corpus (in chapter 1), we mentioned, however, the existence of a few exceptions to this rule. RS 15.111 (KTU 3.2), RS 15.125 (KTU 2.19), RS 16.191+ (KTU 3.4), and RS 16.382 (KTU 3.5) are royal deeds drawn up in Ugaritic (to which perhaps RS 15.117 [KTU 7.63] should be added). In addition, two documents recording a royal transaction recently found in the house of Urtēnu (RS 94.2168 and RS 94.2965) are also written in the Ugaritic language. The latter two examples, however, bear no seal impression and do not even present the usually reserved space for it on the tablet. The same holds true for the two "private" legal documents RS 19.66 (KTU 3.8) and RS [Varia 14] (KTU 3.9) also written in Ugaritic.[89] Given the find-spot and the atypical features of these texts (it should be remembered that the seal impression is not a sufficient but indeed a necessary condition for distinguishing a legal document) we already proposed to regard them as examples of memoranda or private copies of non-preserved (or not yet found) original deeds perhaps written in Akkadian and deposited in their corresponding archive. As for the undoubtedly original Ugaritic royal deeds, we argued above that since scribes or notaries were admittedly biliterate around 1250 BC, why would they not have written, if only exceptionally, legal documents in their own tongue? It is possible that they felt occasionally tempted to use their mother tongue and the less complex alphabetic script to draw royal deeds. Perhaps they once even addressed their king a request similar to the one formulated centuries later (in a similar biliterate context) by a certain Sin-iddina of Ur to his lord Sargon of Assyria. "If it is acceptable to the king," he proposed, "let me write and send my messages to the king in Aramaic." The reply of the king of Ugarit, say of ᶜAmmiṯtamru II, would in all likelihood have been as fast and firm as the one issued by Sargon. "Why would you not write and send me messages in Akkadian? To be sure, the message you write must be drawn up in this very manner!"[90] That was indeed the customary, conventional language of Assyrian official writings (for no other reason was Daniel obliged more than one century after Sargon's reply to spend three years of scribal training at the court of Nebuchadnezzar). And that was too the conventional language of deeds in Ugarit.

Back to the language of our texts, we mentioned above that the rigid and stereotyped formulas, the stylistic tradition, and the conventions of layout of the documents were learned and transmitted from one genera-

---

[89] For a full survey and discussion of the Ugaritic legal texts, see my contribution "The Legal Texts from Ugarit," pp. 411-420.

[90] Now published as SAA 17 2. See the comments of Manfried Dietrich in the opening page of the volume (p. XV).

tion to the next in a well-established fashion. It is this pedagogical specialization that a notary had to accomplish. We also said in chapter 3 above that the difficulty to master the rigid formal language of legal documents was a relative one. Scribes had to learn what must have been obscure, archaic and technical words and expressions, but the practiced repertoire and pattern of phrases and formulas was rather limited and indeed stereotyped. The code, in sum, was made of a restricted number of stock phrases that did not vary through at least one century and a half, and of which many can presumably be traced back to a much older usage. To the readers familiar with some knowledge of legal writing these general features will be readily recognized. Moreover, followers of legal theorist Herbert L.A. Hart's views on legal language will find in this ancient cuneiform province of law fairly suitable evidence.[91] Indeed, one can hardly disagree with the argument that the wording of the royal deeds of Ugarit had no direct relation to ordinary language, let alone to the language spoken. As we have seen, the Akkadian language not only was not the vernacular in Ugarit, but also it was probably not used as lingua franca at the royal court during the Late Bronze Age period. Akkadian was simply unfamiliar to almost every Ugaritian and chiefly served as a vehicle for written communication, so that the language was intelligible only to those who wrote the texts. We have also seen that the ability to produce notarial documents was an essential part of the training and education of a royal secretary, precisely because he was meant to become both the sender and receiver of such messages.

On the other hand, there can be little doubt that the Akkadian of the legal documents was different from ordinary Akkadian. I am not, or not only, referring to the fact that a native Mesopotamian would certainly notice the "foreign accent" of the texts, for example in the orthography, vocabulary or syntax. Even if "pronounced" in a proper Mesopotamian way, the wording of legal documents would have no direct relation to the language spoken by a Babylonian. Such texts, we have insistently argued, basically contain recurrent formulas. It is this specialized repertoire of phrases and clauses (together with other conventional formal aspects) that manifestly sets them apart from other kinds of scribal products. I would not, however, go so far as to suggest that apparently ordinary Akkadian words such as the indefinite personal pronoun *mamman* or the verb *leqû* take on a special legal meaning when used, say, in the warranty clause against eviction (see chapter 6). The distinctiveness of legal language lies rather in the conventional, pre-established, and often specialized, usage of words and word order seeking stability and conti-

---

[91] See "Definition and Theory of Jurisprudence," 70 Law Q. Rev. 37 (1954), reprinted in Hart, *Essays in Jurisprudence and Philosophy* (Oxford, 1983), pp. 21-48.

nuity and therefore offering resistance to linguistic (but also structural) innovation and change. By sticking to frozen and stereotyped formulas and lexicon, the texts indeed became effective and functional. In other words, legal language is one of various languages for special purposes, a technical language or "technolect," generally viewed as an "artificial" linguistic variety in the sense referred to above that it is not related to the "natural" spoken language.

This last remark raises then a fundamental question about the nature of the so-called Akkadian of Ugarit. For when we look at the body of texts that constitutes the basis for the study of the grammar of the Akkadian written by scribes of Ugarit, we cannot fail to realize that most of the language material comes from the legal corpus.[92] This is especially true in the field of syntax. Literary texts constitute "a faithful copy of the Akkadian texts that served as vorlage"[93] and are not therefore relevant for this picture. On the other hand, the laconic language of so-called economic texts presents by its very nature very little syntax and the extant letters written by Ugarit scribes are indeed very scanty, so that, as stated by van Soldt, the evidence that can be extracted all together from them is rather limited.[94] Especially significant with this regard is the picture offered by the examination of the tenses in Ugarit Akkadian. As van Soldt put it himself, since the legal texts form the large majority within the group of texts composed by Ugarit scribes, the "material under discussion is rather one-sided,"[95] the one side being what we have called the specialized language of the deeds. Indeed, one can say that as a result of this state of affairs, much of the grammar of the Akkadian of Ugarit thoroughly depicted by Huehnergard and van Soldt derives from the grammar of a *written language for legal purposes*. I hasten to say that this conclusion agrees well with the picture we have drawn above of the Akkadian language in Ugarit. For Akkadian in Ugarit, we said, is a language that can only be defined by reference to a particular occupation or activity, namely the scribal art, among the practitioners viz. notaries or secretaries of which it was current.

Although it is in the vocabulary that the technical language is most readily detectable, other features in the fields of morphology or syntax, or orthography are also characteristic. No doubt one of the main features of legal language is its conservative character. Archaic spellings and forms can thus be expected to appear in these texts.[96] Before closing the

---

[92] See for example the list in Huehnergard, *The Akkadian of Ugarit*, p. 14.

[93] *SAU*, p. 475. See also the remarks of Huehnergard, *The Akkadian of Ugarit*, p. 9.

[94] *SAU*, p. 475.

[95] Ibid., p. 494.

[96] Van Soldt, for example, suggested to take spellings of forms of the verb *nadānu*

chapter I should like to briefly look at one noteworthy example.

As we shall see in more detail in the forthcoming chapters, legal texts from Ugarit begin conventionally and invariably with the phrase *ištu ūmi annîm* "from today." What interests us here is not the number of attestations, the legal meaning, or the legal tradition of this opening formula, but the fact that (word-final) mimation is not a regular feature of the Akkadian of Ugarit or, for that matter, any other variety of Akkadian of the Late Bronze Age period. Nevertheless, the final *–m* of the demonstrative adjective is generally expressly spelled (by means of the sign IM for /im/). The fact that mimation is never used for the noun qualified (genitive *ūmi*) points to the stereotyped formulaic nature of the phrase, allowing us to consider the inconsistent case of mimation as an archaism or conservative spelling.[97] This interpretation becomes clearer in the light of a number of texts in which the traditional spelling and what we might call the "ordinary" one of the same word appear side by side. In RS 15.136, for example,[98] the same demonstrative adjective *annû* appears without mimation throughout the text (lines 9, 14, and 19) except precisely in the introductory standard formula *ištu ūmi annîm*. As significant are the examples in which the ordinary Late Bronze Age, i.e. Middle Babylonian/Assyrian form *ultu* of the preposition *ištu* is used in the text although the traditional spelling is kept for the introductory phrase (see RS 16.133:12, RS 16.158:5, and RS 16.263:22, 23).[99] These archaic forms are especially interesting because by following the (cultural) connecting threads in the documentary evidence we can obtain more insight into the stream of legal tradition that flowed through Ugarit in the fourteenth century. But this is another story that will be addressed in chapter 7 below.

---

with the sign DIN (e.g., *id-din-nu* for *iddinū* in RS 15.Z:18) as archaisms (see *SAU*, p. 395 n. 34); on the scribal preference of CVC signs over a CV-VC sequence, see Huehnergard, *The Akkadian of Ugarit*, p. 30.

[97] Cf. also the parallel case of *urram šēram* (for this adverbial phrase see also chapters 6 and 7). See Arnaud, "Ras Shamra. La culture suméro-accadienne" (sub C. "La morphologie de l'accadien d'Ugarit"), Supplément au Dictionnaire de la Bible 9 (1979):1352; Huehnergard, *The Akkadian of Ugarit*, pp. 99-100; van Soldt, *SAU*, p. 411.

[98] As noted by Huehnergard, *The Akkadian of Ugarit*, p. 99 n. 3.

[99] See Huehnergard, *The Akkadian of Ugarit*, p. 110, and van Soldt, *SAU*, p. 385 n. 7.

CHAPTER 5

THE SCHEME OF THE DEEDS

It is the opinion of many a scholar devoted to documentary research that the true task of his or her discipline, also called diplomatics, is the examination of the formal aspect, rather than the interpretation of the legal content.[1] Although I believe that both tasks are difficult to divide, this and the following chapters will primarily, though not exclusively, focus on the former given the scope of the book.[2] We have insisted in the previous chapter that formalism is a salient feature of legal writing. This formalism, however, does not only affect the linguistic usage, namely the choice of a centuries-old stable, prestigious language (Akkadian), and the use of a technical, specialized style, standard phrases, and an archaic lexicon, as outlined above. The layout and the structural arrangement of the document are also endowed with a definite form that contributed to insure its validity and regularity. No doubt scribes at Ugarit had to learn beside the complex Mesopotamian writing system and the Akkadian language (and whatever knowledge of Sumerian was considered necessary) the "strict rules as to the shape and physical preparation of the tablets and the arrangement of the writing."[3]

We have seen that the royal deeds of Ugarit present a characteristic physical appearance. As already stated in the introduction to the book, their formal aspect (shape, sealing, arrangement of the inscription) is so distinctive that even an illiterate Ugaritian from the 14th to the early 12th centuries BC, and also a modern scholar with little or no knowledge of cuneiform, would be able to identify such a document if confronted with a varied group of cuneiform tablets (see our prototype in chapter 1 above). On the other hand, any Assyriologist who has read through a number of these tablets would also readily recognize a royal deed of Ugarit by the characteristic standard Akkadian formulas and terminology used.

---

[1] As stated, for example, by Wilhelm Hoenebach, author of the study *Spanisch-Islamische Urkunden aus der Zeit der Nasriden und Moriscos* (Berkeley, 1965).

[2] I have decided to divide such a dense and important subject into three chapters mainly for the sake of convenience of the reader and of the correlation of the chapters of this book.

[3] Oppenheim, *Ancient Mesopotamia*, p. 239.

It is to the conventional physiognomy and scheme of the deeds that we shall first turn to analyze, accordingly including a detailed study of the royal or dynastic seal that is regularly impressed on the tablets as well as the corresponding notarial sealing practice. The examination of the documentary formulary and lexicon together with some considerations on scribal habits and the important legal tradition of Ugarit will be dealt with in the next chapters.

The size of a clay tablet fashioned by a royal notary at the palace audience hall of Ugarit or at his private scriptorium obviously depended on the body of the dictated or otherwise suggested content of the text. Apart from a few exceptions (such as the extraordinary *Sammeltafel* RS 15.109+), royal deeds are inscribed on relatively small, hand-size tablets; our prototype, it will be remembered, measures 68 x 55 x 25 mm. Every text is written on a single tablet, and clay envelopes were not used at Ugarit. Although the number of inscribed lines varies from deed to deed (note e.g. the nine-line text of RS 15.91 contrasting with RS 16.138 containing 39 lines), the average can be estimated to be approximately 21. Scribes at Ugarit wrote the lines of the text parallel to the shorter side of the tablet, so that a royal deed invariably has a vertical form, as opposed for example to the contemporary so-called "Syro-Hittite" shaped tablets.[4]

Once the tablet was carefully fashioned, the notary (or perhaps the king himself) rolled the cylinder seal of the hereditary kings of Ugarit over the smooth and plastic surface of the damp clay, namely over the top of the obverse, parallel to the shorter side; and then he would begin to inscribe the cuneiform text with his stylus, sometimes after drawing a ruling or two immediately below the seal impression. The seal impression forms therefore without exception the beginning of a royal deed. As regards the text, we already mentioned (in chapter 3) that the shape of the inscribed signs in royal deeds is remarkably neat and regular, the only objection to the careful art of notaries being the occasionally imperfect "mise en page."

What we turn to consider now is the scheme of the deeds. To the best of my knowledge, five schemes have been proposed so far. The first one to deal with the structure of legal texts was not surprisingly Nougayrol in *PRU* 3, p. 24. His scheme, however, was not restricted to the royal deeds

---

[4] At use at the neighbouring chanceries of Emar or Carchemish; see Arnaud, "Les textes d'Emar et la chronologie de la fin du Bronze récent," Syria 52 (1975):88 (with n. 3), where he coined the expression to designate those (Emar) tablets in which writing runs parallel to the longer side and the seal impression(s) appear on the reverse. For the Carchemish texts, see my summary in "The Legal Texts from Ugarit," p. 406.

but was meant to cover all kinds, namely his three types of legal documents from Ugarit ("actes devant témoins," "actes devant le roi," and "actes du roi"):

A, *"date"*;
B, *modalité définissant le type*;
C, *description de l'acte*;
D, *clauses secondaires*;
E, *authentification (mention des témoins ou du sceau "dynastique")*.

Nougayrol's scheme was then reproduced, or one should rather say "reinterpreted," by Kienast in his article "Rechtsurkunden in ugaritischer Sprache":[5]

1. *"Inkraftsetzungsvermerk"*
2. *Angabe der Publizitätsfrom*
3. *Geschäftsvermerk*
4. *Schlußklauseln*
5. *Zeugen*
6. *Siegelvermerk*
7. *Schreiber*

The same author had suggested in an earlier contribution the structure of the deeds of sale of Ugarit, which had been formerly dealt with by Haase. The latter's proposed scheme of sale documents, no doubt influenced by Nougayrol's original interpretation, is the following:[6]

1. *"Datum,"*
2. *Angaben über die Publizitätsform beim Abschluß des Geschäfts*,
3. *Angaben über Erwerb oder Veräußerung eines bezeichneten Objekts mit Preisangabe*,
4. a) *Perfizierungsklausel*,
   b) *Nichtanfechtungs- oder Verzichtsklausel*,
   c) *Verfallklausel*,
5. *Angaben über die Mitwirkung des Königs beim Geschäft*,
6. *Angaben über Lasten des Grundstücks*:
   a) *Lastenfreiheit*,
   b) *Befreiung des Erwerbers von Diensten*,
   c) *Erfüllung bestehender Dienstpflichten*,
7. a) *Zeugen*,
   b) *Siegelvermerk*,
   c) *Schreiber*.

---

[5] "Rechtsurkunden in ugaritischer Sprache," p. 433.

[6] "Anmerkungen zum ugaritischen Immobilienkauf," ZA 58 (1967):196.

Although Haase's suggested scheme seems rather complete at first sight, from a general point of view it is less satisfactory. For strictly speaking, it consists of an exhaustive repertoire of the clauses attested in sale transactions. That is to say that one should not expect to find a sale document from Ugarit containing all the indexed elements. As a matter of fact, no text can include them all; neither do the clauses of a text appear always in that same, strict order. The author himself seems to be well aware of this fact when he next describes the scheme of every particular listed deed of sale according to, and presented as a sequence of, the numbered clauses; it is indeed significant that no two documents show the same sequence of clauses.[7] Kienast was neither convinced; in his own, later treatment of the deeds, he qualified Haase's scheme as being "geringfügig abweichend[es]," and proposed accordingly a reductive or less elaborate version of it that clearly anticipates his 1979-scheme of legal documents mentioned above. "Das Formular der echten Kaufurkunden —as he put it— besteht aus folgenden Elementen":[8]

1. *Inkraftsetzungsvermerk*
2. *Angabe über die Publizitätsform*
3. *Kauf- bzw. Verkaufsvermerk*
4. *Perfizierungsvermerk*
5. *Garantieklausel*
6. *Verzichtklausel*
7. *Lehnsklauseln*
8. *Zeugen*
9. *Siegelvermerk*
10. *Schreiber*

The author immediately noted thereafter that not all elements are present in the sale documents, only the third (viz. the clause specifying the nature of the transaction) and either the eighth or ninth (i.e. Nougayrol's "authentification") being requisitely expressed. On the other hand, he wrote, "die Sammelurkunden und die Grundkaufbestätigungen können die gleichen Klauseln enthalten, die hier aber oft, entsprechend dem Charakter der Dokumente im Wortlaut leicht modifiziert sind." Despite the lack of complete uniformity the two schemes proposed for sale documents (by Kienast and Haase) differ little from each other, and roughly agree with the scheme proposed for deeds in general as designed by Nougayrol (and later by Kienast himself).

---

[7] Only RS 16.261 and RS 16.154 coincide in full; the difference, however, as shown in his list (on pp. 196-197), is that the latter text describes two sale transactions (this question will be discussed below).

[8] In "Kauf. E. In Alalaḫ und Ugarit," RlA 5, p. 533.

The last and most recent consideration of the scheme of the legal documents of Ugarit (suggested by myself)[9] differs from the former ones in a more substantial manner. The reason lies in a different understanding of the notion of "scheme." Two main, preliminary aspects need to be considered. To begin with, it is convenient and, I believe, also necessary to distinguish between a document and a transaction. And secondly, a further distinction should be made between the elements of the structure of a legal document and the formulas or standard phrases used in the text. Concerning the former, not otiose, aspect, we have referred to in earlier chapters (and it can be seen by a glance at our catalogue of royal deeds) that some tablets are inscribed with more than one transaction (I may simply recall once again the extraordinary tablet RS 15.109+).[10] In the light of such examples, that are far from exceptional, the drawback of the schemes proposed by these scholars makes itself apparent. RS 16.154, for instance, describing two sale transactions had to be split in two in Haase's catalogue.[11] Not less significant is the fact that the various transactions inscribed in one same tablet may belong to different legal categories. RS 16.142, for example, records a royal grant beside the grantee's promotion by the king to a higher status. None of the reviewed schemes, we should note, would properly represent this, and other documents. In this regard, I can hardly take it as a coincidence that Nougayrol introduced immediately after the discussion of the scheme his so-called "actes multiples, homogènes ou hétérogènes."[12] But the problem still remains. Let us take the example we offered beside the prototype of a royal deed in chapter 1. RS 16.250 records a grant made by king Niqmepa^{c} to a certain ^{c}Abdu; this transaction is followed by ^{c}Abdu's transfer of the granted property to one of his sons; the text then goes on to describe a provision concerning the status of one his wives, namely the mother of the beneficiary son, and her own rights to the property. Whatever "slight modifications" are made and whatever notions are introduced (*Sammelurkunden*, *actes multiples*, etc.), an important, relevant part of the legal text is lost in the schemes discussed. It should be noted in this regard that provisions such as the ones contained in RS 16.250 are present in other documents.

---

[9] In "The Legal Texts from Ugarit," p. 397.

[10] Here lies one of the essential problems of modern classifications of the royal deeds of Ugarit. As mentioned in the introduction to the book, the attempts by Miller and Libolt to classify and analyze royal grants, deeds of adoption, or deeds of sale have proven to be on this very account less adequate than expected and often misleading.

[11] See "Anmerkungen zum ugaritischen Immobilienkauf," p. 197.

[12] *PRU* 3, p. 25.

The second distinction we pointed out is, I believe, also a fundamental one. Although a legal phrase or formula typically belongs to the text, it need not correspond or constitute an isolated part of the scheme of the document. This remark applies to the first two elements of the scheme proposed by Nougayrol, almost uncritically adopted by later studies. Let us review these opinions in more detail (the phrases and formulas as such will be dealt with in the next chapter).

What Nougayrol designated as "date" corresponds to the standard introductory phrase of the legal texts of Ugarit, namely *ištu ūmi annîm* "from today," already mentioned in the previous chapter. The author accordingly translated it "à dater d'aujourd'hui" and rightly noted that it is often completed later in the (conveyance) clause with the phrase "forever."[13] "Les greffiers d'Ugarit —he then explained— ne se soucient pas de dater leurs tablettes d'une façon plus précise : il leur suffit de marquer que l'acte est intervenu à un certain moment, et qu'il vaut —sauf stipulation contraire— pour l''éternité'."[14] Thureau-Dangin had been more succinct and drastic in his publication of the first legal documents unearthed at Ras Shamra. "A la différence des contrats babyloniens ou assyriens —he wrote—, ceux-ci ne sont pas datés."[15] True, Nougayrol defined the formula "from today" as a date, presumably having in mind that this element is almost regularly and traditionally taken as an essential feature of a legal text. But he had been careful enough to write the word with quotation marks, manifestly denoting the special character he attached to it. It was Guy Kestemont who finally discerned the ambiguity, suggesting a new, specific legal meaning to the introductory phrase. In his study of the formal aspect of the Late Bronze Age Near Eastern diplomatic documents (viz. treaties and inter-state agreements) published in 1974, he defined it as "la formule d'entrée en vigueur."[16] In a footnote he then explained that this kind of formula constitutes "l'indication chronologique du moment où la convention sort ses effets; elle diffère de la date —he continued— qui est l'indication chronologique du moment

---

[13] Nougayrol's original translation can still be found in the most recent literature; so, for example, Lackenbacher in her *Textes akkadiens d'Ugarit*, or Josef Tropper and Juan-Pablo Vita in "Texte aus Ugarit" in *Texte zum Rechts- und Wirtschaftsleben* (TUAT NF 1), ed. B. Janowski and G. Wilhelm (Gütersloh, 2004), p. 111 ("[datiert] vom heutigen Tag").

[14] *PRU* 3, p. 24.

[15] "Trois contrats de Ras-Shamra," p. 245. There he noted that the Ugarit tradition was not the only exception to the Mesopotamian rule; the legal texts from Nuzi, for example, are neither dated.

[16] *Diplomatique et droit international en Asie occidentale (1600-1200 av. J.C.)* (Louvain-la-neuve, 1974), p. 172.

où l'instrument est rédigé."[17] In other words, the formula "from today," often completed especially in conveyance texts with "forever," would not concern the instrument itself but the legal relationship established therein, thus constituting an entry-into-effect formula rather than a date. It seems that Kienast independently reached the same interpretation. The introductory phrase, he wrote, "enthält aber keinerlei absolute Zeitbestimmungen nach Jahr, Monat und Tag, sondern korrespondiert mit der besonders im Perfizierungsvermerk so häufigen Phrase *adi dārīti* 'für immer';" "es handelt es sich also —he concluded— weniger um ein Datum als um einen Inkraftsetzungsvemerk, der als typisches Merkmal ugaritischer Rechtsurkunden gelten darf."[18] Nevertheless, possibly due to the important and particular character of the phrase and also influenced by Nougayrol's authoritative study, the German scholar kept the formula (now identified as "Inkraftsetzungsvermerk") in quotation marks heading his own general scheme.

The question we want to raise, however, is whether an adverbial phrase that grammatically belongs to and introduces the clause specifying the nature of the transaction, completed in turn (as explicitly pointed out by Nougayrol, Kestemont and Kienast) by another adverbial phrase, can legitimately stand as a structural part of the document. The same doubts can be raised regarding the second element of the schemes discussed above. The so-called "modalité définissant le type" or "Angabe über die Publizitätsform" as a rule follows the phrase "from today," and consists too of a simple introductory adverbial phrase, namely in translation "before king so-and-so" or "before witnesses." Syntactically speaking, one should note that the formula also belongs to the first sentence of the text that specifies the nature of the transaction. Of course I agree with Kienast that the first phrase "from today" serves *us* as an indicator that we are probably dealing with a legal text (of Ugarit); and I likewise agree with Nougayrol that the second phrase helps *us* in turn define the type of deed.[19] But the fact is that they are single elements, viz. complements, of

[17] Ibid., n. 76.

[18] "Kauf," p. 533. This interpretation has been followed since; see e.g. Liverani, "Ras Shamra. Histoire," col. 1338, Miller, *Studies in the Juridical Texts*, p. 356, Libolt's relevant English translation "as of today" (*Royal Land Grants*, p. 30), Vita, "Datation et genres littéraires à Ougarit," in *Proche-Orient ancien : temps vécu, temps pensé*, ed. F. Briquel-Chatonnet and H. Lozachmeur (Paris, 1998), p. 40 (note however his translation with Tropper quoted in footnote 13 above), or Malbran-Labat, "Langues et écritures à Ougarit," p. 80 (where the formula, however, appears misquoted as *ina ištu ūmi annîm*).

[19] Nougayrol wrote immediately before proposing his scheme of legal documents (*PRU* 3, p. 24) that royal deeds can be easily identified because they all bear: "1° Sauf en de très rares occasions: l'empreinte du *sceau 'dynastique'*; 2° Aussitôt après

the textual, legal discourse, rather than essential, independent aspects of the scheme itself. Eloquent in this regard is the fact that the second phrase is consistently absent from the major group of "actes du roi" and occasionally omitted in the other types of documents. The reason for the absence of this formula in the former deeds is of a practical, notarial nature. The king's direct participation in the transaction, his name appearing as main (very frequently donor) party immediately after "from today," obviously rendered otiose the reference "before RN."

My final discrepancy, rather than objection, to my predecessors' proposed schemes concerns the so-called "final or secondary clauses" ("Schlußklauseln," "clauses secondaires"). It is customary, and no doubt legitimate, among Assyriologists to separate the so-called "Geschäftsvermerk" or "description de l'acte" from the "final clauses" in their proposed schemes of cuneiform legal documents.[20] Nevertheless, it is a basic assumption that provisions contained in, say, the warranty clause against eviction or the taxation clause do contribute to define the legal relationship(s) established in the document. In other words, it is not possible to regard "final clauses" as non-operative. In designing the scheme of the deeds, I would therefore choose not to isolate these sentences keeping them apart from the "Geschäftsvermerk." We may simply recall again the deed RS 16.250. Should the provision concerning the status of one the grantee's wives and her corresponding rights to the property recorded at the end of the document be kept aside from the description of the transaction (namely a royal grant later transferred to the grantee's son)? From a legal point of view, I believe the question should be answered negatively. And the same holds true for other, shorter deeds. The clause describing the transaction is obviously related to whatever expressly written provisions or rules are applicable to the transaction proper. This set of related sentences formed by operative words represents the discourse or textual unit we propose to recognize in our scheme as the operative part.

The scheme we suggest for the royal deeds is then the following:

1. Impression of the dynastic seal
2. Operative part
3. Statement specifying the owner of the seal, i.e. the king
4. Name of the scribe (sometimes as witness)

---

la 'date', la mention: *devant A (fils de B), roi d'Ugarit*; 3° En fin de texte, sauf exception, *aucun nom de témoin*, si ce n'est celui du scribe" (his own italics).

[20] See for example Postgate, *Fifty Neo-Assyrian Legal Documents* (Warminster, 1976), pp. 13ff., or Piotr Steinkeller, *Sale Documents of the Ur-III Period* (Freiburg, 1989), pp. 11ff.

Before discussing each section in more detail, there is one aspect that still deserves our attention. A glance at the tablets or at the beautiful copies of them made by Nougayrol shows that scribes did occasionally draw horizontal lines to divide paragraphs or sections within the document. It is tempting to see in these visual marks made on the soft clay potential indications of the way the notaries themselves, or at least some of them, understood the scheme of their documents (no doubt all of them had learned by heart the order and arrangement of a deed). Some rulings may of course be more relevant than others. The ruling drawn sometimes at the end of the text, for example, is of little help to gain an image of the ancient structural design of the deed. But the lines used to divide each of the different transactions put together in the *Sammelurkunde* RS 15.109+ or the one drawn to visually distinguish the two sale transactions recorded in RS 16.154, to put two of the examples discussed above, are naturally of more significance for us.[21] The same holds true of some examples of rulings that set apart individual clauses such as certain provisions in adoption contracts (e.g. RS 15.92 or RS 16.200) or wills (e.g. RS 15.120). It may be interesting to note one case (RS 18.285) of a ruling incorrectly drawn by the scribe presumably meant to separate the grant-clause from the taxation-clause.[22]

Especially from the reign of ᶜAmmiṯtamru II on it is possible to discern a certain notarial habit to divide the deed into more definite, perhaps standard, sections. The most common ruling (occasionally double) mentioned already in previous chapters and attested for all reigns, is the one that separates the seal impression from the beginning of the inscribed text of the deed. Also in accordance with our own proposed scheme, scribes would often distinguish the name of the scribe and/or the state-

[21] Other examples of different transactions recorded in the same tablet divided by a ruling are RS 15.119, RS 15.139, RS 16.239, RS 16.263 or RS 18.21. Note that after the ruling the next transaction and paragraph is usually introduced by the adverb *šanītam* "moreover."

[22] RS 18.285 is the only royal deed known to us written by Iliramu. Although not reproduced in the handcopy of Nougayrol, Iliramu drew a horizontal line on the lower edge of the tablet between lines 10 and 11 (collated), that means splitting up the clause that records the service to be fulfilled by the grantee. One should further note that the scribe drew up again this clause written in lines 9-11 in the following lines 12-14, an unusual, indeed exceptional notarial practice. Did he try to mend the lapse he had made by re-writing the clause once more in an appropriate way, wishing to avoid any possible ambiguity? Note that Lackenbacher (*Textes akkadiens d'Ugarit*, p. 235 n. 800) suggests in turn that the repetition either stipulated that the service in question was to be fulfilled by different people or was meant to stress the provision; the French author, however, does not mention (perhaps did not notice) the important ruling drawn by the scribe.

ment specifying the owner of the seal from the rest of the text, what we have called the operative part. Indeed, a considerable number of deeds would be divided, viz. structured in the following way (the hyphen representing a ruling): seal impression - operative part - name of the scribe or/and seal identification (e.g. RS 16.204, RS 16.241+, RS 16.256, and RS 16.282). More in accordance with other proposed schemes (discussed above) is the well-attested practice of drawing a ruling after the king's name at the beginning of the text, that is, either in his role as party to the transaction or presiding over it (what was termed by Nougayrol "modalité définissant le type").[23] Some examples show a more elaborate scheme. The deed RS 15.140, for example, presents six sections or paragraphs and its scheme would roughly agree with that suggested by Nougayrol himself and more particularly the one offered by Kienast for sale documents: "From today, RN (followed by patronymic and title)" – grant clause – guarantee clause – taxation clause – seal identification – name of the scribe. It is interesting to remark that the notary who drew up the deed, Iltaḫmu, did not always, or usually, divide his texts into such sections.[24] Similar divisions of the text can be found in RS 15.155 from the time of ᶜAmmiṯtamru II, RS 16.186 from the time of Ibirānu, and RS 18.21 from the time of Niqmaddu III.

Let us now turn to the sections of our proposed scheme and discuss them in more detail.

1. Impression of the dynastic seal

The impression of a seal or other personal mark on a clay tablet is a chief characteristic of, since it is the main means of authenticating, cuneiform legal documents. At Ugarit only seal impressions are attested; that is to say that the practice of making marks on the soft clay tablet with one's finger-nail or the hem of one's garment (as valid and symbolic a means to authenticate a deed) common at other places and periods in the ancient Near East was not used. On the other hand, as a rule only one seal (usually a cylinder seal) is impressed covering the upper part of the obverse, thus constituting the head of a document fashioned by a notary of Uga-

[23] E.g. RS 15.127, RS 15.139, RS 15.155, RS 16.178, RS 16.201, or RS 16.198[B]; see also the Ugaritic (copy?) RS 94.2168.

[24] Note, for example, that the long royal deed RS 16.353 presents only one ruling, the one used to mark the end of the text. Only part of the text from the reverse is preserved on the tablet RS 19.128; here Iltaḫmu did draw a ruling before writing the name of the scribe and the statement specifying the owner of the seal. Compare also the (non-royal) deeds RS 17.88, RS 17.356 or RS 17.358.

rit.[25] We mentioned at the beginning of the study that royal deeds are readily recognized because of the seal impression they bear. "La caractéristique la plus frappante des 'actes royaux' —remarked Nougayrol in his introduction to the Akkadian texts published in *PRU* 3— c'est qu'ils portent tous *la même empreinte* au sommet du *recto*, sous n'importe quel règne."[26] It will be remembered that this feature indeed constituted the main criterion to identify the documents of our corpus.

Nougayrol's statement should, however, be slightly modified. For the impression preserved at the head of royal deeds does not correspond to one and the same "dynastic" cylinder seal. The French Assyriologist himself pointed out one page later that there existed an official replica of the seal, and that either the original or the duplicate was indistinctively used to sign the deeds from Niqmaddu II on.[27] The existence of an official copy of the seal of the hereditary kings of Ugarit already in the 14th century is fairly extraordinary. We do not know under what circumstances did a king of Ugarit (presumably one of Niqmaddu II's predecessors) order his best seal-cutter to duplicate the dynastic seal in almost exact replica and size. In view of the use of both seals, the replica was obviously not made to take over the official duties of the original. One should note, for example, that the latter was impressed on a royal deed of the time of Niqmaddu III and also on what seems to be the only extant example dated to the last king ᶜAmmurapiᵓ.[28] It is most likely, on the

---

[25] This very usage is found at Alalakh in the late Middle Bronze Age period (i.e. in Level IV tablets) and in Amurru in the Late Bronze Age period. Different practices are attested for example in the contemporary Hittite chancery: stamp seals had by then completely replaced the cylinder seal; Hittite tablets unearthed at Ras Shamra usually show a highly raised surface on the centre of the obverse where the deep impression of the circular stamp seal (such as the seal of the Hittite emperor, viz. the Tabarna seal) is to be found. Also different is the practice attested for the so-called "Syro-Hittite" tablets such as the ones from contemporary Carchemish; there the cylinder seal impression is usually found on the reverse closing the legal text.

[26] *PRU* 3, pp. XL-XLI (his own italics). The statement by Miller (*Studies in the Juridical Texts*, p. 20) according to which "most of these (viz. royal deeds) bear the dynastic seal or the royal private seal or both" is not correct. He was actually misled by Haase ("Zum Recht von Ugarit," RIDA 11 [1964]:13ff.) who mistook the statement specifying the owner of the seal in the text for the impression of the king's personal seal (see below under section 3).

[27] On the next page XLII.

[28] The distribution of the use of either version of the dynastic seal according to reign, as studied by Nougayrol (*PRU* 3, p. XLIII), has hardly changed after the discovery and publication of new material. My own computation is the following: of the deeds presided over by Niqmaddu II preserving the seal impression, 21 were sealed with the original and 10 with the replica; for those dated to the short reign of

other hand, that both seals were in the custody of the king, who either personally rolled them or had them rolled perhaps in his presence and necessarily with his consent. A possible explanation is of course the king's or notaries' growing realization of the risk of constantly using the same old seal (its old age will be examined below). What if it would suddenly and accidentally break? Nougayrol through his usually painstaking examination remarked that the original seal had indeed suffered from a little accident, the result of which was a slight scratch in the design (a scratch that interestingly the king's seal-cutter faithfully reproduced in the replica).[29] Perhaps the royal decision to have the official replica made was taken precisely after that little accident happened.[30] In any case, the replica did not replace the original seal which kept being used by the successive kings of Ugarit down to the end of the kingdom, and rulers such as Niqmaddu II and ^{c}Ammiṯtamru II seem to have preferred sealing their deeds with the latter.[31]

Arḫalbu, three are sealed with the original and four with the replica; for Niqmepa^{c}, 12 deeds bear the original seal impression and eight the impression of the replica; as for the major group of deeds presided over ^{c}Ammiṯtamru II, 42 are sealed with the original and 13 with the duplicate; of the only two extant deeds of Niqmaddu III, one bears the original seal impression and the other the replica; and the only deed that can be assigned to the last king ^{c}Ammurapi$^{\supset}$ (RS 17.322) bears the original seal impression.

[29] See *PRU* 3, pp. XLII-XLIII.

[30] Schaeffer proposed another interpretation in *Ugaritica* 3, pp. 73-77. The replica he believed on archaeological grounds to be one to two centuries later than the original seal and accordingly dated it to the centuries he called of economic and social distress in ancient Western Asia, namely between 1750 and 1500 (see also below). The picture he suggested on p. 77 is the following: in those days of economic and social disorder the kings of Ugarit were bound to (provisionally) go into exile; the original seal became then for some time inaccessible to the kings of Ugarit; the dynasty being accordingly in need of their seal decided to have a replica made. The problem of Schaeffer's speculative reconstruction or guess, however interesting it may be, is that nothing in his account finds support in what is at present known of the ancient history of Syria and Ugarit in particular.

[31] See footnote 28 above. It may be interesting to note that the deeds drawn up by the royal notaries Karrānu, Munaḫḫimu, Nu^{c}merašpu, and Ya^{c}ḏirānu were all signed with the original dynastic seal. This circumstance may of course be coincidental (the number of deeds is for example relatively small) and thus bear little or no notarial significance. With this regard, the expert notary Šapšumalku is known to have written four deeds bearing the original seal impression and nine bearing the duplicate impression, and Ya^{c}didu in turn wrote at least four sealed with the former and one with the latter.

Most interesting for archival research is the discovery in the main find-spot of the remains of the archive of royal deeds, i.e. in the small passage between palace rooms 132 and 152, of a clay tablet (RS 16.393A) that exclusively presents on its obverse the impression of the two versions of the dynastic seal: the original above and the replica below.[32] It is reasonable to argue in view of the aspect of this non-inscribed tablet and its find-spot that RS 16.393A was a sort of "signature card," that is, a permanent file that permitted the royal notaries (and of course the rulers themselves) to compare the "signature" on the tablet with the seal impression present on any royal deed. As a clear means to discover potential fakes, it is possible that RS 16.393A was produced at the royal court of Niqmepa^{c} during the trial described in RS 16.249, providing definite evidence about the forgeries (lit. *ṭuppātu sarrūtu* [*sic*]) that had been made, or perhaps it was made as a result of and therefore after the incident. As already mentioned above, the falsification and subsequent unlawful use of the dynastic seal was qualified as a "great crime" (*ḫiṭṭu rabû*) and accordingly punished by the ruler. Because no document from the archive of royal deeds antedates Niqmaddu II, it seems reasonable to assume that the so-called "signature tablet" was made during this reign or later.

Neither the original nor the duplicate of the dynastic cylinder seal has come to light in the course of archaeological excavation work carried out at Ras Shamra. The number and quality of the impressions preserved on our deeds nevertheless provide us with a relatively good picture. Relative because we do not know the material of the two seals, neither can we ascertain whether they had removable metal caps, and their dimensions must necessarily be approximate. Of course we can assume that both versions of the dynastic seal were made of a relatively hard stone, perhaps haematite, and also that they bore metal, possibly gold caps.[33] We do know that the replica was slightly smaller than the original seal. The latter must have measured around 2.25 cm in height and 1.35 cm in diameter; and the replica must have been some 2.1 cm in height. But it is obviously the cylinder seal design carved in intaglio that we can comment in more detail.

---

[32] See the photograph in *PRU* 3, Pl. XVII, and in *Ugaritica* 3, fig. 99 (enlarged). For the drawing of both impressions, see *PRU* 3, pl. XI fig. 14, and *Ugaritica* 3, p. 73 fig. 96.

[33] As stated by Dominique Collon in her seminal handbook *First Impressions. Cylinder Seals in the Ancient Near East* (London, 1993), p. 110, in Syria at this time and earlier "caps were relatively frequent, especially for royal seals, judging from the evidence of the Alalakh impressions;" and she further writes that "the evidence from tombs would indicate that in the second half of the 2nd millennium BC seals frequently had gold caps."

Nougayrol provided an excellent description and study.[34] The design shows the well known presentation scene or, in more recent terminology, audience scene with three figures, namely the deified king, the intermediary goddess, and the worshipper (the owner of the seal).[35] In the audience scene, such as this one, the goddess stands behind the worshipper who directly faces then (to the right) the seated deified king. The design, as stated by Nougayrol, is fairly uncomplicated, free of additional ornamental features, pointing as we shall see to its early date.[36] The goddess wearing a flounced garment stands with both hands raised; the beardless worshipper before her is robed and bare headed with his hands clasped standing before the deified king. As for the latter, bearded figure, he is shown with a brimmed cap seating on a throne that rests on a dais holding a conical cup in his right hand. As is typical of presentation scenes, an astral symbol appears over the outstretched hand, that is, between the seated deified king and the worshipper; the astral symbol depicted here is the so-called star-disc-crescent. Behind the seated deified king and the intermediary goddess a three line inscription carved in archaic cuneiform script identifies the owner of the seal, namely by name, patronymic, and title. The inscription written from top to bottom and from right to left on the impression reads: ^{P}*ia-qa-rum* / dumu *ni-iq-ma*$^{!}$*-du* / lugal ^{uru}*ú-ga-ri/-it*, "Yaqaru(m), son of Niqmaddu, king of Ugarit."[37] The question immediately to be raised is of course, when did Yaqaru(m), the owner of the seal, rule the city-state of Ugarit? Two different answers have been proposed, one by Nougayrol, that has been commonly followed, and another, more recent one by Arnaud. Let us briefly discuss them.

It is well known that the shape, size, type of material and design of a cylinder seal vary from period to period and from one area to another; this means that on iconographic grounds it is normally possible to place a seal in its historical context. Nougayrol had already pointed out that the presentation scene and more particularly the "hommage au roi déifié" as a glyptic design was developed in Babylonia during the Third Dynasty

---

[34] In *PRU* 3, pp. XLI-XLIII.

[35] Two recent PhD dissertations have thoroughly dealt with this cylinder seal design, namely on tablets of the Third Dynasty of Ur: Rudi H. Mayr, *The Seal Impressions of Ur III Umma* (Rijksuniversiteit te Leiden, 1997), and Atsuko Hattori, *Texts and Impressions: A Holistic Approach to Ur III Cuneiform Tablets from the University of Pennsylvania Expedition to Nippur* (University of Pennsylvania, 2002).

[36] The impression of the replica can be seen in the drawing of RS 16.250 we made at the end of chapter 1.

[37] For the reading of the inscription, which slightly but significantly differs from that offered by Nougayrol, see the remarks below.

of Ur, when rulers were deified and received worship in their lifetime as well as after death; and he also noted that this design became a typical motif in the cylinder seals of the so-called Isin/Larsa period in the next century. The Isin/Larsa presentation, however, did not survive into the 18th century BC, and "was gradually replaced by scenes in which only standing figures were depicted."[38] On the basis of the iconography but also the archaic ductus of the inscription, Nougayrol eventually concluded that "c'est à l'époque Isin-Larsa: soit au XIXe ou XVIIIe siècle avant J.-C. qu'il faut attributer le cylindre 'dynastique' d'Ugarit." He accordingly suggested that Yaqarum and his father Niqmaddu were the founders of the dynasty of Ugarit, belonging to the line of Amorite kings who took power of most lands of Syria and Mesopotamia after 2000 BC.[39]

Arnaud in turn has recently challenged Nougayrol's interpretation dating the dynastic seal to the 15th century.[40] This new date is neither based on the design of the seal nor on the cuneiform signs of its inscription, but on newly excavated and partly unpublished documents from Ras Shamra. "Yaqaru —he has written—, fils de Niqmaddu, cela est sûr, se place au milieu du XVe siècle." In reviewing his predecessor's interpretation, Arnaud rightly argues that the assignment of the seal to the beginning of the second millennium is chiefly based on the presentation-scene design. This, however, is in his opinion not possible. In support of this drastic, negative answer he mentions a similar glyptic design, namely two standing figures almost identical to the ones of the dynastic seal, impressed on two deeds and a label recently unearthed at Ugarit, all of them unpublished; the cylinder seal, he notes, is identified in one of the texts as belonging to a certain Uriteššub who apparently lived at Ugarit by the end of the 13th century. Both the dynastic and Uriteššub's seals, argues Arnaud, were made after the same prototype that in his opinion was fairly fashionable in Late Bronze Age Ugarit.[41] As for the inscription, Arnaud has improved Nougayrol's reading (the sign MÁ! in the

---

[38] Collon, *First Impressions*, p. 45.

[39] In *PRU* 3, pp. XLI-XLII. As stated by van Soldt, the name Yaqaru appearing in RS 16.145 and RS 17.53 "was obviously copied from the seal" (*SAU*, p. 14 n. 130); for RS 16.145 see the discussion in chapter 1 above.

[40] In "Prolégomènes à la redaction d'une histoire d'Ougarit I. Ougarit avant Suppiluliuma I," SMEA 39 (1997):158-161.

[41] See "Ougarit avant Suppiluliuma I," p. 158, where he quotes (in note 40) a fragmentary seal impression on a piece of a jar (RS 33.26) whose design he considers to parallel too the one of the dynastic seal (published by Elisabeth and Jacques Lagarce in Henri de Contenson et al., "La XXXIIIe campagne de fouilles à Ras Shamra en 1972. Rapport préliminaire," Syria 50 [1973]:308 fig. 13).

second line should rather be read MA[!]) and has interestingly related the archaic shape of the cuneiform signs with the school series called "Paleographic Sa" which was taught at Ugarit to train apprentice scribes in the cuneiform ductus of old days (see chapter 3 above).

The fifteenth-century date of the seal proposed by Arnaud presents, however, some problems. We mentioned above that the design of a cylinder seal varies from period to period and from one area to another. We know that Near Eastern kings and emperors (and more common individuals) during the 15th century clearly used and favoured other styles, and the Syrian region to which Ugarit belonged had one of its own.[42] The classic Syrian style of Middle and Late Bronze Age seals has manifestly very little in common with the design of the royal seal of Yaqaru(m).[43] On the other hand, and more importantly, should a seal-cutter from fifteenth-century Ugarit have attempted to faithfully reproduce a nineteenth-century Babylonian design in a cylinder seal measuring c. 2.25 x 1.35 it is most likely that his hand would have betrayed his origin and school. As a matter of fact, the replica of the dynastic seal provides an excellent instance, for it certainly betrays a different, presumably later (though no doubt skilful) hand, as observed by Nougayrol. The "what's-different" game properly illustrated by two enlarged pictures of both impressions was magisterially played by the French Assyriologist.[44] What I wish to stress now, however, is not the list of differences brilliantly discovered between the original and the replica, but rather his eloquent, authoritative conclusion. "Enfin —he summed up— rien n'est plus différent que le 'style' des deux empreintes: l'un est purement 'babylonien' dans sa fermeté expressive et 'classique', l'autre est mou, baroque, 'hourritisant', en un mot."[45] Nougayrol left us with an

---

[42] See Collon, *First Impressions*, pp. 69ff. A glance at the examples of cylinder seals dug up from the different levels of Ras Shamra, especially the relevant Middle and Late Bronze Age levels (in Schaeffer-Forrer, *Corpus des cylindres-sceaux de Ras Shamra-Ugarit et d'Enkomi-Alasia*, I [Paris, 1983], and Pierre Amiet, *Corpus des cylindres de Ras Shamra-Ougarit II. Sceaux-cylindres en hematite et pierres diverses*, [Paris, 1992]), will suffice to realize the foreign and distant origin of the dynastic seal (see also below). A summarized view can be found in Amiet, "Les sceaux-cylindres de Ras Shamra au IIe millénaire," in *Le pays d'Ougarit autour de 1200 av. J.-C.*, pp. 239-244.

[43] With this regard, one should note that the faint seal impression on RS 33.26 quoted by Arnaud in support of his hypothesis does not really parallel the design of the dynastic seal. Not only the iconography (two standing figures facing each other, and a disc and a crescent between them), but the seal-cutter's style rather seem to point to a Syrian origin.

[44] In *PRU* 3, pp. XLII-XLIII.

[45] Ibid., p. XLIII.

implicit though I believe unmistakable judgment. The replica obviously antedated too the Hittite conquest of Ugarit and was probably made during the time of Hurrian viz. Mittannian influence in Syria. This interpretation was then made explicit by the excavator of Ras Shamra who placed the replica on iconographic grounds between 1750 and 1500.[46] As for the original, Nougayrol had no doubt that it was considerably earlier than Hammurapi of Babylon.[47] To quote once more his thoughtful words, should the seal have appeared in the antiquity market, as keeps on happening unfortunately too often, the modern specialist would have very likely assigned it to period IVb in Dominique Collon's authoritative nomenclature.[48]

But, as we mentioned above, Arnaud's dating is not based on the analysis of the seal itself, but on complementary, partially unpublished documentary evidence. According to these new sources and the synchronisms established thereby, there seems to be little doubt that king Yaqaru, son of Niqmaddu, ruled the kingdom of Ugarit some time in the course of the 15th century BC (thus roughly contemporary to Idrimi of Alalakh).[49] This evidence comes in part from the newly discovered Akkadian version of the Ugaritic well-known and long-debated list of divinized kings of Ugarit. This king list also makes particularly clear that Yaqaru(m), the owner of the seal, is not the founder of the alleged dynasty (neither his father Niqmaddu).[50]

The problem we are faced with is one that is not uncommon in ancient history research, namely how to reconcile the archaeological and

---

[46] Schaeffer, *Ugaritica* 3, p. 73. Note that on pp. 71-72 he sates that Nougayrol considers the replica to be "vraisemblablement contemporaine des tablettes qui en portent la marque, c'est-à-dire des XIVe et XIIIe siècles av. n. è." I could not, however, find this reference in Nougayrol's text.

[47] As stated in *PRU* 3, p. XLII. Note that Collon agreed with this date in her *The Seal Impressions from Tell Atchana/Alalakh* (Neukirchen-Vluyn, 1975), p. 170.

[48] Compare, for example, the Isin/Larsa cylinder seals in Collon, *Catalogue of the Western Asiatic Seals in the British Museum. Cylinder Seals III. Isin-Larsa and Old Babylonian Periods* (London, 1986), Plates VII-IX.

[49] As stated by Arnaud ("Ougarit avant Suppiluliuma I," p. 155 n. 28), Yaqaru seems to have immediately preceded Ibirānu, the receiver of the message RS 4.449 found at Ras Shamra addressed by Niqmepa^{c} of Alalakh, son of Idrimi. For the date of Idrimi's reign, see now the study of van Soldt, "Syrian Chronology in the Old and Middle Babylonian Periods," Akkadica 119-120 (2000):110-113.

[50] See Arnaud, "Les bordereaux de rois divinisés," pp. 153-173. See also Pardee, *Ritual and Cult at Ugarit* (Leiden/Boston/Köln, 2002), pp. 203-204, where the author provides a thorough discussion of the Akkadian text (RS 94.2518) and the Ugaritic quasi-counterpart RS 24.257-reverse (pp. 201-210), as potentially reflecting aspects of the *kispu*-rite.

the written evidence. Our own analysis, which of course partially but importantly rests on both Nougayrol's and Arnaud's studies, has left us with the following two essential facts: on the one hand, the Isin/Larsa design of the original dynastic seal of Ugarit is to be assigned to, viz. was undoubtedly made in, the early second millennium; and on the other hand, the owner of the seal who had his name, patronymic, and title, inscribed on it, ruled Ugarit around the 15th century BC. After what has been discussed above, I believe one simple explanation presents itself, however improbable it may be.[51]

Anyone who is familiar with the study of cylinder seals knows well that the practice of re-using or re-cutting old seals was fairly common in the Near East. A glance at any modern illustrated catalogue or collection would suffice to realize the numerous cases of re-cut seals at all periods and areas. As stated by Collon, "the inscription was, naturally enough, the part of the design which was most likely to be altered."[52] I would therefore like to suggest that the dynastic seal of Ugarit is to be added in this long list of re-cut seals; that is to say that the fifteenth-century king Yaqaru ordered his most skilful seal-cutter to erase the inscription of a much older and prestigious cylinder seal that stemmed from a typical Isin/Larsa workshop and have his name inscribed instead. Indeed, why not? It was a general practice in the Near East that "a new seal owner would make some change to a seal he had inherited or acquired by some other means."[53]

That Nougayrol counselled caution immediately after his early dating of the seal design precisely on account of the shape and arrangement of the cuneiform signs of the inscription should not come as a surprise (what is surprising is that no serious attention has been paid to his statement).[54] The lines of the inscription are certainly not straight; only the second one is framed, and the first one borders and unskilfully avoids the standing figure of the intermediary goddess. Moreover, the seal-cutter miscalculated the length of the last line, so that the last sign ID had to be carved below the previous one (so indicated in our transliteration above).[55] It is interesting to note that the seal-cutter who later made the official replica had to faithfully reproduce this irregular feature like any

[51] For both Nougayrol (*PRU* 3, p. XLII n. 3) and Arnaud ("Ougarit avant Suppiluliuma I," p. 158) considered it highly unlikely.

[52] *First Impressions*, p. 120.

[53] Ibid.

[54] Literally he wrote: "Cependant, la forme et la disposition de ses caractères auraient, sans doute, tempéré ce diagnostic" (*PRU* 3, p. XLI).

[55] It seems that the inaccurate "mise en page" of scribes in Late Bronze Age Ugarit had a longer tradition.

other carved trace, but felt apparently free to arrange the lines of the text in a more standard, perpendicular manner. On the other hand, as mentioned above, the archaic sign MA is not correctly shaped. Nougayrol also pointed out (and this was stressed by Arnaud) that the use of the sign QA to phonetically express /qa/ (in the first line) is not known before Middle Babylonian times (except in the area of the Middle Euphrates and beyond the Tigris).[56]

Finally, I would like to suggest one more argument in favour of the later date of the inscription, a feature that has apparently escaped the attention of early commentators, the reason possibly being Nougayrol's lapse or omission in his transliteration of the text. The vertical-wedge sign, namely the personal marker, before the king's name Yaqaru(m) in the first line would be indeed exceptional for a seal dated to before 1600, and more particularly to the relevant Ur III or Isin/Larsa periods.[57] The presence of the personal marker is well attested, in turn, in fifteenth-century seals from Nuzi or Alalakh.[58]

If our suggestion proves correct, Yaqaru, son of Niqmaddu, who ruled Ugarit in the 15th century BC, either inherited or acquired by some means we can only guess a (royal?) cylinder seal[59] that had been originally made and carved some four hundred years earlier by a seal-cutter from a Babylonian workshop.[60] As new owner of the precious and pres-

---

[56] It is indeed attested in Old Babylonian Mari and Eshnunna. Nougayrol's remarks on the use of the sign MÁ for /ma/ are not relevant in view of the corrected reading MA$^{!}$ pointed out by Arnaud.

[57] It is worthwhile referring to the fact that the personal marker is not attested in any seal inscription on Ur III tablets. This categorical and reliable piece of information was kindly made available to me by Manuel Molina on the basis of his impressive and complete database (btds.filol.csic.es). One should indeed note that the standard use of the "personal wedge" as the classifier or determinative for male personal names was developed in Middle Babylonian / Assyrian times (see Edzard, "Personenkeil," RlA 10 [2004]:431). It would be interesting to trace and study the origin and development of this particular scribal usage (see presently Rykle Borger's *Mesopotamisches Zeichenlexikon* [Münster, 2003], p. 417).

[58] Note for example the Alalakh seals no. 192 of Irkabtu(m) and no. 193 of king Ilimilimma (cut in reverse) in Collon's *The Seal Impressions from Tell Atchana/Alalakh*.

[59] For favoured and attested designs of royal and dynastic seals, cf. Collon, *First Impressions*, pp. 123-130 (where she does not include the one of Ugarit).

[60] It may be worthwhile to note that seals of Ur III or Isin/Larsa date showing the design of the presentation scene were in common use in an area as far north as the Assyrian colony of Kanesh in the 19th and 18th centuries (see Béatrice Teissier, *Sealing and Seals on Texts from Kültepe Kārum Level 2* [Leiden, 1994], nos. 595-620, and also the remarks by Morgens Trolle Larsen and Eva Møller, "Five Old

tigious seal, Yaqaru would have decided to have it re-cut with his name, patronymic and title. His scribes, well trained in the reading and writing of archaic signs (as pointed out by Arnaud), would have written the text, which was eventually carved (in reverse) by a royal seal-cutter, perhaps after erasing the original inscription. The seal was then subsequently handed over from one generation to the next, probably at the solemn "coronation" ceremony, becoming thereafter the seal of the hereditary kings of Ugarit (for the formula identifying the owner of the seal in the royal deeds, see section 3 below). Aware of the precious, symbolic value of the dynastic seal, Yaqaru himself or one of his successors on the throne of Ugarit had then an official replica made, perhaps as a result of a little accident in which the original seal suffered a slight damage. Although the practice of inheriting and employing the predecessor's or ancestor's royal seal is also known from other Near Eastern kingdoms outside Mesopotamia, the case of the dynastic seal of Ugarit is unique in its consistent, continuing and prolonged use namely for three centuries, down to the destruction of the palace and city.[61]

Every rule has nonetheless its exception. Nougayrol remarked that there were only two examples of royal deeds published in *PRU* 3 (and known hitherto) with the impression of a seal other than the dynastic. In RS 16.197, recording an exchange of real property between king

---

Assyrian Texts," in *Marchands, diplomates et empereurs*, p. 247).

[61] Note for example that Niqmepa^{c} of Alalakh used the older seal of king AbbaAN of Aleppo; Šauštatar king of Mittanni used his predecessor Šuttarna (I)'s seal; and the same seal was affixed on diplomatic documents by the kings of Amurru, namely Aziru and his sucessor DU-Teššub; king Padiya of Siyannu used his predecessor Sasiya's seal; and a dynastic seal was also used by the Late Bronze Age kings of Emar; see Allan R. Millard, "Königssiegel," RlA 6, pp. 139-140; for the seal of Amurru, see the remarks of van Soldt, *SAU*, pp. 14-15; and for Emar, see Masamichi Yamada, "The Dynastic Seal and Ninurta's Seal: Preliminary Remarks on Sealing by the Local Authorities of Emar," Iraq 56 (1994):59-62. But in contrast to the evidence of the dynastic seal of the kings of Ugarit, it should be mentioned that Niqmepa^{c} of Alalakh also affixed his predecessor Idrimi's seal (on AT 17 and AT 69) and that his successor Ilimilimma usually signed with his own royal cylinder seal (see Collon, *The Seal Impressions from Tell Atchana/Alalakh*); on the other hand, as shown by the Tell Brak tablets, Šauštatar king of Mittanni also had his own seal which was used by his successors Artashumara and Tushratta (see Diana Stein, "Mittan[n]i. B. Bildkunst und Architektur," RlA 8, p. 297); and finally, ^{c}Abdianati of Siyannu also affixed his own seal (on RS 17.123). In view of these "peripheral" examples and the fact that the regular use of an ancestor's seal is not attested in Babylonia or Assyrìa, it is perhaps worthwhile recalling Nougayrol's remark (in *PRU* 3, p. XLIII n. 3): "on pourrait admettre —he wrote— qu'[une telle idée] a été apportée en Syrie par les dynastes indo-européens qui dominaient ses confins du Nord ou de l'Est (Hittites, Mitanniens)."

ᶜAmmiṯtamru II and a certain Šumaddu, the seal impressed on top of the obverse, apparently without inscription, belonged to the king's mother "Aḫatmilku, queen of Ugarit," as stated in the text (see section 3 below). It is possible that the queen-mother exceptionally presided over the transaction, acting on behalf of his son who was perhaps absent from Ugarit at that time. If so, one should incidentally refer to the fact that she did not use the dynastic seal, which was probably worn by the king, but her own one.[62] The second irregular case in *PRU* 3 is RS 16.206. This text describing a land conveyance by king Niqmepaᶜ bears a non-inscribed seal impression. Although no statement specifying the owner of the seal is mentioned or preserved, it is reasonable to argue, following the editor of the text, that it belonged to the wealthy merchant Sinarānu on the basis of the terms of the transaction; indeed, the transfer of ownership (a sale?) expressly entails the payment of an amount of silver to Sinarānu.

RS 16.270, published too in *PRU* 3 and included in our list of royal deeds, also deserves our attention. This text, as already mentioned, belongs to the large dossier concerning the dynastic divorce between ᶜAmmiṯtamru II and the daughter of the king of Amurru. The king of Ugarit exceptionally signed the document with two seals: the dynastic seal and his personal signet ring, perhaps marking and assuming his personal responsibility beside the one of the dynasty in this agreement and delicate matter.[63] It should be noted that it is the only text of the dossier unearthed at Ugarit sealed by the divorced king. A remark on notarial practice is here in order: the signet ring was stamped twice, side by side.[64] The reason is to be sought in the nature of the seal itself for, unlike cylinder seals, stamp seals cannot be rolled leaving a continuous impression and covering thus more or less regularly the sealing surface of the tablet, as seems to have been prescribed.[65]

---

[62] As opposed to the procedure described in RS 16.145. There, it will be remembered, the *sākinu*-official rolled the dynastic seal on the tablet on behalf of his lord probably due to the latter's incapacity.

[63] As already suggested by Nougayrol in *PRU* 3, p. 44 n. 2. The signet ring of ᶜAmmiṯtamru has no carved design only bearing the reversed Ugaritic inscription: *mišmn / ᶜmyḏtmr / mlk ugrt* "Seal of ᶜAmmiṯtamru, king of Ugarit." Note that the same seal was impressed on a bulla discovered at Ras Ibn Hani (RIH 83/21); see Bordreuil and Pardee, "Le sceau nominal de ᶜAmmīyiḏtamrou, roi d'Ougarit," Syria 61 (1984):11ff. (= KTU 6.23).

[64] See the photo in *Ugaritica* 3, p. 83 fig. 104, enlarged on the next page fig. 105.

[65] Compare for example the continuous impression of the design of the dynastic seal on the extraordinarily large tablet RS 15.109+ where the seal had to be rolled almost three complete times (see the photo on pl. XII in *PRU* 3). Other examples of seals stamped more than once so as to more or less cover the sealing space of the

Further evidence of the existence and use of royal personal seals comes from three other exceptional cases that appeared after *PRU* 3. The signet ring of king Niqmaddu is affixed on two royal deeds: RS 16.191+ describing in Ugaritic the redemption of a number of people from the city-state of Beirut, and RS 17.147, a grant of ᶜAmmiṯtamru II.[66] Here too, the seal was stamped twice on the reserved space at the head of both documents.[67] The third example is RS 18.280 that presents some faint traces of a cylinder seal other than the dynastic seal. The owner of the seal is identified in the text (see section 3 below) as Ibirānu, king of Ugarit. Finally, one should mention the small fragment RS 17.408 that preserves traces of the impression of a "grand cyl.-sceau anépigraphe(?) au sommet du recto," of which this time no identification is mentioned or preserved.[68] The text seems to describe a conveyance of real property by king ᶜAmmiṯtamru II; it is of course possible that the nature of the transfer of ownership and corresponding obligations is similar to the one recorded in RS 16.206.

---

tablet can be found in the Ras Shamra corpus: RS 17.251 exceptionally presents three stamps of the same seal in a clear attempt to leave no space for other "signatures" (see the photo in *Ugaritica* 3, p. 41 fig. 55 and p. 42 fig. 56); two stamps of two different seals can be seen in RS 17.371+; and RS 17.316 and RS 17.319 illustrate the different usage of stamp seals beside cylinder seals (viz. two stamp seals below the impression of a cylinder seal).

[66] The carved design is a common royal motif, namely a figure (the king?) fighting a lion (see e.g. the "dynastic" seal of Shuttarna of Mittanni). Niqmaddu's signet ring shows a man in kneeling position spearing a lion; the royal name and title is inscribed in Akkadian across the seal's field. The owner of the seal has been generally identified with Niqmaddu II taking RS 17.147 as a *terminus ante quem*. Singer, however, has challenged this common view ("A Political History of Ugarit," p. 693), suggesting to ascribe the seal to Niqmaddu III. Concerning the only datable evidence RS 17.147, he writes that "if the seal belongs to Nimqaddu II we have to assume that ᶜAmmiṯtamru II used in this document the seal of his grandfather instead of using the dynastic seal, which would be the normal procedure. A better alternative seems to be that an original deed of ᶜAmmiṯtamru II was later ratified by Niqmaddu III." In our opinion, however, the problem remains. For a ratified deed (such as RS 15.109+) would also normally be sealed with the dynastic seal. I believe a definite answer cannot be given for the time being. We agree with Singer when he concludes that "perhaps a decisive argument will appear in the new documents of Niqmaddu III found in the Urtenu archive."

[67] See the photo of the seal impression on RS 16.191+ in *Ugaritica* 3, p. 79 fig. 101.

[68] See Nougayrol, *PRU* 6, p. 34.

To sum up, there is evidence that at least some kings of Ugarit had their own personal seals.[69] What is important to stress in this conclusion is that they only used them exceptionally to sign royal deeds for reasons we can only guess. The rule, as stated above, was to roll the cylinder seal of the ancestor king Yaqaru, either the original or the duplicate, both jealously guarded by the hereditary rulers of Ugarit. There can be little doubt that the seal of Yaqaru was a symbol of power and right, especially for the subsequent kings we are here concerned with (from Niqmaddu II to ᶜAmmurapiᵓ).[70] The one who possessed it had been granted the right to rule the kingdom. The dynastic seal materialized and therefore emphasized a reality that is apparent from the versions and duplicates of the king list unearthed at Ras Shamra and the *kispu*-rites they may reflect, namely the prestige of the legitimacy, continuity and great antiquity of the ruling royal house.[71]

Boyer accordingly believed that the seal impressed on the documents (which was directly linked to the complete absence of witnesses in the text) bestowed on each deed the protection not only of the ruler who personally signed it but of the entire dynasty, that is to say, of future kings. In other words, it was his opinion that the juridical object of the dynastic seal, communicating both legitimacy and timelessness,[72] was to impart to the given act a presumption of permanence or perpetuity.[73] I

---

[69] One should refer here to the existence of an unpublished signet ring inscribed in Akkadian with the name of ᶜAmmurapiᵓ possibly coming from Ugarit (see Schaeffer, "Les fouilles de Ras Shamra-Ugarit. Quinzième, seixième et dix-septième campagnes [1951, 1952 et 1953]," n. 2 pp. 34-35). The seal, as reported by Nougayrol (*PRU* 4, p. 205 n. 1), turned up in a private collection in the United States and was studied by Edith Porada. The French Assyriologist remarked that the orthography of the alleged king was not the usual or expected one; despite of it, he considered it likely that the owner of the seal would be the last king of Ugarit.

[70] For a suggested early history of the seal, see Arnaud, "Les bordereaux de rois divinisés," p. 167. There he suggests that Ibirānu (V), viz. the successor of Yaqaru according to the king list, may have used the seal "dynastically" so as to officially bridge the succession interrupted by a hypothetical "repudiated" ruler.

[71] These three aspects were pointed out by Nougayrol in *PRU* 3, p. XLIII; cf. also Elise Auerbach, "Heirloom Seals and Political Legitimacy in Late Bronze Age Syria," Akkadica 74-75 (1991):19-36.

[72] See Auerbach, "Heirloom Seals," p. 28.

[73] As summarized by Speiser in his "Akkadian Documents from Ras Shamra," p. 157. Because the seal had the authority of the state behind it, Speiser was for substituting "the designation 'state seal' for the felicitous yet unduly committing 'dynastic seal'." Although the label "state seal" is certainly relevant and legitimate (perhaps prompted by the fact that in some deeds it is called "The king's *great seal*," see below), I believe the description and discussion we have presented above

agree with the view that what we may call the "magical" transfer of the "legitimacy and timelessness" of the seal to the deed viz. the rights recorded thereupon, naturally materialized in the impression, cannot be overemphasized. But it is no less important to stress that the affixing of the dynastic seal of Ugarit on a tablet should in principle also agree with the formal legal usage of affixing any kind of personal mark, such as a signature, on a document.[74]

By definition, and as we mentioned in opening the section, seals or signatures are affixed to an instrument for the purpose of authenticating it or to give it effect as the act of the one who seals or signs. Like a signature too, the impression of the dynastic seal of Ugarit on royal deeds must thus be regarded as a personal mark in token of knowledge, approval, acceptance, or obligation. In his thoughtful discussion of the legal meaning of the dynastic seal, Skaist remarked that seals in the ancient Near East are normally affixed by witnesses and/or the participant who relinquishes rights or assumes obligations. The same must be true, he argued, of the affixing of the dynastic seal in Late Bronze Age Ugarit.[75] Concerning this relevant and interesting argument, one should further recall that at Ugarit only one seal is usually impressed on legal documents. There is therefore every reason to assume in agreement with Skaist that the seal impression does not only imply that the king of Ugarit was present at, giving his consent to, the recorded transaction(s), but also that by signing the deeds the king, and accordingly the dynasty, undertook obligations presumably relinquishing certain property rights. This reading of the seal impression is of special importance for the interpretation of the royal documents as title deeds in particular and for the question of land tenure at Ugarit in general.[76]

The dynastic seal impression, we already said above, forms without exception the beginning of all the royal deeds. The notarial practice at

---

has shown that Nougayrol's designation "dynastic seal" we have followed throughout the book is far from being "unduly committing." One should note that "state seals" constituted type XIX in Gelb's "Typology of Mesopotamian Seal Inscriptions," where he included the "dynastic seals" of Yaqarum of Ugarit, Aziru of Amurru, AbbaAN of Alalakh, and Tabarna of Hatti (in *Seals and Sealing in the Ancient Near East*, p. 125).

[74] Thus in disagreement with Boyer who considered that the use of the dynastic seal "a certainement pour but d'obtenir des effets juridiques différents de ceux qui résultent de l'emploi du sceau personnel de l'aliénateur dans les actes de transfert de propriété immobilière" (*PRU* 3, p. 285).

[75] "A Unique Closing Formula," p. 158.

[76] For the latter subject, I refer to my forthcoming contribution "Land Tenure and Royal Administration in Late Bronze Age Ugarit."

Ugarit was to roll the cylinder seal (or exceptionally stamp the signet ring) immediately after the clay tablet had been fashioned. Only then would the scribe begin to write the text of the deed.[77] We also stated above that the notary could draw a ruling or two to divide the seal impression from the text.[78] On the other hand, some deeds interestingly show, or rather confirm the assumption, that the space covered by the continuous impression of the dynastic seal was not to be transgressed by the scribe's stylus, even if there would be hardly any space left to complete the legal text.[79]

2. *The operative part*

We have discussed and concluded above that the adverbial phrases "from today" and "before king so-and-so" are both by their very nature components of one and the same sentence and should not, therefore, be divided and treated as independent parts of the scheme of a document. In accordance too with the scope of the operative part defined above, we include under this discourse unit any element of the text which participates in determining the newly created rights of the transaction or transactions involved. As a result, not only the "description of the act," as defined by Nougayrol (Kienast's "*Geschäftsvermerk*"), but also those clauses specifying for example the liability for services, the warranty of the new right-holder(s) against eviction or also the exclusion of future litigations (grouped by Nougayrol under "*clauses secondaires*" and by Kienast under "*Schlußklauseln*") are also comprised in the operative part.

The content of the operative part obviously varies in accordance with the nature of the transaction(s). And yet, as we shall see in more detail in dealing with the formulary proper (in the following chapter), certain standard formulas usually recur in these documents regardless of the kind of transaction involved. As for the "*Sammelurkunden*," we already suggested that their operative part often incorporates the different single operative parts of the allegedly original joined documents; and this for the simple reason that the raison d'être of joining documents lies probably in the purpose of gathering together the rights and obligations of the

[77] That the first lines of the written text are made after the sealing is fairly apparent in some cases; see for example the photos of RS 15.86 (in *Ugaritica* 3, fig. 98), RS 15.91 (ibid., figs. 94 and 97), RS 16.143 (ibid., fig. 95). For examples of legal documents other than royal deeds, see the photos of RS 17.36 (in *Ugaritica* 5, fig. 7) or RS 17.149 (ibid., figs. 4 and 4A).

[78] Examples indented with one line are RS 15.89, RS 15.136, RS 15.155, RS 16.204, and RS 16.262; two rulings are drawn in turn in RS 16.279.

[79] See, for example, the deeds RS 15.86 or RS 16.131.

new holder, including at the same time those of the former holder(s).

As a rule, the notarial style at Ugarit is objective.[80] Since written legal transactions by definition record completed actions which bear upon present and future (and, in a sense, also former) rights and obligations, we find clauses phrased both in the past and the present-future tenses. Verbs used to build up the formulas that specify the nature of the transaction, namely the completed action, obviously appear in the past: perfect or preterite in Akkadian and the (morphologically) so-called suffix-conjugation in the few Ugaritic examples; thus, the king has given or transferred, the seller has sold for such an amount of silver, or the king has set free, promoted, or exempted from services.[81] On the other hand, verbs used to describe provisions that create the resulting obligations (the so-called "final clauses") are styled in the durative in Akkadian and in the prefix-conjugation in Ugaritic; thus, for example, no one shall take the conveyed property from the transferee, the sum of the penalty in case of further litigation amounts to so much silver, no one shall raise claims against the transferee, or the latter is, or is not, to carry out a certain kind of service. Beside the durative, the stative (or permansive) can also be found in such Akkadian clauses for, although temporally unmarked, it "is frequently used to indicate the result of a previously described act;"[82] thus, it is normally used to describe the new status of the person who has been set free (viz. he or she is now free).

Mention should be made to the fact that certain clauses in the operative part are not always drawn up from the same point of view. By this we do not, or not only, mean that the two parties of a transaction, say, of a royal land grant, appear each fulfilling his or her respective part: the donor king has granted and the grantee then undertakes his obligations, viz. he is to fulfil a certain kind of service. What is of interest for the notarial practice of Ugarit is that a transaction such as a real property sale was not bound to one standard formulation; indeed we can find it phrased either *ex latere emptoris* (e.g. RS 15.119, RS 16.147, RS 16.241+, RS 16.281, RS 16.284) or *ex latere venditoris* (e.g. RS 15.136,

---

[80] See my comments on the scribal point of view in chapter 3 footnote 56.

[81] The distinct use of the preterite or the perfect seems to be rather arbitrary. Huehnergard concluded that "these two forms are almost completely interchangeable, although one or the other tends to be preferred in certain circumstances, or with certain verbs" (*The Akkadian of Ugarit*, p. 249). Very few exceptions are also attested, namely where the present or durative is used instead of the past like in RS 16.269:1-10. These, however, may be taken as "simple mistakes" (see van Soldt, *SAU*, pp. 497-498). Each formula, on the other hand, will be dealt with in more detail in the next chapter.

[82] Van Soldt, *SAU*, p. 498.

RS 16.137, RS 16.154, RS 16.156, RS 16.207, RS 16.353).[83] This inconsistency is manifest in the "*Sammelurkunde*" RS 15.109+; here the notary put together the different transactions/deeds without attempting to make the phrasing uniform (his task naturally consisting in faithfully reproducing the original deeds). Still more inconsistent is the description of barter transactions. In these texts, the exchange can be unilateral (e.g. RS 15.70, RS 16.140, RS 16.158, RS 16.371), bilateral (e.g. RS 16.246, RS 16.277, RS 16.343, RS 16.383), or also phrased from the point of view of both parties together such as in RS 15.123+; moreover, concerning the unilateral phrasing, it can also be expressed either *ex latere alienatoris* (e.g. RS 15.70 or RS 16.140) or *ex latere emptoris* (RS 16.158). The verbs and expressions used in each case will be analyzed in the next chapter.

On the other hand, four royal deeds contain clauses in subjective style. It is significant that three of them (RS 16.143, RS 16.239 and RS 16.250) belong to the same "dossier," namely the one of ᶜAbdu discussed in chapter 3 above. In two of these documents (RS 16.143 and RS 16.250) the clauses in subjective style are parallel, following the same pattern designed by the "expert notary" Šapšumalku who was responsible for the registration of the deeds (viz. "new entries") in the royal archive. The clauses in question contain ᶜAbdu's provisions concerning the rights of his sons' different mothers (RS 16.143:23ff., RS 16.250:21ff.). In RS 16.239:21ff., ᶜAbdu speaks giving part of his property to one of his sons. Since the language of wills and other deeds dealing with the division of inheritance occasionally has recourse to subjective style at Ugarit,[84] it seems reasonable to argue that the three paragraphs in question are influenced by the nature of the transaction proper. Written close to the end of the document, the three of them are introduced by the same

---

[83] See already the remarks of Haase "Anmerkungen zum ugaritischen Immobilienkauf," p. 198, and Kienast, "Kauf," p. 534.

[84] See the private deeds RS 8.145, RS 17.36, RS 17.378A and RS 20.146. In all cases the donor father speaks, often introduced by the formula "he has spoken as follows" (*akanna iqtalebi*, so e.g. RS 8.145:3 or RS 20.146:3). One should also note the subjective style used in another private document, namely the deed of manumission RS 8.279bis, lines 7'ff. (see also l. 15'), introduced again by the same expression. As for RS 8.303, another deed of manumission, the spelling *aš-ta-pá-ak* in l. 7 contrasts with the objective style of the rest of the document; although one cannot discard a mixed composition and translate the verbal form accordingly "I have poured" (as is so far accepted), it is by no means unlikely that the scribe made a lapsus or mistake for *ištapak* (note that exceptionally no marker of direct speech is used: for the reading of the previous sign, namely *ù* instead of Nougayrol's KIMIN, see Huehnergard's collation in his *The Akkadian of Ugarit*, p. 349).

sentence, "On the other hand, thus (has spoken) ᶜAbdu" (spelled in the same way: *ša-ni-tam um-ma* ᴾìr-*dì*, in ll. 22, 20 and 20, respectively).[85] Likewise the exceptional document known as "Arḫalbu's last wishes" (RS 16.144) is completely phrased in subjective style. Here the fact that the text is clearly a disposition in contemplation of death ("when I die," ll. 4-5)[86] explains the style of the text, introduced this time by the expression "he (viz. the king) has spoken as follows" (*akanna iqtabi*, l. 3).[87]

---

[85] Only RS 16.143 and RS 16.250 are signed by Šapšumalku (see chapter 3 above). It is possible, however, that he was also the author of RS 16.239 (on the basis of the orthography of the text —see chapter 7).

[86] Line 5 reads *a-na-ku* ba.ug$_7$.meš *mi-ta-ku*. Arnaud, however, has recently suggested to read instead *a-na* dúr ba.ug$_6$.meš *mi-ta-ku* translating "Je suis un mort dans le séjour des morts" or, as a better choice, "Je suis un mort dans le trône des morts" ("Les bordereaux de rois divinisés," p. 169 n. 57). In my opinion, the latter interpretation poses several problems (note also the typo of the subscript number of the Sumerogram for "to die"). To begin with, the third sign (KU) is clearly inscribed "together" with the previous two forming a unit; secondly the religious connotation of the resulting translation does not conveniently suit a disposition *mortis causa*; and finally, the disposition itself is not properly rendered since it is introduced in the previous line (4) by the conditional conjunction and the adverbial phrase marking the future condition.

[87] Quite apart from this small corpus the passage in the provision contained in RS 16.353:17-20 belongs to the examples of legal speech acts discussed in chapter 3. The passage in question reads: "If PN or his children, his children's children, his progeny, his progeny's progeny speak to the king of Ugarit as follows (*akanna iqabbū*, l. 19): 'You are not our lord, another king is our lord'." Nougayrol interpreted also a passage in the deed of RS 15.86 describing a barter transaction, namely lines 7-9, as drawn up in subjective style on the basis of the readings *šub-ši* in l. 7 and *a-di-in*(??) in l. 9. Both readings, however, have been later amended. The former was already identified by Speiser as part of the Hurrian word *pu-ḫu-ka-ru-ši* ("Akkadian Documents from Ras Shamra," p. 164); van Soldt (*SAU*, p. 350 n. 209) has more recently analyzed this word glossing the Sumerogram ki.bi.gar.ra as *puǵ=ugar=oš=i* with the resulting meaning "she has made an exchange." As for the latter case, Huehnergard suggested a new collated reading, namely *ma-a-*⌜*ar(?)*⌝ with the tentative meaning "is exchanged(?)" ("RS 15.86 [PRU 3, 51f.]," UF 18 [1988]: 169-170; see also his *Ugaritic Vocabulary*, pp. 145-146; followed by Malbran-Labat, "Langues et écritures à Ougarit," p. 81). My own collation, however, suggests a different, I believe more plausible reading that also discards the subjective style of the passage (for my reading, see next chapter, footnote 41).

3. Statement specifying the owner of the seal

After the operative part, that is, at the end of the document, the text can, and often does, include a statement specifying the owner of the seal impressed at the head of the tablet.[88] The owner of the dynastic seal is of course the king. This formula did not remain unchanged through the one and a half century covered by our documentation, indeed presenting some interesting variations. These variations can be divided into two main groups: one in which the owner of the seal is "anonymously" identified viz. as the king, and one in which he is "personally" identified, that is, by name and patronymic as well as title.[89] The fact that the statement in question could also be omitted suggests that the use of one or another formula had no legal significance. Nougayrol suggested in his edition of the texts that the two main variations may have been determined by an evolution in notarial forms as well as in royal prestige, rather than reflecting, for example, different scribal habits.[90]

The anonymous formula, as the qualification indicates, describes the dynastic seal as simply belonging to the king, without specifying the name of the ruler who rolled it or had it rolled on the surface of the damp clay of the royal deed. The seal is thus described as "The king's seal" (*kunuk šarri* or *kunukku ša šarri*)[91] or also as "The king's great seal" (*kunuk šarri rabû*)[92]. The anonymous formula was almost completely replaced by the personal one during the reign of ᶜAmmiṯtamru II. In-

[88] Note that in RS 15.138+ and RS 16.135 this statement appears inscribed at the top of the obverse of the tablet. This, however, is due to the fact that the text of the operative part leaves no space on the reverse for the formula in question (one should recall here the non-specialists that cuneiform tablets unlike the pages of a book turn from bottom to top); the notary decided then to write it on the obverse (note that in RS 15.138+ the scribe drew a ruling line before inscribing the formula). RS 16.160 and RS 16.167, however, exceptionally show the formula deliberately inscribed with the seal impression on top of the obverse. Also exceptional is the fragmentary attestation in RS 15.120 which includes the formula in the text, namely in its second line.

[89] See Nougayrol, *PRU* 3, p. XXXIX.

[90] Ibid., p. XL. See our remarks in chapter 7.

[91] Note the different spellings ^{na4}kišib lugal(-*ri*) (e.g. RS 16.156, RS 16.167, or RS 16.385) and ^{na4}kišib *ša* lugal (only in RS 15.90, RS 15.120 and RS 16.275, the three from the reign of Niqmaddu II). The former, namely ^{na4}kišib lugal, is used to designate "The king's seal" (or "The royal seal") that was exceptionally obtained and rolled by the state official on the deed RS 16.145.

[92] Usually spelled ^{na4}kišib lugal gal (e.g. RS 15.Y, RS 16.158, RS 16.166, or RS 16.245); note the exceptional writing with phonetic complements ^{na4}kišib lugal-*ri* gal-*bu* in RS 16.263.

deed, his notaries chiefly identified the seal with which the impression had been made with “The seal of ^{c}Ammiṯtamru, son of Niqmepa^{c}, king of Ugarit.”[93] This personal formula had already been commonly used by the scribes of his father and predecessor Niqmepa^{c}, and was consistently followed by his successors Ibirānu and Niqmaddu III (accordingly of course with their respective name and patronymic).[94] Although the variation seems indeed to describe an evolution in notarial forms, as suggested by Nougayrol, it is no less true that the anonymous longer formula “The king’s great seal” was almost exclusively used by one scribal hand, namely that of Šapšumalku.[95]

Two exceptional, hybrid variations of the formula are attested, both from the time of ^{c}Ammiṯtamru II. RS 15.118:15 reads “The king’s/royal seal of ^{c}Ammiṯtamru, son of Niqmepa^{c},” and RS 16.132:30-31 “The <<great>>$^{?}$ king’s great seal of ^{c}Ammiṯtamru.”[96] Mention should also be made of the awkward fragment RS 17.53 in which the impression of the dynastic seal is here identified as “The seal of Yaqaru(m).”[97] On the other hand, it is interesting to note that in two deeds, RS 15.138+ and RS 16.135, the formula that is exceptionally written on the obverse of the tablet[98] significantly specifies that the seal (viz. “The king’s seal” and “The seal of Niqmepa^{c}, the king” respectively) is impressed “on the tablet” (*eli ṭuppi*).

---

[93] Of the 40 extant preserved formulas, only one uses the “anonymous” one (RS 18.285). In contrast, of the ten attestations in the deeds of Niqmaddu II only one uses the personal formula (RS 15.Z). Compare the data in this and the next footnote with the table of Nougayrol in *PRU* 3, p. XXXIX (note that his example of “formule personnelle” in the deeds of Niqmaddu II should be corrected). One should refer here to Haase’s misunderstanding of the formula and the seal impression in “Zum Recht von Ugarit,” pp. 13ff. (see footnote 26 above).

[94] Ten deeds of Niqmepa^{c} use the personal formula (note that two of them omit the patronymic, namely RS 16.135 and RS 18.53) and nine the anonymous one. The three extant formulas in the deeds of Ibirānu (RS 16.186, RS 18.265[A], RS 18.280) and the two surely dated to Niqmaddu III (RS 15.113 and RS 18.21) identify the seal as belonging to them “personally” (note, however, that the seal impressed on RS 18.280 is not the dynastic).

[95] As already observed by van Soldt (in *SAU*, p. 516). To his attestations one should add the fragment RS 16.149 also written by Šapšumalku, and probably the fragmentary RS 18.285(:20) written by Iliramu. See also chapter 7 below.

[96] Spelled respectively, ^{na4}kišib lugal ^{P}*a-mis-tam-ri* dumu *níq-me-pa*, and ^{na4}kišib gal / lugal gal ^{P}*a-mis-tam-ru*. Indeed the latter formula may perhaps be interpreted as a scribal mistake (viz. dittography of gal).

[97] Spelled ^{na4}kišib ^{P}*ia-qa-rum*.

[98] See footnote 88 above.

As for the Ugaritic examples, the formula identifying the owner of the seal is only fully preserved in RS 15.125 (KTU 2.19). The upper part of the tablet, however, where the impression was presumably to be found, is unfortunately broken off. Lines 6-7 read "The seal of Niqmaddu, king of Ugarit."[99] I would like to incidentally refer to the interpretation of the next lines (viz. ll. 8-9) we suggested in chapter 1 above, according to which the Ugaritic scribe would have stated that Niqmaddu himself "signed the document" (*ktb spr hnd*). Because the seal impression is lost, however, it is not possible to ascertain that the seal used by king Niqmaddu was the dynastic seal. We have seen above that a signet ring owned by a king of the same name was exceptionally stamped on two royal deeds, one written in Ugaritic (RS 16.191+ [KTU 3.4]) and one in Akkadian describing a grant by ᶜAmmiṯtamru II (RS 17.147). RS 15.111 (KTU 3.2) in turn preserves the impression of the dynastic seal at the head of the deed but the inscribed formula that identifies it is badly damaged.[100]

Regarding the exceptional cases of royal deeds bearing an impression other than the dynastic seal, we have mentioned above that only two of them are properly identified in the text. The formula in RS 16.197 states that the impression at the head of the document belongs to that made with "The seal of Aḫatmilku, queen of Ugarit."[101] On the other hand, the personal formula of Ibirānu used to identify the dynastic seal impressed on his deeds (RS 16.186 and RS 18.265[A]) is also used to identify the seal impressed on RS 18.280, which is not the one of the hereditary kings of Ugarit.

---

[99] Spelled *mišmn . nqmd / mlk ugrt*.

[100] Two different restorations of the preserved traces of signs have been proposed. Kienast ("Rechtsurkunden in ugaritischer Sprache," p. 447) suggests reading lines 19-20 as follows: [*mišm*]*n* ᶜ*m*[*ṯtm*]*r* / [*mlk*] *ugr*[*t*]. Lipiński in turn ("Aḫat-Milki, reine d'Ugarit," p. 113) prefers reading lines 20-22 as follows: *mi*[*šmn*] / [ᶜ*mṯtmr*] / *b*[*n nqmp*ᶜ] (see, however, the forthcoming remarks in section 4). A last, very recent collation of the other royal land grant written in Ugaritic, also bearing the impression of the dynastic seal on top of the tablet (RS 16.382), has been made. The authors (Robert Hawley and Dennis Pardee) suggest to read the faint traces on the upper edge and the upper part of the obverse the following: [*m(i)š*]⸢*mn*⸣ / [ᶜ*mṯtmr* .] *b*⸢*n*⸣ / [*nqmp*ᶜ . *ml*]⸢*k*⸣ / [*ugrt*]; see provisionally Bordreuil and Pardee, *Manuel d'ougaritique*, text no. 38 (the article in Semitica 52-53 by the authors of the collation was not yet available to me when I wrote these lines).

[101] Another document bearing the impression of a queen's seal is the unpublished deed RS 22.02. The formula used is the anonymous "The queen's seal" (spelled [na4]kišib mí.lugal).

4. Name of the scribe (sometimes as witness)

The scribe who drew up the deed sometimes wrote his name usually followed by his title at the end of the text. The name of the scribe was written in at least 53 royal deeds. We already noted that Šapšumalku, the expert scribe (*ṭupšarru emqu*) as he called himself once (in RS 16.142), regularly wrote down his name on "his" deeds. The names of thirteen notaries of Ugarit are known to us from the time between the earliest records down to the end of the kingdom.[102] The list of notaries and the kings they served can be found in the Appendix to chapter 3 above. What we have to consider now is that the scribes themselves often appear also as witnesses in the deeds. Indeed, in at least 19 royal deeds the scribe wrote before his name the Sumerogram igi for Akkadian *šību* "witness."[103] The presence or absence of the logogram presumably had no legal significance. For it goes without saying that the notary of every deed was witness to the corresponding recorded transaction(s). On the other hand, a closer examination of the documents shows that the presence or absence of igi rather reflects particular scribal habits. Of the 17 deeds explicitly written by Šapšumalku, only three (RS 15.88, RS 16.142 and RS 16.208) omit the logogram.[104] As for the deeds written by Karrānu and Ḫuṣānu, all of them bear the explicit reference to their role as witness. And notaries such as Iltaḫmu, Munaḫḫimu and Nuᶜmerašpu did never write the word "witness" before their names.[105]

We have insistently referred to the fact that what distinguishes a royal deed from other legal documents is the total absence of witnesses, aside from the scribe, we should now add. Exceptions to this rule are however attested. No more cases than the four listed by Nougayrol have appeared since the edition of *PRU* 3. In these four royal deeds the notary wrote his

---

[102] Note also the broken name AN-[ ] in RS 18.265A, a royal deed of king Ibirānu.

[103] RS 15.118, RS 15.119, RS 15.138+, RS 15.Y, RS 16.133, RS 16.143, RS 16.149, RS 16.156, RS 16.157, RS 16.191A, RS 16.207, RS 16.245, RS 16.250, RS 16.251, RS 16.263, RS 16.283, RS 16.284, RS 16.285, and RS 17.127. Note also the private deeds in which the scribe appears as witness: RS 11.856, RS 17.356, RS 17.360, RS 22.223, and possibly also RS 14.16, RS 18.264, and RS 18.267. Cf. the list in *PRU* 3, p. 230. For the Ugaritic royal deed RS 15.111 (KTU 3.2), see below. That igi is to be read *šību* (and not *maḫar*, for example) is shown by the nominative case of the names of the witnesses; note that in Ugaritic the equivalent in legal texts is also the noun *ypḥ* "witness."

[104] Note that the space before the scribe's name is broken in RS 16.147 and RS 16.254D. Whether or not the sign IGI was written cannot therefore be ascertained.

[105] This would in principle speak against the restoration [*ypḥ*] before *nᶜm*[*ršp*] suggested by Lipiński for RS 15.111 (KTU 3.2):19 (see chapter 3 note 32).

name after mentioning other individuals who acted as witnesses to the recorded transaction(s). To be precise, in RS 16.192A+ the name of one individual followed by the one of the notary (Ya^{c}ḏirānu) are inscribed without the explicit reference to their role as witnesses, that is, without the Sumerogram igi.[106] Nevertheless, the fact that the names are inscribed on the left edge of the tablet, thus isolated and separate from the rest of the text, seems to speak for the adopted interpretation. To explain these exceptional cases, the French Assyriologist wrote that "sans doute doit-on voir là des actes auxquels le roi n'assistait pas *en personne*."[107] Although I believe this is probably the case with RS 16.145 already discussed above (an example Nougayrol did not actually include in his list),[108] I would simply ask the question we have raised (and will keep on raising) as far as the formulary of the texts is concerned, namely whether such exceptions really have any legal significance. The fact that RS 16.192A+ deals with property rights resulting after litigation may account for the presence of an alleged witness beside the notary himself (perhaps he was a witness to the former legal procedure). It is significant, on the other hand, that RS 15.138+ and RS 16.285, that is to say, half of the corpus of exceptional documents, are drawn up by the same scribe, Ḫuṣānu. Since no more documents signed by this scribe are known to us, it is tempting to see his mentioning of witnesses as a scribal idiosyncrasy.

Following his first evaluation, Nougayrol noted that "de toute façon, il faut remarquer que, dans ces rares documents, les témoins sont en bien plus petit nombre et d'un rang plus uniformément relevé que dans les actes de Type 1 [viz. the private legal documents performed before witnesses]." We find two witnesses in RS 16.192A+ and RS 16.285, three in RS 16.156, and four in RS 15.138+, including in all cases the respective notary. This number indeed contrasts, for example, with the six-witness list in the royal deed RS 16.145.[109] As for the identity of the witnesses, RS 16.156 lists two notaries (one of them Šapšumalku) and one judge (one should incidentally note that it is the only attestation of a "judge" [*dayyānu*, spelled logographically di.ku$_5$] in the Ugarit corpus); RS

[106] Note that the same scribe wrote the Sumerogram for "witness" preceding his name in RS 15.118 but omitted it in RS 16.282.

[107] *PRU* 3, p. 230 (his italics).

[108] Note that this extraordinary royal deed does not include the scribe in the list of witnesses. The last one mentioned is instead the official "who obtained the dynastic seal" and sealed the deed.

[109] Between four and six is the common number of witnesses found in deeds explicitly recorded "before witnesses" (e.g. RS 8.145, RS 8.207, RS 8.303, RS 17.22+, RS 17.36, RS 17.61, RS 17.149, RS 17.356, RS 17.358, RS 17.360, RS 22.02, RS 23.36, RS 25.137, RS 26.155, RS 28.56, RS 29.100).

15.138+ states that one of the witnesses is a minister or vizier; and RS 16.285 lists beside the notary Ḫuṣānu the well-known and influential merchant Sinarānu. The number and quality of these witnesses immediately reminds us of the situation reflected in the royal deeds of fifteenth-century Alalakh. There, the king appears presiding over transactions that were as a rule witnessed by a group of nobles that seemed to serve as deputies of the court.[110] As we already discussed and described in chapter 3 above, it is possible that a similar picture applies to Ugarit too during the Late Bronze Age period. The fact that as a rule royal deeds do not mention any witnesses would not contradict it. It is more than likely, as we have stressed throughout the book, that the seal of the hereditary kings of Ugarit impressed at the head of the documents rendered otiose the mentioning of the witnesses that were present at the royal palace audience hall. With this regard it is interesting to note that the only time the dynastic seal was not rolled directly or indirectly by the king, but by his minister, we find the list of witnesses that is characteristic of private deeds. Also significant is the royal RS 15.85 that describes two related transactions, one of which took place "before witnesses." Since the document is signed and therefore authenticated by the ruler, it is more than likely that it was considered unnecessary to list the names of the witnesses in question. Although our remarks are bound to be tentative, they nevertheless should remind us of the important historian's premise we ought to keep in mind especially in reading the next chapter. And that is that title deeds and legal documents in general from any society, particularly if they are not drawn up by professional lawyers as is presently the case, often and inevitably omit information about a lot of aspects of interest to us and give a partial view of others.

To conclude this chapter, and also before we begin to analyze the formulary of the deeds proper, I believe it is appropriate to give one or two examples of royal deeds in transliteration. This indeed will serve as an illustration of what we have been discussing so far, and to rightly introduce us into the next chapter. We have chosen two documents, RS 16.142 and RS 16.201.[111] One is dated to the reign of Arḫalbu and the other to his nephew's, ᶜAmmiṯtamru II. They both show the stereotyped character of the formulas and arrangement of the text, as well as the potential slight formulaic or orthographic deviations that can be found

---

[110] See my "Alalakh" in *A History of Ancient Near Eastern Law*, pp. 704-705.

[111] Apart from Nougayrol's first treatment, note the following translations: of RS 16.142, Miller, *Studies in the Juridical Texts*, pp. 68-69, Libolt, *Royal Land Grants*, p. 243 (including the transliteration as well), and Lackenbacher, *Textes akkadiens d'Ugarit*, p. 238; and of RS 16.201, Miller, *Studies in the Juridical Texts*, pp. 57-58 (it is surprisingly not included by Libolt in his corpus).

among the different deeds. RS 16.142 is a remarkable example since it was drawn up by the well-known notary Šapšumalku and it is this document he signed as "expert scribe." As for RS 16.201, it is representative enough. To begin with, it suits well the prototype of a royal deed as we defined it in chapter 1: the finely inscribed cuneiform text written in Akkadian (by the also well-known notary Munaḫḫimu) records in sixteen lines a conveyance of real property, namely a grant by king ^{c}Ammiṯtamru II. Furthermore, the tablet found in the passage connecting the palace rooms 132 and 152, was (like RS 16.142) stored and kept in the royal palace archive located on the upper floor at the center of the building. On the other hand, the fragmentary state of the tablet shows that the partial information we have does not only depend on the nature of the evidence itself but also on the incomplete state in which the material usually comes down to us. In the following transliteration of the texts, we have kept the arrangement of the lines as inscribed on the tablets.

RS 16.142	
Obverse	(impression of [the replica of] the dynastic seal)
	iš-tu u$_4$.1.kam *an-ni-im*
	^{P}sum-*ḫal-bu* dumu *níq-ma-*^{d}iškur
	lugal ^{uru}*u-ga-ri-it*
	it-ta-ši é a.šà
	ša ^{P}dumu-*ḫa-at-ti-yi-ma*
	ù id-din-šu
Lower edge	*a-na* ^{P}*um-bi-ia-na*
	ù pí-il-ka
Reverse	*ša* ^{lú}ašgab
	ú-bal
	ú-ra še-ra
	ma-am-ma la i-laq-qè-šu
	iš-tu šu ^{P}*um-bi-ia-n*[*a*]
	ù šu-*ti* dumu.meš-*šu*
	^{na4}kišib lugal
	^{pd}utu-lugal dub.sar kù.zu

In translation:

From today Arḫalbu, son of Niqmaddu, king of Ugarit, has produced the house (and) field of Binḫattiyīma and has given it to Umbiyānu.[112]

[112] We prefer to read here, although of course tentatively, the sign UM rather than DUB, usually indistinguishable from each other, on the basis of the personal name alphabetically written *ubyn* (= Ubbiyānu?). Note that Huehnergard follows Nougayrol and reads *tup-pí-ia-na* (*The Akkadian of Ugarit*, p. 368). For the ambiguous

And he (i.e. Umbiyānu) is to perform the service of the leatherworker(s). Tomorrow at dawn no one shall take it (i.e. the property) from Umbiyānu or from his sons. The king's seal. Šapšumalku, expert scribe.

RS 16.201

Obverse (impression of the [original] dynastic seal)

---

iš-tu u$_4$*-mi an-ni-i-im*
^{p}*a-miš-tam-ru* dumu *níq-me-pa*
lugal ^{uru}*ú-ga-ri-*[*i*]*t*

---

it-ta-ši é *ša* ^{p}*sí-gil-da* ^{lú}šà.tam
[*ša*] *i-na* ^{uru}*ma-ra-bá*
ù a.ša.meš *ša* ^{p}*sí-g*[*i*]*l-da-na* ^{lú}šà.tam
[*ša*] a.ša.meš ^{uru}*ma-ra-bá*
qa-du an.za.gàr-*šu* *qa-du* ^{giš}gi.dìm.meš-*šu*
qa-du ^{giš}geštin.na.meš-*šu*
qa-du gáb-bi mim-mu-šu
ù a.ša.meš *ša* lugal
ša a.ša.meš *gu-wa-li*
qa-du an.z[a.g]àr-*šu*[ ]
(broken off)

Reverse (broken off)
[ ]-*ti*
[-*t*]*a*$^{(?)}$*-ru-qa*
[ ]
[*píl-*]*ku ia-nu ina* sum lugal *an-nu-ti*
[ ]

---

^{n}[$^{\mathrm{na4}}$kišib ^{p}*a-miš-tam-ri* dumu] *níq-me-pa*
lu[gal ^{uru}*ú-ga-ri-it*]
^{p}*m*[*u-na-ḫi-mu* dumu *ia-r*]*i-mì* ^{lú}dub.sar

In translation

From today ᶜAmmiṯtamru, son of Niqmepaᶜ, king of Ugarit, has produced the house of Sigildā(nu), the steward, which is in the town of Maᶜrabā, and the field of Sigildānu, the steward, which is (in) the area of the town of Maᶜrabā, including its farmhouse, its olive grove, its vineyard, and everything else, as well as the king's field which is (in) the area of Guwalu, including its farmhouse, ... (rest broken off). [And] there is no *pilku*-service in these royal gifts. Seal of ᶜAmmiṯtamru, son of Niqmepaᶜ, king of Ugarit. Munaḫḫimu, son of Yarimmu, the scribe.

---

reading of the elements *umb-/ub*(*b*) and *tumb-/tubb* in personal names, see van Soldt, *SAU*, p. 354 n. 214.

CHAPTER 6

THE FORMULARY OF THE DEEDS

It is to the language of the legal discourse unit we have called the operative part of the royal deeds that we now turn. This language, we have said in previous chapters, basically consists of a restricted set of recurrent formulas. To be sure, by sticking to stereotyped phrases and expressions structured in a conventional, rigid fashion, the code of the legal message of royal deeds could be properly and accurately conveyed through time (time, we will remember, is the measurement of the distance between the sender and receiver, viz. the notaries). This explains why the code did not vary through the one century and a half covered by our documentary material. No doubt the communicative effectiveness, not to say the validity and regularity, of any written legal message rests upon such pre-established textual structure and wording, which constitutes in fact the distinctiveness of legal language.

The formulas presented in the following catalogue are not arranged according to any strict order, although, as will be readily seen, we have tried to keep as far as possible to the relative order of appearance in the deeds. They are neither arranged in the form of dictionary entries, nor is it meant to be an exhaustive catalogue (we should bear in mind that the list is basically restricted to the vocabulary of royal deeds).[1] The stereotyped structure of the documents probably accounts for the fact that, as will be noticed, some clauses appear inscribed in the same section, viz. number of lines, of certain deeds. On the other hand, it is probably to the stereotyped nature of the phrases and formulas that must be attributed the lack of concordance (between subject and verb, noun and adjective, antecedent and pronoun) that is found in a significant number of examples.[2]

---

[1] As a matter of fact, we are preparing such a dictionary, arranged in alphabetical order and containing exhaustively the legal vocabulary of Ugarit. The most thorough repertoire of terms and phrases to date is the one provided by Nougayrol in *PRU* 3, pp. 215-231; see also the glossary in Miller's *Studies in the Juridical Texts*, pp. 353-362, and the "paradigmatic analysis" of phrases and formulas of Libolt's corpus of royal land grants (Chapter 2, pp. 26-146).

[2] See Huehnergard, *The Akkadian of Ugarit*, pp. 231-236 and 265-267, and the relevant, conclusive remarks on p. 237. As he interstingly observes on pp. 143-144, this kind of mistakes is more frequent in legal texts than in letters.

1. The two "introductory" formulas

Although the operative part obviously varies from one document to the other, especially when we take into account the potentially diverse nature of the recorded transaction(s), two formulas are invariably found at the beginning of the text. As a matter of fact, when the opening two to three lines of the text are more or less well preserved on the clay tablet any reader has in principle no difficulty in identifying a royal legal document from Ugarit. The notaries who composed these documents were themselves well aware of the importance of these lines to judge from the fact that they sometimes drew a ruling after them, as if they would underline what we call the second "introductory formula," indeed "interrupting" the grammar of the text (modern scholars have attached too a special significance to these two formulas considering them parts of their schemes, as we have referred to in the preceding chapter).

Any royal deed, and for that matter any legal text from Ugarit, begins with the words *ištu ūmi annîm* (in Ugaritic spelled *l ym hnd*, probably */lê yômi hannadī/*), that is, "from today" or "as of today," usually inscribed in one (viz. the first) line. As discussed above, what the formula implies is that the transaction described in the following lines takes effect immediately. This opening adverbial phrase is rather frequently completed by another one closing the conveyance sentence with the meaning "forever" (see below under 21).

The notary of royal deeds wrote immediately after the phrase "from today" the name of the ruling king of Ugarit, followed by his patronymic and title.[3] As a rule, and not surprisingly, when the king is party to the transaction (for example, when he gives real property, exempts from services, or promotes somebody to higher status) the document is drawn up *ex latere regis*. Given this major group of royal deeds, one finds very often as opening words "From today RN_1, son of RN_2, king of Ugarit" (*ištu ūmi annîm* RN_1 *mār* RN_2 *šar Ugarit* [in Ugaritic *l ym hnd* RN_1 *bn* RN_2 *mlk ugrt*]). When the king is no explicit party to the transaction, especially in sales or barters between individuals, but also in adoptions or litigations for example, he appears then as presiding over it also immediately after the opening phrase "from today." His name, patronymic and title occur then in the formula *ana pāni* RN_1 *mār* RN_2 *šar Ugarit* (in Uga-

[3] Exceptions to the rule are the following; without patronymic: RS 16.158, RS 16.269, RS 16.279, the extraordinary deed recording Arḫalbu's "last wishes" RS 16.144, and the unusual deed RS 16.145 (we noted in chapter 1 that this omission could be deliberately meant to stress the "impersonal" character of Yaqaru); without tile: RS 16.248. Note that the patronymic can also be exceptionally missing in the formula specifying the owner of the seal (see the discussion in the previous chapter); the examples are: RS 16.135, RS 16.252, RS 16.269 and RS 18.35.

ritic, *l pn RN_1 bn RN_2 mlk ugrt*),[4] "before RN_1, son of RN_2, king of Ugarit."[5] As stated above, the scribe of the text would sometimes drew a ruling after writing the royal title, as though he would mean to stress the royal character of the deed.

2. *The* našû-nadānu *formula*

We mentioned already in the first chapter that conveyances, namely of real property, constitute the bulk of the transactions recorded in royal deeds, viz. more than 90 per cent of the entire corpus. On the other hand, of all the conveyances recorded in royal deeds those made by the king are by far the commonest. These, as we said above, are all phrased from the point of view of the king, i.e., *ex latere alienatoris*. Now, although the transfer of ownership in texts styled *ex latere alienatoris* is normally expressed in Akkadian with the verb *nadānu* "to give," royal notaries of Ugarit used preferably a different, coordinate expression. Indeed, the formula most commonly found in these texts is the two-sentence clause: "king so-and-so (followed then by: son of king so-and-so, king of Ugarit) has produced O (the object, usually real property) and has given it to PN," often adding "and to his sons forever." The verb in the first sentence is a past form of *našû* (preterite *išši*, and more often perfect *ittaši*) and in the second a past form too of *nadānu* proper (preterite *iddin*, and more often perfect *ittadin*).[6] Several attempts have

---

[4] In the only extant example RS 94.2168:2-4: "before ᶜAmmiṯtamru son of Niqmepaᶜ, king of Ugarit" (see Bordreuil and Pardee, *Manuel d'ougaritique*, text no. 38). RS 15.117 (KTU 7.63):1-3 could be another attestation if we would accept a restoration [*l pn*] at the beginning of line 1 (see my contribution "The Legal Texts from Ugarit," p. 414).

[5] Note that the formula is exceptionally missing in the deeds RS 16.200, RS 16.207, RS 16.252, RS 16.277 and the Ugaritic deed RS 16.191+ (KTU 3.4).

[6] As put by Huehnergard, there is a tendency for the first verb in legal documents, after the two introductory phrases, to be a perfect (*The Akkadian of Ugarit*, p. 250; see also van Soldt, *SAU*, p. 496); in the case of *našû*, he added: "overwhelmingly" (the suggestion to interpret the form as Gt preterite, as proposed by Kienast in "Rechtsurkunden in ugaritischer Sprache," p. 436 n. 19, is highly unlikely; see Huehnergard, *The Akkadian of Ugarit*, p. 171 n. 254). The stereotyped character of the perfect form of the verb, probably accounts for the exceptional use of *ittaši* in the private deed RS 17.36:11 with future meaning (see Huehnergard, *The Akkadian of Ugarit*, pp. 254-255, and van Soldt, *SAU*, p. 505). As for *nadānu*, see the distribution of preterite and perfect forms in Huehnergard, *The Akkadian of Ugarit*, p. 252 and n. 187. As for the syntactical order of the first clause (after the opening expressions), Subject-Verb-Object, it has been suggested that, in contrast to the unmarked Akkadian order S-O-V, it probably served to draw attention to the verb

been made to understand or derive some legal significance from the combination of *našû* and *nadānu*, especially as opposed to *nadānu* alone. Kienast, for example, suggested that *našû*, literally meaning "to raise, to lift up" is to be understood here in elliptical use for the Akkadian expression (attested in Middle and Neo-Babylonian as well as in Neo-Assyrian texts) *rēš O našû*, that is, "das Objekt O überprüfen" ("to check on O").[7] Likewise, Libolt considered that "*našû* is used when the property rights must be cleared of potential claims by other parties," and he accordingly suggested to translate it as "to clear of encumbrances."[8] Such interpretations, however, are not without problems.[9] In RS 15.114 and RS 16.202, for example, the object in both grants by king ^{c}Ammiṯtamru II, formulated with the *našû-nadānu* clause, is, or include, an entire village. As is explicitly mentioned in the former deed (but is also true of the latter as well as other grants of villages), what the grantee was given are some rights of management of its own finances and taxes. In RS 15.114 and also, as we suggest, in RS 16.202, the village is said to be ruined or abandoned (its restoration being often explicitly provided for in the former as an obligation of the grantee).[10] Less appropriate (viz.

---

and thus to the type of transaction recorded (see Thomas J. Finley, *Word Order in the Clause Structure of Syrian Akkadian* [PhD. Dissertation, University of California, 1979], p. 139, and Huehnergard, *The Akkadian of Ugarit*, p. 220). This would be supported by the fact that the second sentence of the formula, related to the preceding one in an irreversible temporal sequence, as put by Finley (*Word Order*, p. 98; see also Huehnergard, *The Akkadian of Ugarit*, p. 222), always has the verb (*nadānu*) directly after the conjunction. Note that chiasm, namely S-V-O followed by V-S, is frequently used by notaries of ^{c}Ammiṯtamru II. Such stylistic device actually expands the formula by adding the subject again, viz. the word *šarru* "king," after *nadānu* (the object being normally expressed by an accusative suffix; see van Soldt, *SAU*, pp. 476, 493).

[7] "Rechtsurkunden in ugaritischer Sprache," p. 442.

[8] *Royal Land Grants*, pp. 38 and 42 respectively.

[9] As stated in his introduction to *Royal Land Grants* (p. 21), Libolt's second methodological assumption is that "differences, even small differences in how a clause is stated, are significant". "At times in the study— he went on— we attribute differences to 'style', but most of the differences seem to have legal significance." The author, therefore, makes a case for separating different kinds of conveyances (denoting different rights of the tranferee) according to the different use of verb formulas (pp. 38-50). His distinctions, however, like his methodology can hardly be sustained (as will be shown in this and the next chapter; see also our objections to part of his premises in our introduction).

[10] In RS 15.114:7, the granted village of Šaknā is qualified as *at-ka*, probably representing the Ugaritic word */^{c}atqal/* with the meaning "ruined, abandoned" (this translation was suggested without further commentary by Libolt, *Royal Land*

ill-suited) are these proposed meanings for texts describing a royal grant of specific taxes (RS 16.244) or the conveyance of a deed (RS 16.356:10-12), both expressed with the *našû-nadānu* formula too. Speiser, in turn, in his review of *PRU* 3, concluded that "what characterizes virtually every occurrence of the *n.-n.* formula is the fact that three parties are involved," chiefly meaning the king, the grantee, and the individual whose name serves to identify the property conveyed (thus taken as the former owner of the property).[11] Whatever the identity of the person "naming" the property (for which see 6 below), most of the examples of the *našû-nadānu* formula quoted above do not describe a tripartite situation. That statistically speaking a much larger number of texts agrees with this scheme may be misleading; we should keep in mind that what we have here are exclusively royal documents that to a large extent contain royal grants. With this regard, one should further note that the formula *našû-nadānu* is also used to describe gifts from a father to his son (RS 16.143, RS 16.157, RS 16.250), a father-in-law to his daughter-in-law (RS 15.85), or from a husband to his wife (RS 16.263), as well as to describe other kinds of conveyance such as sales and barters (the nature of the giving further defined, for instance, in the former case by the complement "for X shekels of silver;" for a discussion and examples see section 3 below).[12]

In view of the different attestations and use of the conveyance verb formulas, I would agree with Casper J. Labuschagne's impression that

---

Grants, p. 392; see my comments in the review to Juan A. Belmonte Marín's volume 12/2 of the *Répertoire géographique des textes cunéiformes* [Wiesbaden, 2002] published in ZA 93 [2003]:291). Our tentative restoration in RS 16.202:3 [uru]*ku-um-ba* : *a*[*t*][?]-*ka* is based on the faint traces preserved on the tablet, the clear parallel in RS 15.114, and the presence of the gloss mark that would agree with our interpretation of [c]*atqa* (in accusative) as a Ugaritic word (note that Huehnergard proposed in turn to restore [*am*]-*qà* in RS 16.202:3 and accordingly translated tentatively the end of the line as "Kumba the fort" in his *Ugaritic Vocabulary*, p. 160). RS 15.147 describes in turn the grant of two villages or hamlets (Upper and Lower Yēnā, for the reading of this toponym, see van Soldt, *The Topography of the City-State of Ugarit* [Münster, 2005], p. 25) and provides that the grantee is to restore them as well as resettle them.

[11] "Akkadian Documents from Ras Shamra," p. 160.

[12] Libolt is thus forced to conclude in an intricate way (building up a rule out of what is obviously casuistic) that, although "*našû* is the language of the gift" (*Royal Land Grants*, p. 38; see also Miller, *Studies in the Juridical Texts*, pp. 33-34), "*našû-nadānu* is used among non-grant transactions when the transfers involve transfers from a man to a woman or from a woman to a man, when transfers involve granted properties, and when it is important to separate a transfer of property from another, adjacent legal action" (p. 42). See also below footnote 40.

the simple (*nadānu*) and the full term (*našû-nadānu*) were used promiscuously, and that there seems to be no rule as to the context in which either of the terms fitted.[13] Note that in RS 15.85 the *našû-nadānu* conveyance (in lines 13-21) is recapitulated in the following lines (22-23) as a *nadānu* conveyance.[14] "The only conclusion that can be drawn," the author then added, "is that the term *našû-nadānu* predominates and that it is very often substituted by the simple term *nadānu*."[15] Once more, one needs to read and quote in full Nougayrol's first appreciation: "Il semble d'ailleurs [and he referred to our example RS 16.356:10-12] qu'on ne doive pas attacher une grande importance au verbe *našû*: un particulier 'lève' parfois ses propres biens avant de les céder, comme le roi donne parfois les biens d'un tiers sans les 'lever'. Si *našû (u) nadānu* est plutôt usité dans le premier cas, et *nadānu* dans le second, *c'est sans doute parce que la formule longue, plus emphatique, relève du style officiel*" (our italics).[16] Indeed it is to the last sentence that we shall finally turn given the scope of the chapter and the whole book.

If, as deduced by a number of scholars including now myself, the combined use of *našû* and *nadānu* basically denotes the transfer of ownership (Speiser was the first to suggest that they add up to a kind of hendiadys with the meaning "to transfer"), just as *nadānu* alone, why did notaries write down the formula *našû-nadānu* and not simply *nadānu* alone? It is interesting and, I believe, significant in this regard that in four or five examples of royal grants the verb *nadānu* actually appears substituting *našû* in the double-sentence formula.[17] What we have then is the odd iterative formula "king so-and-so has given O and he has given it to PN" (*RN ... iddin / ittadin O u iddinšu / ittadinšu ana PN*). The number of examples as well as the fact that it is the formula used in the extant Ugaritic examples (*RN ... ytn O w ytn.nn l PN*)[18] renders the interpretation of a scribal mistake (namely *i-din*, *id-din* and *it-ta-din* for *i-ši*[!],

[13] That the scribal hand may be held responsible for the choice of one expression over the other will be shown in chapter 7 below.

[14] See section 8 below.

[15] "The *našû-nadānu* formula and Its Biblical Equivalent," in *Travels in the World of the Old Testament, Studies Presented to Prof. M.A. Beek at the Occasion of His 65th Birthday*, ed. M.S.H.G. Heerma van Voss, Ph.H.J. Houwing ten Cate and N.A. van Uchelen (Assen 1974), p. 178.

[16] *PRU* 3, p. 224.

[17] The texts are: RS 16.189 and RS 16.206 from the reign of Niqmepa[c], and RS 15.126 and RS 17.379A from [c]Ammiṯtamru II, possibly including too the fragmentary RS 15.127. Cf. also RS 16.136. For the collated reading [*it-t*]*a-din* in RS 17.379[A], see my "Collations à RS 15.140 et 17.379[A]," NABU 1992/94.

[18] The texts are: RS 15.111 (KTU 3.2) and RS 16.191+ (KTU 3.4).

it-<ta->ši! and *it-ta-ši*! respectively in the first sentence of the clause) unlikely and indeed unnecessary.[19] I would rather prefer to understand this scribal variation as evidence that in Late Bronze Age Ugarit there was no real difference in legal meaning between the formulas *našû-nadānu* and *nadānu(-nadānu)*. According to Labuschagne, the original, distinct, meaning of the hendiadys was no longer clearly understood by the scribes in Ugarit. The alleged original action of "lifting up" or "taking away" property from its owner, he wrote, had lost its meaning. Following Nougayrol, he concluded that scribes seem to have preferred *našû-nadānu* to *nadānu* "because they considered it more suitable for the solemn, juridical language in their documents."[20] The question, however, still remains: why did they prefer *našû-nadānu* to *nadānu*? Why and how did it become more "official," as Nougayrol would put it, or "solemn," as described by Labuschagne? The answer in these cases is probably to be sought in the tradition of legal terminology. Indeed, the verb *našû* had lost whatever meaning it originally had becoming in this Late Bronze Age province of cuneiform law a frozen expression. Although the question of tradition will be the subject of the next chapter, mention should be made here to the fact that the same formula *našû-nadānu* was used by Hittite notaries, spelled as an Akkadogram, to draw up Hittite royal grants as early as the sixteenth century.[21] The tradition of the verb formula, as we shall see, stretched long not only into the past but also into more recent times. It is this centuries-old usage and prestige that provided solemnity and official character to the wording. Now, what about its original meaning?

I would like to close the discussion by offering an alternative interpretation to the "original action" of taking away viz. deliberately alienating property. My suggestion, or rather guess, is based precisely on the long tradition of the formula and on the well-known fact that it is in procedure that terminology tends to remain unchanged, even if no longer corresponding to reality.[22] My piece of evidence is attested in a royal

---

[19] The scribal mistake first suggested by the editor of the texts Nougayrol (followed i.a. by Speiser, "Akkadian Documents from Ras Shamra," p. 161, Finley, *Word Order*, p. 114, Miller, *Studies in the Juridical Texts*, p. 147 n. 170, Huehnergard, *The Akkadian of Ugarit*, p. 97) was argued for on the basis of the similarity of the cuneiform signs ŠI and DIN. See the objections to the interpretation of a scribal mistake already raised by Labuschagne, "The *našû-nadānu* formula and its biblical equivalent," pp. 178-179, Libolt, *Royal Land Grants*, p. 52, van Soldt, *SAU*, p. 496 n. 49, and my own amending note "Correction à N.A.B.U. 1992/94," NABU 1992/107.

[20] "The *našû-nadānu* formula and its biblical equivalent," pp. 178-179.

[21] As already put forward by Boyer in his "Étude juridique," p. 288.

[22] As stated by Reuven Yaron, *Introduction to the Law of the Aramaic Papyri*

deed of Ugarit proper, RS 16.356, and more particularly its lines 10 to 12, which, as I suggest, may preserve the original reality. Here, the king of Ugarit, Niqmaddu II, presides over a lawsuit concerning the ownership of real property and his decision consists in "producing" the tablet (i.e. the title deed) "and giving it" to the winning party. The expression used is *našû-nadānu*, and it is known that to produce or bring tablets or documents is commonly expressed in Akkadian with the verb *našû*.[23] Our conjecture would then be whether the formula *našû-nadānu* could not reflect the traditional physical or rather ceremonial act of "producing" and "giving" the title deed (in an irreversible temporal sequence), and with it of course the transfer of ownership to the transferee (note that the warranty clause immediately following in RS 16.356 has the conveyed field as object).[24]

3. *The* nadānu *formulas*

Although conveyances in royal deeds styled *ex latere alienatoris* are most commonly formulated by means of the coordination of the verbs *našû* and *nadānu*, it is the latter term, as we have seen, that actually denotes the transfer of ownership. This is clearly shown by the other grant clauses concurrently used at Ugarit: *RN ... iddin / ittadin O ana PN* "king so-and-so ... has given O to PN" (cf. also the Ugaritic sentence *O d ytn mlk l PN* "O [i.e. property] that the king has given to PN" in RS 94.2168:5-6), and more significantly, the examples in which *nadānu* appears substituting *našû* in the coordinated formula discussed above.[25]

(Oxford, 1961), p. 28, and as clearly shown for the Akkadian formulary by Malul's *Studies in Mesopotamian Legal Symbolism*.

[23] For the use at Ugarit itself, see e.g. the formula in the penalty clause of the private legal document RS 17.36:10-11: "Should PN produce another deed" (*šumma PN ṭuppa šanâ ittaši*).

[24] It is noteworthy that Nougayrol consistently translated the verb *našû* in this formula of conveyance with French "produire" in *PRU* 3 (later in *PRU* 6 he preferred the verb "prélever"). Note also that in the Ugaritic deed RS 15.125 (KTU 2.19) the warranty clause has the royal deed (*sipru malki*) as the object (see below section 9).

[25] For the preferred perfect form of the verb (especially during the later reigns), see Huehnergrad, *The Akkadian of Ugarit*, pp. 251-252 with n. 187, and van Soldt, *SAU*, p. 505. Following his methodological premises, Libolt is again forced to develop the more than doubtful conclusion that "*nadānu*-only is preferred for domain property grants because these cannot be 'lifted up' [in reference to *našû*] in the same sense that family properties can be" (*Royal Land Grants*, p. 44). The distinction between domain and family property is not only arbitrary but also wrong (for a detailed discussion see my forthcoming "Land Tenure and Royal Administration in Late Bronze Age Ugarit").

Sales phrased *ex latere venditoris* add then to the verb *nadānu* the complement *ina / ana kaspi* "for silver" (usually specifying the amount of silver) and/or *ina / ana šīmišu gamri* "for its full price."[26] As stated above, one can find the *nadānu* clause with the sale-defining complements preceded by the *našû* clause. Thus we would have after the opening stereotyped phrases "from today, before king so-and-so, son of king-so-and-so, king of Ugarit," the formula *PN_1 ittaši O u ittadinšu ana PN_2 ina X kaspi (ina šīmišu gamri)*, "PN_1 has produced O and has given it to PN_2 for X shekels of silver (for its full price)."[27] Sales can also be formulated by means of two juxtaposed *nadānu* clauses describing mutual conveyances, one of real property and the other of silver or gold, between the two parties. Thus we can have clauses of the type "the king has given O to PN and PN has given X shekels of silver/gold to the king."[28]

Because legally speaking there is hardly any distinction between sale and barter, the use of *nadānu* to describe the latter transactions is very similar to the one just described. The verb can thus appear alone or in combination with *našû*, too. The giving is further defined by adding of course a different technical word or expression, namely with the meaning "in exchange of": *kīmū* (in RS 16.140, RS 16.371, and RS 16.197), *kīma* (in RS 16.383 and possibly to be restored in RS 15.70:6), *ana pūḫat* (in RS 16.277:8), and *pūḫa* (in accusative, in RS 18.53:7').[29] The closeness in wording between both kinds of transaction is shown by RS 15.109+:16 where the sale is described with the clause *nadānu kīmū X kaspi* (followed in the next line by *šīmišu gamri*), "to give in exchange for X (shekels of) silver (its full price)." Like sales too, barters can be described without the addition of a defining technical word, simply by means of two juxtaposed *nadānu* (or *našû-nadānu*) clauses describing

[26] See RS 15.109+:19, RS 16.131:5-7, and possibly also RS 16.133:8-9. For the formulary of sale clauses, see Kienast, "Kauf," p. 534. As for the use of the prepositions, *ana* occurs occasionally instead of the expected (normative Mesopotamian) *ina*, probably as a result of Ugaritic influence (see van Soldt, *SAU*, pp. 449, 452 and 456; and cf. also Huehnergard, *The Akkadian of Ugarit*, p. 184).

[27] See RS 16.145:10-15, RS 16.156, RS 16.207, RS 16.263, and RS 17.61.

[28] E.g. RS 16.135 or RS 16.285 (in both cases it is specified that the silver is the "price" of the real property conveyed), and cf. also RS 15.Z, RS 16.167, RS 16.189, RS 16.282, RS 16.283, RS 16.286, and the fragmentary RS 15.118 and RS 16.184. Note that in RS 16.206 the payment is not made to the king but to a third party (the wealthy merchant Sinarānu). The syntactical order of the sentences follows the same rules described above for *našû-nadānu*. Cf. also section 8 (the confirmation clause) below.

[29] Cf. the expression *bīta pūḫat bīti* in RS 16.147:9 (collated by van Soldt, see *SAU*, p. 418 n. 45). Note that the preposition *kīmū* is only attested in legal texts (see van Soldt, *SAU*, p. 460).

mutual conveyances between the two parties ("PN_1 has given O_1 to PN_2 and PN_2 has given O_2 to PN_1"). A variant of mutual conveyance is denoted by the expression "PN_1 has given (or produced and given) O to PN_2 as *tapdētu* of his (i.e. PN_2's) field." Because the three deeds in which this technical term appears (RS 16.246, RS 16.131 and RS 16.343) involve an exchange of real property between two people, it has generally been taken to mean something like "exchange."[30] That the word is probably Ugaritic (a *taqtal* form of PDY "to redeem, to ransom") is suggested by the gloss mark that precedes it in RS 16.343:9.[31] Due, however, to the very restricted number of relevant documents and the laconic context in which the term *tapdētu* appears, it is not possible for the time being to determine the exact nature of the transaction described (perhaps an exchange of land previously held as pledge?).[32]

In a number of deeds, after the conveyance clause proper (viz. a royal grant), sometimes close to the end of the document, there is the statement that the transferee "has given" (*ittadin*) a certain amount of silver or gold to the king distinctively defined as an "honouring gift for the king, his lord" (*kubuddāt šarri bēlišu*).[33] In another document (RS 16.251) the word *kubuddātu* (either spelled syllabically or with the logogram kubud) is omitted and the verb form *uktabbid/t* (< KBD/T literally "to honour") is used instead of *ittadin*.[34] This sort of countergift,

---

[30] See Nougayrol, *PRU* 3, pp. 219 and 229, and Huehnergard, *Ugaritic Vocabulary*, p. 166.

[31] Otherwise a form *tapras(t)* of *padû* would also be possible; for *padû* in the meaning "to redeem, to ransom" (especially in Mari and Emar), see e.g. Durand, review of *Recherches au pays d'Aštata. Emar VI.3* by D. Arnaud, RA 83 (1989):174.

[32] Note the equivalence between Ugaritic PDY and Akkadian *paṭāru*; see also section 5 below.

[33] The deeds are RS 15.122, RS 16.256, RS 16.260 and RS 17.01. RS 16.256:17 and RS 17.01:26-28 and the traces on the tablet (collated) suggest to restore RS 15.122:27 as: [dugud lugal e]n-*šu it-ta-din* (as already pointed out by Miller, *Studies in the Juridical Texts*, p. 91 and n. 154, followed by Libolt, *Royal Land Grants*, pp. 384-85). Incidentally lines 28-31 should then be restored in the following way: [^{na4}kišib ^{p}*a-m*]*iš-tam-ri* dumu ^{p}*níq-me-pa* / [lugal ^{uru}*ú*]-*ga-ri-it* / [*ù p*]*íl-ka-šu ša* ^{lú}šà.tam^{meš} / [*ubbal*].

[34] For the time being it is, I believe, safer to follow Nougayrol (*PRU* 3, p. 221) and leave open the interpretation of the verb, viz. either as a genuinely Akkadian form (from *kubuttu*) or as an Akkadianized Ugaritic verb (KBD). For the noun *kubuddātu*, understood as Ugaritic, see Huehnergard, *Ugaritic Vocabulary*, p. 135, who refers to the form spelled *ku*$_8$-*ub-bu-*[*da-ti*$^?$] in the Amarna letter EA 26:57, and the Biblical Hebrew hapaxlegomenon *k*^{e}*buddâ* in Judg 18:21. Although etymologically related, I do not think that *kubuddāʾu* in Mari or Emar correspond to the Ugaritic word (see Durand and Joannès, "*kubuddâʾu* à Mari et à Emar," NABU

according to Boyer, would entitle the transferee to enjoy the benefits of an actual grant (the author preferred therefore to include these deeds under the category of "fictional grants").[35]

The verb *nadānu* is also used in penalty clauses to denote the payment of the penalty imposed (see section 22 below).

Finally one should mention under the *nadānu* formulas the clauses "(this is) a royal gift" (*nidnu šarri*)[36] and "this gift has been given" (*nidnu annû nadin*)[37] that occasionally close or appear by the end of the operative part.

4. The leqû *formulas*

Conveyances, namely sales and barters can also be phrased in Ugarit *ex latere emptoris*. As a matter of fact, we find sales more often phrased *ex latere emptoris* than *ex latere venditoris*. The verb used is then *leqû* "to take, to receive." The same defining technical complements we have seen for the formulas styled *ex latere alienatoris* are added to *leqû* to form sale and barter clauses. Thus, we find the clause *PN_1 ilte/aqe O ištu (qāti) PN_2 ina X kaspi (ina šīmišu gamri)*, "PN_1 has taken O from PN_2 for X

1990/70, and Eugen J. Pentiuc, *West Semitic Vocabulary in the Akkadian Texts from Emar* [Winona Lake, IN, 2001], pp. 106-107). More significant seems to me one of the meanings of *kbd* in Middle Hebrew, namely "to offer a gift" (see Marcus Jastrow, *Dictionary of the Talmud* [New York, 1950], p. 606).

[35] See his "Étude juridique," in *PRU* 3, pp. 286 and 294 (and cf. Miller, *Studies in the Juridical Texts*, pp. 84-85). This formula has been also compared to the one describing payments to the king discussed above. See e.g. the independent formula closing the document RS 15.126: "And PN has given X shekels of silver to the king" (cf. section 8 below). Note that Libolt understood that these payments are in lieu of services (*Royal Land Grants*, pp. 130 and 406); this was also put forward by Miller (*Studies in the Juridical Texts*," p. 85) but obviously rightly discarded in view of some examples containing both payments and services.

[36] In RS 16.247:14, RS 16.286:15-16 and RS 16.243:18-20; in the latter two deeds adding "to PN and to his sons" and in RS 16.243 also "forever." As already mentioned in chapter 4, it is common in the Akkadian of Ugarit that bound forms have a case ending, the one required by context, reflecting the Ugaritic language (see Huehnergard, *The Akkadian of Ugarit*, pp. 150-154, and van Soldt, *SAU*, pp. 417-424). Despite its non-normative character, we have kept this peculiar morpho-syntactic feature in our transcriptions when it is consistently marked in the relevant texts.

[37] In RS 16.136:15, RS 16.171:4'-5', RS 16.282:14-15, RS 16.383:14-15, and possibly also on the left edge of RS 16.206. For this formula, see our discussion in the next chapter. Note that since RS 16.383 describes an exchange of real property, one should include this deed in the discussion of so-called "fictional grants."

shekels of silver (for its full price)."[38] Note that *ina kaspi* is omitted in several texts.[39] And in one deed (RS 16.158) the notary used the formula *leqû* + *kīmū* to describe the daughter's acquisition of her paternal house in exchange for her brideprice. In RS 15.70, the barter transaction is described by two sentences: first, the king received (*ilteqe*) the property and then he gave (*ittadin*) another one in exchange for it.[40]

The same verb *leqû* is used in the stereotyped warranty clause against eviction we shall discuss separately in 9 below, as well as in adoptions in which the adopter is a woman (see 18 below).

5. *Other technical terms and expressions denoting conveyance*

It should be mentioned that occasionally barter transactions described with *nadānu* or *našû-nadānu* clauses are defined at the beginning of the text, i.e. after the so-called introductory words "from today RN_1, son of RN_2, king of Ugarit," with the formula "PN_1 has exchanged O (the real

---

38 See RS 15.109+:2-3, 7, 18-19, 52 (with the form *ilqe* and the Sumerogram šu.ba.an.te), RS 15.119:4-6, RS 15.190:4-7 (fragmentary), RS 15.163+:14-15, RS 16.241+:4-16, RS 16.254C+:10-11, and RS 16.281:4-11. For the formulary of sale clauses, see Kienast, "Kauf," p. 534. For the preferred perfect form, see Huehnergard, *The Akkadian of Ugarit*, p. 250, and van Soldt, *SAU*, p. 496. As for the Babylonian and Assyrian forms (*ilteqe* and *iltaqe* respectively), see Huehnergard, *The Akkadian of Ugarit*, pp. 54-55, and van Soldt, *SAU*, p. 433 (both including an analysis of their chronological distribution).

39 RS 16.133:4-10, RS 16.139:4-19, or RS 15.139:4 (where the complement *ina šīmišu gamri* defines the transaction).

40 The preposition *kīma* is probably to be restored in line 6 (following Nougayrol's edition). This wording should accordingly be distinguished from the *našû-nadānu* formula. Libolt, however, included RS 15.70 in his corpus of royal land grants and put forward a *leqû-nadānu* formula analogous to the common *našû-nadānu*. The difference, in his opinion, is that "in a *našû-nadānu* transaction the king 'lifts up' but does not acquire the property in question. *Leqû* marks the property as an acquisition for the king. In modern terms approximately applicable to the ancient situation —he then concludes—, *leqû-nadānu* marks the transaction as private, not official" (*Royal Land Grants*, p. 34). The difference, in our view, is both of formulary and content. As we have mentioned above, *našû* in the *našû-nadānu* formula has no legal efficacy, unlike *leqû*. And a *leqû-nadānu* formula does not exist as such in Ugarit (the other example he quotes, namely RS 15.109+, is based on a misunderstanding of the text: *leqû* and *nadānu* have a different subject and accordingly refer to two different transactions, the transferee's acquisition [*leqû*] and the king's transfer [*nadānu*]). On the other hand, there is nothing to suggest that the notions of "private" and "official" (no doubt irrelevant here) can be deduced from the use of one or other verb formula.

property) with PN_2." The expression used is *pūḫata epēšu* the literal meaning of which is "to make an exchange" (RS 16.140 and RS 16.371); once, in RS 15.86, the verb is written in Hurrian, namely *puḫ=ugar=oš=i* glossing the Sumerogram ki.bi.gar.ra.[41]

Two other verbs describe conveyance transactions, namely *paṭāru* "to redeem" and *pašāru* "to release," both further defined with *ina kaspi* "for silver." One may say that they both denote the same kind of transaction, the former from the point of view of the receiver (buyer) and the latter from the point of view of the giver (vendor). Whereas in general it is difficult legally speaking to distinguish a transaction described with the expression *pašāru ina kaspi* from another using *nadānu ina kaspi*, the verb *paṭāru* (cf. in Ugaritic PDY) leaves less room for ambiguity.[42] The meaning of the latter, viz. "to redeem, ransom," makes clear that the subject is actually buying *back* a (real or moveable) property from the vendor. Note the clause (in RS 18.21) *PN_1 iptaṭar ina X kaspi O ištu qāti PN_2*.[43]

A form (possibly Ugaritic) of *paṭāru* is found in a royal deed (RS 15.123+) involving an exchange of real property between two people. Lines 4-5 read: *PN_1 u PN_2 na-ap-ṭa-ru eqla ina eqli*. Because of the am-

---

[41] As mentioned in the last chapter, namely note 87, this reading was already suggested by Speiser in "Akkadian Documents from Ras Shamra," p. 164 (correct therefore Malbran-Labat, "Langues et écritures à Ougarit," p. 81); see also Huehnergard, "RS 15.86 (*PRU* 3, 51f.)," p. 170, and van Soldt, *SAU*, p. 350 n. 209. For the attestations of this Hurrian verb in Nuzi, see Jeanette Fincke, "Beiträge zum Lexikon des Hurritischen von Nuzi," SCCNH 7 (1995):17-19. Huehnergard suggested "with all due reservation" that his reading *ma-a-⌜ar⌝* (instead of Nougayrol's *a-di-in*[??]) in RS 15.86:9 may render the *qatal(a)* form a hitherto unattested Ugaritic verb MW/YR meaning "to exchange" (see also his *Ugaritic Vocabulary*, pp. 145-146, followed e.g. by Malbran-Labat "Langues et écritures à Ougarit," p. 81). After collation, what we read and accordingly restore is the common phrase *a-di ⌜da⌝[-ri-ti]*, closing the conveyance clause (see section 21 below); so that a Ugaritic verb MW/YR "to exchange" would remain unattested for the time being.

[42] Regarding *pašāru*, Arnaud has recently remarked that this verb (in particular in RS 17.238) "ne signifie pas 'vendre' etc., mais 'vendre à vil prix sous l'effet de la necessité" (review of *Sobre "el modo de producción asiático" en Ugarit* by J.-A. Zamora, Syria 77 [2000]:321). Kienast includes it in his sale formulas (in "Kauf," p. 534). Note that only preterite forms are attested for this verb (see van Soldt, *SAU*, p. 495).

[43] The nature of the transaction is clearly revealed by the fact that the plot of land (6 *ikū*s) is acquired (viz. bought back) from an individual from the neighbouring country of Siyannu. Cf. the Ugaritic ransom clause *PN_1 pdy O* [viz. seven people] *w pdyhm PN_1 X ksp byd GN* (i.e. gentilic) in RS 16.191+ (KTU 3.4) (note the iterative [and chiastic] formula syntactically parallel to the Ugaritic grant formula mentioned above in 2).

biguity of the form (presumably to be analyzed as *napṭarū*),[44] it is not possible for the time being to determine the exact nature of the transaction (perhaps an exchange of land previously held as pledge?).[45]

6. The description of real property

As a rule, real property is the object of the conveyance described in royal deeds. It basically consists of houses (*bītu*, Ug. *bt*) and land (*eqlu*, Ug. *šd*), sometimes including vineyards (*karānu*, Ug. *krm*) and olive groves (*serdu*, Ug. *zt*) as the most characteristic cultures of this Mediterranean area. Farms housing oil and wine pressing installations are rather frequently listed with them (*dimtu*, Ug. *gt*). Occasionally other buildings such as barns and stables as well as other kinds of groves and orchards are also object of conveyances.[46] When the property includes more than a house or a field, like in RS 16.201 (see the transliteration of the text in chapter 5), the complementary estates are often coordinated with the preposition *qadu* (Ug. *yd*) "including, together with," and generally concluded with the formula *qadu gabbi mimmûšu* (and variants, in Ugaritic *yd klklh*) "together with everything else that belongs to it (probably meaning the movables attached to the property)."[47]

The description of the property conveyed, however, is usually laconic providing only the name of a person, presumably the previous tenant. No measurements or boundaries (according to the cardinal points or *inter adfinis circumcirca*) are given, and sometimes a brief geographical refer-

[44] See Huehnergard, *Ugaritic Vocabulary*, p. 167.

[45] Cf. also the technical term *tapdētu* discussed above in 3.

[46] The expressions for barns and stables are *bīt sīsî* (RS 16.239:21; after collation I read é.ḫi.a anše.kur.ra.[m]eš), *bīt tarbaṣi* (RS 16.189:17), *bīt alpī* (ibid. l. 17); note also among the buildings what might be a sort of granary or storehouse (Ugaritic *ḫ/ḥāyu*, *ḫ/ḥēyu*, *ḫ/ḥīyu*; see Huehnergard, *Ugaritic Vocabulary*, pp. 127-128, and del Olmo and Sanmartín, *Dictionary of the Ugaritic Language*, p. 380 s.v. ḥwy). As for other, specific kinds of fields or plantations, orchards (*kirû*) are sometimes mentioned, as well as forests or woods: *qištu* (RS 15.132:6, RS 16.255D rev. 7'), an oak wood (*allanu* in RS 15.122:9), a palm grove (*gišimmaru* in RS 16.204:15), and perhaps a cedar wood (in RS 15.140:10: a.šà.meš er[ín]$^{(?)}$.meš); salt marshes (in Ugaritic *ṣī/ēṣūma*) are also conveyed in RS 15.147:4', RS 15.163+:12 and RS 17.379[A]:2').

[47] Note that in RS 16.295, the house and field conveyed viz. granted also includes oxen, donkeys and small cattle, and is also followed by the expression *gabba mimmîšu*. For the different writings of this expression, see Huehnergard, *The Akkadian of Ugarit*, pp. 141-142. The preposition *qadu* seems to be almost exclusively used in these descriptions of property (see Huehnergard, *The Akkadian of Ugarit*, p. 189).

ence to its location is added.[48] The examples given in transliteration in chapter 5 are illustrative enough. The granted property (obviously in the accusative) in RS 16.142 is formulated in lines 4-5 simply as *bīta eqla ša PN* "house (and) field of PN." In RS 16.201, a reference to the location of the property is added (line 5): *ša ina TN* (toponym) "(house) which is in TN" (cf. also line 7). The Ugaritic counterpart is spelled *d b TN*.[49] The fact that notaries did not provide a more accurate description of houses and fields contrasts with the practice in other cuneiform chanceries (such as Emar for example), but interestingly follows very closely the provision found in the so-called Middle Assyrian laws concerning land sale, discussed in chapter 2. Indeed, the property to be sold as announced by the Assyrian herald (and indeed recorded in proper Middle Assyrian sale documents) is described as "the field or house of so-and-so, son of so-and-so, (situated) within the area of the town in question" (*eqla u bēta ša annanna mār annanna ina ugār āle annie).* One should also refer to the similar wording used to describe the property purchased by Jeremiah quoted in chapter 1, Jer 32:9: "And I bought the field of Hanamel my uncle's son, that was in Anathot (*ʾšr b ʿntwt*)."

The name of the former tenant that identifies the real property transferred is sometimes qualified with a title or condition. Of special legal interest are the terms *nayyālu*, attested in 15 deeds (as well as in Middle Assyrian records in similar contexts) and which possibly designates a person who died without legitimate descendants, and *bēl arni* a "criminal" only once attested (RS 16.145:4).[50] As shown, however, by RS 15.Y

[48] Note that some deeds describe the conveyed real property in *ikūs*, the surface measure at Ugarit, borrowed at some early time from Mesopotamia (the value at Ugarit cannot be determined [see Liverani, "Ras Shamra. Histoire," col. 1318] but it probably did not differ much from the Mesopotamian "dike" [ca. 0.36 ha.]). This indication, however, is not really meant as a description of the field but rather serves to determine the rights to the partial surface of the field conveyed; note in this regard the reference to "half of the field" (*mišil eqli*) conveyed in RS 16.160:6. What is significant, nevertheless, is that this evidence suggests that the plots in question were indeed measured; it is therefore possible that other, perhaps all property conveyed was actually measured (following the text of the Middle Assyrian laws and deeds), but not recorded in royal deeds (see our remarks in chapter 2).

[49] The Ugaritic text has *d b šd* followed by the toponym (in RS 16.382 [KTU 3.5]:6), the counterpart of Akkadian *ša ina eqli*. See Huehnergard, *The Akkadian of Ugarit*, p. 246, and van Soldt, *SAU*, pp. 484, 492-494, who includes an analysis of the chronological distribution of the variant constructions *ša ina X* (Ug. *d b*) and *ina X*.

[50] The royal deeds in which *nayyālu* appears qualifying the person naming the conveyed property are: RS 15.89, RS 15.122, RS 15.141, RS 15.145, RS 15.168, RS 15.Y, RS 16.86+, RS 16.141, RS 16.174, RS 16.248, RS 16.255A+, RS 17.379[A], RS 18.22, and probably to be restored in RS 16.262 and RS 19.98 (cf.

and RS 16.142, both recording the same conveyance, the qualification of the former tenant as *nayyālu* did not seem to be a requisite.[51] It is therefore possible that more ex-tenants in our corpus belonged to this category.

We mentioned above that in a few cases entire towns or villages can

---

RS 17.61); the Middle Assyrian documents are KAJ 160, KAJ 162 and KAV 212 (the parallel was pointed out by Paul Garelli, "Le problème de la 'féodalité' assyrienne," Semitica 17 [1967]:10). The term *nayyālu* has been generally understood since the edition of *PRU* 3 as a kind of defaulter in his liabilities for royal service (see e.g. Michael Heltzer, *The Rural Community of Ancient Ugarit* [Wiesbaden, 1976], pp. 52-57; Haase, "Anmerkungen zum ugaritischen Immobilienkauf, pp. 202-203; Liverani, "Ras Shamra. Histoire," col. 1343; Kestemont, "Remarques sur les aspects juridiques du commerce dans le Proche-Orient du XIVe siècle avant notre ère," Iraq 39 [1977]:198-199; Kienast, "Rechtsurkunden in ugaritischer Sprache," p. 439; or Gary N. Knoppers, "Ancient Near Eastern Royal Grants and the Davidic Covenant: a Parallel?," JAOS 116 [1996]:688 n. 103). Estates so qualified have therefore been understood as real property escheating to the king for disciplinary reasons (incidentally taken to support the meaning of *našû* as "taking away," see the discussion above). Although forfeiture of land is clear in the case of someone who turned against his king (*bēl arni*), the case of the *nayyālu* is not beyond doubt. As a matter of fact, the original interpretation given by Nougayrol ("Textes de Ras-Shamra en cunéiformes syllabiques," p. 185) seems more likely to me (and to Libolt, *Royal Land Grants*, pp. 19 and 88, and Schloen, *The House of the Father*, pp. 248-249). There, the French Assyriologist wrote that "il s'agit explicitement, selon moi, de: biens de défunts (noting the literal translation "gisant"), tombés sans doute en déshérence." Note that this very meaning perfectly suits the Middle Assyrian evidence (Postgate first understood the term as "a man with no living father and no male heirs," in "Land Tenure in the Middle Assyrian Period," p. 509). Nougayrol later changed his mind on account of RS 16.174 recording the sale of real property of a *nayyālu* (*PRU* 3, p. 29 n. 5; cf. also Postgate's "Second Attempt" on land tenure in the Middle Assyrian kingdom [p. 311]). In our opinion, what the text attests to is the sale of property *of* (i.e. that belonged to) a *nayyālu* but not *from* a (living) *nayyālu*. A full discussion of the evidence and the legal situation will appear in my forthcoming article "Land Tenure and Royal Administration in Late Bronze Age Ugarit." What I would still like to point out here is the semantic, viz. etymological parallel between the Akkadian term *nayyālu* (from the verb *nâlu* "to lie down [sleep]") and the Latin technical term *hereditas iacens*, which significantly designates the "lethargic" state of a property between the death of its owner/tenant and the acquisition by its heir.

[51] In RS 15.Y as opposed to RS 16.142 (see the transliteration at the end of chapter 5) Binḫattiyīma is called *nayyālu*. Note also that in four deeds the ex-tenant bears the title of *šatammu* "steward" (RS 15.141, RS 16.143 quoted above, RS 16.148+, and RS 16.201); and a number of transferees are also stewards (RS 16.174 and RS 16.178).

also be the object of royal grants.[52] Some of them seem to be small villages or hamlets needing rebuilding work and even resettlement.[53] As explicitly provided by RS 15.114 and RS 15.147, the restoration of the granted village, in the latter also its resettlement, is actually the condition stipulated by the donor-king.[54] At any rate, what the grantee of a village or town was given was the right of management of its own finances and taxes. Note that the same deed RS 15.114 states that the king has exempted the village from royal services, RS 16.153 records the different local taxes that belong to the grantee (such as the tithe or the grazing tax), and in another royal deed, namely RS 16.244, the object of the transfer is not the town itself (Biʾru) but explicitly a number of its taxes.

7. The ṣamādu *formula*

A formula occurring rather frequently in deeds of conveyance, especially although not exclusively in sales and barters,[55] states after the conveyance clause that the property conveyed "is bound" (*ṣamid*) to the transferee (*ana PN*), more often than not adding also "and to his sons."[56]

---

[52] Upper and Lower Yēnā in RS 15.147 (for the reading of this toponym, see van Soldt, *The Topography of the City-State of Ugarit*, p. 25), Šaknā in RS 15.114 (for the reading see my comments above n. 10 and my review in ZA 93 [2003]:291), Kumba in RS 16.202 (see my comments too in n. 10), Uḫnappu in RS 16.276, and the fragmentary E…iš in RS 16.153.

[53] See above section 2.

[54] Note also that the obligation of rebuilding or restoring real property is also provided for in the royal grant of a house that had formerly belonged to a *nayyālu* (RS 15.168).

[55] RS 16.134, RS 16.162, RS 16.242, RS 16.363, and RS 17.01, record royal grants. Examples of sales are RS 15.136, RS 16.131, RS 16.137, or RS 16.154; and for barters, see RS 15.70, RS 15.86, RS 16.131, RS 16.246, or RS 16.343.

[56] I would once more agree with Nougayrol when he wrote in *PRU* 6, p. 154 n. 2 that "dans l'état actuel de notre information, il ne me paraît pas indispensable d'admettre un verbe *ṣamâtu* particulier à Ugarit," namely with the meaning "to transfer," as has been suggested by a number of scholars (see Huehnergard, *Ugaritic Vocabulary*, pp. 171-172, who includes a review of the previous proposals). Van Soldt has pointed out (in my opinion, convincingly) the arguments in favour of Nougayrol's reading (see *SAU*, p. 244 n. 9). To his arguments I would like to add the semantically and significantly related use (also in Ugarit) of the verbs *paṭāru* "to untie" and *pašāru* "to loosen" in legal context with the respective meanings "to redeem" and "to release" (as we have seen in 5; cf. also *rakāsu* in 18). It is in fact this relation that allows an extended meaning of "to bind beyond redemption" for *ṣamādu* (or "to alienate" as understood by Westbrook, "The Price Factor in the Redemption of Land," pp. 124-126, also in the light of Hebrew *li-ṣᵉmīṯūṯ* in Lev

The "binding" clause is naturally to be understood in a technical sense, and is presumably meant to make clear or emphasize the rights of the transferee, or even specify them (as a non-redeemable transfer?).[57] In about a dozen cases, the verb form *ṣamid* is immediately followed in the clause by the phrase *ina šam/pši ūmi* "in broad daylight,"[58] probably denoting the publicity of the transfer and thereby seeking to prevent challenges to the "binding" transfer by the other party or other individuals. Note that in one deed (RS 16.147) the properties conveyed were bound to the transferee (*ṣamadū ana PN*) "before the king" (*ana pāni šarri*).

8. The sequential ("1st-2nd") formula or royal confirmation clause

Some royal deeds, almost all of them of conveyance, contain a double formula describing a sequence of transactions.[59] The two clauses are introduced by the ordinals "first" (*ištēn*[*šu*], once *ittilta*) and "secondly" (*šanâm*[*ma*], *šanītam* or *ina šanīšu*), both used adverbially.[60] This for-

---

25:30; see also Yochanan Muffs, *Studies in the Aramiac Legal Papyri from Elephantine* [New York, 1973], p. 20 and n. 3). The aspect of redemption may be supported by the fact that the word is written with the logogram šám.til.la (RS 16.356:9) or šàm.til.la (RS 15.123:7, 9 and 14, and RS 16.207:9); cf. šàm.til.la.bi.šè in RS 16.147:13 followed by the glossed word *ṣamadū* (cf. RS 16.174:12). One needs to recall and quote in full the subtle remark made by Nougayrol (*PRU* 3, p. 226): "quant au fond de la question, on peut admettre qu'un transfert de type $ŠAM_{2/3}$.TIL.LA.BI.ŠÈ avait pour effet immédiat un état *ṣamid*."

[57] See the previous footnote. It is simply called "Perfizierungsklausel" by Haase ("Anmerkungen zum ugaritischen Immobilienkauf," p. 200, followed in turn by Kienast, "Kauf," p. 535).

[58] The translation given by CAD Š/1, p. 338 "from today on" should be corrected (probably mistaken for *ištu ūmi annîm*). The reference given by CAD and quoted by Lackenbacher (*Textes akkadiens d'Ugarit*, p. 247 n. 844), namely *ina šam/pši ūmi adi dārīti* in the unpublished private deed RS 22.399+:8 is in fact the end of a fragmentary *ṣamādu*-formula and has therefore nothing to do with the phrase "from today - forever."

[59] RS 15.85:22-26, RS 15.109+:3 and 51-52, RS 15.119 rev. 12'-17' (cf. lines 11ff.), RS 15.139:14-17, RS 15.Z:16-18, RS 16.140:18-20, RS 16.174:9-15, RS 16.192+:14-17, RS 16.200:4-8 and 25-28, RS 16.249:7-9, RS 16.277:9-14, and the fragmentary RS 15.150:3'-5'. The *Sammelurkunde* RS 15.109+ presents the formula at the beginning and at the end of the text; and RS 16.200 contains two different double formulas. For the formula, see also Kienast, "Rechtsurkunden in ugaritischer Sprache," p. 443.

[60] See Huehnergard, *The Akkadian of Ugarit*, pp. 197-198 and 200, and van Soldt, *SAU*, pp. 411 and 468-469. For the syntactical order, see Finley, *Word Order*, p.

mula seems in some cases to further define the rights proper of the transferee. Of the nine deeds of conveyance that preserve this double formula, eight record that "secondly, the king has given the property to the transferee" (phrased either with *nadānu* or with *našû-nadānu*).[61] What is recorded "first" is that the transferee has acquired the property for silver (*leqû ina kaspi*) or that the transferor viz. donor, vendor or exchanger has conveyed it (*nadānu*). Thus, for example, after describing the gift (with the formula *našû-nadānu*), presumably the dowry, of a father-in-law to his daughter-in-law (namely the king's sister), RS 15.85:22-26 runs: *ištēnšu* PN_1 *emuša ittadinšu u ina šanîšu RN šarru ittašīšunu u ittadinšunu ana* PN_2 *aḫātišu*. In the remaining deed of conveyance (RS 15.Z) the first clause states that the king has given the property to the transferee, and the second that the transferee has given a certain amount of silver to the king. This kind of mutual conveyance can be found in other deeds phrased in independent clauses, that is, without the use of the sequential "first ... and secondly" clause (as we have seen above in section 3), so that it is reasonable to argue that the sequential formula has in principle no legal significance at least in this last example. In contrast, in deeds describing sales or barters between two individuals, the presence of this formula and especially its second part seems to denote the royal confirmation of the transfer and possibly also the benefits of a royal grant proper bestowed onto the transferee.[62]

Royal confirmation is not only attested for conveyances of real property between individuals. Immediately after describing the adoption of a son by his adoptive mother (phrased with the verb *leqû*, see 18 below), RS 16.200:4-8 states that "first (*ištēn*) PN (the adopter) has taken him (the adoptee) and secondly (*šanâm*) RN_1, son of RN_2, king of Ugarit, has given him (*ittadinšu*) as her son."[63]

The last example of the formula appears in a deed (RS 16.192A+) recording a case of litigation and the resulting verdict of the king: first, it says, the sons of PN have freed him (presumably from family claims), and secondly RN has freed him.[64]

111.

[61] With *nadānu* alone: RS 15.109+, RS 15.119, RS 15.139, RS 16.140, RS 16.249, RS 16.277, cf. also RS 16.200; with *našû-nadānu*: RS 15.85, RS 16.174. Note that the phrase "and to his (the transferee's) sons" is added in RS 15.119, RS 15.139, and RS 16.277, and the adverb "forever" in RS 15.119 and RS 15.139.

[62] See Boyer, "Étude juridique," pp. 285-286.

[63] In the first clause the verb form *ilteqēša* shows a scribal lapse (note the correct form *taltaqe* in line 3), clearly mixing up (the gender of) subject and object (perhaps due to Hurrian influence?).

[64] The same formulary and kind of dispute is attested in the non-royal deed RS

9. The warranty clause against eviction

As important and indispensable as the clause defining the conveyance and the new rights accordingly established in royal deeds of conveyance is the clause recording the warranty against the transferee's dispossession of the acquired property.[65] The connection between these two clauses is clear: the former refers to the completed transaction (accordingly formulated in the past tense), and the latter provides for the continuity of the resulting legal situation, that is, as having effect also in the future (and so formulated in the future tense). The parallelism is not only of content but also formal. Indeed, just as the former is introduced by the adverbial phrase "from today," the latter is very often introduced by the adverbial (accusative) phrase *urra(m) šēra(m)* literally "tomorrow at dawn," naturally meaning "any time in the future" (some notaries, especially from the reign of Niqmepa^{c} on, seemed to consider it otiose and simply dropped it).[66] The Ugaritic counterpart is attested in RS 16.382 (KTU 3.5);[67] following a new epigraphic collation by Robert Hawley and Dennis Pardee, the phrase (in line 15) should read *šḥr ṯlṯt* "tomorrow (or) the day after."[68]

17.67, in which the *sākinu* official appears presiding over the lawsuit instead of the king.

[65] This kind of clause and the legal notion underlying it should be distinguished from a no-contest clause (see below under 19, and correct thus Lackenbacher, *Textes akkadiens d'Ugarit*, pp. 111-112; see also Skaist, "A Unique Closing Fromula," p. 154). The presence of this clause in a deed of adoption (RS 16.200) may point to the fictional nature of the transaction (as pointed out by Nougayrol, *PRU* 3, p. 65 n. 2), but it may also be due to the stereotyped character of the formula itself. For another potential fictional adoption (grandfather-grandson), cf. RS 16.295 (see my chapter on "Ugarit" in *A History of Ancient Near Eastern Law*, p. 728). For the absence (rather than omission) of this clause, see footnote 76 below.

[66] Note that in the diplomatic document RS 16.270:30 *urram šēram* (spelled *ur-ra-am še-ra*) is immediately followed by the expression *ina arkat ūmi* literally meaning "after today," emphasizing the meaning "in the future" of both phrases.

[67] Like in some Akkadian deeds, it is also omitted in RS 15.111 (KTU 3.2) and RS 94.2965.

[68] The new readings are to be discussed in their common study "Le texte juridique RS 16.382 (KTU 3.5): nouvelle étude épigraphique" scheduled for Semitica 52-53 (2002-2003) [2004], unavailable to me when I wrote these lines. As shown by the photograph (and copy) of the tablet provided by Bordreuil and Pardee in their *Manuel d'Ougaritique* (the text is no. 37 in their "Choix de textes"), the first sign indeed looks more like {ṯ} than {^{c}}, rendering the reading *ṯl⌜ṯ⌝t* in line 15 more likely than *^{c}lmt*, as generally accepted since the *editio princeps* (see e.g. del Olmo and Sanmartín, *Dictionary of the Ugaritic Language*, p. 159 who propose the unlikely literal meaning "the dawn of eternities" and the inaccurate resulting transla-

The clause is actually formulated as a prohibition against any interference with the transferee's enjoyment of the property in the future. What it states is "in the future no one shall take it (i.e. the property) from PN (the transferee)," very often adding "or from his sons" followed by the adverbial phrase "forever" like in the conveyance clause (see 20 and 21 below).[69] In Akkadian it reads *urra(m) šēra(m) (amīlu) mamma(n) ul / lā ila/eqqēšu ištu qāti PN* (in some texts, the phrase *ištu qāti PN* precedes the verb, and in others the indefinite personal pronoun is *mannumma/mê*).[70] The four extant Ugaritic examples use variant formulas. RS 16.382 (KTU 3.5) has: *šḥr ṯlṯt bnš bnšm l yqḥnn bd PN* "tomorrow (or) the day after nobody shall take it from PN;" RS 15.111 (KTU 3.2) reads: *mnk mnkm l yqḥ O bd PN* "no one shall take O (the property) from PN," both deeds adding "or from his sons forever." RS 94.2965 has: *bnš l yqḥ O bd PN*, and RS 15.125 (KTU 2.19) (having "the royal deed" as object) reads: *w mnkm l yqḥ spr mlk hnd b yd PN*, the latter two adding also the adverbial expression "forever."[71]

---

tion "forever"). Samuel E. Loewenstamm in his review of *PRU* 2 appeared in Tarbiz 28 (1959):244-250 (reproduced in English translation in id., *Comparative Studies in Biblical and Ancient Oriental Literatures* [Neukirchen-Vluyn, 1980], pp. 81-90) already remarked that the expression *ᶜlmt* is obscure (ibid., p. 84 n. 12), and later in his review of *Ras Shamra Parallels vol. 1*, ed. L.R. Fisher (Rome, 1972) appeared in Biblica 56 (1975):115, he suggested to translate the hapaxlegomenon as "evening" in view of parallel expressions. The meaning of the expression, namely the indefinite future, and its potential parallels in other provinces of law (such as the Elephantine colony in fifth-century Egypt) will be dealt with in the next chapter; as for the use of *ṯlṯt* to denote "the day after tomorrow (literally, the third day)," see the recently published Ugaritic letter RS 94.2406:8 (*Manuel d'Ougaritique*, text no. 31).

[69] Note also the parallel syntactical order (S-V-O) with the conveyance clause; see Finley, *Word Order*, p. 96, and Huehnergard, *The Akkadian of Ugarit*, pp. 220-221.

[70] As stated by van Soldt, the prepositional phrase can either follow or precede the verb, but the former possibility is preferred in more than 70 per cent of all occurrences (*SAU*, p. 482). For the use of the different forms of indefinite pronouns (*mamman, mamma, mannumma, mannummê*), and their chronological distribution, see Huehnergard, *The Akkadian of Ugarit*, p. 137 (and p. 138 n. 68 for the use of *amīlu mamma[n]*), and van Soldt, *SAU*, p. 408. For the prohibitive, either *ul* or *lā* may be used in Ugarit; see Huehnergard, *The Akkadian of Ugarit*, p. 239, and van Soldt, *SAU*, p. 510 (with an analysis of their chronological distribution); Huehnergard (on p. 274) takes this interchangeability as one more example of reduction of allomorphism. For the formula and its variants, see also Kienast, "Rechtsurkunden in ugaritischer Sprache," p. 443.

[71] RS 94.2965 is published in Bordreuil and Pardee's *Manuel d'Ougaritique* as text no. 39. Concerning the Ugaritic subject of the clause in RS 16.382 (KTU 3.5),

Note that although the stereotyped verb of the clause is *leqû* (Ug. LQḤ),[72] the verb *ekēmu* "to take away" is used in five deeds.[73]

Nougayrol already pointed out that in royal deeds this clause "met surtout le bénéficiaire à l'abri des caprices du souverain, ou de ses successeurs."[74] Because the formula only seems to appear in royal deeds, with the exception of RS 17.61 (where a state official appears possibly acting on behalf of the king)[75], and also in view of potential parallels from Hittite and Alalakh treaty texts, Skaist concluded in agreement with the editor of the texts that the clause is to be interpreted as the king's promise "that no one —himself, a future king or officials in charge of

---

although we agree with, and follow, the reading *bunušu bunušuma* (i.e. the latter word also in singular with the enclitic suffix) proposed by Bordreuil and Pardee (ibid., vol. II, p. 104, cf. *bunušu* alone in RS 94.2965, *mnk mnkm* and *mnkm*, the latter word also clearly with the enclitic, in RS 15.111 [KTU 3.2] and RS 15.125 [KTU 2.19] respectively; for the interpretation of the word as a plural form, see Libolt, *Royal Land Grants*, p. 105, or del Olmo and Sanmartín, *Dictionary of the Ugaritic Language*, p. 230), we prefer to translate the expression as "nobody" rather than "aucun membre du personnel royal." Their translation seems to follow the long accepted, although far from unquestionable, equivalence between *bunušu* and *bunušu malki* (see my objections in "The King's Men in Ugarit and Society in Late Bronze Age," JESHO 45 [2002]:5-7); on the other hand, our favoured, impersonal translation "no one, nobody" rather agrees with the Akkadian counterpart *(amīlu) mamma(n)*, or also the attested indefinite pronoun *mannum-ma/ê* in a few deeds (e.g. RS 15.91, 16.140, RS 16.356, or RS 16.200) as well as with the alternative Ugaritic expressions *mnk mnkm* or *mnkm*.

72 For the forms *ileqqe* and *ilaqqe*, see Huehnergard, *The Akkadian of Ugarit*, pp. 55-56, and van Soldt, *SAU*, p. 433, both with an analysis of the chronological distribution of the forms. Note that there are three cases (RS 16.167, RS 16.200 and RS 16.240) in which the preterite form (*ilqe*) is used instead of the expected durative (see Huehnergard, *The Akkadian of Ugarit*, p. 253, and van Soldt, *SAU*, pp. 501-2; Huehnergard's fourth example, RS 15.140:17, is not to be included, after van Soldt's collation: ⌜*i-laq*⌝[-*qè*] [kindly made available to me]). Both authors (*The Akkadian of Ugarit*, p. 255, and *SAU*, p. 501) propose to explain these cases as a result of Ugaritic influence (viz. the use of /YQTL/ + Ø for the prohibitive).

73 RS 15.85 (collated by van Soldt [see *SAU*, p. 430 n. 63]), RS 16.140, RS 16.150, RS 16.156, and RS 16.262. It is noteworthy that in RS 16.140 the warranty clause is curiously repeated, the first formula with *leqû* (l. 15) and the second closing the text with *ekēmu* (line 23).

74 In *PRU* 3, p. 30. See also Haase, "Anmerkungen zum ugaritischen Immobilienkauf," p. 200.

75 As pointed out by Heltzer, *The Rural Community*, p. 56. Note, however, that the same wording also appears in RS 18.274 (perhaps a fragment of a royal deed, as mentioned in chapter 1) and RS 17.20:2'-4' (discussed below).

royal lands— would take the property from the current recipient."[76] It is indeed reasonable to assume that warranty of real property in the royal deeds of Ugarit was primarily a means of protecting conveyances against royal challenge or eviction. A king wishing to take back, say, a granted property may have thus been unable to eject the transferee (see also the curse formulas in 22 below, presumably addressed to a king or any person or official with access to the deeds and/or recorded rights). But it is also possible that the king's promise of non-interference (we should not forget that royal deeds are presided over by the monarch and sealed with the dynastic seal) did not mean so much that he or a successor of his would not interfere, but that the property was his, and that accordingly his was first and ultimately the right to give it. It is significant in this regard that tenants did not seem to have the right to convey property presumably given by the king without the latter's consent or due authorisation, judging from the fact that the ruler appears presiding over allegedly private transactions and eventually confirming the resulting transfer (see 8 above). On the other hand, in view of the famous case of forgery of the dynastic seal and of royal deeds (RS 16.249), as well as the few cases of litigation on title to land recorded in royal deeds (RS 16.245, RS 16.254C and RS 16.356, whose purpose is of course the resulting transfer of rights), one wonders whether the party against whose eviction the warranty clause is meant should be taken to be exclusively the ruler himself.[77] Furthermore, in some deeds, the warranty clause is followed by a no-contest clause (RS 16.145, RS 16.276, see below 19) or a penalty clause against potential litigants (RS 15.86, RS 16.189, see below 22). It is eloquent that in RS 15.86, the penal stipulation is formulated with the

---

[76] "A Unique Closing Formula," p. 155 (for the external parallels, see chapter 7 below). Perhaps the translation "member of the royal personnel" of Ugaritic *bunušu* in this clause suggested by Bordreuil and Pardee (see note 71 above) has been influenced by this argument. To the remark made by Skaist (p. 158) that "there are a few grants in which the *lā ileqqe* clause is entirely omitted," further suggesting that they "would then appear to be revocable gifts," one should object that his examples (in footnote 23), namely RS 15.90 and RS 15.Y are not fully relevant (neither for that matter the additional four deeds listed by Libolt [*Royal Land Grants*, p. 107]). RS 15.90 is not a grant but a division of shares among brothers, and RS 15.Y is an "updating" of RS 16.142: as we suggested above in chapter 3, it does contain a grant clause (actually a confirmation of a grant made by Niqmepa^{c}'s predecessor), but the text primarily concerns the grantee's promotion to a higher status (see section 16 below), and the same holds true of the other examples put forward by Libolt. What interests us here is the fact that the *lā ileqqe* clause in RS 15.Y is indeed present in RS 16.142 (perhaps the reason why this earlier deed was not discarded).

[77] Kienast, "Kauf," pp. 535-36, also considered that the warranty was meant too for a potential third party i.e. other than the king.

same words used in the warranty clause: "whoever takes O from PN or his sons" (*ša ilaqqe O ištu qāti PN u mārišu*),[78] similar to the one found in the private deed RS 17.20:2'-4': *šumma urra šēra amīlu mamma ša ilaqqe eqla ištu qāti PN* ("if somebody in the future takes the field [conveyed] from PN").

10. The (p)ilku-*service clause*

Royal deeds of conveyance often contain stipulations on the services to be performed (or not) by the transferee. This clause that can either precede or follow the guarantee clause is only attested in royal deeds, which means that we are dealing here with obligations of property owed to the king. The most common is the statement that the property is or is not liable to the royal service traditionally called *ilku* in Mesopotamia, but whose favourite by-form at Ugarit is *pilku*, in Ugaritic *ᵓunuṯṯu*.[79] The

[78] No doubt the reason why the notary wrongly added *lā ilaqqe* (at the end of line 22), mixing up the two formulas.

[79] That the Akkadian terms *ilku* and *pilku* and Ugaritic *ᵓunuṯṯu* denote the same notion (viz. royal service) in Late Bronze Age Ugarit is clearly revealed by the context viz. formulas in which they appear (note that the Ugaritic word is used, spelled syllabically, in three Akkadian deeds of the time of Niqmaddu II: RS 15.89:20, RS 16.156:15 and RS 16.167:17). It is important to note with this regard that the three words are always used independently, i.e. two of them never appear together in the same text (the restoration of the word *pilku* in RS 16.156:11 suggested by Nougayrol [only the sign PÍL can be distinguished in this damaged line] is by its very nature tentative and does not quite agree with the structure of the text). Moreover, as will be shown in the next chapter, the use of one form or the other in a deed seems to be directly related to the scribal hand (see already my "Royal Land Grants and *ilku*-Service in Ugarit. The Legal Mechanism," in *Landwirtschaft im alten Orient*, ed. H. Klengel and J. Renger [Berlin 1999], p. 172). As for the meaning of the words, the etymology of the by-form *pilku* cannot stray far from the verb *palāku*, as stated by Speiser ("Akkadian Documents from Ras Shamra," p. 162), and clearly echoes the classical Mesopotamian noun derived from *alāku* (the suggestion to read the word as *[y]ilku*, put forward by Dietrich and Loretz ["*pilku* = *ilku* 'Lehenspflicht'," UF 4 [1972]:165-66], is not possible, as stated by Huehnergard, [*Ugaritic Vocabulary*, p. 168]). Ugaritic *ᵓunuṯṯu*, in turn, is clearly of Hurrian etymology; probably to be analyzed as *un=o=(š)še*, the word is derived from the verb *un-* "to come" (like Akkadian *ilku*, see already Igor M. Diakonoff, "Some Remarks on I 568," ArOr 47 [1979]:41). What is interesting and of relevance for our discussion of the formulas is that the same Hurrian verb can have a transitive meaning, namely "to bring, to bear" (in Akkadian *abālu*). Different meanings for the terms have been mainly proposed by Heltzer (see especially his "Zum Steuersystem in Ugarit [pilku-ubdy und Ähnliches]," in *Vorträge gehalten auf der 28. Rencontre Assyriologique Internationale in Wien* (AfO Beiheft 19), ed. H. Hirsch and H.

verb used to denote the liability to or the performance of the service is *abālu* "to bear, carry" (in Ugaritic YBL). Because the provision concerns the future obligations due to the king, the verb is conjugated in the durative (the forms being *ubbal* [3s] or *ubbalū* [3p], and in Ugaritic in the /YQTL/ conjugation, *ybl* [3s] to be probably vocalized */yabilu/*).[80] In Ugarit one finds two kinds of *(p)ilku*-service owed by the tenement, one explicitly related to the tenant's property or house and another connected to the tenant's personal profession or category. Thus we find the formula "and (PN) is to carry the *pilku* / *ˀunuṯṯu* -service of (his) house" beside another of the type "and (PN) is to carry the *pilku*-service of the X-men" (such as the leatherworkers, merchants or guards).[81] Note for the former the following examples: *u (PNN) ˀunuṯṯa ša bīti ubbalū* in RS 15.89:20, and *u PN pilka ša bīti ubbal* in RS 15.123+:18-19; and for the latter, *pilka ša aškapūti ubbal* in RS 15.Y:16, and *u pilka šatammūti ubbal* in RS 17.01:30.[82] An illustrative example of these two kinds of service is found in RS 15.123+, describing an exchange of properties. Here (namely in lines 16-19) it is provided that one of the parties is to perform the guard obligation and the other the service of his house (*u* PN_1 *pilka*

Hunger [Horn 1982], pp. 112-19), and also Libolt (*Royal Land Grants*, p. 113); their argument that they appear in different contexts cannot be sustained as will be shown in the following discussion and the next chapter (see already the doubts raised by Postgate concerning Heltzer's interpretation in his "*Ilku* and Land Tenure," p. 313 n. 19, and more recently and thoroughly Schloen, *The House of the Father*, pp. 246ff.). For further discussion, see chapter 7.

80 Huehnergard hesitated to identify the verbal forms as representing *abālu* G or *apālu* D, considering the latter more likely (*The Akkadian of Ugarit*, pp. 60, 176 and 178). After the discovery and publication of the Ugaritic text RS 94.2965, there can be no doubt that they are all to be understood as representing forms of *abālu* (see below). Note that only preterite forms are attested for this verb (see van Soldt, *SAU*, p. 495).

81 No example of "classical" *ilku* is attested in these formulas. The following *pilku*-services are attested: of the officials called *ˁaširu*'s (RS 15.137:8-9, RS 16.242:12), of the leatherworkers (RS 16.142:8-9, cf. RS 15.Y:9 and 15), of the "lancers" (RS 15.Y:16), of the "sons of the queen" (RS 16.138:35, RS 16.204:10'-11'), of the *maryannu*'s of Ugarit (RS 19.98:22-23), of the guards (RS 15.123+:16-17), of the commanders of (prince) Ibirānu (RS 16.348:5), of the commanders of the *sākinu* official (RS 16.139:14), of the *namû*'s (of the town of Raˀšu, RS 16.148+ rev. 10'-11'), of the *ša rēši* officials (RS 16.162:24), of the stewards (RS 15.122:30, RS 16.173:6'-7', RS 17.01:30), and of the merchants (RS 18.285:9-10, cf. 12-13). For the plurals in *-ūtu*, see Huehnergard, *The Akkadian of Ugarit*, pp. 146-147 and 274 (interpreted as a further example of allomorphism reduction), and van Soldt, *SAU*, pp. 426-427.

82 For the vowel-case of the bound form, see above note 36.

ša maṣṣārūti ubbal u PN_2 *pilka bītišu ubbal*). In one case (RS 16.246) we find the exemption from service with the negated formula (*ul ubbal*; cf. *l ybl* in the Ugaritic text RS 94.2965:22). Concerning the syntactical order, the object always precedes the verb usually placed at the end of the clause (O-V, S-O-V and O-S-V are used indistinctly). On the other hand, the hereditary character of the obligation (normally implicitly understood by the transfer of rights in either the conveyance clause or the warranty clause, or both) can be explicitly made by adding the phrase "and his sons" after the transferee's name in the *pilku*-clause (so in RS 16.148+, RS 16.204, RS 19.98 and probably also in RS 17.363); and in two of these deeds (RS 16.148+ and RS 16.204, and also in RS 16.138) the recurrent adverbial-formula "forever" closes the clause (see also sections 20 and 21 below).

Exemption from service can also be formulated with the verb *zakû* (see below 15); for example, *zaki* PN_1 *ištu pilku bīti* PN_2 "PN_1 is free from the *pilku*-service of the (conveyed) house of PN_2" (RS 16.140:11-12), or also *šarru uzakki TN ina pilki* "the king has freed TN (the conveyed village) from *pilku*-service" in RS 15.114:12-13 (cf. RS 16.133:12f.). But by far the commonest formula of exemption from service, mainly attested in deeds of the time of ᶜAmmiṯtamru II, is the clause that has as predicate the particle of non-existence *yānu*, functioning as a verb. The formula simply states that "there is no *(p)ilku*-service on the conveyed property."[83] Note, for example, *u (p)ilku/a yānu ina eqli annî* "and there is no *(p)ilku*-service on this field" (in RS 15.136, RS 15.143+, RS 15.155, RS 16.154, RS 16.241+, RS 16.243).[84] The Ugaritic counterpart has *w unṯ in bh* "and there is no *ˀunuṯṯu*-service on it (i.e. the property)" (in RS 15.111 [KTU 3.2] and RS 16.382 [KTU 3.5]). As for the syntactical order of the clause, the noun always precedes the particle *yānu* (Ug. *in*); the adjunct phrase (viz. "on the property") usually follows the particle of non-existence but may also precede it.[85] Note that the use of the

[83] The formula was very likely already used before the reign of ᶜAmmiṯtamru II; see RS 16.149:1', written by the expert notary Šapšumalku, who worked for Niqmaddu II, Arḫalbu and Niqmepaᶜ, and RS 15.119:17' (where *yānu* is probably to be restored).

[84] Or *ina eqli šuwāti* (in RS 16.139:13), and "in his field" (in RS 15.163+:18). Obviously depending on the nature of the property conveyed we find other expressions for the adjunct phrase such as "this house" (RS 15.131:2'), "(this) house (and) field" (RS 19.98:21), "these fields" (RS 15.140:23, RS 15.145:19, RS 16.162:26, RS 17.379[A]:12', RS 18.21:27), "these salt-marshes" (RS 15.147:4'), or "these royal gifts" (RS 16.148+ r. 10', RS 16.201:4'). Note the variant formula *u pilkašu yānu* (RS 16.343:17) and *u pilkušunu mimma yānu* (RS 16.134:7), the suffix referring to the property conveyed (cf. also RS 16.147:17).

[85] See Huehnergard, *The Akkadian of Ugarit*, p. 217.

accusative (*pilka*) in some instances must reflect Ugaritic influence.[86]

It is difficult to decide from these formulas and deeds whether the *(p)ilku* services due to the king rested on the conveyed landed property or personally on the tenants, or (more probably) on both. It would seem a priori that formulas such as "and there is no *pilku*-service on this field but he (i.e. the tenant) is to carry the *pilku*-service of the prefect's commanders" in RS 16.139:13-14, or "and there is no *pilku*-service on the house and the field which are in TN but PN and his sons (the grantees) are to carry the *pilku*-service of the *maryannu's* of Ugarit" (in RS 19.98:21-24)[87] would rather point to two kinds of service distinctively resting on the property and the tenant respectively. But a formula like the one inscribed on the left edge of the tablet RS 16.162 would speak against this interpretation. Here we find "he (the grantee) is to perform the *pilku*-service of the officers (and) there is no other *pilku*-service on these fields."[88] This interpretation would be further supported by a formula such as "and there is no *pilku*-service whatsoever (*mimma*) on the property."[89] But that the question is not conclusively answered is shown by the newly published Ugaritic text RS 94.2965 which reads: "and PN (the grantee) is to carry no *ʾunuṯṯu*-service whatsoever on these fields but is to carry the *ʾunuṯṯu*-service of his house."[90] What the tenant's house

[86] See Huehnergard, *The Akkadian of Ugarit*, pp. 240 and 280, and van Soldt, *SAU*, p. 413.

[87] They read respectively: *u pilku ina eqli šuwāti yānu pilkama murʾī sākini ubbal*, and *u ina bīti eqli ša TN pilku yānu pilkama ša maryannūti ša Ugarit ubbal PN u mārūšu*; note the lack of concordance of subject-verb in the latter example, and the use of the enclitic *-ma* to denote contrast (see Huehnergard, *The Akkadian of Ugarit*, p. 204, and van Soldt, *SAU*, pp. 514-515), a phenomenon that also occurs in the parallel Ugaritic clause quoted below. As already mentioned, we believe that the lack of concordance is due to the formulaic language of the texts, so that an alleged value CVCv for a number of signs (such as BAL here, as pointed out by van Soldt, *SAU*, pp. 438-40) seems unnecessary.

[88] Lines 24-26: *pilkušu ša ša rēši ubbal šanû pilku yānu ina eqlēti annâti*; note the use of the proleptic suffix before the genitive, not infrequent and exclusive of legal texts (see Huehnergard, *The Akkadian of Ugarit*, pp. 227-229, and van Soldt, *SAU*, p. 517). For the use of the adjective *šanû* qualifying the service, cf. also the fragmentary text RS 15.55:8'.

[89] See RS 16.134:7, RS 16.148+ rev. 9', RS 18.21:26, and possibly RS 17.351[B] A:4'; note also the Ugaritic counterpart (using the impersonal independent pronoun *mnm*) in RS 15.111 (KTU 3.2):18.

[90] Lines 19-24 of this alphabetic text read: *w PN b šdm hnmt unṯ mhkm l ybl unṯm bth ybl*; note the parallel in the use and meaning of the enclitic *-m* (suffixed too to the word for service) with the Akkadian examples cited above. Note also the Akkadian counterpart of the latter sentence in RS 16.343:18-19: *u PN pilka bītišu*

(*bth*) means here is obviously not the conveyed viz. granted property (here, identified as "the fields"), but presumably his own household.

11. Clauses exempting from services with alāku *and* epēšu

Akkadian *alāku*, from which *ilku* is derived, is the classic verb used to denote the performance of service to the king.[91] Although Akkadian *pilku* and Ugaritic *ʾunuṯṯu* are construed with *abālu*, as we have seen in 10 above (see also 14 below),[92] *alāku* appears in a number of formulas describing (in negative) the exemption from services. Exemption from some kind of military service is probably meant by the expression *u PN ana rēṣūti lā illak* literally "and PN is not to come to help" in RS 16.239:14-15 (cf. also RS 16.132:16ff.).[93] The service most commonly found in lists of immunities is the so-called work for the palace or the king (*šipir ekalli* or *šipir šarri*). It is construed with *alāku* probably in RS 15.114:16-17 and RS 16.348:13-14, and possibly also in RS 16.188:2'-5' (all passages rather fragmentary). In the former text the exemption from going or serving is said of the oxen, donkeys and inhabitants of the granted and exempted village (in RS 16.188, oxen and donkeys are mentioned too). In the *Sammelurkunde* RS 15.109+ the kind of service meant by the word *šipru* is more explicit. Line 54 provides that the transferee "is not to go i.e. serve as emissary" (*ina mār-šiprūti lā illak*).[94] Note

---

ubbal.

[91] The classic use of *ilku* with *alāku* is only attested in one administrative record, namely RS 19.32, curiously spelled *il-ka la-lak* (line 4) and *la-li-ku ša il-ki* (line 9), probably as a result of crasis (*lā allak* and *lā ālikū* respectively); see Rainey, "Gleanings from Ugarit," IOS 3 (1973):41, Huehnergard, *The Akkadian of Ugarit*, p. 108, and van Soldt, *SAU*, p. 438. What is interesting mentioning here is that the text belongs to the so-called "South-Palace archive" that, as discussed above in chapter 4, precisely shows a strong Mesopotamian influence as far as the Akkadian written there is concerned. The exceptional use of the classic expression would thus support the hypothesis (put forward by van Soldt) that the scribe was of Assyrian origin.

[92] Note that linguistically speaking, *abālu* corresponds to the active transitive meaning of (the active intransitive) *alāku*. This feature is clearly evidenced in a language like Hurrian in which the same verb root *un-* (from which significantly *ʾunuṯṯu*, the Ugaritic word for service derives, see above note 79) has an intransitive meaning ("to come") and a transitive one ("to bring").

[93] The same formula (this time as an obligation) is attested in a diplomatic document found at Ugarit, namely RS 19.68:32, an agreement between Aziru of Amurru and Niqmaddu II.

[94] For the (collated) reading *ši-ip-ru-ti* instead of *ši-ip-ru* lugal(?), see van Soldt, *SAU*, p. 427. Note that the same expression is attested in a broken letter from

also the exemption "to serve as a courier" (^{lú}*kalla lā illak*) with the inhabitants of the town of Ma^{c}rabā in RS 16.188:6'-7', and the reference to the routes, i.e. the caravans or embassies (from Ugarit) to Hatti and Egypt,[95] before the clause providing that the beneficiaries in RS 16.386:7'-9' "are not to do (*epēšu*) any kind of service whatsoever for the palace or for the palace overseer" (*ana ekalli u ana akil ekalli šipra mimma lā eppušū*).[96]

12. Clauses exempting from taxes and obligations with erēbu

Exemption from taxes on agriculture products and livestock is rendered by the formula *ana / ina ekalli ul / lā i/errub*.[97] The products that are exempted from entering the palace are usually grain, beer (or wine), and oil (RS 16.132:22-23, RS 16.238+:7-8, RS 16.269:18-20, RS 16.348:2'-3', perhaps also in RS 16.384:10-12).[98] Beside agriculture products, RS 16.132:22 lists the tenant's oxen, donkeys and sheep and goats (as well as any other chattel [*gabbu mimmûšu*]); small cattle is also mentioned in RS 16.269:19 (perhaps oxen should be restored immediately before).

Boghazköy (KUB 3 61:4), significantly translated as "diplomatic relations" by CAD M/1, p. 265.

[95] Note also in line 6' the reference to what may be some sort of couriers. The term can tentatively be normalized as *sīsāḫalīma* (the Ugaritic form viz. case-ending of the word seems clear, see Huehnergard, *Ugaritic Vocabulary*, pp. 193-194). The proposed meaning is based on an alleged derivation from *sīsû* "horse" (see Liverani, "Ras Shamra. Histoire," col. 1328, or Libolt, *Royal Land Grants*, p. 295; preferable to the interpretation of the word as a toponym, as suggested by Miller, *Studies in the Juridical Texts*, p. 79, cf. CAD S, p. 321). Note the relevant Biblical Hebrew parallel between *rkb hsws* in 2Kings 9:17f. and the term for "messenger" (cf. John T. Greene, *The Role of the Messenger and Message in the Ancient Near East* [Atlanta, 1989], pp. 122-123).

[96] In view of the latter formula, it is possible to restore a durative form of *epēšu* in RS 16.384:15. Note that in these prohibition clauses the verb is usually final (see Huehnergard, *The Akkadian of Ugarit*, p. 223).

[97] We have already seen the interchangeability of the prepositions *ana* and *ina*, probably to be explained on account of Ugaritic influence. Here we find *ina* for expected *ana* (see van Soldt, *SAU*, p. 447).

[98] Nougayrol restored the verb form *ušerab* because he took the phrase "PN and his sons" in line 17 as the first words, and thus the subject, of the following sentence. It is more likely, however, that these words belong to the preceding clause as the subject of *zaki* in line 16 (despite the lack of concordance, not unusual in these formulas —see 15). It is, therefore, more likely to restore in line 20 *i/errub*. As for RS 16.348:3', one should correct the typographical error in *PRU* 3, p. 163 (see the copy) and read *e-ru-ub* (instead of *e-ru-bu*).

Concerning the nature of the taxes, it is interesting to note that RS 16.153 recording the grant of a village further provides that the grain and the beer (or wine) of the town's tithe (Ug. *ma*ᶜ*šaru*) and the sheep of its grazing tax (Ug. *maqqadu*) belong to the grantee.[99] In RS 16.132:23, the agricultural products are defined as the tax normally due to the king.[100]

Exemption from agricultural labour is once described as "(PN) is not to enter royal land" (*ina eqli šarri ul ir*[*rub*], RS 16.348:9). And the obligation of (perhaps exemption from) bringing a present to the king, said of the merchant Sinarānu with regard to his trading journeys to Crete, is formulated also once as *tāmartašu ana šarri (lā) ušerrab* (RS 16.238+:11).[101]

Other obligations to the palace include billeting *ḫapiru* troops as well as housing foreign visiting agents or emissaries (*ubru*). The formula exempting the transferee of real property from these obligations in the three documents in which it is attested, states that the *ḫapiru's* or the foreign agent are not to enter his house: *ḫapiru / ubru ana bītišu ul / lā irrub* (RS 15.109+:53, 54-55, 16.132:20-21, and RS 16.157:23, where the verb form appears as *ušerrebū*).[102]

13. Clauses exempting from royal mobilization

Another variant of exemption from services to the king is expressed with a formula that refers to the immunity of the beneficiary vis-à-vis certain palace officials, that is, of summons. It is noteworthy that we find these formulas of exemption in deeds describing the privileges of people belonging to the category of "friends of the king."[103] In RS 15.137 and RS

---

[99] Note that the tithe of Biʾru is given among other taxes in the royal grant RS 16.244:7.

[100] The reading nì.⌜ku$_5$.da⌝ (*miksu*) in line 23 was collated by van Soldt who kindly made it available to me.

[101] The left edge of the tablet is broken off. It is not unlikely therefore to restore the negative *lā* (used rather than *ul* in lines 8 and 14) at the beginning of line 13: [*la*]*ú-še-ra-ab*. The resulting exemption, on the other hand, would agree with the clause that introduces the provision in question, namely line 9 stating that "his ship is free i.e. exempted (from obligation)" (*eleppašu zakât*; see also section 15). For the most recent treatment of the traditional interpretation, i.e. understanding the clause as the only exceptional duty to be perfomred by the Sinarānu, see Lackenbacher, *Textes akkadiens d'Ugarit*, p. 307.

[102] Or *ušēribū*; see Huehnergard, *The Akkadian of Ugarit*, p. 252 n. 189, and van Soldt, *SAU*, p. 434 n. 81. Note again that in these prohibition clauses the verb is usually final (see Huehnergard, *The Akkadian of Ugarit*, p. 223).

[103] For these royal courtiers, see the next section 14.

16.239 the provision states that "such-and-such official will have no authority over the transferee," that is to say, shall not call up the transferee for palace works or military service. In RS 15.137:15-16 it is the mayor (*ḫazannu*) and the overseer of the fields (*akil eqlēti*)[104] who are not to have authority (*lā imallik*) over him (*elišu*), and in RS 16.239:31-33 it is the overseer of the chariots (*akil narkabti*) who is not to have power (*lā umaᵓᵓer*) over (*eli*) the transferee and his sons. This very exemption, however, is formulated differently in the deeds RS 16.157 and RS 16.250 (belonging to the ᶜAbdu dossier too, and corroborating the heritability of the exemption mentioned in the previous record). Here we find the formula *(NP) ištu qāti akil narkabti u hazanni zaki* "(PN) is free from the overseer of the chariots and the mayor" (for the *zakû* formulas, see section 15). More eloquent still is the summarizing formula in the same deed RS 16.250:19 *mamma ana muḫḫišu lā iqarrib* "no one shall approach him," meaning: "and mobilize him." The same verb is attested in the immunity clause in RS 16.238:14-15: "the herald shall not approach his house" (*nāgiru ana bītišu lā* [*iqa*]*rrub*). In view of this formula, I would prefer to restore a form of *qerēbu* in RS 16.348:10 and read: "the mayor (*ḫazannu*) shall not approach his house (*ana bītišu*)."[105]

14. Clauses describing services with abālu

We have seen (in section 10) that *abālu* (Ug. YBL) is the verb used by the notaries of Ugarit to denote the performance of (*pilku*, Ug. *ᵓunuṯṯu*) service to the king. It is probably in this connection that must be seen the use of *abālu* in the formula describing the payment due to the king or queen as a result of membership in the category of friends of the king or queen respectively (*mūdû šarri / šarrati*).[106] Clearly as part of their *pilku*-

---

[104] For the plural form of *eqlu* in Ugarit, see Huehnergard, *The Akkadian of Ugarit*, p. 149.

[105] Rather than *erēbu*, as suggested by Nougayrol (*PRU* 3, p. 163). Note again that in these prohibition clauses the verb is usually final (see Huehnergard, *The Akkadian of Ugarit*, p. 223), except for the ones in RS 15.137 and RS 16.239 (perhaps due to Ugaritic influence: *imallik* is a clear Akkadianized form of Ugaritic MLK [see Huehnergard, *Ugaritic Vocabulary*, p. 147], and Akkadian *umaᵓᵓer* may have been construed by analogy [cf. van Soldt, *SAU*, p. 454]).

[106] For this category, see especially the studies by Peter Vargyas, "Le *mudu* à Ugarit. Ami du roi?," UF 13 (1981):165-79, and Heltzer, *The Internal Organization of the Kingdom of Ugarit* (Wiesbaden 1982), pp. 161-163. Of interest is the parallel offered by Tryggve N.D. Mettinger in his *Solomonic State Officials. A Study of the Civil Government Officials of the Israelitic Monarchy* (Lund, 1971), pp. 66ff. (who considered it to be the origin of the use at Ugarit), namely the Egyptian title *rḫ-nsw.t* (cf. the king's *philoi* in Alexander's court).

service, members of this status had to bring (*ubbal*) annually (*ina šanāti* in RS 16.157:21 and RS 16.254D:11') to the king (*ana šarri* in RS 16.254D:11' and RS 16.239:19), or alternatively to the queen (*ina qāt šarrati* in RS 16.348:22), a fixed amount of silver: 10 shekels of silver (in RS 16.143:21, RS 16.157:21, RS 16.250:16, RS 16.254D:10', and presumably also RS 16.239:19)[107] and 20 shekels of silver (in RS 15.137:14) as friend of the king, and 5 shekels of silver (RS 16.353:31) as friend of the queen.[108]

In RS 16.239, the verbs *alāku* and *abālu* are used side by side in two respective sentences describing exemption from two different kinds of service. The formula *u PN ana reṣūti lā illak*, probably denoting military service has been discussed above (in section 11); then follows *u napṭāra lā ubbal*, that is, "and he (the beneficiary) shall not carry / bring the *napṭāru*." Because of the use of *abālu* in connection with payment obligations in Ugarit, and the fact that no other meaning seems to rightly suit this example, I would follow Nougayrol's interpretation and understand the term as a by-form of *ipṭeru* "ransom (money)."[109] If this translation is correct, one can relate this royal obligation with the Ugaritic royal deed RS 16.191+ (KTU 3.4) that records the redemption by a certain Iwrikili of a family of five members plus two other people that had been enslaved abroad, namely by Berutians (the ransom money [the *napṭāru*?] amounting to 100 shekels of silver). Note that the text provides then that the ransomed people will get back to their *ʾunuṯṯu*-service only once they have paid back the ransom money to their redeemer, meaning that they are not free, and accounting for the involvement of the king in this (kind of) transaction.

Finally, the verb *abālu* is probably to be restored in the fragmentary

[107] The space at the beginning of the line in RS 16.239 agrees with such restoration (see already Miller, *Studies in the Juridical Texts*, p. 73, and Libolt, *Royal Land Grants*, p. 209; cf. Vargyas, "Le *mudu* à Ugarit," pp. 177-178).

[108] Note that in RS 16.348:7 the amount of silver not preserved in the text is to be brought to the palace overseer (*ana akil ekalli ubbal*). In view of the evidence, the verb form *ubbal* is probably to be restored in RS 16.254D:10' rather than a form of *nadānu* (as suggested by Nougayrol, *PRU* 3, p. 79, followed by Libolt, *Royal Land Grants*, p. 204); see already Vargyas, "Le *mudu* à Ugarit," p. 172 (one should further note that the notary Šapšumalku is also the author of the other deeds of the ᶜAbdu dossier where *ubbal* is written).

[109] See *PRU* 3, p. 223. The word is not necessarily to be taken as Ugaritic (as tentatively suggested by Huehnergard, *Ugaritic Vocabulary*, p. 167), and should not be equated with the form /*napṭarū*/ in RS 15.123+:5 (as has been frequently suggested: e.g. CAD N/1, p. 324, Malul, "Susapinnu, the Mesopotamian Paranymph," JESHO 32 [1989]:258, 273-74, or Charpin, dealing with the hosting of foreign emissaries in ARM 26/2, p. 142 n. 16).

text RS 19.128 that stipulates exemption from some kind of (*pilku*?) service. Lines 4'-5' read: *u itti mārī māti* [broken] *mimma ul ubbal* "and (PN) shall not carry whatever [service?] with the people of the land."[110]

15. The zakû *formulas*

To be free of claims or to be free or exempted from services are both expressed by the adjectival form of the verb (or the predicate state of the adjective)[111] *zakû* (the more common form being 3ms *zaki*).[112] When the king is literally the one who frees or exempts, namely a subject or servant of his, then the form *uzakki* (from *zukkû*) is used. Thus we find the formula *RN uzakki PN* (as the first clause of the text),[113] *šarru* (*bēlšu*) *uzakki PN*, or also in V-S order, *uzakkišu šarru* (*bēlšu*), that is, "RN / the king (his lord) has freed PN/him."[114] Apart from RS 16.238+:9, in which the object of royal immunity (viz. the grammatical subject of *zakât*) is the beneficiary's ship (*eleppašu*), and RS 15.114:12-13 where the object of immunity (viz. of *uzakki*) is the granted village, the ones free(d) of/from claims or services are always individuals. The claims and services in question can be mentioned in the clause always preceded by a preposition or prepositional expression with the meaning "from." The more common is *ištu*, extended with *muḫḫi* or *qāti*, but *ina* and *eli* are also attested.[115] Thus we find exemptions from royal service (*ištu šipri*

---

[110] Indeed, the end of line 5' should read *ú-ba-a*[*l*, rather than *ú-ba-q*[*ar*(?) as suggested by Nougayrol in *PRU* 6, p. 34; cf. van Soldt, *SAU*, p. 452 n. 158.

[111] See van Soldt, *SAU*, p. 499.

[112] The use of *zaki* instead of expected (normative Mesopotamian) *zaku* may be due to a general levelling of III-weak verbs to III-i, as stated by Huehnergard, *The Akkadian of Ugarit*, p. 185 (n. 212); likewise see van Soldt, *SAU*, pp. 437-438. Its formulaic nature and use is evidenced by the examples in which it appears without agreement with its noun phrase subject (see below).

[113] In RS 16.132 (see the promotion clause in 17 below), RS 16.238+, and RS 16.267. Only preterite forms are attested for the verb *zukkû* (see van Soldt, *SAU*, p. 495).

[114] In the verdict 16.192+ it is said of both the king (twice) and one of the parties involved (lines 13, 15 and 17); note the lack of concordance in lines 14-15 (*mārū PN uzakkišu*). A similar case is recorded in RS 17.67 presided over by the *sākinu* official. Gerhard Ries (in "Lastenfreiheit," RlA 6, pp. 510-511), provides a brief summary of the evidence with reference to Nougayrol's study in *PRU* 3.

[115] That *ištu* usually replaces expected (normative Mesopotamian) *ina* with *zakû* is probably due to Ugaritic influence (see Huehnergard, *The Akkadian of Ugarit*, p. 281, and van Soldt, *SAU*, pp. 450-452). For the reading *eli* of the Sumerogram ugu, see the remarks of van Soldt, *SAU*, p. 454.

ekalli, *ištu* or *ina pilki*, or simply *ištu* followed by the kind of service, as well as *ištu qāti* followed by royal officials),[116] and release from royal slavery (*ina ardūti ša šarri* and *ištu amūti*).[117]

Concerning claims on family property, we find the provision that PN forfeits his claim to the paternal estate, literally he/she is free from his/her father's house (*eli bīt abīšu* in RS 15.120:15, and *ištu bīt abiša* in RS 15.92:23), and/or from his brother(s) (*eli aḫḫēšu* in RS 15.120:16, *ištu muḫḫi PN* [his/their brother] in RS 15.90:9, RS 16.143:12-13, RS 16.250:14, and cf. RS 16.158:7-10). In two deeds, the latter provision is followed by the stereotyped formula *zaki amīlu ištu (muḫḫi) amīli* the meaning of which is "they (i.e. the two parties) are free (of claims) from each other."[118]

In three deeds (RS 16.238+, RS 16.267, and RS 16.269), immediately after the clause stating that "RN has freed PN" we find the formula "like the Sun who is free, PN is free," meant to confirm or emphasize the new status of the person in question.[119] This stereotyped expression is found in other deeds.[120] Because it is only attested in Ugarit, once in Ugaritic, and the sun deity is of feminine gender in most cases, it is most likely that the formula is of Ugaritic origin. Note the following examples: *kīma Šapši zakâti zaki PN u mārūšu* (RS 16.269:16-17),[121] or RS 16.238+:5-6:

---

[116] RS 15.114:13, RS 15.Y:15, RS 16.133:14, RS 16.140:12, RS 16.147:17, RS 16.157:22, RS 16.250:17-18, RS 16.269:15, and probably also RS 19.128:5'-6'. A form of *zakû* is probably to be restored in the fragmentary RS 16.386 (note the complements "from [*ištu*] the routes [i.e. caravans / embassies that go from Ugarit] to Hatti and Egypt" and from some sort of courier service(?) [*ina sīsāḫalīma*[(?)]] in lines 4' to 6'; see above note 95).

[117] RS 16.250:22, RS 16.267:5, and RS 18.21:29.

[118] Note that the noun phrase subject appears nearly always after the adjective; see Huehnergard, *The Akkaadian of Ugarit*, p. 216. "It is likely," he wrote, "that the adjective appears first in these formulaic clauses simply to render the type of clause instantly identifiable;" see also van Soldt, *SAU*, p. 477. In RS 15.90:12 (and also l. 14) the second noun is spelled LÚ-*lum*, that is, with the incorrect vowel of the complement, probably due to the formulaic, frozen writing of the form (see Huehnergard, *The Akkadian of Ugarit*, p. 80). In the Ugaritic document RS 94.2168, the verb BHL seems to have the same meaning as Akkadian *zukkû* denoting the emancipation of sons from the paternal house.

[119] For a possible symbolic significance of the expression, see Malul, *Studies in Mesopotamian Legal Symbolism*, pp. 49-50.

[120] In royal deeds: RS 15.120:14-15, RS 16.252:3-4, RS 16.276:17-20, and probably also in RS 15.138+:21 and RS 15.146+:9-10, both fragmentary. See Huehnergard, *The Akkadian of Ugarit*, pp. 188 and 249, and van Soldt, *SAU*, p. 460.

[121] That "PN and his sons" are part of this sentence is shown by the syntactical order typical of the formula. The lack of agreement of the subject "PN and his sons"

kīma [*Šapši*] *zakât zaki (PN)*. In RS 16.276:17-20, we find the variant formula *PN zaki kīma Šapši* "PN is free like the Sun," followed by the phrase "forever."[122] The expression can also specify the kind of exemption involved with the addition of the corresponding complement. Thus, RS 16.267:5-6 states that "like the Sun who is free, so is PN free from slavery (*ištu amūti*)," and RS 15.120:14-15 provides that "like the Sun who is free, so is PN free from the house of his father and from his brothers (*eli bīt abišu eli aḫḫēšu*)." Likewise, the Ugaritic example reads (RS 15.125 [KTU 2.19]:2-5): *km špš d brt kmt br PN b unṯ ᶜd ᶜlm* "like the Sun who is free, so is PN free of *ᵓunuṯṯu*-service forever."

16. The promotion formula

The king could also grant certain types of offices understanding thereby special rights and obligations tied to a particular royal service, namely the *pilku*-service of a social or professional category (see section 10 above). It is therefore not surprising to find what we have called promotion clauses or formulas recorded beside conveyances of real property (RS 15.137, RS 15.Y, RS 16.132, and probably also the fragmentary RS 16.173). RS 16.348, on the other hand, records exclusively one such royal promotion. The stereotyped formula states that the king has removed or released PN from his former office or service and has placed him into a new one. The verb form of the first sentence is *unakkir* (preterite of *nukkuru* "to remove")[123] in two texts (15.137 and RS 16.348) and *ipṭur* (preterite of *paṭāru* "to redeem") in another (RS 15.Y), both construed with the preposition *ištu* "from." In RS 16.132 the releasing is formulated as "RN has freed (*uzakki*) PN and his sons" without specifying their former status.[124] As for the raising to a higher rank the verb used is always *šakānu* "to place" construed with the preposition *ina* (sometimes in the preterite, *iškun* [in RS 15.Y and RS 16.348], and sometimes in the perfect, *iltakan* [in the other examples]). The service or office is called *pilku* in three deeds, in two (RS 15.137 and RS 16.348) qualifying the former and in another (RS 16.173) the new office.[125] So,

---

appears in other formulas too (see e.g. the *pilku*-clause in RS 19.98 quoted above).

[122] Note that in RS 16.267 it is repeated in line 8 with the expression *u uzakkišu kīma Šapši*.

[123] Only preterite forms are attested for this verb (see van Soldt, *SAU*, p. 495).

[124] For *zakû*, see also 15 above. Note that in RS 15.Y the notary wrote after the promotion clause that the beneficiary is free (*zaki*) from his former service.

[125] Note also that RS 15.Y provides in line 16 that the beneficiary is to carry the corresponding *pilku*-service (cf. also RS 16.142).

for example, the first sentence of the operative part in RS 16.348, viz. lines 1-6 read: *ištu ūmi annîm RN$_1$ mār RN$_2$ šar Ugarit unakkir PN$_1$ mār PN$_2$ u mārīšu ištu pil<ki> murʾi ibirāna u iškunšu ina mūdê šarrati* "From today RN$_1$, son of RN$_2$, king of Ugarit, has removed PN$_1$, son of PN$_2$, and his sons from the *pilku*-service of Ibirānu's commanders and has placed him (*sic*) among the friends of the queen."[126]

17. The anāḫu *formula*

In four deeds it is explicitly mentioned that the royal grants, promotions or immunities in question are in fact a reward for faithful service.[127] The formula generally coming at the end of the text (in RS 16.157 and RS 16.238+ immediately before the divine curses [see section 22]) states that "PN has exerted himself/herself for the king's sake." The verb used is *anāḫu*, with the meaning "to exert oneself, to become exhausted," occurring both in the perfect (*ētanaḫ*, RS 16.238+:16, RS 16.267:7) and the adjectival form (*aniḫ*, RS 16.132:29, RS 157:24).[128] In RS 16.132 and

---

[126] Note here too the lack of agreement (between pronoun and referent). These formulas naturally inform us about the relative position or rank in status of a number of services. Thus, the friends of the queen are higher in rank than the commanders of Ibirānu (RS 16.348), the friends of the king are higher than the officials called *ᶜaširu's* (RS 15.137), and the "lancers" are higher than the leatherworkers (RS 15.Y). In RS 16.173 the office lower than the stewards is not preserved, and in RS 16.132 the former status of the man and sons who are granted "maryannuship" is not specified. According to RS 15.Y:12-13, the promotion required the consequent "degradation" of someone else, as though the number of members at least for the categories involved (lancers and leatherworkers) would be fixed or scheduled.

[127] RS 16.132, RS 16.157, RS 16.238+, and RS 16.267 (a release from slavery by the king); cf. also RS 16.386:13'. RS 16.269 records too a royal grant and exemptions from service that probably were made as a result of the grantee's service described in lines 7-11; there it is said that he put to death an enemy of the king. The fact that the formula under discussion is not used in this text is probably due to the fact that the loyal service rendered by the grantee in RS 16.269 was a punctual one and therefore differed from the sustained, continuous and lasting effort or service denoted by the verb *anāḫu* (see below).

[128] For the past meaning and the possible Ugaritic influence of the latter form (viz. of the suffix-conjugation QTL), see Huehnergard, *The Akkadian of Ugarit*, p. 259 (cf. van Soldt, *SAU*, p. 499, who prefers to regard it as referring to the present or future; see also e.g. Moshe Weinfeld, "The Covenant of Grant in the Old Testament and the Ancient Near East," JAOS 90 [1970]:187 [translated as present], and Knoppers, "Ancient Near Eastern Royal Grants," p. 688 [as future]). Note that in RS 16.269 quoted above the disloyal *past* behaviour of the culprit is denoted too by the *paris* form (*nakir* in line 7). Kestemont (*Diplomatique et droit international*, p. 557) has proposed a legal, indeed far-flung and farfetched meaning for *anāḫu*,

probably also in RS 16.238+, the loyalty is further emphasized by adding to *ana (muḫḫi) šarri* the attribute *bēlišu* "his lord."[129] In RS 16.132:29-30, it is said that the loyal subject of the king "had indeed exerted himself very much for the king his lord" (*ana šarri bēlišu aniḫ danniš dannišma*).[130]

18. The adoption formulas

Four royal deeds (RS 15.92, RS 16.200, RS 16.295, and RS 16.344) contain a clause describing an adoption, always phrased *ex latere adoptantis*. What is of special interest here is the fact that the verb used to denote the adoption seems to be different whether the adopter is a man or a woman. In the former case, the verb is *rakāsu* (note the perfect and preterite forms *irtakus* and *irkus*), and in the latter *leqû* (*taltaqe* in RS 16.200:3).[131] Both verbs, "to bind" and "to take," have a person as object, viz. the adoptee, and are then further defined with the expression "as his/her son" or also (in RS 16.344) as "his brother" (*adoptio in fratrem*). In RS 15.92, the adoption is said to be in "*ammati* sonship" (*mārūt ammati*), an expression that also occurs in other, private deeds of adoption.[132] I wonder whether the (presumably Ugaritic) word could be

---

namely "être dans l'état de celui qui s'est engagé envers NP;" on the other hand, his interpretation of *ētanaḫ* and *ītanaḫ* (see footnote 130 below) as Gt forms (with a meaning "devenir l'allié de NP") is also highly unlikely (Libolt also understood them as Gt forms, see *Royal Land Grants*, p. 129).

[129] Cf. also the same use and denotation of royal loyalty in the *kubuddātu* formula (discussed in section 3).

[130] A similar formula is attested in the treaty text between Šuppiluliuma I and Niqmaddu II (RS 17.340). Line 13' reads: *ana Šamšī šarri rabî bēlišu ītanaḫ danniš* "he (i.e. the king of Ugarit) has exerted himself very much for My Sun (i.e. the Hittite emperor), the great king, his lord." Cf. the use of the derived substantive *mānaḫtu* in the inscription of the Statue of Idrimi to denote precisely the faithful service rendered by his forefathers (CAD M/1, p. 206, translates the word ad hoc as "vassal service"); *mānaḫtu* is also attested in the fragment RS 19.55:2 and 5, here describing the mutual loyalty of the kings of Ugarit and Carchemish.

[131] As already pointed out by Nougayrol, *Ugaritica* 5, p. 173 n. 2; see also van Soldt, *SAU*, pp. 426-427 n. 52. Note that the latter is confirmed by the king using the formula *nadānu ana mārīša* (see the sequential formula in section 8).

[132] See the section on adoption in my "Ugarit" chapter in *A History of Ancient Near Eastern Law*, pp. 727-728. For the word, cf. Huehnergard, *Ugaritic Vocabulary*, p. 189 (left without translation). The etymology put forward by Sanmartín in "Glossen zum ugaritischen Lexikon (VI)," UF 21 (1989):336-337, namely an alleged, unattested Ugaritic verb ᵓMD (with reference to Akkadian *emēdu*) seems to me rather unlikely.

connected with Hurrian *ammade* (glossing Akkadian *labīrūtu* [and spelled *am-ma-ti*] in the Amarna letter EA 59:11) meaning "grandfather, ancestor," and denoting then in the Ugarit deeds something like "inherited sonship" (i.e. as an ordinary son).

Also typical of the deeds of adoption are the clauses that stipulate the dissolution of the relationship. The verb denoting the repudiation of either adopter or adoptee is *zêru* the literal meaning of which is "to hate." The formula then runs "if in the future (*urram šēram*) PN_1 (the adoptee/adopter) repudiates (*izeʾʾer*) PN_2 (the adopter/adoptee)."[133] Since the relationship could be terminated on the initiative of either party, one often finds the two provisions consecutively formulated (so in RS 15.92 and RS 16.344). It is in these clauses where symbolic expressions are more usual: in RS 15.92, if the adoptee repudiates his adoptive father, the former "is to wash his hands and leave," and in RS 16.344, if the adoptee repudiates his adoptive brother, the former "is to hold his ears and leave."[134] Of interest too, given its polyvalent and frequent use in legal context, is that the stereotyped verb used to denote the act of leaving the father's (or brother's) house is *paṭāru*, sometimes further defined with *ana / ina sūqi* literally "on the street" (see RS 15.92:14 and 21, RS 16.200:22, RS 16.344:11 and 16, and cf. also RS 16.141:15 and RS 16.143:27).[135]

19. The no-contest clause

Two deeds recording the division of shares among brothers contain the clause that provides that "one against the other will not contest." In RS 15.90:13-15, it reads *mamma mimma amīlu ana muḫḫi amīli lā iraggum*, and in RS 16.143:14-15 *amīlu ana amīli lā iraggum.*[136] RS 16.252, a

---

[133] For the verb form, see Huehnergard, *The Akkadian of Ugarit*, p. 254 n. 205.

[134] For these symbolic acts, see our discussion in chapter 3 section 1 above. For these ones in particular, see in addition Yaron, "Varia on Adoption," Journal of Juristic Papyrology 15 (1965):182-183, and Anne Draffkorn Kilmer, "Symbolic Gestures in Akkadian Contracts from Alalakh and Ugarit," JAOS 94 (1974):180-181.

[135] Note again the use of *ina* for expected *ana*, probably as a result of Ugaritic influence (see van Soldt, *SAU*, pp. 447 and 450 n. 141).

[136] In RS 15.90:14 (and also l. 12) the second noun is spelled LÚ-*lum*, that is, with the incorrect vowel of the complement, probably due to the formulaic, frozen writing of the form (see Huehnergard, *The Akkadian of Ugarit*, p. 80). Note again that in these prohibition clauses the verb is usually final (see Huehnergard, *The Akkadian of Ugarit*, p. 223). For the clause, see Skaist, "A Unique Closing Formula," pp. 158-159; Joachim Oelsner (in "Klageverzicht[sklausel]," RlA 6, p. 15) provides a brief summary of the evidence with reference to Nougayrol's study in *PRU* 3.

deed also about family property and freedom of claims, contains a no-contest clause expressed in a different fashion. Lines 6-8 state that no one will make any complaint whatsoever against PN or against her children, the prohibition denoted by *lā uttazamūni* (from *nazāmu*).[137] The same provision formulated with the stereotyped verb *ragāmu* is attested in RS 16.145 and RS 16.276, both recording a conveyance of real property. In the former, it appears after the warranty clause (see section 9) and refers to the transferee (*ana muḫḫišu*), and in the latter it refers to the conveyed town (*ana TN*).[138]

Other formulas safeguarding against challenge or contest (cf. *ša dīna iṣabbat* or *ša dīna inammuš / unammiš*) appear in penalty clauses (see below section 22).

20. The heritability phrase

As we have referred to in previous sections, the transfer of real property in royal deeds of conveyance very often provides that it is made to the transferee "and to his sons" (*u ana mārīšu*, in Ugaritic *w l bnh*).[139] The provision that the children of the transferee are to succeed to his position is also frequently contained once more in the text in the warranty clause against eviction; here the text provides that in the future no one is to take the property from the transferee "or from his sons" (*u ištu qāti mārīšu*, in Ugaritic *w bd bnh*). We also have seen (and will see in the next section) that this provision is usually, and significantly, accompanied by the adverbial phrase "forever," indicating the perpetual character of the transfer. Eloquent in this regard is the occasional addition to the phrase *ana mārīšu* or *ištu qāti mārīšu* in the conveyance clause or the warranty clause respectively the expression *mārmārīšu*, that is, "(and/or) his grandsons" (e.g. RS 15.109+, RS 15.123+, RS 16.136, RS 18.21). Sometimes

---

[137] Although spelled *it-ta-za-mu-nim* in line 7 (see van Soldt, *SAU*, p. 436 n. 91).

[138] The verb *baqāru* viz. *buqquru* also with the meaning "to contest, challenge" is not attested in RS 19.128:5' (note that the reading *ú-ba-q*[*ar*(?) proposed by Nougayrol, and followed i.a. by Huehnergard in his *The Akkadian of Ugarit*, p. 139, should probably be corrected into *ú-ba-a*[*l*, see above 14). On the other hand, the restoration suggested by Huehnergard (*The Akkadian of Ugarit*, pp. 139 and 154 n. 161) to read ⸢*ú*⸣-*ba*!-*qar*! instead of [*mi-i*]*m-ma-am* in RS 16.252:11, as copied and interpreted by Nougayrol, seems speculative to me. My skepticism, however, may have to be revised in view of Lackenbacher's collation and reading *ú-ba-qar*! (*Textes akkadiens d'Ugarit*, p. 332 n. 1207).

[139] See above sections 2, 3, 5, 7, 8. In Akkadian documents, the word for "son" is always written with the Sumerogram dumu. For the Ugaritic expression, see RS 15.111 (KTU 3.2):11, RS 16.382 (KTU 3.5):13-14, and RS 94.2168:7.

the conveyance is made "to PN and to his grandsons" (e.g. RS 16.153, RS 16.167). In both cases, the phrases are obviously meant to emphasize and ensure the perpetual heritability of the transfer.

Because some conveyances, especially made by the king, do not include the wording of heritability, that is to say, they simply state that the property is given to PN, it has been argued that they do denote the time limit of the transfer.[140] Although this seems clearly to be the case of the deeds that explicitly provide that the transfer is made "for the transferee's lifetime" (see the next section), I believe a grant just "to PN" does not necessarily prevent PN's heir(s) from succeeding to the granted property. On the other hand, that the wording of the conveyance clause should not be taken too literally is proven by several deeds that omit the phrase "and to his sons" in this clause but include the analogous phrase "or from his sons" in the warranty clause (e.g. RS 16.142, RS 16.150, RS 16.262). One should note that conversely, a deed like RS 16.239 omits the phrase in the warranty clause, i.e. it does not explicitly protect the heirs against potential future interferences, but the property is explicitly conveyed "to PN and his sons."[141] Moreover, it is interesting to remark that part of the father's patrimony could be granted to his sons during his lifetime, as clearly shown by the so-called "ᶜAbdu's dossier" to which the latter example RS 16.239 precisely belongs (cf. also RS 15.120 or the Ugaritic document RS 94.2168).[142]

But not only conveyances are explicitly heritable (viz. secure and lasting). Duties too, or alternatively exemptions from them, can be explicitly formulated as attached to "PN and his sons." Thus, as stated above (in section 10), deeds such as RS 16.148+, RS 16.204 and RS 19.98 stipulate that the grantee and his sons (*u mārūšu*) are to carry a certain kind of *pilku*-service. As for exemptions, in RS 16.239 it is provided that the overseer of the chariots should not have any authority over the transferee and his sons, and RS 16.269 declares "free like the Sun" (see section 15) concerning service for the palace the grantee and his sons. Likewise, royal promotions can be explicitly made for PN and

---

[140] See Skaist, "A Unique Closing Formula," p. 157, and especially Libolt who makes a case for separating heritable and non-heritable land grants on the strict basis of the different wording (the main subject of his PhD dissertation *Royal Land Grants*). The latter's arguments have been thoroughly discussed by Schloen in his *The House of the Father*, pp. 242-245, who concludes that Libolt's distinction cannot be sustained.

[141] As pointed out by Skaist, "A Unique Closing Formula," p. 157 n. 22.

[142] The so-called "ᶜAbdu's dossier" was discussed in chapter 3. Note that another royal deed, RS 15.90 records the division of shares (probably of property given to the father by the king) among brothers presumably after the death of the father.

his heirs (so RS 16.132 and RS 16.348, see above section 16). Noteworthy is the wording of RS 16.348, already mentioned above: "From today RN_1, son of RN_2, king of Ugarit, has removed PN_1, son of PN_2, and his sons from the *pilku*-service of Ibirānu's commanders and has placed him among the friends of the queen;" the accusative suffix in singular clearly referring to the antecedent "PN and his sons."

Prohibitions of challenge or interference are also explicitly meant for the beneficiary's children. Thus, as we have seen, PN can appear together with his sons safeguarded in the warranty clause, but also in the "free-of-claims" formula (RS 15.90, see section 15), in no-contest clauses (RS 16.252, see section 19), as well as in penalty clauses (RS 15.86, see sections 9 and 22).

Before closing this section, reference should be made to two isolated but related formulas. One is attested in RS 15.89:15-16 and provides that "to the one (son) who honours her (i.e. the mother), she shall give it." The object of the transfer is of course the family property, and the requisite of the good son, denoted by the verb *kubuttu*, is naturally to look after her mother.[143] In the Ugaritic document RS 94.2168 it is the father who is given the power of appointment to the property he was granted by the king: he may give it to the son he loves (*d ihb*). Finally, one should also mention the *ul / lā summuḫ* formula attested in three royal deeds (RS 15.146+, RS 15.190 and RS 16.353, the verb always in the predicative adjective form)[144] meant to exclude people other than the tenant among the heirs to the property (including his brothers and sons, as explicitly provided for in RS 16.353).

21. The formulas for "forever" and "for the transferee's lifetime"

In most royal deeds of conveyance the transfer is made "forever" (usually accompanying the so-called heritability phrase, just discussed). As we mentioned in the previous chapter, the adverb "forever" closing the conveyance clause is syntactically and semantically related to the opening adverbial phrase "from today." In Akkadian, the adverb "forever" can be expressed with different formulas, all based on the word *dāru* "perpetuity, eternity."[145] Thus we find *ana dāri dūri* and *ana / adi dārīti*

[143] See especially Jonas Greenfield, "*Adi balṭu*: Care for the Elderly and its Rewards," in *Vorträge gehalten auf der 28. Rencontre Assyriologique Internationale in Wien*, p. 312.

[144] See van Soldt, *SAU*, p. 502.

[145] Cf. The recent study of the semantic range of the word by Jean-Jacques Glassner, "Le devin historien en Mésopotamie," in *Historiography in the Cuneiform World*, ed. T. Abusch et al. (Bethesda, 2001), pp. 182-86.

as the most common.[146] The Ugaritic counterpart is spelled *ʿd ʿlm*.[147] What the combination of the adverbial expressions "from today ... for ever" seems to denote is that the transfer in question, framed within both phrases, is not a priori limited in time: it takes effect at that very moment and it is to be perpetual.[148]

On the other hand, there is a small number of conveyances (RS 16.189, RS 16.244, and RS 15.122, cf. also the fragmentary RS 16.208) that are explicitly limited in time, namely to the lifetime of the new holder. This is recorded with the expression *ana / ina ūmēti balāṭišu* "for his (i.e. the transferee's) lifetime."[149] The use in one of these documents (RS 16.189) of the verb *akālu* leaves no doubt that we are here dealing with usufruct and not ownership.[150] What we cannot know, however, is whether the occasional absence of the adverbial phrase in the text is of any significance, that is, whether the conveyance is made with or without time limit. One should note in this regard that in some deeds the adverbial expression "forever" is missing in the conveyance clause but appears instead in the following warranty clause, the latter then, and not the former, providing the perpetual character of the transaction (e.g. RS 15.89, RS 15.168, and RS 16.282). Indeed, the formula "(tomorrow at dawn) no one shall take it (i.e. the property) from PN (the transferee)," very frequently adds "forever" too, as though completing and emphasizing in the corresponding cases the adverbial phrase "tomorrow at dawn" (given the prohibitive nature of the clause, a suitable translation would then be "never in the future"). It is rather frequent therefore to find this adverb

---

[146] There are definitely more than two expressions (viz. *ana dāri dūri* and *ana dārīti*, cf. Malbran-Labat, "Langues et écritures à Ougarit," p. 80). See the full list provided by Huehnergard (*The Akkadian of Ugarit*, p. 202). As pointed out by van Soldt (*SAU*, p. 458), the preposition *adi* only occurs in this phrase, probably as a result of Ugaritic influence (see the chronological distribution of the usage of *ana* and *adi* on p. 459).

[147] Note the Ugaritic equivalent expression to (*ana*) *dāri dūri* spelled *dr dr* in the story of Aqhatu (RS 3.66 [KTU 1.19] iv:6).

[148] See the relevant comments by Yaron in *The Law of the Aramaic Papyri*, pp. 80-81.

[149] Note here again the indistinct use of both prepositions *ana* and *ina* (probably as a result of Ugaritic influence). For the formula, see also Skaist, "A Unique Closing Formula," p. 157.

[150] In one case, RS 15.122, the real property is paradoxically given to the transferee "for ever (and) for his lifetime" (*adi dārīti ina ūmēti balāṭišu*). This exceptional example may actually point to a scribal lapse caused by the stereotyped, frozen character of the formula *adi dārīti* (as also pointed out by Schloen, *The House of the Father*, p. 244 n. 52).

both in the conveyance clause and the warranty clause (e.g. RS 15.145, RS 15.155, 15.Z, RS 16.138, RS 16.141, RS 16.247, RS 16.275, RS 16.353, and also the Ugaritic deeds RS 15.111 [KTU 3.2] and RS 16.382 [KTU 3.5]).

The scope of the transfer was obviously to define also a priori the scope of the obligation to the king. Indeed, if the property was the transferee's for no fixed period, i.e. of a permanent nature, so must have been the services attached to the property and tenant due to the palace. Accordingly, notaries occasionally added too the phrase "forever" to the obligation clause. Thus, for example, RS 16.204 provides that "PN (the grantee) and his sons are to carry the *pilku*-service of the sons of the queen forever." And the same holds true for the exemptions from service (for "permanent" exemptions see e.g. RS 16.269:21, RS 16.276:19).

22. Penalty and curse formulas

Penal stipulations are significantly rare in the royal deeds of Ugarit. In the few examples, worldly penalties and divine maledictions never appear together. The former are always pecuniary in nature. What the formula provides is that whoever, i.e. either one of the parties involved in the transaction or a third party, takes legal steps against the other party (or the transferee in RS 15.86 and RS 16.189), he shall have to pay a certain sum of silver or/and gold.[151] The expression used is "to start suit," *ša dīna iṣabbat* or *ša dīna inammuš* / *unammiš*, the latter construed with *itti* ("against").[152] In RS 15.86, however, it is significantly phrased fol-

[151] The attestations are RS 15.86:17-25, RS 15.90:16-21, RS 16.189:14-16, RS 16.192A+:17-24, RS 16.239:25-30; see also the diplomatic document RS 16.270:30-43, and the fragmentary deed RS 16.280:1'-4'.

[152] It is used in RS 15.90, RS 16.192A+, RS 16.239, RS 16.280, and RS 16.270 (as well as RS 17.318+, also belonging to the dossier of the dynastic divorce; cf. RS 17.59 and RS 17.82 both issued on behalf of the Hittite emperor). For the use of *unammiš*, that is, a preterite form instead of the expected durative, see Huehnergard, *The Akkadian of Ugarit*, pp. 252-255. Huehnergard refers to Kestemont as having suggested that the expression is a calque of Hittite *nini(n)k-* (and so included in his list of "Hittite Features" in *The Akkadian of Ugarit*, p. 283, and apparently followed by Malbran-Labat in her "Langues et écritures à Ougarit," p. 81 n. 93, who also takes it as a calque from Hittite). Nevertheless, what Kestemont means by the abbreviation "trad. litt. hitt." (found throughout his Akkadian lexicon in *Diplomatique et droit international*) is the literal equivalent or counterpart in Hittite; thus we find on p. 614 s.v. *ninink-* (in the Hittite glossary) the abbreviation "trad. litt. acc." followed by *namāšu*. What Kestemont did take as a Hittite interference (not beyond doubt in my opinion) is the use of the Akkadian preposition (wrongly quoted as *ištu* on p. 577).

lowing the wording of the warranty clause against eviction; it states "whoever takes the conveyed property from the hands of the transferee and his heirs" (see section 9 above).[153] When the potential litigant is not impersonal, such as in RS 16.239 (the name of the party's brother) or the diplomatic document RS 16.270 (ᶜAmmiṯtamru II), the sentence is formulated as a conditional sentence with the phrase "if tomorrow at dawn i.e. in the future" (*šumma urra*[*m*] *šēra*[*m*]). The penalties are indeed heavy, consisting of round sums. We find 2,000 shekels of silver plus 1,000 shekels of gold in RS 16.189, one talent (= 3,000 shekels in Ugarit) of gold plus 5 talents of silver in RS 16.192A+, 2 talents of silver in RS 15.86, 10 talents of silver in RS 16.239, and one talent of silver plus one talent of gold in RS 15.90 (since we know very little about the value of the transactions it is hardly possible to evaluate whether or not there is any relationship between the sum and the transaction).[154] The transgressor then has to give (normally *nadānu*, once *mullû*)[155] the sum either to the king (RS 15.90), to the protected party (RS 16.189, RS 16.239) or both (RS 16.192A+: the one talent of gold is for the king and the 5 talents of silver for PN). The challenging party would also have to give the property to his brother in RS 15.90, and in RS 16.239 he additionally would have to return to his father's house.

Divine curses are also rarely used to secure transactions.[156] They all come towards the end of the document, and are explicitly meant to protect the transferee against the changing of the text viz. its content, therefore presumably addressed to a king or any person or official with access to the deeds and rights recorded therein (the verbs used are *nakāru* or *nukkuru*, and *šubalkutu*). Two of the extant examples significantly belong to the same dossier of the merchant Sinarānu (the *Sammelurkunde* RS 15.109+ and RS 16.238+). RS 15.109+:56-57 reads "whoever discards this deed, may the gods destroy his name!" (*ša ṭuppa annâm unakkir ilānu šumšu liḫalliq*),[157] and the fragmentary lines 18-20 in RS

[153] Note that the clause "whoever takes it" in RS 15.86, and "whoever starts suit" in RS 16.192A+ is repeated at the end of the clause. For this unusual word order, see Huehnergard, *The Akkadian of Ugarit*, p. 223.

[154] Compare, for example, these sums with the pecuniary stipulation, namely 1,000 shekels of silver in the deed of adoption RS 16.344.

[155] The forms *inaddin* and *iddin* are used, and *umalli* in RS 18.280:4'; note again the use of a preterite form for the expected durative, see Huehnergard, *The Akkadian of Ugarit*, pp. 252-255, and van Soldt, *SAU*, pp. 500-501.

[156] We have therefore not included under this category the so-called "last wishes" of king Arḫalbu (RS 16.144) that basically contains maledictions addressed to he who would marry his wife after his death.

[157] Note again the use of the preterite instead of the durative, and the wrong declination of the object spelled *ṭup-pu*.

16.238+ have Ba^{c}lu the Lord of the Mount Cassius protect too the words of the document. The same patron-god of Ugarit is to punish (*šâlu*) in RS 16.157:25-28 "he who invalidates this gift" (*ša ušbalkit nidna annâ*).

For the seal formula and the name of the scribe that close the deed, which do not properly belong to the operative part, see chapter 5, sections 3 and 4 respectively.

CHAPTER 7

SCRIBAL HABITS AND NOTARIAL TRADITION

As the title of this final chapter indicates, two last aspects of legal language need to be discussed. One concerns the formulaic variants attested in the royal deeds of Ugarit and the other concerns the use (both synchronic and diachronic) of certain formulas in other ancient Near Eastern provinces of law. In dealing in the previous chapter with the wording of phrases and terms in royal deeds, we have indicated for some examples the existence of variant forms for the same stereotyped expression. Although only incidentally, we have also referred to the relation between notarial usages, say of a particular variant phrase, and a chronological situation or generation (naturally within the one century and a half covered by our documentation). Indeed, as we shall see in the first part of this chapter, the choice not only of a word but also of a sign over another in drawing up a legal formula (and text) is in most cases the result of scribal training. We shall also point out in what follows that the preference of a sign or a word over another can reflect not only a notarial fashion but also the hand or style of an individual scribe.[1] Needless to say, the analysis of these variants must proceed with great care. When faced to formulaic deviations, it is difficult but of course desirable to distinguish between what is of legal significance and what may be a simple feature of style. On the other hand, once scribal idiosyncrasies are conclusively identified, it is possible to establish to a certain extent the hand or the (approximate) chronology of an otherwise "anonymous," fragmentary or undated deed.

The historical analysis of some formulas, or in other words, a study of the notarial stream of tradition that flowed through Late Bronze Age Ugarit constitutes the second, closing section of the chapter. As we have mentioned on several occasions throughout the last chapters, law shows at all times an overriding concern for precise, consistent, and traditional linguistic usage. It is therefore the conservative nature of notarial language that can importantly help us to trace back the source, as well as follow the fate, of some particular items of terminology.

---

[1] Nougayrol announced in *PRU* 3 (p. 237) a forthcoming study of the different notarial hands that was never published to the best of my knowledge. Huehnergard and van Soldt include in their studies of the Akkadian of Ugarit occasional relevant remarks on scribal habits that will be duly noted in the following examination.

1. A note on scribal habits

In our discussion on the Akkadian language written in Ugarit (in chapter 4), we referred to the conclusion reached by van Soldt after his thorough analysis of the whole relevant corpus that there exists a clear and significant shift in the orthography and grammar of the texts. Indeed, in the documents written under the earlier kings of Ugarit, especially as far as the syllabary is concerned, one can observe a strong Hurrian viz. Mittanian influence, whereas the documents written under the later kings evidence a growing Assyrian influence, and even more clearly, a growing Ugaritic influence. Because, as we also stated in chapter 4, the legal documents constitute an important, and in some areas of grammar (such as syntax) an essential part of the corpus (they are on the other hand the texts more accurately dated), it will not come as a surprise that these observable orthographic and grammatical developments apply too to the linguistic style of royal deeds. Let us list some examples. The form *adi dārīti* (instead of *ana dārīti*) is only attested in late texts, namely from ᶜAmmiṯtamru II on (presumably under the influence of the Ugaritic preposition *ᶜd*);[2] the use of the (Assyrian) form *ilaqqe* increases at the expense of (Babylonian) *ileqqe* also around the time of this king;[3] and the same is true of the increasing use of the negative *lā* over *ul*, probably due to either Assyrian or Ugaritic influence;[4] and a shift from *ina TN* to *ša ina TN* in the description of conveyed real property (reflecting Ugaritic *d b TN*) seems also to take place under ᶜAmmiṯtamru II.[5] As for the orthography, we may note the development of the spellings for /qe/ to write the forms of *leqû*: under the earlier kings Niqmaddu II and Arḫalbu only GI is used; then under Niqmepaᶜ KI begins to be used as well and becomes the favoured sign to represent /qe/ under his son and successor ᶜAmmiṯtamru; during the reign of Ibirānu QI is introduced and is prominently used under Niqmaddu III.[6]

Other clear developments in grammar and terminology are the following: the chiastic word order S-V-O—V-S (the latter S = *šarru* "king")

---

[2] See Huehnergard, *The Akkadian of Ugarit*, p. 202, and van Soldt, *SAU*, pp. 458-459, 472.

[3] See Huehnergard, *The Akkadian of Ugarit*, pp. 55-56, and van Soldt, *SAU*, pp. 433-434, 473.

[4] Assyrian has only *lā* as negative and *lā* is also the general negative particle in Ugaritic, as stated by van Soldt, *SAU*, p. 511; see also ibid., pp. 510 and 518, and Huehnergard, *The Akkadian of Ugarit*, pp. 239-240.

[5] See van Soldt, *SAU*, pp. 484, 492-494, 518.

[6] See van Soldt, *SAU*, p. 263.

in the *našû-nadānu* clause is only attested in deeds of ^{c}Ammiṯtamru II;[7] the odd iterative formula *nadānu-nadānu* is not attested before Niqmepa^{c} and then only continued under ^{c}Ammiṯtamru II; the phrase *amīlu mamman* in the warranty clause is also introduced in times of Niqmepa^{c} becoming especially frequent in deeds of ^{c}Ammiṯtamru II;[8] the verb *ekēmu* is used instead of *leqû* in the warranty clause only in deeds dated to the reign of Niqmaddu II;[9] and also exclusively attested in Akkadian deeds of Niqmaddu II is the Ugaritic word for royal service *ʾunuṯṯu*; the classical Akkadian form *ilku*, on the other hand, does not appear before ^{c}Ammiṯtamru II; the title "king of the land of Ugarit" as a variant of "king of Ugarit" is also used from ^{c}Ammiṯtamru II on; the stereotyped formula of exemption from royal service ([*p*]*ilku/a yānu*) is not found before Niqmepa^{c} and is especially frequent in the deeds of ^{c}Ammiṯtamru II;[10] and the so-called "anonymous" formula used to describe the dynastic seal impressed on the tablet is almost completely replaced by the "personal" one during the reign of ^{c}Ammiṯtamru II.[11]

However minor (one should keep in mind the conservative nature of our material), it seems that a change in notarial or scribal practice must have taken place in Ugarit sometime during the first half of the 13th century. One should note that beside the linguistic stylistic features listed above, the notarial habit of dividing the text in sections by means of rulings is also mainly attested from the reign of ^{c}Ammiṯtamru II on.[12] Whether chance or fashion played their part is difficult to say, especially in view of the limited number and quality of the relevant documents we have. On the other hand, whether or not the change or the "fashion," at least in Akkadian grammar and terminology, is to be related to the political international situation following the influence of Assyria, now controlling the entire area of upper Mesopotamia, must remain open for the time being.[13] What may not be coincidental and may speak for a significant development within the scribal or cultural activity at Ugarit is that probably around the same time the alphabetic script was invented to

[7] See van Soldt, *SAU*, pp. 476 and 493.

[8] See Huehnergard, *The Akkadian of Ugarit*, p. 138 n. 68.

[9] See van Soldt, *SAU*, p. 472.

[10] See my "Royal Land Grants and *ilku*-Service in Ugarit," pp. 171-178.

[11] See our remarks in chapter 5.

[12] And the same is true, for example, of the shape of the cuneiform sign KAM used to write the word *ūmu* in the opening phrase. As pointed out by Huehnergard (*The Akkadian of Ugarit*, p. 396), the variant KÁM (ḪIxBAD) of KAM (ḪI+BAD) is not attested before ^{c}Ammiṯtamru II.

[13] See van Soldt, *SAU*, p. 522.

write the native Ugaritic language.[14] Perhaps as relevant is the fact that, as we stated in chapter 1, a salient increase in notarial activity is attested for the reign of ᶜAmmiṯtamru II: over forty percent of the corpus is written under his reign, and a total of nine known notaries did work for this king (it may not be otiose to mention that it was during this reign that was established the so-called "Pax Hethitica," following the battle of Qadesh, which brought along a period of unsurpassed prosperity for Ugarit).[15]

Be that as it may, I believe one should not underestimate, let alone ignore individual decisions that could be taken in the chancery (including the invention of the alphabetic cuneiform itself). The following survey into scribal individual idiosyncrasies will possibly illustrate the point.

After an examination of the different royal deeds that preserve the name of the notaries who wrote them (see the appendix to chapter 3), we get the following examples of individual orthographic and linguistic habits.

1.1. The phrase "from today"

Concerning the writing of *ūmi annîm* in the opening formula of the legal text,[16] Šapšumalku uses the spelling u_4.1.kam *an-ni-i-im* in his earlier compositions (RS 16.133 and RS 16.263 dated to Niqmaddu II) but consistently writes u_4.1.kam *an-ni-im* in his more mature texts (RS 15.88, RS 15.Y, RS 16.142, RS 16.143, RS 16.157, RS 16.208, RS 16.250 and RS 16.251). The spelling u_4-*mi an-ni-i-im* is in turn favoured by Karrānu (RS 15.119), Munaḫḫimu (RS 15.147, RS 15.190, RS 16.201, RS 16.243, cf. also the private deed RS 17.22+), Iltaḥmu (RS 16.353, cf. also the documents RS 17.88 and RS 17.356), and Yaᶜdidu (RS 15.136, RS 16.138, RS 16.204, RS 16.241+ and RS 19.98).[17]

1.2. The expressions for "forever"

As for the adverbial phrase "forever," Šapšumalku uses either *ana dārīti* (RS 15.88, RS 16.147, RS 16.157 and RS 16.283) or *ana dāri dūri* (RS 16.245 and RS 16.254D). The latter expression is also used by Yaᶜḏirānu

---

[14] See our discussion in previous chapters.

[15] As described by Singer, "A Political History of Ugarit," pp. 646ff.

[16] Cf. Huehnergard, *The Akkadian of Ugarit*, pp. 58 and 391, and van Soldt, *SAU*, pp. 409-410, 508 n.99.

[17] Note that as shown by other legal documents, Ilimalku prefers the spelling u_4-*mi an-ni-im* (RS 17.61 and RS 17.67) and Nuᶜmerašpu u_4.1.kam *an-ni-i-im* (RS 17.77, RS 17.371+, RS 18.02, RS 29.100).

(RS 16.282A+B); but Munaḫḫimu (RS 15.145, RS 15.147 and RS 16.243), Nu^{c}merašpu (RS 15.131 and RS 15.143+), Iltaḥmu (RS 15.140) and Ya^{c}didu (RS 15.136, RS 16.138, RS 16.204, RS 16.241+ and RS 19.98) favour *adi dārīti*.

1.3. The warranty clause

If we now turn to the warranty clause, we find that Šapšumalku spells the opening phrase *urra(m) šēra(m)* as *ú-ra še-ra* (RS 16.142, RS 16.143 and RS 16.250)[18] but more frequently he omits it (RS 15.88, RS 16.147, RS 16.157, RS 16.208, RS 16.245 and RS 16.251). The same is true of Ya^{c}didu: in one deed he uses *ur-ra-am še-ra-am* (RS 16.138) and in three other deeds he omits the phrase (RS 15.136, RS 16.204 and RS 16.241+). Karrānu in turn writes *ur$_5$-ra še-ra* (RS 16.207 and probably also RS 16.284); whereas Munaḫḫimu seems to consistently omit it (RS 15.145, RS 15.147 and RS 16.243).[19]

As for the indefinite personal pronoun in the same clause, Šapšumalku uses either the form *mamman* (RS 16.133, RS 16.147, RS 16.208, RS 16.245, RS 16.251, RS 16.254D and RS 16.263) or *mamma* (RS 15.88, RS 16.142, RS 16.143, RS 16.250 and RS 16.283). The form *amīlu mamman* is favoured by Karrānu (RS 16.207 and RS 16.284), Munaḫḫimu (RS 15.145, RS 15.147), Nu^{c}merašpu (RS 15.168), Iltaḥmu (RS 15.140) and Ya^{c}didu (RS 15.136, RS 16.138, RS 16.204, RS 16.241+ and RS 19.98).[20] Ya^{c}didu, on the other hand, always adds the complement *-lum* to the Sumerogram lú (to write *amīlu*).[21]

The verb in the warranty clause is usually spelled *i-laq-qè* by Šapšumalku (RS 15.88, RS 16.142, RS 16.147, RS 16.157, 16.208, 16.245, 16.263) preceded by either *ul* (RS 15.88, RS 16.147, RS 16.157, RS 16.208, RS 16.245 and RS 16.243) or *lā* (RS 16.142, RS 16.251, RS 16.254D and RS 16.283). Karrānu in turn prefers the negative *lā* (RS 16.207 and RS 16.284) as well as the spelling *i-la-qè* (RS 16.207). Munaḫḫimu (RS 15.145 and RS 15.147), Nu^{c}merašpu (RS 15.143+ and RS 15.168), Iltaḥmu (RS 15.140), and Ya^{c}didu (RS 15.136, RS 15.138, RS 16.204 and RS 16.241+) employ too the negative *lā*, always spelled *la-a*, and the form *ilaqqe*: Munaḫḫimu spells it *i-la-aq-qè*, Nu^{c}merašpu

---

18 In RS 16.263 he spelled it *ú-ra-am še-ra*.

19 Note that Ilimalku spells it *ur-ra še-ra-am* in the private deeds RS 17.61 and RS 17.67.

20 After collation I could read the sign AN (of *ma-am-ma-an*) at the end of the broken line 5' of RS 16.204.

21 See Huehnergard, *The Akkadian of Ugarit*, p. 79. Note that Ilimalku uses in turn the pronoun *mannumma* in the private deeds RS 17.61 and RS 17.67.

i-laq-qè and Ya^cdidu either spelling.[22]

Finally, the expression *ištu qāti* in this clause is as a rule spelled *iš-tu* šu(*-ti*). Distinctively, however, Ya^cdidu always spells it syllabically *iš-tu qa-ti* (RS 15.136, RS 16.138, RS 16.204, RS 16.241+ and RS 19.98).

1.4. The (p)ilku*-clause*

If we now take a look at the *(p)ilku*-clause, we find that Šapšumalku uses always the term *pilku* (RS 15.Y, RS 16.133, RS 16.142, RS 16.147 and RS 16.149), just like Karrānu (RS 15.119), Munaḫḫimu (RS 15.145, RS 15.147, RS 16.243, and RS 16.255D), Ya^cdidu (RS 16.138, RS 16.204, RS 16.241+ and RS 19.98), and Iliramu (RS 18.285). Nu^cmerašpu (RS 15.131 and RS 15.143+), Iltaḫmu (RS 15.140) and Eḫliteššub (RS 18.21), in turn, use the term *ilku*. In the formula with *yānu* Munaḫḫimu usually writes the noun in accusative (*pilka* in RS 15.145, RS 15.147, and RS 16.243; cf. however *pilku* in RS 16.201),[23] whereas Ya^cdidu, for example, declines the word always in the nominative (RS 15.136, RS 16.241+ and RS 19.98), like Nu^cmerašpu who uses, however, the Mesopotamian form *ilku* (RS 15.131 and RS 15.143+). As for the clause itself, Ya^cdidu writes the same formula in two royal deeds (RS 16.138 and RS 16.204).

1.5. The seal identification formula

As regards the phrase identifying the dynastic seal impressed on the tablet, Šapšumalku prefers the "anonymous" formula (RS 15.88, RS 15.Y, RS 16.142, RS 16.143, RS 16.147, RS 16.149, RS 16.157, RS 16.191A, RS 16.208, RS 16.245, RS 16.250, RS 16.251, RS 16.254D and RS 16.283).[24] The "personal" formula is favoured instead by Karrānu (RS 15.119 and RS 16.207), Munaḫḫimu (RS 15.145, RS 15.147, RS 16.86+, RS 16.201, RS 16.243 and RS 16.386), Nu^cmerašpu (RS 15.131, RS 15.143+, RS 15.168, and cf. RS 18.280), Iltaḫmu (RS 15.140, RS 16.353 and RS 19.128), and Ya^cdidu (RS 15.136, RS 16.138, RS 16.204, RS 16.241+ and RS 19.98).

---

[22] Note that Ilimalku uses the negative *ul* and the form *ileqqe* in RS 17.61.

[23] Cf. van Soldt, *SAU*, p. 413.

[24] See van Soldt, *SAU*, p. 516.

1.6. The toponym "Ugarit"

The writing of the toponym Ugarit (always preceded by the proper classifier uru)[25] in the royal title following the king's name and patronymic also show minor variations from one notary to another.[26] Thus, for example, Šapšumalku prefers to spell it *u-ga-ri-it* (that is, with the initial U sign: RS 15.88, RS 15.Y, RS 16.133, RS 16.142, RS 16.143, RS 16.157, RS 16.245, RS 16.250, RS 16.251 and RS 16.263) and hardly uses the classifier ki written after the toponym (only in RS 16.147, RS 16.251, RS 16.263). As for Karrānu, he never writes the classifier ki and spells the toponym with Ú (RS 15.119 and RS 16.207). Munaḫḫimu, in turn, also prefers the spelling of the name with Ú (RS 15.145, RS 15.147, RS 15.190, RS 16.201 and RS 16.243) but favours writing the additional classifier ki (RS 15.145, RS 15.147, RS 15.190, RS 16.86+ and RS 16.243), just like Yaᶜdirānu (RS 16.192A+ and RS 16.282A+B). Interestingly, both Nuᶜmerašpu (RS 15.131, RS 15.143+, RS 15.168, RS 18.280, and cf. RS 17.371+), and Yaᶜdidu (RS 15.136, RS 16.138, RS 16.241+, and RS 19.98) write before the toponym the Sumerogram kur for "land" (omitting then the classifier ki).[27]

1.7. The royal name "ᶜAmmiṯtamru"

Of interest too are the various spellings of the royal name ᶜAmmiṯtamru.[28] Šapšumalku, for example, spells the name of Niqmaddu II's father as *am-mi-iš-tam-rV* (RS 16.133 and RS 16.263), whereas Munaḫḫimu (RS 15.145, RS 15.147, RS 15.190, RS 16.201 and RS 16.243), Iltaḫmu (RS 15.140 and RS 16.353), and Yaᶜdidu (RS 15.136, RS 16.138, RS 16.204, RS 16.241+ and RS 19.98) prefer *a-miš-tam-rV* to write the name of Niqmaddu II's grandson.[29] Yaᶜdirānu in turn favours the spelling *am-mi-is-tam-rV* (RS 16.192A+ and RS 16.282A+).

---

[25] Also present (collated) in RS 16.244 (the copy and transliteration of Nougayrol should accordingly be corrected).

[26] See Huehnergard, *The Akkadian of Ugarit*, pp. 32 and 84.

[27] Cf. van Soldt, *SAU*, p. 31 and note 248, and Huehnergard, *The Akkadian of Ugarit*, p. 32.

[28] Cf. the survey made by Huehnergard in *The Akkadian of Ugarit*, pp. 380-381.

[29] The last sign can be RU, RA or RI, depending on the case of the name (nominative or genitive) and the scribal favoured system of declension (diptotic or triptotic, see Huehnergard, *The Akkadian of Ugarit*, p. 145), as well as the potential mistakes. It is relevant to observe here that Munaḫḫimu makes the same mistake of declension (he spells it with RI when the king is the subject of the sentence) in two deeds (RS 15.145 and RS 15.147); see van Soldt, *SAU*, p. 414.

1.8. Restoration of damaged passages

As a matter of course, the instances of scribal idiosyncrasies can be multiplied. One could add, for example, the exceptional writing of an.za.gàr in the description of the transferred real property followed by the classifier ki. Ya^{c}didu is significantly the author of the three extant examples in the whole corpus (RS 16.138, RS 16.204 and RS 16.241+).[30] The immediate interest and importance of discovering scribal writing habits for the Assyriologist is obviously the possibility to reconstruct passages that are damaged or not preserved on the tablet. Take for example RS 19.98, a tablet written by Ya^{c}didu himself, the right edge of which is broken off. In view of his favoured spellings, the end of line 17 can be restored beyond doubt as *a-d*[*i da-ri-ti*] and the phrase *urram šēram* was very likely not written afterwards; in the next line the complement *–lum* is to be restored after lú as well as the form *ilaqqe* at the end of the line. Likewise, on the damaged reverse of RS 16.204, drawn up by the same scribe, the complement *–lum* after lú is to be restored at the end of line 5'. If we concentrate now on Munaḫḫimu's texts, one can restore in all likelihood the sign PÍL and not IL (to complete the word *pilku*) in the first intelligible line (line 4') on the broken reverse of RS 16.201. Likewise, the fragmentary *pilku*-clause in RS 16.86+16.172, also drawn up by Munaḫḫimu, can safely be restored as [*ù píl-ka/ku ia-nu i-na* a.šà].ḫi.a *an-nu-ti* in view of the analogous formulas in RS 15.145, RS 15.147 and RS 16.201.

In other cases, however, a restoration must remain tentative. Indeed, sometimes the same scribe may use one form or another. This, we have seen, is the case of Šapšumalku. Thus, for example, the corrected restoration proposed by Huehnergard to Nougayrol's reading in RS 16.133 rev. 16, namely [*ú-ul i-laq*]-*qè-šu-nu* for [*la-a i-le*]-*qè-šu-nu*, is not beyond doubt. As we have seen above, the "expert" notary does not always use the negative *ul* in the warranty clause (neither does he always spell it *ú-ul*, see *ul* in RS 16.147:16); and although he does usually favour the form *ilaqqe*, *ileqqe* is inscribed in one of his deeds (RS 16.251:14; note furthermore that he not always spelled the Assyrian form *i-laq-qè*, see *i-la-qè* in RS 16.283:9). Still more significant regarding the individual free choice in drawing up a deed is the fact that the same scribe can use two variants of the same expression in the same text. Thus, for example, the indefinite personal pronouns *mamman* and *mannumma* appear side by side in RS 16.140, and the negatives *lā* and *ul*

---

[30] The spelling of the title "scribe" with the Sumerogram dub.sar either with or without the complement *–rum* is, for example, surveyed by Huehnergard in *The Akkadian of Ugarit*, pp. 78-79.

are used for the same formula in RS 16.154.[31] More eloquent is the attestation of the three forms *ana dārīti*, *ana dāri dūri* and *adi dārīti* to denote "forever" in the same deed RS 16.182+.[32]

1.9. Who wrote it, and when was it written?

The Assyriologist can further profit from these observations and attempt to identify the scribal hand of a deed that has not preserved or does not record the name of the scribe who wrote it. Thus, for example, it is tempting to recognize some of the notarial habits of Šapšumalku in the deed RS 16.144, namely the so-called "last wishes" of king Arḫalbu.[33] Or the habits of Karrānu in RS 16.260, RS 17.331 and RS 29.98, the three of them dated to the relevant reign of Niqmepaᶜ;[34] or still those of Ilimalku in RS 16.356 dated to the corresponding reign of Niqmaddu III.[35] On the basis too of the personal preferences, it is possible, for example, to decide that Yarimmu and not Šapšumalku is the author of RS 16.156, both names written at the end of the document and followed by the title "scribe."[36]

---

[31] As already pointed out by Huehnergard in *The Akkadian of Ugarit*, pp. 137-138 and 239.

[32] See Huehnergard, *The Akkadian of Ugarit*, p. 202. One should none the less take into consideration that the use of these variants side by side could be the result of putting together two different deeds, i.e. drawn up by two different notaries, into one same document (a *Sammelurkunde*). On the other hand, the examples listed above could be taken as an argument for the restoration of the word *pilku* in RS 16.156:11 beside *ᵓunuṯṯu* in line 15, as suggested by Nougayrol, and followed by Heltzer (note his variant restoration in "La signification de *unṯ* / *unuššu* à Ougarit," Semitica 30 [1980]:7); see, however, our objections above and the remarks that follow.

[33] Note the spellings u_4.1.kam *an-ni-im*, ᴾsum-*ḫal-bu* (like in RS 16.142), ᵘʳᵘ*u-ga-ri-it*, or *ú-ra še-ra*.

[34] Note the spellings u_4-*mi an-ni-i-im*, ᵘʳᵘ*ú-ga-ri-it* or lú *ma-am-ma-an la i-la-qè-šu*.

[35] Note the spellings u_4-*mi an-ni-im*, *ur-ra še-ra-am*, *ma-an-nu-um-ma*, or *ú-ul i-leq-qè*.

[36] The authorship was cautiously left open, for example, by Huehnergard, *The Akkadian of Ugarit*, pp. 344-345. But note indeed the following spellings, different from Šapšumalku's writing habits: *a-miš-tam-ri*, ᵘʳᵘ*ú-ga-ri-it*ᵏⁱ; the use of *ekēmu* instead of *leqû* in the warranty claus,e and of *ᵓunuṯṯu* instead of *pilku*, as well as the expression *ana kaspi* (Šapšumalku seems to favour the preposition *ina*, see RS 16.133 and RS 16.147). Note also here the examination carried out by van Soldt in his attempt to distinguish or identify two hands of the same name Nuᶜmerašpu (*SAU*, p. 31).

Likewise, the chronological or generational developments in scribal habits discussed above can help determine at least an approximate date of an otherwise undated document. I would like to particularly refer to two documents, a royal deed inscribed in alphabetic cuneiform and an unpublished deed recording a conveyance of real property by the queen of Ugarit. The former document is RS 16.191+ (KTU 3.4). In the first chapter, we mentioned that the only clue we have as to its date is the impression on top of the obverse of the tablet of the seal of Niqmaddu II. We also mentioned that the same seal was used by ^{c}Ammiṯtamru II to authenticate the royal deed RS 17.147. Because of this evidence and the fact that the Ugaritic alphabet was presumably not invented before the reign of Niqmepa^{c}, one can tentatively suggest that ^{c}Ammiṯtamru II is the king who presided over the transaction recorded in RS 16.191+ (KTU 3.4). In support of this, we can now refer to the chiastic formulation of the ransom clause (spelled in Ugaritic *l ym hnd PN pdy PNN w pdy.hm PN*) and the observation that this word order S-V-O—V-S is typical (with the formula *našû-nadānu*) of the royal deeds of ^{c}Ammiṯtamru II. As for the unpublished Akkadian document RS 22.02, it is noteworthy that the spelling of the opening words u$_4$-*mi an-ni-im* is characteristic of the documents composed during the reign of Niqmaddu II and absolutely unfamiliar in the later deeds. Furthermore, the warranty clause against eviction of the property uses the verb *ekēmu* instead of *leqû*, a feature also distinctive of the earlier documents, as we have seen. I would therefore hesitate to take queen Ašdadā as the wife of ^{c}Ammurapiʾ, the last king of Ugarit,[37] and rather prefer to place her at the other end of the chronological spectrum of dated texts, namely in the 14th century (perhaps then as wife of Niqmaddu II?).

1.10. Differences of style or legally significant?

We now finally come to discuss the question whether or not differences in wording have any legal significance.[38] Aware that it is not always

---

[37] As suggested by van Soldt (see *SAU*, p. 19).

[38] We have already mentioned that the second methodological assumption in Libolt's study is that "differences, even small differences in how a clause is stated, are significant." "At times in the study —he concluded— we attribute differences to 'style,' but most of the differences seem to have legal significance" (*Royal Land Grants*, p. 21). We already raised our objections in the introduction to (and I therefore believe there is no need to dwell longer upon) Libolt's third methodological assumption according to which changes in legal language may reflect changes in the society of Ugarit or even indicate a change in regime. On the other hand, criticisms to his interpretation of the differences in conveyance formulas and the heritability clause can be found in the relevant sections of the previous chapter. More will also

possible to give a definite answer and that one should avoid drawing general conclusions from simple cases, I have chosen four or rather five examples that I hope will suffice to show that a variant or deviation from the usual formulary that can be easily taken to be of legal import may have no more legal significance than the addition of the classifier ki to the Sumerogram an.za.gàr mentioned above.

1.10.1. The witnessing notary

One of the instances has already been dealt with in chapter 5, namely in our discussion of the name of the scribe. A summary of the remarks we made there will accordingly suffice. A documentary aspect of clear legal substance is the mentioning of witnesses. Although, as we have insistently stated on several occasions, royal deeds are characterized by the absence of witnesses (the presence of the king viz. his seal impression rendered their mentioning simply unnecessary), we also said that the name of the notary at the end of the document is sometimes preceded by the Sumerogram igi, the meaning of which is "witness." The writing of the logogram, however, as we pointed out, seems to reflect particular scribal habits. Šapšumalku, for example, used to write it before his name, and all deeds signed by Karrānu and Ḫuṣānu refer always to their role as witnesses. On the other hand, notaries such as Iltaḫmu, Munaḫḫimu or Nu^{c}merašpu never wrote the sign igi before their names. As for the exceptional four royal deeds that mention a reduced number of witnesses, we also mentioned that two, i.e. half, of the attestations are precisely the two documents that have come down to us signed by the notary Ḫuṣānu (RS 15.138+ and RS 16.285), so that the interpretation of the naming of witnesses as a scribal habit can certainly not be ruled out.[39]

---

be said in what follows. As a last word to this note, I would put forward my own methodological issue, namely that one cannot, and must not, assume the degree of precision of words and phrases. With this regard, I would like to underline the tentative character of the suggestion I made some years ago about the significance of the *(p)ilku*-clause in royal grants of real property ("Royal Land Grants and *ilku*-Service in Ugarit," pp. 171-178). There I proposed that the variation in formulary, especially from the reign of ^{c}Ammiṯtamru II on when the formula of exemption is most commonly used, had legal significance, so that the absence of *(p)ilku*-clause before that reign implied the exemption from service (coinciding with and thus possibly following the change evidenced in the Hittite laws).

[39] Note that RS 16.156, another example, is the only record we have drawn up by Yarimmu (for his authorship, see note 36 above).

1.10.2. The perpetual service

Our second example concerns the provision found in some deeds of conveyance that the transferee is to perform royal service together with his sons and in perpetuity. Here too the relevant phrases are of legal interest and significance (see in the previous chapter the respective sections 20 and 21). Their use, however, limited to a small number of texts, seems to reflect again scribal habits. Indeed, the formula "PN and his sons (and the sons of his sons) are to carry the (*pilku*-)service of the sons of the queen forever" is written in RS 16.138:33-36 and RS 16.204:9'-12' by the same notary Yaᶜdidu, who also included the phrase "and his sons" (with the verb in singular) in RS 19.98:22-24 (perhaps the expression *adi dārīti* is to be restored at the end of line 24). The heritability of the obligation and the perpetual nature of the duty attached to the property (conveyed also to the transferee's sons and forever) are only once more attested together (in RS 16.148+ also dated to ᶜAmmiṯtamru II).

1.10.3. The terms for royal service

The use of the terms for royal service, namely Akkadian *ilku* and *pilku* and Ugaritic *ˀunuṯṯu*, also deserves special attention here. As stated in the preceding chapter, the idea that the difference in the use of one or other word has legal significance cannot be sustained. We have discussed above, for example, the indistinctive use of all three terms in exactly the same, stereotyped formula of exemption: *ilku yānu*, *pilku/a yānu*, and in Ugaritic *unṯ in*. And we have also showed that Akkadian *ilku* and Ugaritic *ˀunuṯṯu* share both etymology and meaning, remarking on the other hand the notorious "rhyme" between the classical Mesopotamian Akkadian word and the favoured Akkadian by-form of Ugarit. That *ˀunuṯṯu* appears "in contexts which do not have *pilku/ilku* parallels", as argued by Libolt who refers to the administrative text RS 18.118 (KTU 3.7), should not surprise us much and is probably due to the chance of the indeed very scanty attestations of the words in question (usually appearing in laconic, stereotyped contexts), as well as to the fact that we are specifically dealing with two different languages, rather than to a difference in meaning, as he assumes.[40] And the same may be true of the

[40] *Royal Land Grants*, p. 113. As stated in the previous chapter, Heltzer also distinguished the three terms according to their alleged different use in his contribution "Zum Steuersystem in Ugarit." There (p. 112) he states that "wie es uns gelungen ist zu beweisen, war die Steuer oder Arbeitspflicht vom Familieneigentum, welches nicht mit den Dienstpflichten der 'Leute des Königs' (*bnš mlk*) gebunden war;" "*ilku* (ug. *hlk*)," he then continues, "war die Pflicht oder Steuer, die meistenteils bestim-

extant use of *pilku* to describe the service qualified with an office owed to the king. The administrative text RS 18.118 (KTU 3.7) paradoxically speaks against Libolt's contention and supports our view.[41] To begin with, the first sentence uses an expression, namely *ᶜrb b unṯ*, that parallels Akkadian *ana ilki erēbu*, suggesting therefore the equivalence between the Ugaritic and the Akkadian words for service. On the other hand, this is the only text that attests to the use of Ugaritic *ʾunuṯṯu* to describe the so-called professional or office obligation; lines 2-4 list three people (viz. Egyptians) who are to perform the guard obligation (the office is spelled in Ugaritic *mḏrǵl*). If we now have a closer look at our evidence, we see that the term *ilku* does not appear before ᶜAmmiṯtamru II and that the attestations in our corpus are limited to five records (RS 15.140, RS 15.143+, RS 15.155, RS 18.21 and the small fragment RS 15.131). What is again significant is that its use seems to be related to scribal habits. Indeed, Nuᶜmerašpu is the author of two or perhaps three of these deeds (RS 15.131, RS 15.143+ and possibly also RS 15.155);[42] and that the classic Akkadian word for service seems to have been also the form preferred by Iltaḫmu and Eḫliteššub who drew up RS 15.140 and RS 18.21 respectively.

---

mte Kollektive — Dörfer, oder Gruppen der königlichen Dienstleute (*bnš mlk*) für die Krone leisten mußten. So scheint das Bild wenigstens in Ugarit zu sein." As for the word *pilku*, the notion of which he relates to the obscure Ugaritic term seplled *ubdy*, he would understand it as "den Dienst, den die Personen, die das Feld vom König erhielten, zu leisten hatten" (p. 116). The evidence discussed in the previous chapter already speaks against these arguments (note, moreover, that *hlk* is not the Ugaritic counterpart of *ilku* but a verbal form of "to go", that the generally accepted interpretation of *bnš mlk* as "Diensleute" has been (I believe seriously and I hope convincingly) disputed in my "The King's Men in Ugarit," and that the equivalence between Ugaritic *ubdy* and Akkadian *pilku* is more than doubtful [see now Schloen's *The House of the Father*, p. 247]). That the picture offered by Heltzer does not find support in the relevant sources proper seems to have been realized by the author himself who wrote in another publication (*The Internal Organization of the Kingdom of Ugarit*, p. 17) that *ʾunuṯṯu* "was performed as a corvée-service, in which the royal dependents were sometimes also involved;" or elsewhere ("Private Property in Ugarit," in *Circulation of Goods in Non-Palatial Context in the Ancient Near East*, ed. A. Archi [Rome, 1984], p. 176) that the expression "the *pilku*-service of his house" (in RS 16.343) "can, in this case, be interpreted as the equivalent of the *unuššu* of the house."

[41] For this text, see my "KTU 3.7 Reconsidered. On the *ilku*-Service in Ugarit," AuOr 11 (1993):250-252.

[42] Note the analogous spellings of the opening phrase, the writing of the toponym Ugarit, also preceded by the Sumerogram for "land," the warranty clause, and of course the *ilku*-clause, without neglecting the use of rulings to divide the different sections of the text.

1.10.4. On a nadānu *formula*

Our fourth and fifth examples are clearly related to each other. In closing our discussion of the *nadānu* formulas in the previous chapter (namely section 3), we referred to what has been called "*nidnu*-clauses." These, we said, are formulas that normally appear at the end of the operative part and that define the transaction recorded on the tablet as a royal grant. One of them literally states that "this gift has been given" (*nidnu annû nadin*) and occurs in four deeds (RS 16.136, RS 16.171, RS 16.282A+B and RS 16.383).[43] Although in appearance this clause seems to be pregnant of substantive legal import, especially when compared to other similar deeds in which it is absent, the following remarks will show that its presence is the result of a scribal hand and thus to be interpreted as an individual idiosyncrasy.[44] That the clause is written by the same notary is a priori suggested by its position in the text, always closing the document, as well as its consistent spelling: *ni-id-nu an-nu-ú na-din*. When we come to compare the spelling habits of other formulas present in the four texts, we find the following striking analogies: the opening phrase is spelled u_4.1.kam *an-ni-im*,[45] the unusual combination of the signs MI-IS is employed to write the name of the ruling monarch ᶜAmmiṯtamru II, and also significant is that in the four texts the name is spelled in the genitive (*am-mi-is-tam-ri*) instead of the expected nominative; the toponym Ugarit is spelled with the initial Ú sign and marked with the classifier ki; the conveyance clause uses the verb *nadānu* (in RS 16.136 the same verb is repeated at the end of the sentence), in all cases spelled *i-ta-din*; the relative pronoun is spelled *ša-a*; as for the warranty clause (not preserved in RS 16.171), the opening adverbial phrase *urra(m) šēra(m)* is omitted, the personal indefinite pronoun is *mamma* (spelled *ma-am-ma*),[46] the verb is spelled *i-la-qè*, the expression for "forever" is *ana dāri dūri*, indeed unusual under ᶜAmmiṯtamru II and consistently spelled *a-na da-ri dú-ri*, and the word order in the three preserved examples follows the same pattern S-Prep(ositional phrase)-V; the hereditary phrase (in RS 16.136, RS 16.171 and RS 16.282A+B) is the rather infrequent "his sons (and) his

---

[43] Perhaps in five if we restore the formula on the edge of RS 16.206.

[44] Following his premise, Libolt believed that the presence or absence of this formula had legal significance, although, as he admitted, the precise function of the clause "remains clouded" (*Royal Land Grants*, p. 55).

[45] Note that in RS 16.282A+B the scribe forgot to write the numeral 1 before the sign KAM.

[46] After collation, I read *ma-am-*⸢*ma*⸣ at the end of line 9 in RS 16.282A+B (I have seen no traces whatsoever of the sign AN read by Nougayrol).

grandsons" (spelled dumu.meš-*šu* dumu dumu.meš-*šu*). To these common salient points one should add the unusual feature that none of the four royal deeds includes the formula identifying the seal impressed on the tablet, and that in all of them a horizontal ruling marks the end of the text. That Ya^c^ḏirānu, the scribe of RS 16.282A+B, is the author of the other three deeds is even clearer after my own examination of the ductus of the texts as well as of the format of the tablets which is almost identical.[47] Thus, the reason for the presence of a formula such as "this gift has been given" or the variant use of the verb *nadānu* (instead of the more common *našû-nadānu*) to describe the conveyance of property can simply be attributed to the favoured style of a notary.[48]

2. *A note on the stream of notarial tradition*

Bureaucracy and notarial practice did certainly not start in Ugarit in the 14th century BC despite the image projected by the extant sources. Indeed, the aspect and formulary, viz. the code of the documents that have come down to us already had a long history behind them. Legal forms and language are conservative by definition. In the words of Jacob Rabinowitz, "a legal formulary does not come into being at the behest of some bureaucrat. It takes a very long time for it to develop, and when it is developed, if it is to remain effective and vital, it must be constantly guarded against deterioration at the hands of incompetent practitioners."[49] The use of particular technical phrases, the shape of the clay tablet, the arrangement of the cuneiform text, or also the characteristic

---

[47] Since no photographs are available, I can only quote, apart from my own personal evaluation after collation, the measures of the tablets provided by the Bordreuil and Pardee's catalogue (*TEO*). RS 16.136: 59 x 49 x 23, RS 16.171: 49 x 47 x 24, RS 16.282A+B: 64 x 56 x 26, and RS 16.383:60 x 50 x 25. Ya^c^ḏirānu's writing habits can be further checked since RS 16.192A+ is signed with his name. Here we indeed find the same spelling of the opening phrase *ištu ūmi annîm*, the name of ^c^Ammiṯtamru, and the toponym Ugarit, and also the omission of the seal formula (note the measurements of the tablet: 65 x 59 x 25).

[48] Because, as stated above, [*ni-id-nu a*]*n-nu-ú na-d*[*in*] can be restored on the left edge of RS 16.206, as already suggested by Nougayrol, it is in order to check here the spelling habits of this fragmentary text dated to ^c^Ammiṯtamru II's father and predecessor. Although the evidence available is too small and partial to reach any definite conclusion, it is noteworthy that the spelling of the opening phrase *ištu ūmi annîm* and the toponym Ugarit agrees with Ya^c^ḏirānu's hand, and that RS 16.206 is one of the few documents that use the formula *nadānu-nadānu* (note too the similar measurements of the tablet: 46 x 47 x 24).

[49] *Jewish Law. Its Influence on the Development of Legal Institutions* (New York, 1956), p. 127 n. 9.

sealing practice must each have been learned and transmitted from an earlier, traditional model and usage (and the same holds true, for instance, for the non-use of envelopes). I once therefore mentioned[50] that in a sense the task of the Assyriologist, or for that matter any documentary researcher, when reading legal documents rivals that of astronomers when they look up into the sky and see ancient objects as they were long ago, when the light left them.

Evidence of past images can be found in our documentation and have already been referred to in previous chapters. The use of mimation, for example, is an indication that at least some elements of the language in 1350 BC were already old. On the other hand, the cylinder seal of the Late Bronze Age kings of Ugarit is another good example of the time or tradition factor (in this case obviously linked to the notion of royal legitimacy). As stated by the inscription carved in intaglio, it belonged to Yaqaru who must have ruled the kingdom back in the 15th century; the seal, however, not the (possibly re-cut) inscription, had very likely been made some four hundred years earlier by a seal-cutter from a Babylonian workshop.

Because no examples of deeds earlier than Niqmaddu II have been found so far at Ras Shamra (perhaps some future excavations, especially from layers older than the Late Bronze Age, will bring to light the desired evidence), we can only fill the gaps for the time being with the help of external sources. And this is not only true for the earlier gaps but also for the later ones, since Ugarit ceased to exist after the conflagration that put an end to the city in the first quarter of the 12th century. It is thus the aim of this last section to establish, in so far as it is possible, the relationship of the notarial practice of Ugarit in the 14th-12th centuries to other Near Eastern documentary styles. This will allow us to outline or reconstruct, at least to some extent, the stream of tradition that flowed across Ugarit during the Late Bronze Age period.

In dealing with the scribal curriculum practiced and learned by notaries-to-be in Ugarit, we mentioned that although the system of writing and the main bureaucratic techniques came ultimately from Mesopotamia, both the didactic material and the resulting scribal products unearthed at Ras Shamra suggest that the direct transmission came from some peripheral region. Indeed, not only is Akkadian the language of legal writing, Sumerian being restricted to some rudimentary logograms; also the orthography and grammar of the texts composed at Ugarit show a variety of deviations (i.e. to be attributed not only to Ugaritic influence) from normative Akkadian. Furthermore, regarding the formulary

[50] In my lecture "Classifying Ancient Legal Traditions: The Story of a 'Syrian' Phrase" on the occasion of the 51st Rencontre Assyriologique Internationale held in 2005 at Chicago.

of our documentation proper, we have also pointed out that some clauses and items of terminology are unknown in native Akkadian texts. It is precisely this characteristic technical wording that will help us define more accurately the (peripheral) tradition we are here dealing with.[51]

2.1. The tablet and the seal

In the preceding pages and chapters we have occasionally referred to external sources mainly to point out correspondences with the notarial practice of Ugarit. Thus, for example, we have suggested an analogy between the royal deeds themselves and the so-called "strong deeds" in roughly contemporary Assur. Although no example of the latter has been found so far, the description in Assyrian texts of both the content and legal quality of these documents, including the procedure involved in their composition, suits fairly well the picture offered by the domestic legal corpus kept at the royal palace archives of Ugarit.

We also pointed out that the use of so-called "dynastic seals," although admittedly less consistent than the one of Ugarit, was also common to other chanceries (Mittanni, Alalakh, Amurru, Siyannu, or Emar, with a reference too to the Tabarna seal[s] of the Hittite kings). The significant "peripheral" area covered by the evidence led already Nougayrol to suggest that this practice could have been imported in Syria "par les dynastes indo-européens qui dominaient ses confins du Nord ou de l'Est (Hittites, Mitanniens)".[52]

The sealing practice, however, differs from one chancery to another. To begin with not all dynastic seals are cylinders. The Tabarna seal, for example, was a stamp seal which was normally deeply impressed on the highly raised surface on the centre of the obverse of the tablet. The Mittanni cylinder seal, on the other hand, seems to have been usually rolled once the text was inscribed and after a ruling, that is, closing the document on the reverse of the tablet.[53] The notarial practice in fifteenth-century Alalakh, like in Late Bronze Age Ugarit, Amurru and Siyannu, had in turn the cylinder seal impression on top of the obverse.

As for the design of the dynastic seal itself, we mentioned that the

---

[51] We shall therefore not trace back notions such as "to hate" in the context of dissolution of family ties, or phrases such as "to whom you love you will give it," which are attested in the documents of Ugarit but are common to several Near Eastern traditions alike throughout millennia.

[52] See our discussion in chapter 5. For the Tabarna seal, see the study by Onofrio Carruba, "Zur Datierung der ältesten Schenkungsurkunden und der anonymen Tabarna-Siegel," IstMitt 43 (1993):71-85, with previous literature.

[53] So in AT 13, AT 14, TB 6002, and TB 8001.

typical Ur III or Isin/Larsa presentation scene is common in seals found or used as far north as the Assyrian colony of Kanesh in the 19th and 18th centuries.

2.2. The phrase "from today (forever)"

As for items of legal terminology or phraseology peculiar to Ugarit, our main concern in this chapter, we of course have different kinds of examples. As we shall see in the following list (far from exhaustive), some items will allow us to obtain a better insight into the workings of the stream of tradition because of the number and wider chronological distribution of attestations. Others, for which fewer testimonies are available, obviously present more gaps in the history of their usage, and their origin as well as transmission is more difficult to trace.

I believe the reader is by now well aware that one of the most characteristic items (if not the most characteristic) of legal terminology in Ugarit is the opening phrase *ištu ūmi annîm* (in Ugaritic *l ym hnd*) "from today", very often completed in deeds of conveyance with the adverbial expression meaning "forever" (in Akkadian often *adi dārīti*, in Ugaritic *^{c}d ^{c}lm*).[54] We closed chapter 4 mentioning that mimation is not a regular feature of the Akkadian written in Ugarit, and that the few examples where it is explicitly indicated (i.e. spelled with the final -*V*M sign) are almost exclusively formulaic, and should therefore be considered archaisms. This is certainly the case of the phrase *ištu ūmi annîm* which, as we shall attempt to show in the following discussion, had a long history behind it and also had a long history after 1200 BC.

Travelling downstream across the dark scene of seven centuries, in which relevant documentary material is virtually absent, we find the phrase in an interesting number and variety of documents.[55] In chronological order, we should first refer to the phrase written in Aramaic in the fifth-century legal papyri discovered at Elephantine in Egypt. In many of the deeds of conveyance, one of the expressions denoting transfer or recognition of rights is more often than not followed by the phrase *mn*

---

[54] An outline of the discussion that follows was presented at the 51st Rencontre Assyriologique Internationale held in 2005 at Chicago (the title of my lecture, as already referred to above, was "Classifying Ancient Legal Traditions: The Story of a 'Syrian' Phrase").

[55] This evidence was first discussed by Rabinowitz, *Jewish Law*, pp. 124-136. See also, with reference to the Ugarit material, Loewenstamm, "Notes on the Alalakh Tablets," IEJ 6 (1956):221-222, and id., "The Formula *me^{c}attā w$^{e\,c}$ad ^{c}olām*," Tarbiz 32 (1963):313-316 (the latter reproduced in English translation in id., *Comparative Studies*, pp. 166-170).

ywmʾ znh wʿd ʿlm, that is, "from today and forever." The same formula appears also in marriage contracts actually concluding the bridegroom's declaration: "she is my wife and I, her husband, from today and forever."[56] As stated by Yaron, the adverbial phrase "does not imply the indissolubility of the marriage; this is obvious from the detailed provisions concerning divorce contained in these contracts." "Nor," he continued, "need the formula be regarded as an expression of sentiment, a pious wish that the marriage be a lasting one." Similarly, in conveyances, Yaron observed, "the right of the buyer to alienate what he has acquired is frequently stressed." What "from today and forever" merely denotes then is, just like in Late Bronze Age Ugarit, that the legal situation evidenced by the document is not a priori limited in time.[57] The difference, indeed slight, between the Aramaic and the Ugarit formulas is rather of a formal nature. As pointed out by Muffs, the former combines the two elements into one organic unit (normally, though not always, coordinated with the conjunction *w*) while the Akkadian or Ugaritic one does not.[58] As for the ways of transmission or the direct source of the Aramaic source, we can only guess given the lack of relevant evidence. It is still a problem, on the other hand, to decide with definiteness when the Jewish settlers arrived at Elephantine and where exactly they came from (Mesopotamia or Palestine). One thing, however, is clear; whenever and wherever they came from they brought along the Aramaic documentary formulary that, at least as far as some significant items are concerned, was to remain constant in the Jewish notarial practice until more recent times. This is especially true of our phrase.

Indeed, when Jewish deeds come to light again, namely in the Judean Desert, the words "from today and forever" still stand as an integral part of the formulary of conveyance texts and marriage contracts. In a recently found ostracon from Khirbet Qumran, for example, recording in Hebrew a conveyance of a house, it is expressly stated that the transfer is made *mhywm hzh l<ʿ>wl[m]* (one should note here the absence of conjunction).[59] Further examples, although fragmentary, come from the papyri found in the neighbouring caves of Wadi Murabbaʿat from the

[56] The texts are (following the edition of Bezalel Porten and Ada Yardeni, *Textbook of Aramaic Documents from Ancient Egypt, vol. 2 Contracts* [Jerusalem 1989]): B2.3:9, B2.6:4, B2.8:6-7, B2.9:9 and 10, B2.11:7, B3.3:4, B3.4:11, B3.5:4-5, B3.8:4, B3.11:8, B3.12:23, B5.2:8, B5.5:4 and 8, B5.6:6, and B6.1:4. Note the spelling *ʿlmn* in B3.4:11 and B3.12:23.

[57] *The Law of the Aramaic Papyri*, p. 47.

[58] *Studies in the Aramaic Legal Papyri*, n. 2 pp. 30-31.

[59] See Frank Moore Cross and Esther Eshel, "Ostraca from Khirbet Qumrân," IEJ 47 (1997):18-19.

time of the Bar Kokhba Revolt. Although six hundred years had elapsed after the writing of the Elephantine deeds, the Judean Desert Aramaic texts still preserve the same wording of the formula: *mn ywmᵓ dnh wlᶜlm* (note also the Hebrew formula *mᶜth wᶜd ᶜlm* "from now and forever").[60]

More significant is the fact that when Greek was used, beside Syriac, to draw up Jewish deeds, beginning in the 2nd century and continuing through the 4th century, the phrase survived in its original form. The Hellenization of Jewish documentary practice did not, or could not go beyond the surface of the Greek language, the expression remaining basically Jewish. As shown by the Greek papyri found in the so-called "Cave of the Letters" in the Judean Desert, in Dura Europos on the Euphrates, or in Oxyrhynchus in Egypt, deeds of conveyance and marriage contracts kept using the traditional, standard phrase "from today and forever", although here in the forms of ἀπὸ τῆς σήμερον ἡμέρας καὶ εἰς ἀεί, or also ἀπὸ τοῦ νῦν εἰς τὸν ἀεί / ἅπαντα χρόνον (note the use of the conjunction in the former, which is clearly not Greek in diction, and the asyndetic phrase of the latter, reflecting the Hebrew and the Aramaic formulas quoted above respectively).[61] Mention should be made here too of the attestation in the apocryphal Greek Book of Tobit, now known to have had an original Aramaic *Vorlage*. The passage (from the long recension of the Sinaiticus MS [7:11]) is significant because it occurs immediately after Tobiah's decision to negotiate his marriage with Raguel and clearly echoes the formula of the traditional Jewish marriage contracts. Raguel's words reassuring Tobiah that Sarah will become his wife are the following: "From now on (ἀπὸ τοῦ νῦν) you are brother to her, and she is sister to you. She has been given to you ἀπὸ τῆς σήμερον καὶ εἰς τὸν αἰῶνα (from today and forever)."

In view of the firm tradition in the legal usage of such a single

---

[60] See the Aramaic fragments DJD 2 203-4, 26:2, and the Hebrew text DJD 2 22, and cf. DJD 2 24 B:13 and C:11 (*mn hywm ᶜd*). See also the Aramaic deeds published by John T. Milik, "Un contrat juif de l'an 134 après J.-C.," RB 61 (1954):183, and id., "Deux documents inédits du Désert de Juda," Biblica 38 (1957):258-259, and more recently the deed published by Magen Broshi and Elisha Qimron, "A House Sale Deed from Kefar Baru from the Time of Bar Kokhba," IEJ 36 (1986):203 and 206 (line 6). For the variant Hebrew formula "from now" and its parallels, see already Rabinowitz, *Jewish Law*, pp. 124-126; Loewenstamm, in turn (*Comparative Studies*, pp. 166-170), pointed to the clear Ugaritic equivalent of the full phrase attested in the Story of Aqhatu: *lht wᶜlmh* (RS 3.66 [KTU 1.19] iv 5).

[61] See already Rabinowitz, *Jewish Law*, p. 135 n. 24, who also discusses the third-century Syriac examples, viz. in deeds of sale, from Dura. See more recently Hannah M. Cotton, "The Archive of Salome Komaise Daughter of Levi: Another Archive from the 'Cave of the Letters'," Zeitschrift für Papyrologie und Epigraphik 105 (1995):183-192.

phrase, it is no wonder that the Talmud pays especial attention to it, notably and interestingly to its formulaic, written nature. Rabinowitz, Loewenstamm and, more recently, Frank Moore Cross and Esther Eshel have drawn the attention to these passages as clear illustrations of the Jewish documentary style.[62]

Take, for example, the definition of *mattana*, that is, a deed of gift, given in the Palestinian Talmud (Peah 3:9 17d): "What is a deed of gift? 'All my property is given to so-and-so as a gift from now (*mattana me-ᶜak̲šaw*)', and —it significantly specifies— it should be written on it [i.e. on the deed] (with the words) "from this day" (*me-ha-yom*)'." In the definition of *mattana* given this time in Mishnah Baba Batra (8:7) the importance and the specifically notarial character of the formula is again stressed: "Whoever assigns his goods to his sons —it says— must write: *me-ha-yom u-le-ᵓaḥar mit̲a*, 'from today and after death'."

The rigidity, tradition and effectiveness of the phrase in legal context probably accounts for its introduction into the language of magic. Indeed, Aramaic incantations of Late Antiquity borrowed the formula *mn ywmᵓ dn(n)/dyn wl ᶜ(w)lm*, which became standardized too in the texts of amulets and magic bowls. Note the following examples: "be healed, PN, from all pain, from today and forever. Amen. Amen. Selah,"[63] or "eradicate from the body of PN_1, the daughter of PN_2, all hectic fever and illness and sickness from today and forever. Amen. Amen. Selah,"[64] or also the more common formula that states: "this bond is from today and forever. Amen. Amen. Selah."[65]

As a matter of fact, the phrase "from today" seems to have been so much established and employed that for some particular cases it became ambiguous and accordingly a subject of debate in the Talmudic commentaries. The phrase "from today and after death" in gift, for example, is indeed strange.[66] Rabbi Jose, for one, held that the words "from today" in the Mishnaic sentence quoted above, namely "Whoever assigns his goods to his sons must write, *me-ha-yom u-le-ᵓaḥar mit̲a*," were unneces-

---

[62] See Rabinowitz, *Jewish Law*, pp. 125-135, Loewenstamm, "Legal Documents from Alalakh," p. 222, and *Comparative Studies*, pp. 166-168, and Cross and Eshel, "Ostraca," p. 23.

[63] Joseph Naveh and Shaul Shaked, *Amulets and Magic Bowls* (Jerusalem, 1985), pp. 40-41 (Amulet 1:10-12).

[64] Naveh and Shaked, *Magic Spells and Formulae* (Jerusalem, 1993), pp. 50-53 (Amulet 17:30-33).

[65] See e.g. Naveh and Shaked, *Magic Spells*, pp. 122-123 (Bowl 18:2), and Markham J. Geller, "Eight Incantation Bowls," OLP 17 (1986):107 (Aaron Bowl A:2).

[66] See the discussion of the phrase in Yaron's *Gifts in Contemplation of Death in Jewish and Roman Law* (Oxford, 1960), p. 114.

sary. Was the ownership to pass immediately or rather after the donor's death? If it is written in gifts in contemplation of death, why then was *me-ha-yom* added? As stated by R. Jose, and thoroughly discussed by Yaron, the phrase was simply superfluous. In the time of the late Tannaites, as noted this time by Loewenstamm, the claim was heard that the phrase "from today" should be eliminated.[67] What interests us to point out here is that such intellectual discussion, together with the fact that the legal expression made its way into the magic formulary in Late Antiquity, is probably to be taken as an indication that we are facing the culmination of the millennia-old legal tradition of the formula. Let us accordingly turn back to Late Bronze Age Ugarit, our point of departure, and search now for the source of the phrase.

The Late Bronze Age level of Ras Shamra itself has preserved a few examples of the phrase in legal tablets drawn up by notaries from two southern neighbouring kingdoms, namely Siyannu (which once belonged to the kingdom of Ugarit) and Amurru.[68] There are other more or less contemporary chanceries from the Syrian area that also employed the Akkadian phrase *ištu ūmi annîm* in documentary formulary, in many cases as the standard opening formula too. So is the case of Emar on the Euphrates where I have counted some 40 examples;[69] and also Ekalte where "from today" opens the text of at least 20 documents.[70] The deeds, like those of Ugarit, are not only restricted to conveyances; they also include wills, adoptions or records of debts.

The next stage in our upstream journey is fifteenth-century Alalakh. Here, the phrase *ištu ūmi annîm* appears introducing nine legal documents: two deeds of sale (AT 73 and AT 74), a deed of gift (AT 87), two marriage contracts (AT 93 and AT 94), a royal promotion (AT 15), and three other fragmentary texts (AT 99, AT 102 and AT 104). Two com-

---

[67] *Comparative Studies*, p. 168 n. 16, with reference to the Babylonian Talmud, Gittin 85b and Baba Batra 136a.

[68] The examples from Siyannu are RS 17.123 and RS 18.01; and those from Amurru are RS 17.228, RS 17.360A+, and RS 19.68 (for the attribution of the latter to the chancery of Amurru, see Nougayrol, *PRU* 4, p. 281, Izre'el, *Amurru Akkadian*, p. 21, and my remarks in "The Legal Texts from Ugarit," p. 409).

[69] To the texts quoted by van Soldt, *SAU*, p. 410 n. 23, add now Arnaud, *Textes syriens de l'âge du Bronze Récent* (Sabadell, 1991), nos. 29, 35, 41, 48, 86; ASJ 13 nos. 32, 39, 42; Iraq 54 no. 2; SMEA 30 nos. 12 and probably 22; Beckman, *Texts from the Vicinity of Emar in the Collection of Jonathan Rosen* (Padova, 1996), RE nos. 8, 18, 23, 28, 30, 32, 39, 57, 82, 84 (cf. also nos. 4 and 21).

[70] Walter Mayer, *Tall Munbāqa-Ekalte II. Die Texte* (Saarbrücken, 2001), nos. 1, 17, 20, 23, 24, 25, 26, 28, 36, 37, 38, 42, 46, 51, 67, 70, 75, 76, 90, 91 and perhaps also 87.

ments are, I believe, worthwhile. The first one is that the cuneiform attestations belong so far to a common "Syrian" sphere, roughly corresponding to the vine culture area west of Mesopotamia. And the second, that the consistent orthography of the examples of Alalakh makes clear that the peculiar use of mimation only for the demonstrative pronoun characteristic of the notarial practice in Late Bronze Age Ugarit (as well as Ekalte and Emar) has a tradition that goes back at least one hundred years.[71]

Alalakh still offers us further, rewarding information, since the site of Tell Atchana has yielded two superimposed, different levels with documentary material. We have therefore the great chance to go further upstream in time without moving in space. None of the deeds found in level VII, roughly dated to the first half of the 17th century, begins with the words "from this day." The formula, however, did already exist and was used by notaries to introduce certain clauses. The two attestations we have come from litigation documents concerning disputes over property shares decided by the king of Yamkhad. Once the final distribution of shares is made, one of the texts (AT 7:32) provides that "from today, he (the plaintiff) will not come back (to this decision);" and the other one (AT 8:29) concludes after the prohibition of future claims that "from today there is no debt between them (the litigant parties)." In both texts, the adverbial phrase is spelled *ištu ūmim annîm*, in accordance with the Old Babylonian dialect proper of the documents: mimation is consistently used for both the noun and the adjective. Here then, we may suggest, is the origin of the mimated adjective in the texts of later Alalakh, as well as Ekalte, Ugarit, Siyannu, Amurru and Emar.

Earlier, namely eighteenth-century examples of the formula can be found down the Euphrates in the archives of ancient Mari, thus at the border of our "Syrian" area. One of the few attestations we have is a legal sentence or rather formula quoted verbatim in a long letter reporting the end-result of the so-called Alakhtum affair, a formula that clearly echoes the clauses of seventeenth-century Alalakh / Yamkhad just reviewed. The provision literally states: "from today (*ištu ūmim annîm*) no one is to come near the estate of Alakhtum."[72] At least as significant is the fact that the formula "from today" seems to have been used at the chancery of Mari too to open the text of solemn oaths. Two such texts, identi-

[71] Note that examples without mimation can occasionally be found; note e.g. the royal deed RS 16.140:1 or the non-royal RS 15.37:1; for Emar, Beckman, *Texts from the Vicinity of Emar*, RE no. 18:1 and no. 82:1; and for Ekalte, Mayer, *Ekalte*, no. 38:1 or no. 46:1.

[72] Jean-Marie Durand, *Le culte d'Addu d'Alep et l'affaire d'Alahtum* (Florilegium Marianum 7, Paris, 2002), no. 36:26-27. Perhaps Alakhtum is to be identified with Alalakh itself, as suggested by the editor of the text.

fied by Dominique Charpin as "small tablets" or drafts (the *ṭuppum ṣeḫrum* containing only the clauses of the agreement) have been recovered from the ruins of the palace of Mari.[73] One of them is the draft of the treaty of alliance between Zimri-Lim of Mari and Hammurapi of Babylon (M.6435+M.8987) containing the solemn words that the king of Babylon must swear by the gods Shamash and Addu (no doubt as submitted by, and therefore in the formulaic terms of, the ruler of Mari): "*ištu ūmim annîm adi balṭāku*, that is, from today as long as I live, I shall be at war against Ṣiwapalarḫuḫpak (the Elamite emperor)".[74] The other one (A.96) is part of a vassal treaty and contains the words of the oath to be taken by Atamrum, king of Andarig; introduced too in lines 4-5 by the phrase "from today as long as I live", Atamrum promises not to commit a sin against Zimri-Lim and his country.[75] In view of the stereotyped formula and the content of the so-called "Diviner's Protocol" from Mari, namely the recorded vow of this official to his lord, the king, it is tempting to suggest the restoration [*ištu ūmim annîm adi*] *balṭāku* in ARM 26 1:4'.[76] Durand, the editor of the text, interestingly pointed out in a later contribution the parallelism between such a Mari text and the Neo-Assyrian loyalty oaths (the so-called *adê* texts).[77] What he did not discover, however, is that an *adê*-text such as Assurbanipal's treaty with the Babylonians dating from the time of the Šamaš-šumu-ukin rebellion (SAA 2 9) uses exactly the same formula that characterises the vows in

---

[73] See ARM 26/2, p. 144 and n. 35.

[74] Lines 5-7. The text is published by Durand, "Fragments rejoints pour une histoire élamite," in *Fragmenta historiae elamicae, Mélanges offerts à M.J. Stève*, ed. L. de Meyer et al. (Paris, 1986), pp. 111-114. The text is no. 290 in the author's *Documents épistolaires du palais de Mari* vol. 1 (Paris, 1997).

[75] The text is published by Francis Joannès, "Le traité de vassalité d'Atamrum d'Andarig envers Zimri-Lim de Mari," in *Marchands, diplomates et empereurs, Études sur la civilisation mésopotamienne offertes à Paul Garelli*, ed. D. Charpin and F. Joannès (Paris, 1991), pp. 167-169. The text is no. 291 in Durand's *Documents épistolaires du palais de Mari*. It is therefore probable that the oath, today lost, in the treaty text A.361 (published by Charpin, "Un traité entre Zimir-Lim de Mari et Ibâl-pî-El II d'Ešnunna," in *Marchands, diplomates et empereurs*, pp. 141-144) also began with the same words.

[76] Durand tentatively suggested that the text on the left edge of the tablet where this line is inscribed was divided in two sections and that the first one, namely the left column, is lost (see AEM I/1, p. 15 n. 39). His translation accordingly takes what is preserved almost as the beginning of the line. According to our restoration, however, the sentence or phrase would properly begin at the beginning of the line discarding the presence of columns.

[77] "Précurseurs syriens aux protocols néo-assyriens," in *Marchands, diplomates et empereurs*, pp. 13-71.

Mari more than one thousand years earlier. Indeed, we find in lines 3', 17' and 33' the phrase *ultu ūmi annî adi ūmu mala balṭāni* "from today as long as we live", uttered by the Babylonian subjects to introduce their sworn agreements. Perhaps we have here a key (viz. the key) to understand or at least better follow the transmission from the Akkadian formulary inscribed in cuneiform on clay tablets to the Aramaic language of the Elephantine papyri.[78]

The phrase *ištu ūmim annîm* occurs in another treaty text unearthed this time at Tell Leilan, the ancient Šeḫnā / Šubat-Enlil, roughly contemporary to the Mari counterparts. The agreement is between Till-Abnû of Appum and the city of Assur.[79] The passage preserved in column iii lines 6-13 provides that "from today you (i.e. Till-Abnû) shall observe the content of this document which you swore to the city of Assur, the citizens of Assur, and the *kārum*."[80] A variant of the phrase occurs in a similar context about two centuries later. The text describes a provisional treaty between Idrimi king of Alalakh and Pilliya king of Kizzuwatna (AT 2). Before the curse formula closing the document, the text stipulates (lines 40-45) that the agreement will take effect "from that day" (*ištu ūmi šuwāti*) in which the Mittannian overlord Barattarna takes the required oath with Idrimi.

But Mari and Tell Leilan around 1750 are not the final stop in our journey upstream. That the phrase may be of greater antiquity is suggested by its possible occurrence in a tablet from Ebla. The deed is TM.75.G.2396 recording a grant of real property to Tišar-Lim king of Emar by Irkab-Damu who ruled Ebla some time in the 24th century BC.[81] The second paragraph (ii 3-7) confirms that the ruler of Ebla has given the property, a clause significantly introduced by the phrase "from today" (spelled *áš-du-ma* u_4 in lines 4-5), just like the deeds of Ugarit one thousand years later.[82]

---

[78] Muffs devoted a large part of his conclusion to *Studies in the Aramaic Legal Papyri* (pp. 179-192) to the influence of Neo-Assyrian models on the Aramaic formulary.

[79] The text L87-442+ is published by Jesper Eidem, "An Old Assyrian Treaty from Tell Leilan," in *Marchands, diplomates et empereurs*, pp. 195-204.

[80] Note the phrase *adi balṭāt* in the previous line 5.

[81] The text is published by Pelio Fronzaroli, "Disposizioni reali per Iṯaw-Liʾm (TM.75.G.2396, TM.75.G.1986+)," SEbl 7 (1984):2-4. For the chronology of the Ebla tablets, see Alfonso Archi, "Chronologie relative des archives d'Ébla," Amurru 1 (1996):11-28.

[82] Fronzaroli already remarked the striking parallel with the deeds of Ugarit in his commentary to the text ("Disposizioni reali," p. 7).

2.3. *The formula* našû-nadānu

Another very characteristic item of legal language in Late Bronze Age Ugarit is without any doubt the coordinate use of the verbs *našû* and *nadānu* to form the formula of conveyance. This formula is also preserved in two deeds drawn up in the contemporary chancery of Amurru that were kept in the palace diplomatic archive of Ugarit itself.[83] The relatively few records preserved from Amurru indeed show a very close relation to the formulary of the chancery of its northern neighbour (they both probably belonged to the same school tradition).[84] More interesting for the present discussion is the attestation of the same expression in the earlier Hittite land grants. The presence of this Akkadian expression in the Anatolian chancery of the 16th and 15th centuries is explained by the fact that these deeds are heavily Akkadographic in formulation. Hans Gustav Güterbock, the first one to systematically analyze them, even wondered "ob diese akkadisch oder hethitisch gelesen wurden" (the only non-Akkadian words in some examples being the names of the grantees).[85] The two verbs of the formula are always in the preterite form (the perfect, it will be remembered, was preferred at Ugarit). Thus we have *išši* (always spelled *iš-ši*) and *iddin* (always spelled *id-di-in*).[86] Instead of the conjunction *u*, the Hittite land grants preferred the enclitic *-ma*, attached to *išši*. The formulation of the Hittite grant clause generally fol-

---

[83] The texts are: RS 17.228 and RS 17.360A+.

[84] See Izre'el, *Amurru Akkadian*, p. 377.

[85] See Güterbock, *Siegel aus Bogazköy* (AfO Beiheft 5, Berlin, 1940), p. 50, and also the remarks by Beckman, "Mesopotamians at Ḫattuša," p. 102, and Einar von Schuler, "Landschenkungsurkunden," RlA 6, p. 469. As for the date of the documents, see Kaspar K. Riemschneider, "Die hethitischen Landschenkungsurkunden," MIO 6 (1958):321-330 (who made available all the deeds then known still quoted today with the abbreviation "LS"), von Schuler, "Landschenkungsurkunden," p. 469, Donald F. Easton, "Hittite Land Donations and Tabarna Seals," JCS 33 (1981):3-43, as well as Heinrich Otten, "Das hethitische Königshaus im 15. Jahrhundert v. Chr. Zum Neufund einiger Landschenkungsurkunden in Bogazköy," Anzeiger der phil.-hist. Klasse der Österreichischen Akademie der Wissenschaften 123 (1986):21-34 (Abb. 1-9), and Carruba, "Zur Datierung der ältesten Schenkungsurkunden," pp. 71-85. A recent examination of the chronology can be found in Beckman, "Hittite Chronology," Akkadica 119-120 (2000):19-32.

[86] Except for the plural forms *iššū* and *iddinū* in LS 1:47 (the subject there being the king, the queen and the crown-prince of Hatti). The stereotyped singular formula is fully preserved in KBo 32 185 rev. 4-5 and Bo 90/758 obv. 12-16; see also the fragmentary passages in LS 2 rev. 1-2, LS 7 obv. 9-11, LS 12:1-4, LS 14 obv. 2', LS 19 obv. 7 (it seems that the scribe forgot the second verb of the formula), LS 24 obv. 3-9, KBo 32 184 rev. 12'-13', and KBo 32 189 obv. 2'.

lows then the pattern: "the great king has produced (the property) and has given (it) to PN, his servant, as a gift".[87]

Speiser, Labuschagne and Greenfield have dealt with potential Hebrew and Aramaic equivalents of the *našû-nadānu* formula. Speiser first pointed to the parallel combined use of *nś*ᵓ and *ntn* amply attested in Middle Hebrew denoting "business, dealings, transactions, etc."[88] Labuschagne cast doubts about this equivalence and proposed in turn cognates from Biblical Hebrew, namely *lqḥ-ntn*, *lkd-ntn* and *hnṣl-ntn*.[89] Greenfield's study provides a review of all these earlier alleged equivalents, including, as we have seen, a discussion of the Hittite use of *našû-nadānu*, and suggests further congeners.[90] Concerning Mishnaic Hebrew, the true equivalent of the Akkadian formula according to Greenfield would be *nṭl-ntn*, "for *nṭl* has replaced *lqḥ* in Mishnaic Hebrew in most of the common usages of 'to take'."[91] As for Biblical Hebrew, the formula *lqḥ-ntn* is "truly relevant" in a number of cases, 1Sam 8:14 being the most eloquent.[92] Taken indeed as an echo of "Canaanite precedent"[93]

---

[87] Bo 90/758 obv. 12-16, for example, reads: lugal gal *iš-ši-ma a-na* PN gal [lú.meš]*me-še-di* ìr-*di-šu a-na* níg.ba-*šu id-di-in* (see Christel Rüster, "Eine Urkunde Ḫantilis II.," IstMitt 43 [1993]:64-66). Güterbock already realized in his study published in 1940 (*Siegel aus Bogazköy*, p. 48) that when the property is granted not to an individual but to an institution, namely the "house of Hatti in the town of Šarišša," the formula used is not *našû-nadānu* but *našû-šakānu* (the form *iškun*, spelled *iš-ku-un*, is fully preserved in LS 3 rev. 32, partially in 1312u rev. 4' and therefore presumably to be restored in LS 4 rev. 12, as already suggested by Kemal Balkan in *Eine Schenkungsurkunde aus der althethitischen Zeit, gefunden in Inandik 1966* [Ankara, 1973], p. 50). The formula *leqû-nadānu* is also attested (in the deed found at Inandik [obv. 10-14] and in KBo 32 136 obv. 14-15, cf. also LS 4 obv. 15-16 and 18-20); the evidence we have does not seem to speak for Greenfield's suggestion ("*našû-nadānu* and its Congeners" in *Ancient Near Eastern Studies in Memory of Jacob Joel Finkelstein*, ed. M. de Jong Ellis [Hamden, CT, 1977], pp. 87-88) according to which this formula is used when a person is granted to an institution.

[88] "Akkadian Documents from Ras Shamra," p. 161.

[89] "The *našû-nadānu* Formula," pp. 179-180.

[90] "*našû-nadānu*," pp. 87-91.

[91] Ibid., p. 91.

[92] Ibid., pp. 89-90.

[93] See Isaac Mendelsohn, "Samuel's Denunciation of Kingship in the Light of the Akkadian Documents of Ugarit," BASOR 143 (1956):17-22 (or also the PhD dissertation [in Hebrew] of Zafrira Ben-Barak *The Manner of the King and the Manner of the Kingdom* [Hebrew University, Jersualem, 1972] which was not available to me).

the Biblical expression (*yiqqaḥ wᵉnātan*) would reflect the formula of royal grants of Ugarit, and the same would hold true, in his opinion, for the Hittite pair *arḫa da-* and *pai-* that occurs for example in the deed of Saḫurunuwa. Finally, the Aramaic cognate proposed by Greenfield comes form the Elephantine papyri.[94] There the clause providing that the donor has no longer the right to give the house to anyone else is phrased with the combined use of either *hnṣl-ntn* or *lqḥ-ntn*, the same pairs attested in Biblical Hebrew.

I believe there can be little doubt about "the antique flavour" of the Hebrew and Aramaic terms pointed out by these scholars. Nevertheless, I would hesitate to take all of them as "true" cognates, not only on the basis of the different verbs (or etymologies) adduced but also on account of their meaning and the context in which they appear. Indeed, although the verb denoting the transfer of property is *ntn* like *nadānu* in the deeds of Ugarit, the verbs *lqḥ*, *nṭl* and *hnṣl* (or Hittite *arḫa da-*) are not strictly speaking cognates of Akkadian *našû*, the particular term of the Akkadian formula (possibly the reason why Speiser preferred to suggest as a parallel the phrase *maśśaʾ umattān*). The Akkadian equivalent of the three West Semitic verbs (as well as the Hittite verb) would rather be *leqû*, the literal meaning of which is "to take." This verb, as we have seen in the preceding chapter, is attested in the deeds of Ugarit to precisely denote the eviction of the property in the warranty clause. I believe that this is precisely the same notion that interestingly underlies the terms *hnṣl* or *lqḥ* in the Aramaic deeds written on papyri, as well as *lqḥ* in a Biblical passage such as 1Sam 8:14, and *arḫa da-* in the so-called deed of Saḫurunuwa dated to Tudḫaliya IV (KUB 26 43).[95] Indeed, the donor's declaration in the deeds of Elephantine that he no longer has the right "to take (away)" the property, viz. from the grantee, and "give" it to someone else (also the same phrasing found in the Hittite document) reflects both the formulation and the content of the warranty clause in the royal deeds of Ugarit. And the same holds true for the king taking fields, vineyards, and olive groves from their legitimate tenants to give them to his courtiers, as denounced by Samuel. In all these cases, *lqḥ* (or *hnṣl*, or Hittite *arḫa da-*) denotes exactly the same notion as *leqû* in the warranty clause, and should accordingly be kept apart from *našû*.[96]

---

[94] "*našû-nadānu*," p. 91. The deeds in question are: Cowley 8 (B2.3 in the edition of Porten and Yardeni) and Cowley 9 (B2.4).

[95] See the edition by Fiorella Imparati, "Una concessione di terre da parte di Tudhaliya IV," RHA 32 (1974).

[96] This is the reason why we prefer to translate the term as "to produce" rather than "to take" (see also our proposed original meaning of the expression viz. the formal act of producing the title-deed, in the preceding chapter). See 2.7 below for further discussion.

According to what has been stated above and because form, especially in legal language, lives longer than its own conceptual content, I believe Speiser's proposed parallel is the more convincing one.[97] This does not mean that I disagree with Labuschagne when he wrote that "it is very doubtful, however, whether there is any direct connection between this late Hebrew phrase and the *našû-nadānu* formula" used as early as the 16th century BC in the Hittite chancery.[98] The gap of about 1,000 years certainly rules out the possibility that Ugarit was the source of direct influence, but it is, I believe, likely that the usage in Late Bronze Age Ugarit and in Mishnaic Hebrew attest to the continuation of the same tradition. Riemschneider and Greenfield have pointed out probable intermediate pieces of evidence in the transmission of the formula. The former referred to the expression (*inašši-ma ana PN inamdin*) found in a Neo-Babylonian record used to denote the transfer of a deed (*uʾiltu*).[99] Greenfield in turn, who included in his discussion the Neo-Babylonian example, remarked that the combined use of both verbs denoting the notion of transfer occurs too in a number of Neo-Assyrian records, namely in the formula *šumma* PN_1 PN_2 *lā naṣṣa ana* PN_3 *lā iddin* or its abbreviation *šumma lā naṣṣa lā iddin* "if PN_1 has not handed over PN_2 to PN_3."[100] These Neo-Babylonian and Neo-Assyrian usages evidence the continuation of the tradition in the first millennium before our era, probably under the influence of Aramaic.[101]

Greenfield thus concluded that *našû-nadānu* and its cognates are all clearly from the West, admitting, however, that "it is too early to speculate about the source of the phrase."[102] Two years later, Fronzaroli suggested, if not the source itself, at least the earliest parallel of the phrase with which we would like to close this discussion. The Ebla tablet TM.75.G.1766 records the king's transfer of real property to Ingar, son

[97] See also the comments and additions of Greenfield, "*našû-nadānu*," p. 91.

[98] "The *našû-nadānu* Formula," p. 179.

[99] "Die hethitischen Landschenkungsurkunden," p. 331. Note that the parallel he suggested from Alalakh level VII, namely AT 41, rests on a misreading or wrong restoration: line 7 should read *na-di* not *na-di-*[*in*] (see now Dietrich and Loretz, "Alalaḫ-Texte der Schicht VII (I). Historische und juristische Dokumente," UF 36 [2004]:71-72); the recorded expression is then *ana mazzazzāni nadi* "deposited as pledge."

[100] "*našû-nadānu*," pp. 90-91. To the attestations quoted by Greenfield, one could add SAA 4 215, SAA 14 73 or SAA 14 74. Cf. also a deed such as SAA 4 35 in which the transfer viz. return of a sum of silver (recovered from the thieves) to its owner is described with the combined use of *ittaṣa* and *ittidin*.

[101] See Greenfield, "*našû-nadānu*," pp. 90-91.

[102] Ibid., p. 90.

of the noble minister "Lord" Ibrium.[103] The transfer is described (in obv. ii 2-4) by means of the combination or coordination (with the conjunction *wa*) of two verbs written logographically, namely sag.du$_8$ "and" ì.na.sum(-*kum*). The latter corresponds unmistakably to the verb "to give" (Eblaite NDN, NTN or YTN), whereas the interpretation of the former poses more problems. Fronzaroli, nonetheless, had little doubt that the expression reflects the formula *našû-nadānu* attested one thousand years later in the royal deeds of Ugarit.[104]

2.4. *The description of the real property*

We mentioned in chapter 6 that the description of the property conveyed usually found in the royal deeds of Ugarit has parallels in Middle Assyrian practice and resembles too the description of the estate purchased by Jeremiah (32:9). My main interest here is to draw the attention again to the Ebla tablet TM.75.G.1766 because its simple formulation bears some resemblance too to the wording of the texts of Ugarit written one thousand years later. The property granted to Ingar (for a period of 10 years) is described there as "the house that is in TN of PN" (spelled é *in TN ša PN* in obv. ii 5-iii 3).[105]

2.5. *The term* nayyālu

An interesting Akkadian term attested in the deeds of Ugarit is *nayyālu*, for which we proposed in the preceding chapter the meaning of a person who died without legitimate descendants. As previously mentioned, this word qualifying the former tenant of transferred real property occurs, apart from Ugarit, in deeds from fifteenth or fourteenth-century Assur and in exactly the same context (KAJ 160, KAJ 162 and KAV 212). Whether or not the term was directly borrowed from the Assyrian chancery can obviously not be ascertained on the basis of the scarce available evidence.

---

[103] See Fronzaroli, "Un atto reale di donazione dagli archive di Ebla (TM.75.G.1766)," SEb 1 (1979):4-5.

[104] See "Un atto reale di donazione," pp. 6-7 (followed by Milano, "Bilinguismo," pp. 185-186). Accordingly, the Italian scholar translated the first verb as "rendere disponibile", pointing to the verb GRŠ as a possible reading of the logogram sag.du$_8$ on the basis of the lexical lists of Ebla.

[105] It is generally agreed that the logogram for "property" should rather be read ᵓà in Ebla (so Fronzaroli in his edition of the text). We have kept the Sumerographic reading to show that the sign used is the same we find in the Ugarit texts.

2.6. The phrase "tomorrow at dawn"

We also said above that the opening phrase of the warranty clause is to be related to the adverbial expression introducing the clause describing the transaction, thus forming an interesting and legally significant temporal sequence. Indeed, if "from today" denotes the immediate efficacy of the transaction evidenced by the document, the adverbial phrase *urra(m) šēra(m)*, the literal meaning of which is "tomorrow at dawn," marks the validity of the transaction in the future. The first remark to be made concerns the mimation of the expression frequently indicated (by means of the final –AM sign in the spelling of both words) in analogy with the opening phrase *ištu ūmi annîm* (note that the form *urra šēram*, that is, with mimation only indicated in the last word, also occurs in some deeds).[106] This morphological element therefore suggests a priori that we are dealing here too with a very ancient and highly stereotyped formula.

Ernst Weidner tentatively suggested the Hurrian origin of the phrase,[107] but only a few years later Speiser invalidated such speculation making clear through his translation of the words and resulting expression (viz. "day and dawn") that the phrase is clearly Semitic.[108] Rabinowitz in turn as early as 1956 drew the attention to the striking similarity of the Akkadian expression from the first published Ras Shamra tablets of legal content with the phrases found in analogous context (viz. the no-contest clause) in the later demotic and Aramaic deeds from Egypt.[109] It is significant that precisely in view of the

---

[106] RS 15.85 (collated), RS 15.92, RS 16.262, RS 16.277, RS 16.356, RS 17.61, RS 17.67, the latter two private deeds written by the same scribe Ilimalku.

[107] "Subaräische Gottheiten im Assyrischen Pantheon," AfO 15 (1945-1951):83, namely from *ḫurri* "night" and *šeri* "day", an idea that tantalized Nougayrol in *PRU* 3, p. 230.

[108] See Speiser, "The Alalakh Tablets," JAOS 74 (1954):23. See also the early important remarks of Rabinowitz, *Jewish Law*, pp. 159-161, and Muffs, *Studies in the Aramaic Legal Papyri*, p. 183 n. 7. Because the spelling ḪUR-*ra še-ra* in some deeds of Ugarit should be read *ur*$_5$-*ra še-ra*, the Hurrian etymology revived by Riemschneider ("Die hethitischen Landschenkungsurkunden," p. 333) must definitely be discarded.

[109] *Jewish Law*, pp. 158-161. The Elephantine deeds of conveyance are: B2.1:6, B2.3:18, 20 and 26, B2.4:8 and 13, B5.1:4. One should add that the phrase also occurs in marriage contracts introducing the provision concerning divorce (see B2.6:22 and 26, B3.3:7 and 9, and B3.8:21). The demotic formula that occurs in an Egyptian papyri dated to about 631 BC was translated by Francis Llewellyn Griffith as "to-morrow or the second morrow" (see Rabinowitz, *Jewish Law*, p. 138). On p. 161, Rabinowitz would further compare the absence of conjunction in the Aramaic deed B5.1:4 with the Akkadian asyndetic phrase.

evidence of Ugarit he challenged the hitherto accepted translation of Aramaic *mḥr ʾw ywm ʾḥrn* as "tomorrow and another day" (namely put forward by Arthur E. Cowley and Emil G. Kraeling), suggesting the proper rendering "tomorrow, or the day after (tomorrow)." Although undoubtedly functionally identical, it must be pointed out that Akkadian *urram šēram* is not the literal counterpart of the Aramaic phrase. The exact equivalent occurs, however, in Ugaritic following the new reading of RS 16.382 (KTU 3.5):15 put forward by Hawley and Pardee. Indeed, *šḥr ṯlṯt*, the literal meaning of which is "tomorrow (or) the day after," precisely reflects the Aramaic phrase of the deeds of Elephantine, and would correspond even closer in wording to the Biblical Hebrew phrase *tmwl šlšwm* "yesterday (or) the day before" denoting here the indefinite past instead of the indefinite future, but expressed with the same first (asyndetic) two members in the unending series of days.[110]

Muffs pointed out the possible link between the second millennium evidence on clay tablets and the Aramaic phrase written on papyri. Our phrase constitutes his sixth example of the twelve Aramaic legal formulas said to be derived from the Neo-Assyrian cuneiform tradition. "There can be little doubt," he wrote, "that the common Aramaic expression *mḥr ʾw ywm ʾḥrn* '(If) tomorrow or the day after (PN should undertake some illegal action) …' is derived directly from *ina šērtu ina lidiš*.[111]

Let us now survey the second-millennium evidence. A glance at the entry in the Chicago Assyrian Dictionary suffices to realize that, as stated by Huehnergard, the phrase "is especially frequent in peripheral texts."[112] To make our journey upstream in chronological order, we should first stop at Ras Shamra itself, the Late Bronze Age level of which has yielded evidence from contemporary Amurru and Carchemish.[113] The phrase *urram šēram* in the deeds of Carchemish introduces as a rule the no-contest clause, often formulated as *urram šēram* PN_1 *ana muḫḫi* PN_2 *lā iraggum*.[114] The notaries of Emaṛ and Ekalte also employed the phrase *urram šēram* (usually indicating mimation in both words or only in the latter) to introduce clauses against potential litigants to the recorded

---

[110] See Rabinowitz, *Jewish Law*, p. 159.

[111] *Studies in the Aramaic Legal Papyri*, p. 184. The earlier phrase *urram šēram* and other parallels are discussed in the previous page.

[112] See CAD Š/2, p. 334 (that translates the phrase as "later on, in the future", without including all the relevant sources [examples from Emar, Hazor or Ekalte, for instance, are missing]), and Huehnergard's remarks in *The Akkadian of Ugarit*, p. 276; see also van Soldt, *SAU*, p. 410.

[113] See the Amurru example RS 17.318+:17'.

[114] See RS 17.68:7, RS 17.108:9, RS 17.129:20, RS 17.337:13, RS 17.396:12, RS 27.52:17.

transaction. The notaries of the latter two chanceries, like their colleagues of Ugarit, thus used the sequential pattern "from this day" / "tomorrow at dawn."[115] The same pattern also occurs in the fifteenth-century deed of sale from Alalakh AT 74, where the phrase *urra šēra* (i.e. without mimation) introduces too the no-contest clause. In the fragmentary deed of sale AT 75, the expression (in line 6) is interestingly spelled with the conjunction *ū* (or) and with mimation only in the second last word (*urra ū šēram*). The older archive of Alalakh (from level VII) has also yielded some examples of the phrase in analogous context, showing that *urram šēram*, as it is consistently spelled following the grammatical rules of the Babylonian of the time, was a formulaic expression as early as the 17th century.[116]

It is also significant that the phrase occurs in the only legal document unearthed at a Canaanite site. The Hazor tablet describes a litigation that took place sometime between the 18th and 16th centuries; *urram šēram* introduces here too the clause against future claims.[117] As collected by CAD, the phrase is also used in the roughly contemporary chanceries of Shemshara and Mari. Note that *urram šēram* in the letter ARM 13 147 probably has the literal meaning "tomorrow at dawn", as pointed out by Durand.[118] His more recent translation of the phrase as "tôt ou tard" in A.4251+:59,[119] and "à un moment ou à un autre" in A.1121+:11[120] is in our opinion rather free. It is to be noted that in the latter text, the sentence *ana urram šēram lā ibbalakkatanni* reflects a legal formulation (attested in a contemporary deed of Alalakh, AT 78:11-12) the meaning of which is "he should not contravene my accord (any time) in the future."

That *urram šēram* was a stereotyped legal phrase before the 16th century is shown by its formulaic use as Akkadogram (always with mimation in both words) in the Hittite royal land grants. What is particularly noteworthy here is the stereotyped formulation of the whole no-contest clause, which is syntactically very close to the warranty clause in

---

[115] See the Ekalte documents Mayer, *Ekalte*, nos. 20, 23, 24, 36, 51, 67, 70, 90 and 91. As for the deeds of Emar, see, for example, Arnaud, Emar VI.3 nos. 186, 213, 253, 256, Arnaud, *Textes syriens*, nos. 29, 35, and Beckman, *Texts from the Vicinity of Emar*, RE no. 4.

[116] See e.g. AT 11:25, AT 41:12, AT 58:20, AT 61:13-14, AT 78:11 or also AT 456:43.

[117] See William H. Hallo and Hayim Tadmor, "A Lawsuit from Hazor," IEJ 27 (1977):1-11.

[118] See *Documents épistolaires du palais de Mari*, vol. 1, p. 461.

[119] *Le culte d'Addu*, no. 8, p. 27.

[120] *Le culte d'Addu*, no. 39, p.139.

the royal deeds of Ugarit. The provision runs as follows: *urram šēram ana PN ana mārīšu mamman lā iraggum* "in the future no one shall contest against PN or his sons."[121] As pointed out by Riemschneider, the later Hittite texts drawn up in the Hittite language rendered the phrase *urram šēram* with Hittite *ziladuwa.*[122] Note that the expression *ziladuwa arḫa lē kuiški dāi* in the warranty clause in the deed of Saḫurunuwa (obv. 61) literally corresponds to *urra(m) šēra(m) mamma lā ilaqqe* in the deeds of Ugarit.

2.7. *The verb* leqû *in the warranty clause*

In dealing with the legal significance of the warranty clause in the preceding chapter, we referred to the opinion expressed by Nougayrol and Skaist according to which the clause was meant to protect the transferee's newly acquired property rights against the king's challenge or eviction. In support of his argument, we also said above, Skaist adduced provisions contained in Hittite and Alalakh treaty texts. This is the place to discuss the evidence. The Alalakh treaty in question (AT 456) is the one concluded between the great king of Yamkhad and his younger brother Yarim-Lim installed by the former as ruler of Alalakh around the middle of the 17th century. Following the transfer of the territory of the kingdom, the overlord then declares his promise of non-interference. The oath he then took literally states (line 42): "(May I be cursed) if I take (away) that which I gave you" (*šumma ša addinukkummi eleqqu*). As for the Hittite evidence, Skaist referred to the Ulmi-Teššub treaty as well as other texts quoted by Greenfield in his study of the *našû-nadānu* for-

[121] The texts are: LS 14 rev. 1-3 (see Easton, "Hittite Land Donations," p. 7), LS 18+20 rev. 1'-3' (see Easton, "Hittite Land Donations," p. 13), KBo 32 185 rev. 6-7, KBo 32 194 rev. 1'-3', and Bo 90/758 rev. 17-20; and presumably to be restored in LS 2 rev. 3-4, LS 11 rev. 1-12, LS 12 rev. 1-3, 518z:2'-3', KBo 32 136 rev. 1'-3', KBo 32 184 rev. 13'-15', KBo 32 189 obv. 3'-6' (cf. also LS 16 obv. 3'-5'). LS 1 rev. 48 has *urram šēram ša PN ana mārīšu mārmārīšu mamman lā iraggum.* Note also the Inandik deed rev. 15-18: *urram šēram* PN_1 *u mārīšu ana* PN_2 *u mārīšu mamman lā iraggum.* The deeds in which the property is granted not to an individual but to an institution, namely the "house of Hatti in the town of Šariššа," the formula used obviously has the house in question instead of the grantee and his children (LS 3 rev. 35-36, LS 4 rev. 12-14, and 1312u rev. 5-6'). See Güterbock, *Siegel aus Bogazköy*, pp. 48-49, Riemschneider, "Die hethitischen Landschenkungsurkunden," pp. 332-334, where he compares the formula to the one of the Carchemish documents as well as the deeds of Ugarit.

[122] For example, the Ulmi-Teššub treaty ("Die hethitischen Landschenkungsurkunden," p. 333) and also the deed of Saḫurunuwa (obv. 20, 51, 59, and 61).

mula discussed above.[123] Indeed, we mentioned in the preceding discussion that Greenfield understood the verb *arḫa da-* used in combination with *pai-* as the Hittite cognate of the Akkadian formula *našû-nadānu*. Although *pai-* certainly has the meaning of "to give," we objected above that *arḫa da-* corresponds to Akkadian *leqû* rather than *našû*, and that the direct context in which this phrase occurs is not the transfer or grant proper (where *našû-nadānu* is normally used) but rather the warranty against the transferee's dispossession. And this is what Skaist, in our opinion, rightly points out.[124] In the deed of Saḫurunuwa, for example, we find the divine curses addressed to the person who would challenge the words of the gift and who would accordingly "take" (*arḫa dāi*) the transferred property and "give" it (*pāi*) to someone else (rev. 17, see also obv. 60-64). Greenfield offered other examples of the same formula: in KUB 26 58:18-20 as well as KBo 4 10, the treaty of Ulmi-Teššub; the latter was also given by Skaist in translation: "nobody shall take away (*lē arḫa danzi*) his house or his land from him and give it (*lē piianzi*) to a descendant of someone else."

What is interesting to note here are the parallel formulations found in 1Sam 8:14 and the Aramaic deeds from Elephantine discussed above. As we have mentioned, such parallels were pointed out by Greenfield (who nevertheless understood them in turn as parallels of the *našû-nadānu* formula). Samuel's denunciation of kingship precisely emphasizes the king's power of taking away or back (*lqḥ*) property (fields, vineyards and olive groves) to give it (*ntn*) to someone else of his preference, namely his courtiers. And the Aramaic deeds contain the provision (after the clauses defining the transfer proper) that the donor no longer has the right "to take (away)" (*lqḥ* or *hnṣl*) the property, viz. from the grantee, and "give" (*ntn*) it to someone else.

In the previous discussion on the phrase *urra*(*m*) *šēra*(*m*) we noted the literal correspondence between the Hittite expression *ziladuwa arḫa lē kuiški dāi* that occurs in the warranty clause in the deed of Saḫurunuwa (obv. 61) with the wording of the same clause in the royal deeds of Ugarit: *urra(m) šēra(m) mamma lā ilaqqe*.

As for the earliest occurrence of the use of *leqû* in the warranty clause, which, as we have seen, was typically used in Late Bronze Age Ugarit, I would like to refer again to the Ebla text TM.75.G.1766. After the grant clause discussed above, the donor king declares: "I shall not take it (i.e. the property) back" (spelled *an-na* nu ba_4.ti in obv. iii 4-5,

---

123 The same parallels discussed here were pointed out already by Moshe Weinfeld, "The Covenant of Grant in the Old Testament and the Ancient Near East," JAOS 90 (1970):189.

124 See also Weinfeld, "The Covenant of Grant," p. 189.

the Sumerogram ti possibly hiding an Eblaite form of LQḤ).

2.8. *The word* ʾunuṯṯu

Of interest too are Ugaritic words of Hurrian, i.e. foreign, etymology denoting legal notions. Such is the case of the term for royal service, *ʾunuṯṯu* (the counterpart of Akkadian *ilku*), and possibly also of *ʾammad/tu*, always used to qualify the Akkadian word *mārūtu* "sonship", the resulting meaning of which may be something like "inherited sonship", as discussed above. The borrowing of these terms and their absorption into the cultural property of Late Bronze Age Ugarit has more than a simple linguistic interest, given the legal significance of the notions underlying them. With regard to *ʾunuṯṯu*, it is noteworthy that the word is attested in records from ancient Kanesh, the Assyrian colony in Anatolia, namely its level Ib dated to about 1810-1740.[125] The Old Assyrian term *unuššum* is attested in two legal documents, kt r/k 15 and kt 89/k 383.[126] And in both texts it appears asyndetically paired to the word *arḫalum* also denoting a kind of service.[127] In kt 89/k 383 the service is qualified as owed to the king (*arḫalum unuššum ša rubāʾim*).[128] Both kt r/k 15:9-10 and kt 89/k 383:33-35 provide that the parties to the

---

[125] It was Prof. Klaas R. Veenhof who back in 1994 kindly drew my attention to this Old Assyrian evidence. He and Jan Gerrit Dercksen kindly provided me then with the relevant attestations which I used and quoted with due permission in my PhD dissertation (see now Veenhof, "Old Assyrian and Anatolian Evidence for the Care of the Elderly," in *The Care of the Elderly in the Ancient Near East*, ed. M. Stol and S.P. Vleeming [Leiden/Boston/Köln, 1998], p. 152, and id., "Old Assyrian Period", in *A History of Ancient Near Eastern Law*, p. 448). Here, like in 1995, I want to express my sincere thanks to both of them. Note that Lackenbacher has now referred to part of this evidence in her *Textes akkadiens d'Ugarit*, p. 221 n. 733.

[126] Both published by Veysel Donbaz, the former in "Some Remarkable Contracts of 1-B Period Kültepe Tablets (I)," in *Anatolia and the Ancient Near East. Studies in Honor of Tahsin Özgüç*, ed. K. Emre et al. (Ankara, 1989), pp. 78-79 and 94, and the latter in "Some Remarkable Contracts of 1-B Period Kültepe Tablets II," in *Aspects of Art and Iconography: Anatolia and Its Neighbors. Studies in Honor of Nimet Özgüç*, ed. M.J. Mellink et al. (Ankara, 1993), pp. 134-135. It is also attested in an unpublished text (kt f/k 80:16), see Donbaz and Veenhof, "New Evidence for Some Assyrian Terms," Anatolica 12 (1985):151 n. 13. Note too the possible restoration of the word in kt 89/kt 370 end of line 33, as suggested by Veenhof, "The Care of the Elderly," p. 147.

[127] Note the word in kt 89/kt 370:34.

[128] Lines 28-29 and 33-34 read respectively: *ar-ḫa-lam ú-nu-ša-am ša ru-ba-im* and (*a-na*) *ar-ḫa-lim ú-nu-ší-im ša ru-ba-im*.

transaction are exempted (*ellū*) from (*ana*) service; in the former deed the exemption is restricted to five years after which period they would have to perform it (the verb used [in line 18] being then *epāšum*).[129] Before closing this discussion I would like to point to what may be the Hittite cognate of *arḫalum-unuššum*. As is well known, *šaḫḫan* and *luzzi* are the two words that denote royal service in Hittite.[130] The interesting aspect is that they very frequently appear together and always related asyndetically, just like the Old Assyrian word pair. Apart from the semantic and syntactic parallel, the usage in some formulas also shows striking similarities. So, for example, the specification "of the king" (spelled with the logograms *ša* LUGAL) occasionally added to *šaḫḫan luzzi*, and the clauses that stipulate either exemption (*araw-*) from service or performance (*ešša-* [the equivalent of Akkadian *epēšu*]) of service. Note the parallel clause to kt 89/k 383 in the deed of Saḫurunuwa. There (KUB 26 43, rev. 13) it is provided that the grantee "is exempted (*arawaḫḫan*) from the *šahhan* (and) *luzzi*-service of the king." If the equivalence of word-pairs for royal service is correct, we would have an example of notions and formulas that continued in use (naturally in translation) in this Anatolian region from the eighteenth century until the late thirteenth century.

Note in passing that the same Hittitte deed provides after specifying the nature of the service due to the king that the transferee will be liable to "no other *šaḫḫan*-service" (obv. 59), a wording that bears some resemblance to the Akkadian formula found in the royal deed RS 16.162 discussed above.

2.9. Heritability

It has been suggested that the divine grants of land to the patriarchs in the Old Testament reflect the language of grants or transfers in deeds such as the ones of Ugarit, by which possession is very frequently bestowed upon the transferee and his children for all generations.[131] Indeed

---

[129] Cf. also *a-na ar-ḫa-lam e-lu* in kt 89/k 365:14-15, published by Donbaz in "Remarkable Contracts II," p. 133. As far as the formula of exemption is concerned (see our discussion in the preceding chapter), Muffs interestingly remarked that sometime around 1600 the verb *elēlu* was replaced by *zakû* in legal usage (*Studies in the Aramaic Legal Papyri*, p. 127).

[130] See Fiorella Imparati, "Aspects de l'organisation de l'état hittite dans les documents juridiques et administratifs," JESHO 25 (1982):225-267, Sedat Alp, "Die Verpflichtungen *šaḫḫan* und *luzzi* in einem Masat-Brief," Or 59 (1990):112-113, or also Richard Haase, "Anmerkungen zum sogenannten Lehensrecht der Hethiter," ZAR 2 (1996):135-139.

[131] See Weinfeld, "The Covenant of Grant," pp. 199-200, and Loewenstamm, "The

the phrases "for your descendants forever" in Genesis 13:15, or "for your descendants after you throughout their generations" in Genesis 17:7-8 could echo the formulas of heritability and perpetuity typical of the royal deeds of Ugarit describing conveyances of real property.[132]

The Hittite land grants also contain the provision that the sons of the transferee are to succeed to his position, not, however, in the grant clause but in the no-contest clause: "tomorrow morning no one shall contest against PN or his sons." The later Hittite deed of Saḫurunuwa, in turn, stipulates not only that the transferee's descendants are protected against potential future interferences (i.e. in the warranty clause) but also that the property is given (*piandu*) to the transferee's sons, grandsons, great-grandsons, and future descendants (KUB 26 43 obv. 60-67). The similarity between these examples and the provision contained in the Aramaic deeds of conveyance from Elephantine has also been pointed out.[133] Here, the wording of the (so-called *shallit*) formula closely parallels that of the deeds of Ugarit. It literally states: "you have full rights over it (i.e. the property) from this day forever, and your sons after you."

2.10. The scheme and the position of the formulas

After the comparative study of a number of legal terms and formulas, I believe a comparative consideration, however sketchy, of the relative position of the clauses within the document i.e. of the structure of the deeds as a whole is in order. Let it be stated at once that our comparative material is rather restricted. To begin with, comparison seems really appropriate when based on cuneiform documents written on clay. On the other hand, a comparison with our deeds of Ugarit is only fully reliable if the documents in question are private legal transactions issued by the royal palace. Our first observation to be made is that there is no example or prototype from another ancient Near Eastern chancery that absolutely matches the structure and sequence of clauses characteristic of the deeds of Ugarit. Because the diplomatic nature of the deeds from Amurru and Siyannu, found at the royal palace archives of Late Bronze Age Ugarit, obviously differs from the domestic deeds of Ugarit, it is not possible to go very far in the comparison of the notarial practices. The format of the tablets and sealing practice, the use of dynastic seals, the arrangement of

---

Divine Grants of Land to the Patriarchs," JAOS 94 (1972):509-510.

[132] For the parallels between the phrase in the Bible and the so-called *shallit*-clause in the Aramaic papyri of Elephantine, see already Rabinowitz, *Jewish Law*, pp. 129-131.

[133] Apart from the studies of Weinfeld and Loewenstamm referred to above, one should mention Yaron's *The Law of the Aramaic Papyri*, p. 116.

the text, and the writing of common characteristic formulas (such as the opening phrase *ištu ūmi annîm*, the *našû-nadānu* formula, or the expression *urra*[*m*] *šēra*[*m*]) would, however, point to what is already suggested by the actual closeness both in time and space of the chanceries themselves, namely, that they shared a common notarial tradition and style. Relevant documentary evidence is nevertheless lacking to draw a definite conclusion.

More relevant is the material from other chanceries, such as Ekalte and Emar. The problem, however, is that they are no royal deeds, so that the differences in sealing and witnesses are obvious. The documents drawn up by Emar notaries, on the other hand, fall into two different categories: the so-called "Syro-Hittite type" and "Syrian type". The former, characteristic in Late Bronze Age Carchemish, has the written lines of the text parallel to the longer side of the tablet and normally present the seal impression on the reverse, at the end of the text, whereas the latter (to which the Ugarit or Ekalte deeds belong) has the inscribed lines parallel to the shorter side.[134] The Syrian-type documents of Emar and those of Ekalte have further aspects similar to the deeds of Ugarit. The seal is impressed on top of the obverse (in Ekalte an additional seal impression can be found on the left edge of the tablet), and we have seen that the text is sometimes opened by the phrase "from today", containing also provisions about future claims introduced by *urram šēram*. Moreover, the seal or seals impressed on the tablet are also identified at the end of the document, following the list of witnesses.

The nature of the sources from Alalakh and Hatti offers a more reliable basis for comparison since apart from their domestic legal character they are designed by royal notaries. The deeds of fifteenth-century Alalakh (not the earlier ones) show a considerable number of formal similarities with the royal deeds of Ugarit: the format of the tablets, the sealing practice and the use of dynastic seals, the arrangement of the text, and the writing of common characteristic formulas such as the opening phrase *ištu ūmi annîm*, sometimes followed by "before RN", as well as the adverbial expression *urra*(*m*) *šēra*(*m*) to introduce the no-contest clause. The royal seal, however, is normally not identified, and, despite the royal nature of the deeds, a list of witnesses usually closes the text, including the scribe himself. As for the Hittite royal land grants, we have seen that the format of the tablet and the sealing practice are different from the design of royal deeds of Ugarit.[135] Although the Tabarna seal is

---

[134] See our note 4 in chapter 5 above.

[135] For the scheme of the Hittite royal land grants, see Güterbock, *Siegel aus Bogazköy*, pp. 47-49, Riemschneider, "Die hethitischen Landschenkungsurkunden," pp. 330.

identified, the formula "Seal of the Tabarna, the great king" (spelled with the Sumerograms ^{na4}kišib *ta-ba-ar-na* lugal gal) is as a rule inscribed in the first (not the last) line of the text. What usually closes the document is the reference to the place where the deed was drawn up, the names of the witnesses to the transaction and the scribe who wrote it. The property granted, on the other hand, is described before the verb formula describing the transaction, and the stereotyped clause on royal sanctions is included after the no-contest clause. The similarities with the deeds of Ugarit are thus rather restricted, like the Ebla documents mentioned above, to a number of interesting formulas. A remarkable feature, common to all these "peripheral" cuneiform notarial practices is the absence of a date formula.[136]

2.11. Conclusion

In introducing this study on the notarial historical tradition, I compared, perhaps somewhat pompously, the task of documentary researchers with that of astronomers who when they look up into the sky see ancient objects as they were long ago, when the light left them. It may now be appropriate to open this closing section with the rather matter-of-fact lesson of quantitative astrophysics according to which there is roughly ten times as much dark matter as there is stuff we can identify or see. I believe the image is all the more suitable when we attempt to draw the picture of a stream of tradition that flowed across millennia, largely before our common era. Indeed, numerous (and ever-increasing) as our evidence seems to be, there will always remain serious gaps in our picture. That what we have constitutes but a random selection both in time and space is already shown by the important lack of sources for long stretches of time and for large regions bathed by our stream. Take, for example, the extensive Levantine area; only the fragmentary papyri from the Judean Desert break the silence of several centuries after the fall of Ugarit. As for the available material, the number of relevant documents is relatively small. The domestic legal documents from fifteenth-century Alalakh, for example, amount to thirty-three tablets and fragments; the corpus of Hittite royal land grants does not exceed fifty texts more often than not in fragmentary condition; and not more than seventy legal documents (written on papyrus) have been preserved in more or less good condition from Elephantine. And then there remains the question of whether or not the surviving sample is actually adequate for our purposes, private legal

---

[136] Note that the later Jewish documents referred to throuhgout the survey bear a date formula, possibly as a result of the incorporation of other traditional usages through the centuries.

transactions signed with the king's seal being indeed rare. How, then, are we to connect all these small spots of light of different age and context within the vast darkness and piece them together into a reconstructed serial or continuous story? How can we overcome, for example, the gap that separates the use of *unuššum* in the eighteenth-century Assyrian colony of Kanesh from the use of Ugaritic *ʾunuṯṯu* attested some four hundred years later?

I believe the negative picture we have drawn should warn us against conclusions drawn too quickly about direct formal influences. I cannot imagine, for example, that the formulaic similarities between the royal grants of Ugarit and the Hittite grants have anything to do with the fact that the extant documentation found at Ras Shamra dates to the time of Hittite sovereignty over this Mediterranean region and kingdom.[137] We have insisted enough on the fact that the notarial tradition of Ugarit in all likelihood antedates 1350 BC and thus the Hittite conquests of Šuppiluliuma I. On the other hand, we have also seen that the differences between both styles and models are at least as significant as the similarities. And finally one should stress that none of these Akkadographically written grant texts was drawn up by the Hittite chancery that issued the vassal agreements to the king of Ugarit.[138] The manifest similarities (such as the *našû-nadānu* formula) are probably to be explained on account of a common stream whose waters bathed the banks of both notarial schools, separated from each other by one to two centuries. And here we reach the positive tone in our admittedly tentative attempt to reconstruct the stream in question. For the parallels we have pointed out above, including the important *našû-nadānu* formula used in the Hittite grants, exhibit unmistakable signs of a common tradition, and although we are necessarily bound to a superficial inspection, I believe it is possible to write a reasonable story of the stream.

Let us take precisely the example of the Hittite land grants. That Akkadian, and not Hittite, is used as the language of the documents clearly points to the borrowing of a foreign formulary that no doubt enjoyed the advantage of centuries-old prestige and traditional usage. Following the important results of the development of criteria for the dating of Hittite tablets on the basis of their script, Beckman remarked that "the seventeenth century witnessed the borrowing from a Syrian scribal center of a

[137] As suggested by Lackenbacher, *Les texts akkadiens d'Ugarit*, p. 219.

[138] By that time Hittite had become the language of domestic legal documents and the formulas seem to have significantly developed, as shown for instance by the deed of Saḫurunuwa (see Güterbock, *Siegel aus Bogazköy*, p. 51, von Schuler, "Landschenkungsurkunden," p. 470, Carruba, "Zur Datierung der ältesten Schenkungsurkunden," p. 71, and the discussion of Riemschneider, "Die hethitischen Landschenkungsurkunden," p. 329).

script more like that of the earlier Old Akkadian period than those of contermporary Assyria or Babylonia."[139] Although Ebla had been proposed by a number of scholars, the available evidence, as noted by Beckman himself, is unfortunately too meager to allow relevant comparisons.[140] On the other hand, on the basis of foreign mythological elements in Hittite religion and literature, and in particular in the Kumarbi cycle, it has been suggested that possibly after their Syrian conquests, the Hittites carried back to their capital "from Aleppo (ancient Halab) or Ebla (Tell Mardikh) a number of texts that were the object of later reworkings, themselves often recopied in the thirteenth century BCE."[141] The explanation of this cultural introduction of "Syrian" motifs in Hatti seems to me most interesting and no doubt reasonable but remains vague for lack of definite evidence. It would of course be desirable to have an account of how the traffic of ideas, including literary motifs and legal formularies, worked. In dealing with the channels of notarial transmission in the first millennium, Muffs has thoroughly argued that it was through the Neo-Assyrian formulary or medium that "the archaic norms of the third millennium and the legal practices of Ras Shamra and Alalakh made their way into the Aramaic formulary of the fifth century."[142] But the actual workings, not the parallels, are missing. And the same holds true for the picture of seventeenth-century Hittite schools. The desirable historical account is very unlikely to be discovered, and for that matter, to have existed at all. What every scholar knows well is that these questions together with one of the most serious gaps in our picture (and many of the unsolved problems in the history of this crucial period) would be largely overcome with the discovery of the Middle Bronze Age archives of Aleppo, the capital of the kingdom of Yamkhad. But grumbling will certainly not take us far in our reconstruction of the stream.

Traces of the Amorite past of Ugarit are clearly discernible in the available documentation. Suffice it to mention the names of the Late Bronze Age kings who issued grants and privileges for their subjects and whose deeds are the subject matter of this book. As Singer has put it, "this conservatism in royal name-giving may indicate that ancient dynastic traditions were strictly preserved by the rulers of Ugarit for many centuries."[143] We believe that it is to the Amorite tradition, and not, say,

[139] See "Mesopotamians at Ḫattuša," p. 100. See also Otten, "Das hethitische Königshaus," p. 33.

[140] "Mesopotamians at Ḫattuša," p. 100 n. 17.

[141] So René Lebrun, "From Hittite Mythology: The Kumarbi Cycle," in *Civilizations from the Ancient Near East*, vol. 3, p. 1972.

[142] *Studies in the Aramaic Legal Papyri*, pp. 186-187.

[143] "A Political History of Ugarit," p. 611. For a recent discussion of Amorite re-

to Hittite influence, that one has to attribute many aspects of Ugarit's culture. This may be true of the specific status and title of the queen-mother, for example, as interestingly suggested by Charpin on the basis of a few references in the Mari texts to Gašera queen(-mother) of Aleppo.[144] And it is our contention that it is especially true of the notarial practice. Formulas such as *ištu ūmi annîm*, *urram šēram* or *našû-nadānu*, and even the use of the Akkadian language to draw up legal documents in Late Bronze Age Ugarit are in all likelihood to be understood as the result of a local tradition that goes as far back as the 18th century. And there can be little doubt that the same Amorite tradition that dominated what is nowadays northern Syria was borrowed by the Hittites. Because we do not have any material from the archives of the capital of ancient Yamkhad we cannot decide whether or not the notaries of fourteenth-century Ugarit followed their ancient models literally. But it is very likely that they did not. They probably learned and preserved stereotyped phrases and clauses that, as we have seen, were used at the Amorite chanceries of Mari and Alalakh (and possibly Hazor), but it is as probable that new expressions were developed through the centuries as well as a different structure of the various elements of a deed. With this regard, mention should be made of the similarities in scheme between the royal deeds of Ugarit and the counterparts from fifteenth rather than seventeenth-century Alalakh.

We have also seen that remains of this centuries-old usage can be found in other schools from this Syrian area during the Late Bronze Age period (Emar, Ekalte, Amurru and Siyannu). As for the question, how old the items are, it seems that the evidence from Ebla can throw a dim but interesting light on the great antiquity of at least some of them. It is probable, as we have pointed out, that the Amorite tradition retained traces of this earlier legal practice (cf. the phrases "from today," the verb "to take" in the warranty clause or the conveyance formula combining two verbs the second of which is "to give"). Because some of the formulas appear in later Jewish documents after a long, serious gap in our documentation, the "Syrian" origin of the items, as proposed by Yaron, seems to me quite an appropriate designation, provided, of course, we include like him within the "Syrian" sphere "all the inhabited areas along the Mediterranean coast, roughly from the present-day Turkish border to

---

flexes in Ugaritic culture, see Felice Israel, "La classificazione dell'ugaritico: problema prima storico e poi linguistico," in *Semitic and Assyriological Studies Presented to Pelio Fronzaroli* (Wiesbaden, 2003), pp. 256-262.

[144] See "Mari entre l'Est et l'Ouest: politique, culture, religion," Akkadica 78 (1992):8 n. 50. Cf. also Durand, *Le culte d'Addu d'Alep*, p. 93.

that of Egypt."[145] This label would approximately fit our image of a vine culture area mentioned above (indeed the texts that use such legal items significantly record among the transferred properties vineyards and olive groves); and it would correspond too with Muff's "fringe tradition."[146] Greenfield, it will be remembered, preferred in turn the generic term and notion of the "West" to designate the area where the formula *našû-nadānu* originated. What he did not specify is whether he understood the term in its strictly geographical sense, that is to say, as the region "west" of Mesopotamia, or as the homeland of West Semitic speaking people. In all likelihood, he implicitly meant both aspects. Had he known of the recently interpreted incantations from Ebla mentioning the conflict myth between the triumphant storm god and the serpent, he no doubt would have immediately drawn the parallel.[147] What I of course cannot tell is if he then would have coined a new name for the waters that carried "Syrian" or "West Semitic" myths along with legal formulas through antiquity and beyond, naturally including Ugarit, such as "the stream of Leviathan."

---

[145] *The Law of the Aramaic Papyri*, p. 115. It should be noted that at the time he published the study (in 1961) he could only compare his Elephantine papyri with the material from Alalakh and Ugarit.

[146] *Studies in the Aramaic Legal Papyri*, p. 186.

[147] See Fronzaroli, "Les combats de Hadda dans les texts d'Ébla," MARI 8 (1997):283-290, and his more recent "The Hail Incantation (ARET 5, 4)," in *Festschrift für Burkhart Kienast zu seinem 70. Geburtstage*, ed. G.J. Selz (Münster, 2003), pp. 89-107.

BIBLIOGRAPHICAL ABBREVIATIONS

A.	registration number of tablets excavated at Mari
AfO	Archiv für Orientforschung
AJSL	American Journal of Semitic Languages and Literatures
AoF	Altorientalische Forschung
ARM	Archives royales de Mari
ArOr	Archiv Orientální
ASJ	Acta Sumerologica
AT	D.J.Wiseman, The Alalakh Tablets
AuOr	Aula Orientalis
BASOR	Bulletin of the American Schools of Oriental Research
BiOr	Bibliotheca Orientalis
BM	tablets in the collections of the British Museum
BSOAS	Bulletin of the School of Oriental and African Studies
CAD	The Assyrian Dictionary of the Oriental Institute of the University of Chicago
Cowley	A. Cowley, Aramaic Papyri of the Fifth Century B.C.
CRAIBL	Académie des Inscriptions et Belles Lettres. Comptes rendus
DJD	Discoveries in the Judean Desert
EA	J.A. Knudtzon, Die El-Amarna-Tafeln
Emar VI	D. Arnaud, Recherches au pays d'Aštata: Emar 6
IEJ	Israel Exploration Journal
Inandik	K. Balkan, Eine Schenkungsurkunde aus der althethitischen Zeit, gefunden in Inandik 1966
IOS	Israel Oriental Studies
IstMitt	Istanbuler Mitteilungen
JAOS	Journal of the American Oriental Society
JCS	Journal of Cuneiformm Studies
JESHO	Journal of the Economic and Social History of the Orient
JNES	Journal of Near Eastern Studies
KAJ	E. Ebeling, Keilschrifttexte aus Assur juristischen Inhalts
KAV	O. Schroeder, Keilschrifttexte aus Assur verschiedenen Inhalts
KBo	Keilschrifttexte aus Boghazköi
kt	field numbers of tablets excavated at Kültepe
KTU	M. Dietrich, O. Loretz, and J. Sanmartín, Die keilalphabetischen Texte aus Ugarit
KUB	Keilschrifturkunden aus Boghazköi
L	field numbers of tablets excavated at Tell Leilan
Law Q. Rev.	Law Quarterly Review
LS	number of Hittite landgrant texts after K.K. Riemschneider, Die hethitischen Landschenkungsurkunden
M.	registration number of tablets excavated at Mari

MARI	Mari, Annales de recherches interdisciplinaires
MIO	Mitteilungen des Instituts für Orientforschung
MSL	Materialien zum sumerischen Lexikon; Materials for the Sumerian Lexicon
NABU	Nouvelles assyriologiques brèves et utilitaires
OLP	Orientalia Lovaniensia Periodica
Or	Orientalia
Piepkorn Asb.	A.C. Piepkorn, Historical Prism Inscriptions of Ashurbanipal
PRU	Le palais royal d'Ugarit
RA	Revue d'assyriologie et d'archéologie orientale
RB	Revue biblique
RHA	Revue hittite et asianique
RIDA	Revue internationale du droit de l'antiquité
RIH	field numbers of tablets excavated at Ras Ibn Hani
RlA	Reallexikon der Assyriologie
RS	field numbers of tablets excavated at Ras Shamra
RSO	Rivista degli studi orientali
SAA	State Archives of Assyria
SAU	W. van Soldt, Studies in the Akkadian of Ugarit. Dating and Grammar
SCCNH	Studies on the Civilization and Culture of Nuzi and the Hurrians
Sebl	Studi eblaiti
SEL	Studi epigrafici e linguistici sul Vicino Oriente antico
SMEA	Studi micenei ed egeo-anatolici
TB	field numbers of tablets excavated at Tell Brak
TEO	P. Bordreuil and D. Pardee, La trouvaille épigraphique de l'Ougarit. 1. Concordance
TM	field numbers of tablets excavated at Tell Mardikh
TUAT	Texte aus der Umwelt des Alten Testaments
UF	Ugarit-Forschungen
VO	Vicino Oriente
VT	Vetus Testamentum
WdO	Die Welt des Orients
ZA	Zeitschrift für Assyriologie
ZAR	Zeitschrift für altorientalische und biblische Rechtsgeschichte
ZDMG	Zeitschrift der Deutschen Morgenländischen Gesellschaft
ZDPV	Zeitschrift der Deutschen Palästina-Vereins

Bibliography of Works Cited

Adams, James N., and Simon Swain.

"Introduction." In *Bilingualism in Ancient Society. Language Contact and the Written Word*, edited by J.N. Adams, M. Janse and S. Swain, 1-20. Oxford, 2002.

Alp, Sedat.

"Die Verpflichtungen *šaḫḫan* und *luzzi* in einem Masat-Brief." Or NS 59 (1990):107-113.

Alt, Albrecht.

"Eine neue Provinz des Keilschriftrechts." WdO 1 (1947):78-92

Amiet, Pierre.

Corpus des cylindres de Ras Shamra-Ougarit II. Sceaux-cylindres en hématite et pierres diverses. Paris, 1992.

"Les sceaux-cylindres de Ras Shamra au IIe millénaire." In *Le pays d'Ougarit autour de 1200 av. J.-C.*, edited by M. Yon, M. Sznycer, and P. Bordreuil, 239-244. Paris, 1995.

André-Salvini, Béatrice, and Mirjo Salvini.

"Un nouveau vocabulaire trilingue sumérien-akkadien-hourrite de Ras Shamra." SCCNH 9 (1998):3-40

Archi, Alfonso.

"Chronologie relative des archives d'Ébla." Amurru 1 (1996):11-28.

Arnaud, Daniel.

"Les textes d'Emar et la chronologie de la fin du Bronze recent." Syria 52 (1975):87-92

"Ras Shamra. III. La culture suméro-accadienne." Supplément au Dictionnaire de la Bible 9 (1979):1348-1359.

"Les textes cuneiformes suméro-accadiens des campagnes, 1979-1980 à Ras Shamra-Ougarit." Syria 59 (1982):199-222.

Textes syriens de l'âge du Bronze Récent. Sabadell, 1991.

"Études sur Alalah et Ougarit à l'âge du Bronze Récent." SMEA 37 (1996):47-65.

"Prolégomènes à la redaction d'une histoire d'Ougarit I. Ougarit avant Suppiluliuma I." *SMEA* 39 (1997):151-161.

"Le dialecte d'Alalah: un examen préliminarire." AuOr 16 (1998):143-186.

"Prolégomènes à la rédaction d'une histoire d'Ougarit II: les bordereaux de rois divinisés." *SMEA* 41 (1999):153-173.

"Une bêche-de-mer antique. La langue des marchands à Tyr à la fin du XIIIe siècle." AuOr 17-18 (1999-2000):143-166.

Review of *Sobre "el modo de producción asiático" en Ugarit* by J.-A. Zamora. Syria 77 (2000):317-322.

"Le jargon épistolaire de Sidon à la fin de l'âge du Bronze récent." In *Études Ougaritiques. I. Travaux, 1985-1995*, edited by M. Yon and D. Arnaud, 291-322. Paris, 2001.

Auerbach, Elise.

"Heirloom Seals and Political Legitimacy in Late Bronze Age Syria." Akkadica 74-75 (1991):19-36.

Austin, John L.

How To Do Things with Words. Cambridge, MA, 1975.

Balkan, Kemal.

Eine Schenkungsurkunde aus der althethitischen Zeit, gefunden in Inandik 1966. Ankara, 1973.

Beckman, Gary.

"Mesopotamians and Mesopotamian Learning at Ḫattuša." *JCS* 35 (1983):97-114.

Texts from the Vicinity of Emar in the Collection of Jonathan Rosen. Padova, 1996.

"Hittite Chronology." Akkadica 119-120 (2000):19-32.

Bordreuil, Pierre, and Dennis Pardee.

"Le sceau nominal de ᶜAmmīyiḏtamrou, roi d'Ougarit." Syria 61 (1984):11-14.

La trouvaille épigraphique de l'Ougarit. 1. Concordance. Paris, 1989.

Manuel d'ougaritique. 2 vols. Paris, 2004.

Borger, Rykle.

Mesopotamisches Zeichenlexikon. Münster, 2003.

Bowman, Alan K., and Greg Woolf.

"Literacy and Power in the Ancient World." In *Literacy and Power in the Ancient World*, edited by A.K. Bowman and G. Woolf, 1-16. Cambridge, 1996.

Boyer, Georges.

"La place des textes d'Ugarit dans l'histoire de l'ancien droit oriental, in *Le palais royal d'Ugarit*, vol. 3, 283-308. Paris, 1955.

"Royauté et droit public dans les textes d'Ugarit." In *Mélanges d'histoire du droit oriental,* vol. 2, 153-167. Paris, 1965.

Broshi, Magen, and Elisha Qimron.

"A House Sale Deed from Kefar Baru from the Time of Bar Kokhba." IEJ 36 (1986):201-214.

Brosius, Maria, ed.

Ancient Archives and Archival Traditions. Concepts of Record-keeping in the Ancient World. Oxford, 2003.

Calvet, Yves.

"Les bassins du palais royal." Syria 67 (1990):31-42.

Carruba, Onofrio.

"Zur Datierung der ältesten Schenkungsurkunden und der anonymen Tabarna-Siegel." IstMitt 43 (1993):71-85.

Castel, Corinne.

"Contexte archéologique et statut des documents: les textes retrouvés dans les maisons mésopotamiennes du I millénaire av. J.-C." RA 89 (1995):109-137.

Cavigneaux, Antoine.

"Lexikalische Listen." RlA 6 (1980-1983):609-641.

Charpin, Dominique.

"Le geste, la parole et l'écrit dans la vie juridique en Babylonie ancienne." In *Ecritures, systèmes idéographiques et pratiques expressives*, edited by A.-M. Christin, 65-73. Paris, 1982.

"Une pratique administrative méconnue." MARI 3 (1984):258-259.

"Transmission des titres de propriété et constitution des archives privées en Babylonie ancienne." In *Cuneiform Archives and Libraries*, edited by K.R. Veenhof, 121-140. Leiden, 1986.

"Corrections, ratures, annulations: la pratique des scribes mésopotamiens." In *Le texte et son inscription*, edited by R. Laufer, 57-62. Paris, 1989.

"Un traité entre Zimir-Lim de Mari et Ibâl-pî-El II d'Ešnunna." In *Marchands, diplomates et empereurs. Études sur la civilisation mésopotamienne offertes à Paul Garelli*, edited by D. Charpin and F. Joannès, 139-166. Paris, 1991.

"Les malheurs d'un scribe ou de l'inutilité du sumérien loin de Nippur." In *Nippur at the Centennial*, edited by M. deJong Ellis, 7-27. Philadelphia, 1992.

"Mari entre l'Est et l'Ouest: politique, culture, religion." Akkadica 78 (1992):1-10.

"Le voyage d'un roi de Mari." Le Monde de la Bible 146 (2002):25-29.

Charpin, Dominique, and Nele Ziegler.

Mari et le Proche-Orient à l'époque amorrite. Essai d'histoire politique. Paris, 2003.

Civil, Miguel.

"Lexicography." In *Sumerological Studies in Honor of Thorkild Jacobsen on His Seventieth Birthday, June 7, 1974*, edited by S.J. Lieberman, 123-157. Chicago, 1975.

"Bilingualism in Logographically Written Languages: Sumerian in Ebla." In *Il bilinguismo a Ebla*, edited by L. Cagni, 75-97. Napoli, 1984.

"Sur les 'livres d'écolier' à l'époque paléo-babylonienne." In *Miscellanea Babylonica, Mélanges offerts à Maurice Birot*, 67-78. Paris, 1985.

"An Edubba text from Boghazköy." NABU 1987/47.

"Education in Mesopotamia." The Anchor Bible Dictionary, vol. 2, ed. by D.N. Freedman, 301-305. New York, 1992.

Collon, Dominique.

The Seal Impressions from Tell Atchana/Alalakh. Neukirchen-Vluyn, 1975.

Catalogue of the Western Asiatic Seals in the British Museum. Cylinder Seals III. Isin-Larsa and Old Babylonian Periods. London, 1986.

First Impressions. Cylinder Seals in the Ancient Near East. London, 1993.

Cooper, Jerrold S.

"Sumerian and Semitic Writing in Most Ancient Syro-Mesopotamia." In *Languages and Cultures in Contact*, edited by K. van Lerberghe and G. Voet, 61-77. Leuven, 1999.

Cotton, Hannah M.

"The Archive of Salome Komaise Daughter of Levi: Another Archive from the 'Cave of the Letters'." Zeitschrift für Papyrologie und Epigraphik 105 (1995):171-208.

Dalix, Anne-Sophie.

"Šuppiluliuma (II?) dans un texte alphabétique d'Ugarit et la date d'apparition de l'alphabet cunéiforme." Semitica 48 (1998):5-15.

Diakonoff, Igor M.

"Some Remarks on I 568." ArOr 47 (1979):40-41.

Dietrich, Manfried, and Oswald Loretz.

"*pilku* = *ilku* 'Lehenspflicht'." UF 4 (1972):165-66.

"Alalaḫ-Texte der Schicht VII (I). Historische und juristische Dokumente." UF 36 (2004):43-150.

Dietrich, Manfried, Oswlad Loretz, and Joaquín Sanmartín,

Die keilalphabetischen Texte aus Ugarit. Neukirchen-Vluyn, 1976.

The Cuneiform Alphabetic Texts from Ugarit, Ras Ibn Hani and Other Places (KTU: second, enlarged edition). Münster, 1995.

Donbaz, Veysel

"Some Remarkable Contracts of 1-B Period Kültepe Tablets (I)." In *Anatolia and the Ancient Near East. Studies in Honor of Tahsin Özgüç*, edited by K. Emre et al., 75-98. Ankara, 1989.

"Some Remarkable Contracts of 1-B Period Kültepe Tablets II." In *Aspects of Art and Iconography: Anatolia and Its Neighbors. Studies in Honor of Nimet Özgüç*, edited by M.J. Mellink, E. Porada, and T. Özgüç, 131-154. Ankara, 1993.

Donbaz, Veysel, and Klaas R. Veenhof.

"New Evidence for Some Assyrian Terms." Anatolica 12 (1985):131-155.

Dossin, Georges.

"Fragment de syllabaire de la III Dynastie d'Ur." *Mélanges de l'Université Saint-Joseph* 45 (1969):245-249.

Durand, Jean-Marie.

"Fragments rejoints pour une histoire élamite." In *Fragmenta historiae elamicae, Mélanges offerts à M.J. Stève*, edited by L. de Meyer, H. Gasche, and F. Vallat, 111-128. Paris, 1986.

Review of *Recherches au pays d'Aštata. Emar VI.3. Textes sumériens et accadiens*, by Daniel Arnaud. RA 83 (1989):163-191.

"Précurseurs syriens aux protocols néo-assyriens." In *Marchands, diplomates et empereurs. Études sur la civilisation mésopotamienne offertes à Paul Garelli*, edited by D. Charpin and F. Joannès, 13-71. Paris, 1991.

"Unité et diversités au Proche-Orient à l'époque amorrite." In *La circulation des biens, des personnes et des idées dans le Proche-Orient ancien*, edited by D. Charpin and F. Joannès, 97-128. Paris, 1992.

Documents épistolaires du palais de Mari, vol. 1. Paris, 1997.

"Apologue sur des mauvaises herbes et un coquin." *AuOr* 17-18 (1999-2000):191-196.

Le culte d'Addu d'Alep et l'affaire d'Alahtum. Paris, 2002.

Durand, Jean-Marie, and Francis Joannès.

"*kubuddâʾu* à Mari et à Emar." NABU 1990/70.

Easton, Donald F.

"Hittite Land Donations and Tabarna Seals." JCS 33 (1981):3-43.

Edzard, Dietz O.

"Ein neues Tontafelfragment (Nr. 7) aus Kāmid al Lōz." ZA 70 (1980):52-54.

"Personenkeil." RlA 10 (2004):431.

Eidem, Jesper.

"An Old Assyrian Treaty from Tell Leilan." In *Marchands, diplomates et em-*

pereurs. Études sur la civilisation mésopotamienne offertes à Paul Garelli, edited by D. Charpin and F. Joannès, 185-207. Paris, 1991.

Favier, Jean.

Les archives. Paris, 1959.

Fincke, Jeanette.

"Beiträge zum Lexikon des Hurritischen von Nuzi." SCCNH 7 (1995):5-21.

Finley, Thomas J.

"Word Order in the Clause Structure of Syrian Akkadian." Ph.D. diss., University of California, 1979.

Fisman, Joshua A.

"Who spoke what language to whom and when?", La linguistique 2 (1965):67-88.

Fronzaroli, Pelio.

"Un atto reale di donazione dagli archive di Ebla (TM.75.G.1766)." SEbl 1 (1979):3-16.

"Disposizioni reali per Ti̱taw-Liʾm (TM.75.G.2396, TM.75.G.1986+)." SEbl 7 (1984):1-22.

"Les combats de Hadda dans les texts d'Ébla." MARI 8 (1997):283-290.

"The Hail Incantation (ARET 5, 4)." In *Festschrift für Burkhart Kienast zu seinem 70. Geburtstage*, edited by G.J. Selz, 89-107. Münster, 2003.

Garelli, Paul.

"Le problème de la 'féodalité' assyrienne." *Semitica* 17 (1967):5-21.

Gelb, Ignace J.

"The Word for Dragoman in the Ancient Near East." *Glossa* 2 (1968):93-104.

"Typology of Mesopotamian Seal Inscriptions." In *Seals and Sealing in the Ancient Near East*, edited by Mc Guire Gibson and Robert D. Biggs, 107-126. Malibu, CA, 1977.

Geller, Markham J.

"Eight Incantation Bowls." OLP 17 (1986):101-117.

Gesche, Petra.

Schulunterricht in Babylonien im ersten Jahrtausend v. Chr. Münster, 2001.

Gianto, Agustinus.

Word Order Variation in the Akkadian of Byblos. Rome, 1990.

"Amarna Akkadian as a Contact Language." In *Languages and Cultures in Contact*, edited by K. van Lerberghe and G. Voet, 123-132. Leuven, 1999.

Glassner, Jean-Jacques.

"Le devin historien en Mésopotamie." In *Historiography in the Cuneiform World*, edited by T. Abusch et al., 181-193. Bethesda, Ma, 2001.

Goetze, Alfred, and Selim Levy.

"Fragment of the Gilgamesh Epic from Megiddo." *ᶜAtiqot* 2 (1959):121-128.

Goossens, Godefroy.

"Introduction à l'archivéconomie de l'Asie Antérieure." RA 46 (1952):98-107.

Gray, John.

"Sacral Kingship in Ugarit." In *Ugaritica* 6, 289-302. Paris, 1969.

Greene, John T.

The Role of the Messenger and Message in the Ancient Near East. Atlanta, 1989.

Greenfield, Jonas.

"*našû-nadānu* and its Congeners." In *Ancient Near Eastern Studies in Memory of Jacob Joel Finkelstein*, edited by M. deJong Ellis, 87-91. Hamden, CT, 1977.

"*Adi balṭu*: Care for the Elderly and its Rewards." In *Vorträge gehalten auf der 28. Rencontre Assyriologique Internationale in Wien*, edited by H. Hirsch and H. Hunger, 112-119. Horn, 1982.

Güterbock, Hans Gustav.

Siegel aus Bogazköy. Berlin, 1940.

Haase, Richard.

"Zum Recht von Ugarit." RIDA 11 (1964):3-17.

"Anmerkungen zum ugaritischen Immobilienkauf." ZA 58 (1967):196-210.

"Anmerkungen zum sogenannten Lehensrecht der Hethiter." ZAR 2 (1996):135-139.

Hallo, William W.

ed., *The Context of Scripture. Volume 1: Canonical Compositions from the Biblical World*. Leiden, New York, and Köln, 1997.

"A Model Court Case Concerning Inheritance." In *Riches Hidden in Secret Places. Ancient Near Eastern Studies in Memory of Thorkild Jacobsen*, edited by Tzvi Abusch, 141-154. Winona Lake, In, 2002.

Hallo, William H., and Hayim Tadmor.

"A Lawsuit from Hazor." IEJ 27 (1977):1-11.

Hart, Herbert L.A.

Essays in Jurisprudence and Philosophy. Oxford, 1983.

Hattori, Atsuko.

"Texts and Impressions: A Holistic Approach to Ur III Cuneiform Tablets from the University of Pennsylvania Expedition to Nippur." Ph.D. diss., University of Pennsylvania, 2002.

Heltzer, Michael.

The Rural Community of Ancient Ugarit. Wiesbaden, 1976.

"La signification de *unṯ* / *unuššu* à Ougarit." Semitica 30 (1980):5-12.

"Zum Steuersystem in Ugarit [pilku-ubdy und Ähnliches]." In *Vorträge gehalten auf der 28. Rencontre Assyriologique Internationale in Wien*, edited by H. Hirsch and H. Hunger, 112-119. Horn, 1982.

The Internal Organization of the Kingdom of Ugarit. Wiesbaden, 1982.

"Private Property in Ugarit." In *Circulation of Goods in Non-Palatial Context in the Ancient Near East*, edited by A. Archi, 161-194. Rome, 1984.

Hoftijzer, Jacob, and Wilfred H. van Soldt.

"Texts from Ugarit Concerning Security and Related Akkadian and West Semitic Material." UF 23 (1991):189-216.

Horowitz, Wayne.

"A Combined Multiplication Table on a Prism Fragment from Hazor." IEJ 47 (1997):190-197.

Huehnergard, John.

"RS 15.86 (*PRU* 3, 51f.)." UF 18 (1986):169-171.

Ugaritic Vocabulary in Syllabic Transcription. Atlanta, 1987.

The Akkadian of Ugarit. Atlanta, 1989.

Review of *Canaanite in the Amarna Tablets: A Linguistic Analysis of the Mixed Dialect Used by the Scribes from Canaan* by Anson F. Rainey. BASOR 310 (1998):59-77.

Huehnergard, John, and Wilfred H. van Soldt.

"A Cuneiform Lexical Text from Ashkelon with a Canaanite Column." IEJ 49 (1999):184-192.

Huehnergard, John, and Christopher Woods.

"Akkadian and Eblaite." In *The Cambridge Encyclopedia of the World's Ancient Languages*, edited by R.D. Woodard, 218-280. Cambridge, 2004.

Imparati, Fiorella.

"Una concessione di terre da parte di Tudhaliya IV," RHA 32 (1974).

"Aspects de l'organisation de l'état hittite dans les documents juridiques et administratifs." JESHO 25 (1982):225-267.

Israel, Felice.

"La classificazione dell'ugaritico: problema prima storico e poi linguistico." In *Semitic and Assyriological Studies Presented to Pelio Fronzaroli*, 256-262. Wiesbaden, 2003.

Izre'el, Shlomo.

Amurru Akkadian. A Linguistic Study. 2 vols. Atlanta, 1991.

Review of *The Akkadian of Ugarit* by John Huehnergard. BiOr 49 (1992):168-180.

"The Amarna Glosses: Who Wrote What to Whom? Some Sociolinguistic Considerations." IOS 15 (1995):101-122.

The Amarna Scholarly Tablets. Groningen, 1997.

Canaano-Akkadian. Munich, 1998.

"Vocalized Canaanite: Cuneiform-Written Canaanite Words in the Amarna Letters. Some Methodological Remarks." Dutch Studies (NELL) 5 (2003):13-34.

"Some Methodological Requisites for the Study of the Amarna Jargon. Notes on the Essence of that Language." In *Tell el-Amarna, 1887-1987*, edited by B.J. Beitzel and G.D. Young. Winona Lake, In. (forthcoming).

Jastrow, Marcus.

Dictionary of the Targumim, the Talmud Babli and Yerushalmi, and the Midrashic Literature. New York, 1950.

Joannès, Francis.

"Le traité de vassalité d'Atamrum d'Andarig envers Zimri-Lim de Mari." In *Marchands, diplomates et empereurs, Études sur la civilisation mésopotamienne offertes à Paul Garelli*, edited by D. Charpin and F. Joannès, 167-177. Paris, 1991.

Jursa, Michael.

Das Archiv des Bēl-Rēmanni. Leiden, 1999.

Kestemont, Guy.

Diplomatique et droit international en Asie occidentale (1600-1200 av. J.C.). Louvain-la-neuve, 1974.

"Remarques sur les aspects juridiques du commerce dans le Proche-Orient du XIVe siècle avant notre ère." Iraq 39 (1977):198-199.

Kienast, Burkhart.

"Kauf. E. In Alalaḫ und Ugarit." RlA 5 (1976-80):530-541.

"Rechtsurkunden in ugaritischer Sprache." UF 11 (1979):431-452.

Kilmer, Anne Draffkorn.

"Symbolic Gestures in Akkadian Contracts from Alalakh and Ugarit." JAOS 94 (1974):177-183.

Klíma, Josef.

"Die jüngste Provinz des Keilschriftrechtes." ArOr 24 (1956):123-130.

"Untersuchungen zum ugaritischen Erbrecht (Auf Grund der akkadischen Urkunden aus Ras Šamra)." ArOr 24 (1956):356-374.

"Die Stellung der ugaritischen Frau (Auf Grund der akkadischen Urkunden aus Ras Šamra)." ArOr 25 (1957):313-333 (= "Le statut de la femme à Ugarit d'après les textes accadiens de Ras-Schamra." Recueils de la Société Jean Bodin 11 [1959]:95-105).

"Sulla diseredazione secondo le fonti accadiche di Ugarit." RSO 32 (1957):655-660.

Knoppers, Gary N.

"Ancient Near Eastern Royal Grants and the Davidic Covenant: a Parallel?" JAOS 116 (1996):670-697.

Korošec, Victor.

Keilschriftrecht. Leiden and Köln, 1964.

Koschaker, Paul.

Neue keilschriftliche Rechtsurkunden aus der El-Amarna Zeit. Leipzig, 1928.

"Keilschriftrecht." ZDMG 89 (1935):1-39.

Kühne, Cord.

Die Chronologie der internationalen Korrespondenz von El-Amarna. Neukirchen-Vluyn, 1973.

Labat, René.

L'akkadien de Boghaz-köi. Étude sue la langue des lettres, traités et vocabulaires akkadiens trouvés à Boghaz-köi. Bordeaux, 1932.

"Le rayonnement de la langue et de l'écriture akkadiennes au deuxième millénaire avant notre ère." Syria 39 (1962):1-27.

Labuschagne, Casper J.

"The *našû-nadānu* formula and Its Biblical Equivalent." In *Travels in the World of the Old Testament, Studies Presented to Prof. M.A. Beek at the Occasion of His 65th Birthday*, edited by M.S.H.G. Heerma van Voss, Ph.H.J. Houwing ten Cate, and N.A. van Uchelen, 176-180. Assen, 1974.

Lackenbacher, Sylvie.

"Les textes judiciaires d'Ugarit." In *Rendre la justice en Mésopotamie. Archives judiciaires du Proche-Orient ancient (IIIe-Ier millénaires avant J.-C.)*, edited by F. Joannès, 317-320. Saint-Denis, 2000.

Textes akkadiens d'Ugarit. Paris, 2002.

Lafont, Sophie.

"Middle Assyrian Period." In *A History of Ancient Near Eastern Law*, vol. 1, edited by R. Westbrook, 521-563. Leiden and Boston, 2003.

Lagarce, Elisabeth, and Jacques Lagarce.

apud Henri de Contenson, et al. "La XXXIIIe campagne de fouilles à Ras Shamra en 1972. Rapport préliminaire." Syria 50 (1973):283-309.

Landsberger, Benno.

"Assyrische Königsliste und 'dunkles Zeitalter'." JCS 8 (1954):31-45, 47-73, 106-133.

Larsen, Morgens T., and Eva Møller.

"Five Old Assyrian Texts." In *Marchands, diplomates et empereurs. Études sur la civilisation mésopotamienne offertes à Paul Garelli*, edited by D. Charpin and F. Joannès, 227-252. Paris, 1991.

Lebrun, René.

"From Hittite Mythology: The Kumarbi Cycle." In *Civilizations from the Ancient Near East*, vol. 3, edited by J.M. Sasson, 1971-1980. New York, 1995.

Leemans, Wilhelmus F.

"La fonction des sceaux des contrats vieux-babyloniens." In *Zikir Šumim, Assyriological Studies Presented to F.R. Kraus on the Occasion of his Seventieth Birthday*, edited by G. van Driel et al., xxxx. Leiden, 1982.

Libolt, Clayton T.

"Royal Land Grants from Ugarit." Ph.D. diss., University of Michigan, 1985.

Lieberman, Stephen L.

"Nippur: City of Decisions." In *Nippur at the Centennial*, edited by M. deJ. Ellis, 127-136. Philadelphia, 1992.

Lipiński, Edward.

"Recherches ugaritiques." Syria 50 (1973):35-51.

"Aḫat-Milki, reine d'Ugarit, et la guerre de Mukiš." OLP 12 (1981):79-115.

Liverani, Mario.

Storia di Ugarit nell'età degli archivi politici. Roma, 1962.

"Ras Shamra. II. Histoire." Supplément au Dictionnaire de la Bible 9 (1979):1295-1348.

"Il primo piano degli archivi di Ugarit." SEL 5 (1988):121-142.

Loewenstamm, Samuel E.

"Notes on the Alalakh Tablets." IEJ 6 (1956):217-225.

"The Divine Grants of Land to the Patriarchs." JAOS 94 (1972):509-510.

"Ugarit and the Bible I." Biblica 56 (1975):103-119.

Comparative Studies in Biblical and Ancient Oriental Literatures. Neukirchen-Vluyn, 1980.

Lombard, Pierre.

"Contexte archéologique et données épigraphiques. Quelques réflexions sur l'interprétation du gisement de, 1973-1992." In *Le pays d'Ougarit autour de 1200 av. J.-C.*, edited by M. Yon, M. Sznycer, and P. Bordreuil, 227-237. Paris, 1995.

Loundine, Avraam G.

"L'abécédaire de Beth Shemesh." Le Muséon 100 (1987):243-250.

Malbran-Labat, Florence.

"Langues et écritures à Ougarit." Semitica 49 (1999):65-101.

Malul, Meir.

Studies in Mesopotamian Legal Symbolism. Neukirchen-Vluyn, 1988.

"Susapinnu, the Mesopotamian Paranymph." JESHO 32 (1989):241-278.

Margueron, Jean-Claude.

"Le palais royal d'Ougarit. Premiers résultats d'une analyse systématique." In *Le pays d'Ougarit autour de 1200 av. J.-C.*, edited by M. Yon, M. Sznycer, and P. Bordreuil, 183-202. Paris, 1995.

Márquez Rowe, Ignacio.

"Summaries of Ugaritic Texts and Some New Reading Suggestions." UF 24 (1992):259-262.

"Collations à RS 15.140 et 17.379[A]." NABU 1992/94.

"Correction à N.A.B.U. 1992/94." NABU 1992/107.

"KTU 3.7 Reconsidered. On the *ilku*-Service in Ugarit." AuOr 11 (1993):250-252.

"Syllabic and Alphabetic Texts. A Further Note on Scribal Education at Ugarit." UF 28 (1996):457-462.

"Notes on the Hurro-Akkadian of Alalaḫ in the Mid-Second Millennium BCE." IOS 18 (1998):63-78.

"*Royal Land Grants* and *ilku*-Service in Ugarit. The Legal Mechanism." In *Landwirtschaft im alten Orient*, edited by H. Klengel and J. Renger, 171-178. Berlin, 1999.

"The Legal Texts from Ugarit." in *Handbook of Ugaritic Studies*, edited by W.G.E. Watson and N. Wyatt, 390-422. Leiden, Boston, and Köln, 1999.

"The King of Ugarit, His Wife, Her Brother, and Her Lovers. The Mystery of a Tragedy in Two Acts Revisited." UF 32 (2000):365-372.

"The King's Men in Ugarit and Society in Late Bronze Age." JESHO 45 (2002):1-19.

"Alalakh." In *A History of Ancient Near Eastern Law*, vol. 1, edited by R. Westbrook, 693-717. Leiden and Boston, 2003.

"Ugarit." In *A History of Ancient Near Eastern Law*, vol. 1, edited by R. Westbrook, 719-735. Leiden and Boston, 2003.

Review of *Die Orts- und Gewässernamen der Texte aus Syrien im 2. Jt. v.Chr.* by J.A. Belmonte Marín. ZA 93 (2003):288-292.

"Reflexiones sobre el acadio como lengua de contacto en el antiguo Oriente." In *Lenguas en contacto: el testimonio escrito*, edited by P. Bádenas et al., 17-34. Madrid, 2004.

Review of *Études ougaritiques, I. Travaux, 1985-1995*, edited by M. Yon and D. Arnaud. Or NS 74 (2005):136-145.

"Scribes, Sages, and Seers in Ugarit." In *Scribes, Sages, and Seers. Wise Men and Women in the Eastern Mediterranean World. A Prospectus*, edited by Leo Perdue. Göttingen (in press).

"Land Tenure and Royal Administration in Late Bronze Age Ugarit", (forthcoming)

Mayer, Walter.

Tall Munbāqa-Ekalte-II. Die Texte. Saarbrücken, 2001.

Mayr, Rudi H.

"The Seal Impressions of Ur III Umma." Ph.D. diss., Rijksuniversiteit te Leiden, 1997.

Meier, Samuel A.

The Messenger in the Ancient Semitic World. Atlanta, 1988.

Mendelsohn, Isaac.

"Samuel's Denunciation of Kingship in the Light of the Akkadian Documents of Ugarit." BASOR 143 (1956):17-22.

Mettinger, Tryggve N.D.

Solomonic State Officials. A Study of the Civil Government Officials of the Israelitic Monarchy. Lund, 1971.

Michalowski, Piotr.

"Language, Literature, and Writing at Ebla." In *Ebla, 1975-1985. Dieci anni di studi linguistici e filologici*, edited by L. Cagni, 165-175. Naples, 1987.

Milano, Lucio.

"Osservazioni sul bilinguismo ugaritico-accadico." VO 3 (1980):179-197.

Milik, John T.

"Un contrat juif de l'an 134 après J.-C." RB 61 (1954):182-190.

"Deux documents inédits du Désert de Juda." Biblica 38 (1957):245-268.

Millard, Allan R.

"Königssiegel." RlA 6 (1980-1983):135-140.

Miller, Gerald I.

"Studies in the Juridical Texts from Ugarit." Ph.D. diss., The Johns Hopkins University, 1980.

Moore Cross, Frank, and Esther Eshel.

"Ostraca from Khirbet Qumrân." IEJ 47 (1997):17-28.

Moran, William L.

The Amarna Letters. Baltimore and London, 1992.

"A Syntactical Study of the Dialect of Byblos as Reflected in the Amarna Tablets." In *Amarna Studies. Collected Writings*, edited by J. Huehnergard and S. Izre'el, 1-130. Winona Lake, In, 2003.

Muffs, Yochanan.

Studies in the Aramiac Legal Papyri from Elephantine. New York, 1973.

Naveh, Joseph, and Shaked, Shaul.

Amulets and Magic Bowls. Jerusalem, 1985.

Nougayrol, Jean.

"Textes de Ras-Shamra en cunéiformes syllabiques (campagne de 1951)." CRAIBL 1952:181-191.

"Les nouvelles tablettes accadiennes de Ras Shamra (16e Campagne : septembre-novembre 1952)." CRAIBL, 1953:40-51.

Le palais royal d'Ugarit, vol. 3: *Textes accadiens et hourrites des Archives Est, Ouest et Centrales*. 2 vols. Paris, 1955.

"L'influence babylonienne à Ugarit, d'après les textes en cunéiformes classiques." Syria 39 (1962):28-35.

Le palais royal d'Ugarit, vol. 6: *Textes en cunéiformes babyloniens des Archives du Grand Palais et du Palais Sud d'Ugarit*. Paris, 1970.

Nougayrol, Jean, et al.

Ugaritica, vol. 5: Nouveaux textes accadiens, hourrites et ugaritiques des Archives et Bibliothèques privées d'Ugarit. Paris, 1968.

Oelsner, Joachim.

"Klageverzicht(sklausel)." RlA 6 (1980-1983):6-14.

del Olmo Lete, Gregorio.

La religión cananea según la liturgia de Ugarit. Sabadell, 1992.

Canaanite Religion according to the Liturgical Texts of Ugarit. Bethesda, Ma, 1999.

del Olmo, Gregorio, and Joaquín Sanmartín.

A Dictionary of the Ugaritic Language in the Alphabetic Tradition. Leiden and Boston, 2003.

Oppenheim, A. Leo.

"A Note on the Scribes in Mesopotamia." In *Studies in Honor of Benno Landsberger on His Seventy-Fifth Birthday*, 253-256. Chicago, 1965.

Letters from Mesopotamia. Chicago and London, 1967.

Ancient Mesopotamia. Portrait of a Dead Civilization. 2nd revised ed. Chicago and London, 1977.

Otten, Heinrich.

"Das hethitische Königshaus im 15. Jahrhundert v. Chr. Zum Neufund einiger Landschenkungsurkunden in Bogazköy." Anzeiger der phil.-hist. Klasse der Österreichischen Akademie der Wissenschaften 123 (1986):21-34.

Papritz, Johannes.

"Archive in Altmesopotamien. Theorie und Tatsachen." Archivalische Zeitschrift 55 (1959):11-50.

Pardee, Dennis.

"Le traité d'alliance RS 11.722+." Semitica 51 (2001):5-31.

Ritual and Cult at Ugarit. Leiden, Boston, and Köln, 2002.

Pearce, Laurie E.

"The Scribes and Scholars of Ancient Mesopotamia." In *Civilizations of the Ancient Near East*, vol. 4, edited by J.M. Sasson, 2265-2278. New York, 1995.

Pedersén, Olof.

Archives and Libraries in the Ancient Near East 1500-500 BC. Bethesda, Ma, 1998.

Pentiuc, Eugen J.

West Semitic Vocabulary in the Akkadian Texts from Emar. Winona Lake, In, 2001.

Porten, Bezalel, and Ada Yardeni.

Textbook of Aramaic Documents from Ancient Egypt. Volume 2: Contracts. Jerusalem, 1989.

Posner, Ernst.

Archives in the Ancient World. Cambridge, MA, 1972.

Postgate, John Nicholas.

"Land Tenure in the Middle Assyrian Period: A Reconstruction." BSOAS 34 (1971):496-520.

Fifty Neo-Assyrian Legal Documents. Warminster, 1976.

"*Ilku* and Land Tenure in the Middle Assyrian Kingdom: A Second Attempt." In *Societies and Languages of the Ancient Near East: Studies in Honor of I.M. Diakonoff*, edited by M.A. Dandamayev et al., 304-313. Warminster, 1982.

"Middle Assyrian Tablets: The Instruments of Bureaucracy." AoF 13 (1986):10-39.

Purves, Pierre M.

"The Early Scribes of Nuzi." AJSL 57 (1940):162-187.

Rabinowitz, Jacob.

Jewish Law. Its Influence on the Development of Legal Institutions. New York, 1956.

Rainey, Anson F.

"The Scribe at Ugarit. His Position and Influence." *Proceedings of the Israel Academy of Sciences and Humanities* III/4 (1969):126-147.

"Gleanings from Ugarit." IOS 3 (1973):34-62.

"Two Cuneiform Fragments from Tel Aphek." Tel Aviv 2 (1975):125-129.

"A Tri-Lingual Cuneiform Fragment from Tel Aphek." Tel Aviv 3 (1976):137-140.

Canaanite in the Amarna Tablets: A Linguistic Analysis of the Mixed Dialect Used by the Scribes from Canaan. Leiden, 1996.

Renger, Johannes.

"Legal Aspects of Sealing in Ancient Mesopotamia." In *Seals and Sealing in the Ancient Near East*, edited by Mc G. Gibson and R.D. Biggs, 75-88. Malibu, CA, 1977.

Riemschneider, Kaspar K.

"Die hethitischen Landschenkungsurkunden." MIO 6 (1958):321-381.

Ries, Gerhard.

"Lastenfreiheit." RlA 6 (1980-1983):508-511.

Robson, Eleanor.

"The Tablet House: A Scribal School in Old Babylonian Nippur." RA 95 (2001):39-66.

Roth, Martha T.

"Scholastic Tradition and Mesopotamian Law: A Study of FLP 1287, a Prism in the Collection of the Free Library of Philadelphia." Ph.D. diss., University of Pennsylvania, 1979.

Law Collections from Mesopotamia and Asia Minor. 2nd printing. Atlanta, 1997.

Rüster, Christel.

"Eine Urkunde Ḫantilis II." IstMitt 43 (1993):63-70.

Sanmartín, Joaquín.

"Glossen zum ugaritischen Lexikon (VI)." UF 21 (1989):335-348.

San Nicolò, Mariano.

Beiträge zur Rechtsgeschichte im Bereiche der keilschriftlichen Rechtsquellen. Oslo, 1931.

Schaeffer, Claude F.A.

"Les fouilles de Minet-el-Beida et de Ras Shamra (Campagne du printemps 1929). Rapport sommaire." Syria 10 (1929):285-297.

"Reprise des recherches archéologiques à Ras Shamra-Ugarit. Sondages de 1948 et 1949 et campagne de 1950." Syria 28 (1951):1-21.

"Fouilles à Ras-Shamra-Ugarit (Campagne, 1951)." CRAIBL 1952:234-240.

"Nouvelles fouilles et découvertes de la mission archéologique de Ras Shamra dans le palais d'Ugarit (campagne 1951)." Annales Archeólogiques de Syrie 2 (1952):3-22.

"Nouvelles découvertes à Ras Shamra-Ugarit et à Enkomi-Alasia (Chypre) en 1953." CRAIBL 1954:97-103.

"Les fouilles de Ras Shamra-Ugarit, quinzième, seizième et dix-septième campagnes (1951, 1952, et, 1953), rapport sommaire." Syria 31 (1954):14-67.

ed., *Ugaritica*, vol. 3: *Sceaux et cylindres hittites, épée gravée du cartouche de Mineptah, tablettes chypro-minoennes et autres découvertes nouvelles de Ras Shamra*. Paris, 1956.

ed., *Ugaritica*, vol. 4: *Découvertes des XVIIIe et XIXe campagnes, 1954-1955.* Paris 1962.

Corpus des cylindres-sceaux de Ras Shamra-Ugarit et d'Enkomi-Alasia I, Paris, 1983

Schloen, David.

The House of the Father as Fact and Symbol. Patrimonialism in Ugarit and the Ancient Near East. Winona Lake, In, 2001.

Schuler, Einar von.

"Landschenkungsurkunden." RlA 6 (1980-1983):469-470.

Schulman, Alan R.

"Diplomatic Marriage in the Egyptian New Kingdom." JNES 38 (1979):177-193.

Selinker, Larry.

"Interlanguage." International Review of Applied Linguistics in Language Teaching 10 (1972):209-230.

Singer, Itamar.

"A political History of Ugarit." In *Handbook of Ugaritic Studies*, edited by W.G.E. Watson and N. Wyatt, 601-733. Leiden, Boston, and Köln, 1999.

"The Great Scribe Taki-Šarruma." In *Hittite Studies in Honor of Harry A. Hoffner Jr. On the Occasion of his 65th Birthday*, edited by G. Beckman et al., 341-348. Winona Lake, In, 2003.

Skaist, Aaron.

"A Unique Closing Formula in the Contracts from Ugarit." In *Society and Economy in the Eastern Mediterranean (c. 1500-1000 BC)*, edited by M. Heltzer and E. Lipiński, 151-159. Leuven, 1988.

Soden, Wolfram von.

"Bemerkungen zu einigen literarischen Texten in akkadischer Sprache aus Ugarit." UF 1 (1969):189-195.

Einführung in die Altorientalistik. Darmstadt, 1985.

van Soldt, Wilfred H.

"The Palace Archives at Ugarit." In *Cuneiform Archives and Libraries*, edited by K.R. Veenhof, 196-204. Leiden, 1986.

"The Title *ṯʕy*." UF 20 (1988):313-321.

Studies in the Akkadian of Ugarit. Dating and Grammar. Neukirchen Vluyn, 1991.

"Babylonian Lexical, Religious and Literary Texts and Scribal Education at Ugarit and Its Implications for the Alphabetic Literary Texts." In *Ugarit. Ein ostmediterranes Kulturzentrum im Alten Orient. Ergebnisse und Perspektive der Forschung. Band I: Ugarit und seine altorientalische Umwelt*, edited by M. Dietrich and O. Loretz, 171-212. Münster, 1995.

"The Akkadian of Ugarit: Lexicographical Aspects." SEL 12 (1995):205-215

"Private archives at Ugarit." In *Interdependency of Institutions and Private Entrepreneurs*, edited by A.C.V.M. Bongenaar, 229-245. Leiden, 2000.

"Syrian Chronology in the Old and Middle Babylonian Periods." Akkadica 119-120 (2000):103-116.

"Naḫiš-šalmu, an Assyrian Scribe Working in the 'Southern Palace' at Ugarit." In *Veenhof Anniversary Volume. Studies Presented to Klaas R. Veenhof on the Occasion of His Sixty-fifth Birthday*, edited by W. van Soldt et al., 429-444. Leiden, 2001.

"Studies on the sākinu-Official (2)." UF 34 (2002):805-828.

The Topography of the City-State of Ugarit. Münster, 2005.

Speiser, Ephraim A.

"The Alalakh Tablets." JAOS 74 (1954):18-25.

"Akkadian Documents from Ras Shamra." JAOS 75 (1955):154-165.

Starke, Frank.

"Zur Herkunft von akkad. *ta/urgumannu(m)* 'Dolmetscher'." WdO 24 (1993):20-38.

Stein, Diana.

"Mittan(n)i. B. Bildkunst und Architektur." RlA 8 (1993-1997):296-299.

Steinkeller, Piotr.

Sale Documents of the Ur-III Period. Freiburg, 1989.

Tadmor, Hayim.

"A Lexicographical Texts from Hazor." IEJ 27 (1977):98-102.

Teissier, Béatrice.

Sealing and Seals on Texts from Kültepe Kārum Level 2. Leiden, 1994.

Teixidor, Javier.

La filosofía traducida. Sabadell, 1991.

Thureau-Dangin, François.

"Trois contrats de Ras-Shamra." Syria 18 (1937):245-255.

van der Toorn, Karel.

"Cuneiform Documents from Syria-Palestine. Texts, Scribes, and Schools." ZDPV 116 (2000):97-113.

Tropper, Josef, and Juan-Pablo Vita

"Texte aus Ugarit." In *Texte zum Rechts- und Wirtschaftsleben* (*TUAT* NF 1), edited by B. Janowski and G. Wilhelm, 111-128. Gütersloh, 2004.

Vargyas, Peter.

"Le *mudu* à Ugarit. Ami du roi?" UF 13 (1981):165-179.

Veenhof, Klaas R.

"Cuneiform Archives: An Introduction." In *Cuneiform Archives and Libraries*, edited by Klaas R. Veenhof, 1-36. Leiden, 1986.

"Old Assyrian and Anatolian Evidence for the Care of the Elderly." In *The Care of the Elderly in the Ancient Near East*, edited by M. Stol and S.P. Vleeming, 119-160. Leiden, Boston, and Köln, 1998.

"Old Assyrian Period", In *A History of Ancient Near Eastern Law*, vol. 1, edited by R. Westbrook, 431-483. Leiden and Boston, 2003.

Veldhuis, Niek.

Elementary Education at Nippur. The Lists of Trees and Wooden Objects. Groningen, 1997.

Villard, Pierre.

"Un roi de Mari à Ugarit." UF 18 (1986):387-412.

Virolleaud, Charles.

"Cinq tablettes accadiennes de Ras-Shamra." RA 38 (1941):1-12.

Le palais royal d'Ugarit, vol. 2: *Textes alphabétiques des Archives Est, Ouest et Centrales*. Paris, 1957.

"Six textes de Ras-Shamra provenant de la XIVe campagne (1959)." Syria 28 (1951):163-179.

Vita, Juan Pablo.

"Datation et genres littéraires à Ougarit." In *Proche-Orient ancien : temps vécu, temps pensé*, edited by F. Briquel-Chatonnet and H. Lozachmeur, 39-52. Paris, 1998.

Volk, Konrad.

"Edubba'a und Edubba'a-Literatur: Rätsel und Lösungen." ZA 90 (2000):1-30.

Von Dassow, Eva.

"What the Canaanite Cuneiformists Wrote: Review Article." IEJ 53 (2003):196-217.

Weidner, Ernst.

"Subaräische Gottheiten im Assyrischen Pantheon." AfO 15 (1945-1951):82-84.

Weinfeld, Moshe.

"The Covenant of Grant in the Old Testament and the Ancient Near East." JAOS 90 (1970):184-203.

Weinreich, Uriel.

Languages in Contact. Findings and Problems. The Hague, 1963.

Westbrook, Raymond.

"The Price Factor in the Redemption of Land." RIDA 32 (1985):97-127.

"Introduction: The Character of Ancient Near Eastern Law." In *A History of Ancient Near Eastern Law*, vol. 1, edited by R. Westbrook, 1-90. Leiden and Boston, 2003.

"Old Babylonian Period." In *A History of Ancient Near Eastern Law*, vol. 1, edited by R. Westbrook, 361-430. Leiden and Boston, 2003.

Wilhelm, Gernot.

Untersuchungen zum Hurro-Akkadischen von Nuzi. Neukirchen-Vluyn, 1970.

"Introduction." SCCNH 10 (1999):3-11.

Yamada, Masamichi.

"The Dynastic Seal and Ninurta's Seal: Preliminary Remarks on Sealing by the Local Authorities of Emar." Iraq 56 (1994):59-62.

Yaron, Reuven.

Gifts in Contemplation of Death in Jewish and Roman Law. Oxford, 1960.

"A Document of Redemption from Ugarit." VT 10 (1960):83-90.

Introduction to the Law of the Aramaic Papyri. Oxford, 1961.

"Varia on Adoption." Journal of Juristic Papyrology 15 (1965):171-183.

Yon, Marguerite.

La cité d'Ougarit sur le tell de Ras Shamra. Paris, 1997.

INDICES

1. Terms and phrases

1.1. Akkadian

1.2. Ugaritic

2. Sources

2.1. Cuneiform sources

2.2. Hebrew sources

2.3. Aramaic sources

2.4. Syriac sources

2.5. Classical sources

Ugarit-Verlag Münster

Ricarda-Huch-Straße 6, D-48161 Münster (www.ugarit-verlag.de)

Lieferbare Bände der Serien AOAT, AVO, ALASP(M), FARG, Eikon und ELO:

Alter Orient und Altes Testament (AOAT)

Herausgeber: *Manfried DIETRICH - Oswald LORETZ*

43 Nils P. HEEßEL, *Babylonisch-assyrische Diagnostik.* 2000 (ISBN 3-927120-86-3), XII + 471 S. + 2 Abb., € 98,17.

44 Anja ULBRICH, *KYPRIS. Heiligtümer und Kulte weiblicher Gottheiten auf Zypern in der kypro-archaischen und -klassischen Epoche (Königszeit).* 2005 (ISBN 3-934628-56-7) (i.V.)

245 Francesco POMPONIO - Paolo XELLA, *Les dieux d'Ebla. Étude analytique des divinités éblaïtes à l'époque des archives royales du IIIe millénaire.* 1997 (ISBN 3-927120-46-4), VII + 551 S., € 59,31.

246 Annette ZGOLL, *Der Rechtsfall der En-ḫedu-Ana im Lied nin-me-šara*, 1997 (ISBN 3-927120-50-2) – vergr.

248 *Religion und Gesellschaft. Veröffentlichungen des Arbeitskreises zur Erforschung der Religions- und Kulturgeschichte des Antiken Vorderen Orients (AZERKAVO), Band 1.* 1997 (ISBN 3-927120-54-5), VIII + 220 S., € 43,97.

249 Karin REITER, *Die Metalle im Alten Orient unter besonderer Berücksichtigung altbabylonischer Quellen.* 1997 (ISBN 3-927120-49-9), XLVII + 471 + 160 S. + 1 Taf., € 72,60.

250 Manfried DIETRICH - Ingo KOTTSIEPER, Hrsg., *"Und Mose schrieb dieses Lied auf". Studien zum Alten Testament und zum Alten Orient. Festschrift Oswald Loretz.* 1998 (ISBN 3-927120-60-X), xviii + 955 S., € 112,48.

251 Thomas R. KÄMMERER, *Šimâ milka. Induktion und Reception der mittelbabylonischen Dichtung von Ugarit, Emār und Tell el-'Amārna.* 1998 (ISBN 3-927120-47-2), XXI + 360 S., € 60,33.

252 Joachim MARZAHN - Hans NEUMANN, Hrsg., *Assyriologica et Semitica. Festschrift für Joachim OELSNER anläßlich seines 65. Geburtstages am 18. Februar 1997.* 2000 (ISBN 3-927120-62-6), xii + 635 S. + Abb., € 107,88.

253 Manfried DIETRICH - Oswald LORETZ, Hrsg., *dubsar anta-men. Studien zur Altorientalistik. Festschrift für W.H.Ph. Römer.* 1998 (ISBN 3-927120-63-4) – vergr.

254 Michael JURSA, *Der Tempelzehnt in Babylonien vom siebenten bis zum dritten Jahrhundert v.Chr.* 1998 (ISBN 3-927120-59-6), VIII + 146 S., € 41,93.

255 Thomas R. KÄMMERER - Dirk SCHWIDERSKI, *Deutsch-Akkadisches Wörterbuch.* 1998 (ISBN 3-927120-66-9), XVIII + 589 S., € 79,76.

256 Hanspeter SCHAUDIG, *Die Inschriften Nabonids von Babylon und Kyros' des Großen.* 2001 (ISBN 3-927120-75-8), XLII + 766 S., € 103,--.

257 Thomas RICHTER, *Untersuchungen zu den lokalen Panthea Süd- und Mittelbabyloniens in altbabylonischer Zeit* (2., verb. und erw. Aufl.). 2004 (ISBN 3-934628-50-8; Erstausgabe: 3-927120-64-2), XXI + 608 S., € 88,--.

258 Sally A.L. BUTLER, *Mesopotamian Conceptions of Dreams and Dream Rituals.* 1998 (ISBN 3-927120-65-0), XXXIX + 474 S. + 20 Pl., € 75,67.

259 Ralf ROTHENBUSCH, *Die kasuistische Rechtssammlung im Bundesbuch und ihr literarischer Kontext im Licht altorientalischer Parallelen.* 2000 (ISBN 3-927120-67-7), IV + 681 S., € 65,10.

260 Tamar ZEWI, *A Syntactical Study of Verbal Forms Affixed by -n(n) Endings . . .* 1999 (ISBN 3-927120-71-5), VI + 211 S., € 48,06.

261 Hans-Günter BUCHHOLZ, *Ugarit, Zypern und Ägäis - Kulturbeziehungen im zweiten Jahrtausend v.Chr.* 1999 (ISBN 3-927120-38-3), XIII + 812 S., 116 Tafeln, € 109,42.

262 Willem H.Ph. RÖMER, *Die Sumerologie. Einführung in die Forschung und Bibliographie in Auswahl* (zweite, erweiterte Auflage). 1999 (ISBN 3-927120-72-3), XII + 250 S., € 61,36.

263 Robert ROLLINGER, *Frühformen historischen Denkens. Geschichtsdenken, Ideologie und Propaganda im alten Mesopotamien am Übergang von der Ur-III zur Isin-Larsa Zeit* (ISBN 3-927120-76-6)(i.V.)

264 Michael P. STRECK, *Die Bildersprache der akkadischen Epik.* 1999 (ISBN 3-927120-77-4), 258 S., € 61,36.

265 Betina I. FAIST, *Der Fernhandel des assyrischen Reichs zwischen dem 14. und 11. Jahrhundert v. Chr.*, 2001 (ISBN 3-927120-79-0), XXII + 322 S. + 5 Tf., € 72,09.

266 Oskar KAELIN, *Ein assyrisches Bildexperiment nach ägyptischem Vorbild. Zu Planung und Ausführung der „Schlacht am Ulai".* 1999 (ISBN 3-927120-80-4), 150 S., Abb., 5 Beilagen, € 49,08.

267 Barbara BÖCK, Eva CANCIK-KIRSCHBAUM, Thomas RICHTER, Hrsg., *Munuscula Mesopotamica. Festschrift für Johannes RENGER.* 1999 (ISBN 3-927120-81-2), XXIX + 704 S., Abb., € 124,76.

268 Yushu GONG, *Die Namen der Keilschriftzeichen.* 2000 (ISBN 3-927120-83-9), VIII + 228 S., € 44,99.

269/1 Manfried DIETRICH - Oswald LORETZ, *Studien zu den ugaritischen Texten I: Mythos und Ritual in KTU 1.12, 1.24, 1.96, 1.100 und 1.114.* 2000 (ISBN 3-927120-84-7), XIV + 554 S., € 89,99.

270 Andreas SCHÜLE, *Die Syntax der althebräischen Inschriften. Ein Beitrag zur historischen Grammatik des Hebräischen.* 2000 (ISBN 3-927120-85-5), IV + 294 S., € 63,40.

271/1 Michael P. STRECK, *Das amurritische Onomastikon der altbabylonischen Zeit I: Die Amurriter, die onomastische Forschung, Orthographie und Phonologie, Nominalmorphologie.* 2000 (ISBN 3-927120-87-1), 414 S., € 75,67.

272 Reinhard DITTMANN - Barthel HROUDA - Ulrike LÖW - Paolo MATTHIAE - Ruth MAYER-OPIFICIUS - Sabine THÜRWÄCHTER, Hrsg., *Variatio Delectat - Iran und der Westen. Gedenkschrift für Peter CALMEYER.* 2001 (ISBN 3-927120-89-8), XVIII + 768 S. + 2 Faltb., € 114,53.

273 Josef TROPPER, *Ugaritische Grammatik.* 2000 (ISBN 3-927120-90-1), XXII + 1056 S., € 100,21.

274 Gebhard J. SELZ, Hrsg., *Festschrift für Burkhart Kienast. Zu seinem 70. Geburtstage, dargebracht von Freunden, Schülern und Kollegen.* 2003 (ISBN 3-927120-91-X), xxviii + 732 S., € 122,--.

275 Petra GESCHE, *Schulunterricht in Babylonien im ersten Jahrtausend v.Chr.* 2001 (ISBN 3-927120-93-6), xxxiv + 820 S. + xiv Tf., € 112,48.

276 Willem H.Ph. RÖMER, *Hymnen und Klagelieder in sumerischer Sprache.* 2001 (ISBN 3-927120-94-4), xi + 275 S., € 66,47.

277 Corinna FRIEDL, *Polygynie in Mesopotamien und Israel.* 2000 (ISBN 3-927120-95-2), 325 S., € 66,47.

278/1 Alexander MILITAREV - Leonid KOGAN, *Semitic Etymological Dictionary. Vol. I: Anatomy of Man and Animals.* 2000 (ISBN 3-927120-90-1), cliv + 425 S., € 84,87.

278/2 Alexander MILITAREV - Leonid KOGAN, *Semitic Etymological Dictionary. Vol. II: Animal Names.* 2005 (ISBN 3-934628-57-5), xci + 415 S., € 104,--.

279 Kai A. METZLER, *Tempora in altbabylonischen literarischen Texten.* 2002 (ISBN 3-934628-03-6), xvii + 964 S., € 122,--.

280 Beat HUWYLER - Hans-Peter MATHYS - Beat WEBER, Hrsg., *Prophetie und Psalmen. Festschrift für Klaus SEYBOLD zum 65. Geburtstag.* 2001 (ISBN 3-934628-01-X), xi + 315 S., 10 Abb., € 70,56.

281 Oswald LORETZ - Kai METZLER - Hanspeter SCHAUDIG, Hrsg., *Ex Mesopotamia et Syria Lux. Festschrift für Manfried DIETRICH zu seinem 65. Geburtstag.* 2002 (ISBN 3-927120-99-5), XXXV + 950 S. + Abb., € 138,--.

282 Frank T. ZEEB, *Die Palastwirtschaft in Altsyrien nach den spätaltbabylonischen Getreidelieferlisten aus Alalaḫ (Schicht VII).* 2001 (ISBN 3-934628-05-2), XIII + 757 S., € 105,33.

283 Rüdiger SCHMITT, *Bildhafte Herrschaftsrepräsentation im eisenzeitlichen Israel.* 2001 (ISBN 3-934628-06-0), VIII + 231 S., € 63,40.

284/1 David M. CLEMENS, *Sources for Ugaritic Ritual and Sacrifice. Vol. I: Ugaritic and Ugarit Akkadian Texts.* 2001 (ISBN 3-934628-07-9), XXXIX + 1407 S., € 128,85.

285 Rainer ALBERTZ, Hrsg., *Kult, Konflikt und Versöhnung. Veröffentlichungen des AZERKAVO / SFB 493, Band 2.* 2001 (ISBN 3-934628-08-7), VIII + 332 S., € 70,56.

286 Johannes F. DIEHL, *Die Fortführung des Imperativs im Biblischen Hebräisch.* 2004 (ISBN 3-934628-19-2), XIV + 409 S., € 78,00.

287 Otto RÖSSLER, *Gesammelte Schriften zur Semitohamitistik*, Hrsg. Th. Schneider. 2001 (ISBN 3-934628-13-3), 848 S., € 103,--.

288 A. KASSIAN, A. KOROLËV†, A. SIDEL'TSEV, *Hittite Funerary Ritual šalliš waštaiš*. 2002 (ISBN 3-934628-16-8), ix + 973 S., € 118,--.

289 Zipora COCHAVI-RAINEY, *The Alashia Texts from the 14th and 13th Centuries BCE. A Textual and Linguistic Study*. 2003 (ISBN 3-934628-17-6), xiv + 129 S., € 56,--.

290 Oswald LORETZ, *Götter – Ahnen – Könige als gerechte Richter. Der "Rechtsfall" des Menschen vor Gott nach altorientalischen und biblischen Texten*. 2003 (ISBN 3-934628-18-4), xxii + 932 S., € 128,--.

291 Rocío Da RIVA, *Der Ebabbar-Tempel von Sippar in frühneubabylonischer Zeit (640-580 v. Chr.)*, 2002 (ISBN 3-934628-20-6), xxxi + 486 S. + xxv* Tf., € 86,--.

292 Achim BEHRENS, *Prophetische Visionsschilderungen im Alten Testament. Sprachliche Eigenarten, Funktion und Geschichte einer Gattung*. 2002 (ISBN 3-934628-21-4), xi + 413 S., € 82,--.

293 Arnulf HAUSLEITER - Susanne KERNER - Bernd MÜLLER-NEUHOF, Hrsg., *Material Culture and Mental Sphere. Rezeption archäologischer Denkrichtungen in der Vorderasiatischen Altertumskunde. Internationales Symposium für Hans J. Nissen, Berlin 23.-24. Juni 2000*. 2002 (ISBN 3-934628-22-2), xii + 391 S., € 88,--.

294 Klaus KIESOW - Thomas MEURER, Hrsg., *„Textarbeit". Studien zu Texten und ihrer Rezeption aus dem Alten Testament und der Umwelt Israels. Festschrift für Peter WEIMAR zur Vollendung seines 60. Lebensjahres*. 2002 (ISBN 3-934628-23-0), x + 630 S., € 128,--.

295 Galo W. VERA CHAMAZA, *Die Omnipotenz Aššurs. Entwicklungen in der Aššur-Theologie unter den Sargoniden Sargon II., Sanherib und Asarhaddon*. 2002 (ISBN 3-934628-24-9), 586 S., € 97,--.

296 Michael P. STRECK - Stefan WENINGER, Hrsg., *Altorientalische und semitische Onomastik*. 2002 (ISBN 3-934628-25-7), vii + 241 S., € 68,--.

297 John M. STEELE - Annette IMHAUSEN, Hrsg., *Under One Sky. Astronomy and Mathematics in the Ancient Near East*. 2002 (ISBN 3-934628-26-5), vii + 496 S., Abb., € 112,--.

298 Manfred KREBERNIK - Jürgen VAN OORSCHOT, Hrsg., *Polytheismus und Monotheismus in den Religionen des Vorderen Orients*. 2002 (ISBN 3-934628-27-3), v + 269 S., € 76,--.

299 Wilfred G.E. WATSON, Hrsg., *Festschrift Nick WYATT*. 2004 (ISBN 3-934628-32-X)(i.V.)

300 Karl LÖNING, Hrsg., *Rettendes Wissen. Studien zum Fortgang weisheitlichen Denkens im Frühjudentum und im frühen Christentum. Veröffentlichungen des AZERKAVO / SFB 493, Band 3*. 2002 (ISBN 3-934628-28-1), x + 370 S., € 84,--.

301 Johannes HAHN, Hrsg., *Religiöse Landschaften. Veröffentlichungen des AZERKAVO / SFB 493, Band 4*. 2002 (ISBN 3-934628-31-1), ix + 227 S., Abb., € 66,--.

302 Cornelis G. DEN HERTOG - Ulrich HÜBNER - Stefan MÜNGER, Hrsg., *SAXA LOQUENTUR. Studien zur Archäologie Palästinas/Israels. Festschrift für VOLKMAR FRITZ zum 65. Geburtstag*. 2003 (ISBN 3-934628-34-6), x + 328 S., Abb., € 98,--.

303 Michael P. STRECK, *Die akkadischen Verbalstämme mit* ta-*Infix*. 2003 (ISBN 3-934628-35-4), xii + 163 S., € 57,--.

304 Ludwig D. MORENZ - Erich BOSSHARD-NEPUSTIL, *Herrscherpräsentation und Kulturkontakte: Ägypten - Levante - Mesopotamien. Acht Fallstudien*. 2003 (ISBN 3-934628-37-0), xi + 281 S., 65 Abb., € 68,--.

305 Rykle BORGER, *Mesopotamisches Zeichenlexikon*. 2004 (ISBN 3-927120-82-0), viii + 712 S., € 74,--.

306 Reinhard DITTMANN - Christian EDER - Bruno JACOBS, Hrsg., *Altertumswissenschaften im Dialog. Festschrift für WOLFRAM NAGEL zur Vollendung seines 80. Lebensjahres*. 2003 (ISBN 3-934628-41-9), xv + 717 S., Abb., € 118,--.

307 Michael M. FRITZ, *". . . und weinten um Tammuz". Die Götter Dumuzi-Ama'ušumgal'anna und Damu*. 2003 (ISBN 3-934628-42-7), 430 S., € 83,--.

308 Annette ZGOLL, *Die Kunst des Betens. Form und Funktion, Theologie und Psychagogik in babylonisch-assyrischen Handerhebungsgebeten an Ištar*. 2003 (ISBN 3-934628-45-1), iv + 319 S., € 72,--.

309 Willem H.Ph. RÖMER, *Die Klage über die Zerstörung von Ur*. 2004 (ISBN 3-934628-46-X), ix + 191 S., € 52,--.

310 Thomas SCHNEIDER, Hrsg., *Das Ägyptische und die Sprachen Vorderasiens, Nordafrikas und der Ägäis. Akten des Basler Kolloquiums zum ägyptisch-nichtsemitischen Sprachkontakt Basel 9.-11. Juli 2003.* 2004 (ISBN 3-934628-47-8), 527 S., € 108,--.

311 Dagmar KÜHN, *Totengedenken bei den Nabatäern und im Alten Testamtent. Eine religionsgeschichtliche und exegetsiche Studie.* 2005 (ISBN 3-934628-48-6), x + 514 S. + 42 S. Abb., € 95,80.

312 Ralph HEMPELMANN, *„Gottschiff" und „Zikkurratbau" auf vorderasiatischen Rollsiegeln des 3. Jahrtausends v. Chr.* 2004 (ISBN 3-934628-49-4), viii + 154 S., + Tf. I-XXXI, Abb., € 55,--.

313 Rüdiger SCHMITT, *Magie im Alten Testament.* 2004 (ISBN 3-934628-52-4), xiii + 471 S., € 94,--.

314 Stefan TIMM, *„Gott kommt von Teman . . ." Kleine Schriften zur Geschichte Israels und Syrien-Palästinas. Hrsg. von Claudia Bender und Michael Pietsch.* 2004 (ISBN 3-934628-53-2), viii + 274 S., € 63,--.

315 Bojana JANKOVIĆ, *Vogelzucht und Vogelfang in Sippar im 1. Jahrtausend v. Chr. - Veröffentlichungen zur Wirtschaftsgeschichte Babyloniens im 1. Jahrtausend v. Chr., Bd. 1.* 2004 (ISBN 3-934628-54-0), xx + 219 S., € 56,20.

316 Christian SIGRIST, Hrsg., *Macht und Herrschaft. Veröffentlichungen des AZERKAVO / SFB 493, Band 5.* 2004 (ISBN 3-934628-55-9), xii + 239 S., € 63,--.

317 Bogdan BURTEA / Josef TROPPER / Helen YOUNANSARDAROUD, Hrsg., *Studia Semitica et Semitohamitica. Festschrift für RAINER VOIGT anläßlich seines 60. Geburtstages am 17. Januar 2004.* 2005 (ISBN 3-934628-73-7), v + 539 S., € 98,50.

318 Manfred HUTTER / Sylvia HUTTER-BRAUNSAR, *Offizielle Religion, lokale Kulte und individuelle Religiosität. Akten des religionsgeschichtlichen Symposiums „Kleinasien und angrenzende Gebiete vom Beginn des 2. bis zur Mitte des 1. Jahrtausends v. Chr." (Bonn, 20.-22. Februar 2003).* 2004 (ISBN 3-934628-58-3), 504 S., Abb., € 121,--.

319 Catherine MITTERMAYER, *Die Entwicklung der seitlich abgebildeten Tierkopfzeichen. Eine Studie zur syro-mesopotamischen Keilschriftpaläographie des 3. und frühen 2. Jahrtausends v. Chr.* 2005 (ISBN 3-934628-59-1), 169 S., € 48,80.

321 Galo W. VERA CHAMAZA, *Die Rolle Moabs in der neuassyrischen Expansionspolitik.* 2005 (ISBN 3-934628-61-3), VIII + 203 S., € 58,00.

322 Siam BHAYRO, *The Shemihazah and Asael Narrative of 1 Enoch 6-11: Introduction, Text, Translation and Commentary with reference to Ancient Near Eastern and Biblical Antecedents.* 2005 (ISBN 3-934628-62-1), X + 295 S., € 66,50.

323 Mirko NOVÁK / Friedhelm PRAYON / Anne-Maria WITTKE, Hrsg., *Die Außenwirkung des späthethitischen Kulturraumes. Güteraustausch - Kulturkontakt - Kulturtransfer. Akten der zweiten Forschungstagung des Graduiertenkollegs „Anatolien und seine Nachbarn" der Eberhard-Karls-Universität Tübingen (20. bis 22. November 2003).* 2004 (ISBN 3-934628-63-X), VIII + 496 S., Abb. € 106,00.

324 Wilfred H. van SOLDT, *The Topography of the City-State of Ugarit.* 2005 (ISBN 3-934628-64-8), vi + 253 S., € 64,--.

325 Robert ROLLINGER, Hrsg., *Von Sumer bis Homer. Festschrift für Manfred Schretter zum 60. Geburtstag am 25. Februar 2004.* 2005 (ISBN 3-934628-66-4), ix + 697 S., € 128,50.

326 Ulla Susanne KOCH, *Secrets of Extispicy. The Chapter Multābiltu of the Babylonian Extispicy Series and niṣirti bārûti Texts mainly from Aššurbanipal's Library.* 2005 (ISBN 3-934628-67-2), x + 630 S. + liv pl., € 119,--.

327 Helga WEIPPERT, *Unter Olivenbäumen. Studien zur Archäologie Syrien-Palästinas, Kulturgeschichte und Exegese des Alten Testaments. Gesammelte Aufsätze. Festgabe zum 4. Mai 2003 herausgegeben von Angelika Berlejung und Hermann Michael Niemann.* 2006 (ISBN 3-934628-68-0), x + 522 S., € 94,00.

328 Eva A. BRAUN-HOLZINGER / Ellen REHM, *Orientalischer Import in Griechenland im frühen 1. Jahrtausend v. Chr.* 2005 (ISBN 3-934628-72-9), vi + 208 S. + 39 Tf., € 63,60.

329 Michael HERLES, *Götterdarstellungen Mesopotamiens in der 2. Hälfte des 2. Jahrtausends v. Chr. Das anthropomorphe Bild im Verhältnis zum Symbol.* 2006 (ISBN 3-934628-76-1)(i.D.)

330 Heather D. BAKER / Michael JURSA, *Approaching the Babylonian Economy. Proceedings of the START Project Symposium Held in Vienna, 1-3 July 2004.* 2005 (ISBN 3-934628-79-6), viii + 448 S., € 86,50.

331 Thomas E. BALKE, *Das sumerische Dimensionalkasussystem*. 2006 (ISBN 3-934628-80-X), x + 287 S., € 68,00.

332 Margaret JAQUES, *Le vocabulaire des sentiments dans les textes sumériens. Recherche sur le lexique sumérien et akkadien*. 2006 (ISBN 3-934628-81-8), xxii + 663 S., € 122,00.

333 Annette ZGOLL, *Traum und Welterleben im antiken Mesopotamien. Traumtheorie und Traumpraxis im 3.-1. Jt. v. Chr. als Horizont einer Kulturgeschichte des Träumens*. 2006 (ISBN 3-934628-36-2), vi + 568 S., € 96,00.

335 Ignacio MÁRQUEZ ROWE, *The Royal Deeds of Ugarit. A Study of Ancient Near Eastern Diplomatics*. 2006 (ISBN 3-934628-86-9), 336 S. (i.D.)

Guides to the Mesopotamian Textual Record (GMTR)

Editors: *Eckart FRAHM - Michael JURSA*

1 Michael JURSA, *Neo-Babylonian Legal and Administrative Documents. Typology, Contents and Archives*. 2005 (ISBN 3-934628-69-9), xii + 189 S., € 28,--.

2 Benjamin R. FOSTER, *Choicest Offerings. Akkadian Literature, 1200-200 BC*. 2006 (ISBN 3-934628-70-2)(i.V.)

3 Karen RADNER, *Assyrian Archival Documents. Letters, Legal Records and Administrative Texts*. 2006 (ISBN 3-934628-71-0)(i.V.)

4 Rocio DA RIVA, *The Neo-Babylonian Royal Inscriptions. An Introduction*. 2006 (ISBN 3-934628-83-4)(i.V.)

Elementa Linguarum Orientis (ELO)

Herausgeber: *Josef TROPPER - Reinhard G. LEHMANN*

1 Josef TROPPER, *Ugaritisch. Kurzgefasste Grammatik mit Übungstexten und Glossar*. 2002 (ISBN 3-934628-17-6), xii + 168 S., € 28,--.

2 Josef TROPPER, *Altäthiopisch. Grammatik des Ge'ez mit Übungstexten und Glossar*. 2002 (ISBN 3-934628-29-X), xii + 309 S. € 42,--. — Weiterführung durch Otto Harrassowitz, Wiesbaden.

Altertumskunde des Vorderen Orients (AVO)

Herausgeber: *Manfried DIETRICH - Reinhard DITTMANN - Oswald LORETZ*

1 Nadja CHOLIDIS, *Möbel in Ton*. 1992 (ISBN 3-927120-10-3), XII + 323 S. + 46 Taf., € 60,84.

2 Ellen REHM, *Der Schmuck der Achämeniden*. 1992 (ISBN 3-927120-11-1), X + 358 S. + 107 Taf., € 63,91.

3 Maria KRAFELD-DAUGHERTY, *Wohnen im Alten Orient*. 1994 (ISBN 3-927120-16-2), x + 404 S. + 41 Taf., € 74,65.

4 Manfried DIETRICH - Oswald LORETZ, Hrsg., *Festschrift für* Ruth Mayer-Opificius. 1994 (ISBN 3-927120-18-9), xviii + 356 S. + 256 Abb., € 59,31.

5 Gunnar LEHMANN, *Untersuchungen zur späten Eisenzeit in Syrien und Libanon. Stratigraphie und Keramikformen zwischen ca. 720 bis 300 v.Chr.* 1996 (ISBN 3-927120-33-2), x + 548 S. + 3 Karten + 113 Tf., € 108,39.

6 Ulrike LÖW, *Figürlich verzierte Metallgefäße aus Nord- und Nordwestiran - eine stilkritische Untersuchung*. 1998 (ISBN 3-927120-34-0), xxxvii + 663 S. + 107 Taf., € 130,89.

7 Ursula MAGEN - Mahmoud RASHAD, Hrsg., *Vom Halys zum Euphrat*. Thomas Beran *zu Ehren*. 1996 (ISBN 3-927120-41-3), XI + 311 S., 123 Abb., € 71,07.

8 Eşref ABAY, *Die Keramik der Frühbronzezeit in Anatolien mit »syrischen Affinitäten«*. 1997 (ISBN 3-927120-58-8), XIV + 461 S., 271 Abb.-Taf., € 116,57.

9 Jürgen SCHREIBER, *Die Siedlungsarchitektur auf der Halbinsel Oman vom 3. bis zur Mitte des 1. Jahrtausends v.Chr.* 1998 (ISBN 3-927120-61-8), XII + 253 S., € 53,17.

10 *Iron Age Pottery in Northern Mesopotamia, Northern Syria and South-Eastern Anatolia.* Ed. Arnulf HAUSLEITER and Andrzej REICHE. 1999 (ISBN 3-927120-78-2) – vergr.

11 Christian GREWE, *Die Entstehung regionaler staatlicher Siedlungsstrukturen im Bereich des prähistorischen Zagros-Gebirges. Eine Analyse von Siedlungsverteilungen in der Susiana und im Kur-Flußbecken.* 2002 (ISBN 3-934628-04-4), x + 580 S. + 1 Faltblatt, € 142,--.

Abhandlungen zur Literatur Alt-Syrien-Palästinas und Mesopotamiens (ALASPM)

Herausgeber: *Manfried DIETRICH - Oswald LORETZ*

1 Manfried DIETRICH - Oswald LORETZ, *Die Keilalphabete.* 1988 (ISBN 3-927120-00-6), 376 S., € 47,55.

2 Josef TROPPER, *Der ugaritische Kausativstamm und die Kausativbildungen des Semitischen.* 1990 (ISBN 3-927120-06-5), 252 S., € 36,30.

3 Manfried DIETRICH - Oswald LORETZ, *Mantik in Ugarit.* Mit Beiträgen von Hilmar W. Duerbeck - Jan-Waalke Meyer - Waltraut C. Seitter. 1990 (ISBN 3-927120-05-7), 320 S., € 50,11.

5 Fred RENFROE, *Arabic-Ugaritic Lexical Studies.* 1992 (ISBN 3-927120-09-X). 212 S., € 39,37.

6 Josef TROPPER, *Die Inschriften von Zincirli.* 1993 (ISBN 3-927120-14-6). XII + 364 S., € 55,22.

7 *UGARIT - ein ostmediterranes Kulturzentrum im Alten Orient. Ergebnisse und Perspektiven der Forschung.* Vorträge gehalten während des Europäischen Kolloquiums am 11.-12. Februar 1993, hrsg. von Manfried DIETRICH und Oswald LORETZ. **Bd. I**: *Ugarit und seine altorientalische Umwelt.* 1995 (ISBN 3-927120-17-0). XII + 298 S., € 61,36; **Bd. II**: H.-G. BUCHHOLZ, *Ugarit und seine Beziehungen zur Ägäis.* 1999 (ISBN 3-927120-38-3): **AOAT 261**.

8 Manfried DIETRICH - Oswald LORETZ - Joaquín SANMARTÍN, *The Cuneiform Alphabetic Texts from Ugarit, Ras Ibn Hani and Other Places.* (*KTU: second, enlarged edition*). 1995 (ISBN 3-927120-24-3). XVI + 666 S., € 61,36.

9 Walter MAYER, *Politik und Kriegskunst der Assyrer.* 1995 (ISBN 3-927120-26-X). XVI + 545 S. € 86,92.

10 Giuseppe VISICATO, *The Bureaucracy of Šuruppak. Administrative Centres, Central Offices, Intermediate Structures and Hierarchies in the Economic Documentation of Fara.* 1995 (ISBN 3-927120-35-9). XX + 165 S. € 40,90.

11 Doris PRECHEL, *Die Göttin Išḫara.* 1996 (ISBN 3-927120-36-7) — Neuauflage geplant in AOAT.

12 Manfried DIETRICH - Oswald LORETZ, *A Word-List of the Cuneiform Alphabetic Texts from Ugarit, Ras Ibn Hani and Other Places (KTU: second, enlarged edition).* 1996 (ISBN 3-927120-40-5), x + 250 S., € 40,90.

Eikon

Beiträge zur antiken Bildersprache

Herausgeber: *Klaus STÄHLER*

1 Klaus STÄHLER, *Griechische Geschichtsbilder klassischer Zeit.* 1992 (ISBN 3-927120-12-X), X + 120 S. + 8 Taf., € 20,86.

2 Klaus STÄHLER, *Form und Funktion. Kunstwerke als politisches Ausdrucksmittel.* 1993 (ISBN 3-927120-13-8), VIII + 131 S. mit 54 Abb., € 21,99.

3 Klaus STÄHLER, *Zur Bedeutung des Formats.* 1996 (ISBN 3-927120-25-1), ix + 118 S. mit 60 Abb., € 24,54.

4 *Zur graeco-skythischen Kunst. Archäologisches Kolloquium Münster 24.-26. November 1995.* Hrsg.: Klaus STÄHLER, 1997 (ISBN 3-927120-57-X), IX + 216 S. mit Abb., € 35,79.

5 Jochen FORNASIER, *Jagddarstellungen des 6.-4. Jhs. v. Chr. Eine ikonographische und ikonologische Analsyse.* 2001 (ISBN 3-934628-02-8), XI + 372 S. + 106 Abb., € 54,19.

6 Klaus STÄHLER, *Der Herrscher als Pflüger und Säer: Herrschaftsbilder aus der Pflanzenwelt.* 2001 (ISBN 3-934628-09-5), xii + 332 S. mit 168 Abb., € 54,19.

7 Jörg GEBAUER, *Pompe und Thysia. Attische Tieropferdarstellungen auf schwarz- und rotfigurigen Vasen.* 2002 (ISBN 3-934628-30-3), xii + 807 S. mit 375 Abb., ∈ 80,--.

8 *Ikonographie und Ikonologie. Interdisziplinäres Kolloquium 2001.* Hrsg.: Wolfgang HÜBNER - Klaus STÄHLER, 2004 (ISBN 3-934628-44-3), xi + 187 S. mit Abb., ∈ 40,--.

Auslieferung - Distribution:
BDK Bücherdienst GmbH
Kölner Straße 248
D-51149 Köln

Distributor to North America:
Eisenbrauns, Inc.
Publishers and Booksellers, POB 275
Winona Lake, Ind. 46590, U.S.A.